ie waters. Gen 1:3 And God said, Let there be light: and there was light. Gen 1:4 And God, looking on the light, saw that it was good: and God made a division between the light and the dar
e waters from the waters. Gen 1:7 And God made the arc [illegible] ose which were over it: and it was so.Gen 1:8 And God gave th
een: and it was so.Gen 1:10 And God gave the dry land t [illegible] eas: and God saw that it was good.Gen 1:11 And God said, L
ucing seed of its sort, and every tree producing fruit, in which is its seed [illegible] was good.Gen 1:13 And there was evening and there was morning, the third day.Ge
;Gen 1:15 And let them be for lights in the arch of heaven to give light on the earth: and it was so.Gen 1:16 And God made t [illegible] the ruler of the day, an
for a division between the light and the dark: and God saw that it was good.Gen 1:19 And there was evening and there was [illegible] the waters b
'ull, and every sort of winged bird: and God saw that it was good.Gen 1:22 And God gave them his blessing, saying, Be ferti [illegible] as full, and le
gs moving on the earth, and beasts of the earth after their sort: and it was so.Gen 1:25 And God made the beast of the earth [illegible] ything movin
f the air and over the cattle and over all the earth and over every living thing which goes flat on the earth.Gen 1:27 And Go [illegible] ade him: ma
over the birds of the air and over every living thing moving on the earth.Gen 1:29 And God said, See, I have given you eve [illegible] and every tre
ery green plant for food: and it was so.Gen 1:31 And God saw everything which he had made and it was very good. And the [illegible] y.Gen 2:1 An
e had done.Gen 2:3 And God gave his blessing to the seventh day and made it holy: because on that day he took his rest from all the work which he had made and done.Gen 2:4 These are th
'or the Lord God had not sent rain on the earth and there was no man to do work on the land.Gen 2:6 But a mist went up from the earth, watering all the face of the land.Gen 2:7 And the Lor
n whom he had made.Gen 2:9 And out of the earth the Lord made every tree to come, delighting the eye and good for food; and in the middle of the garden, the tree of life and the tree of th
n goes round about all the land of Havilah where there is gold.Gen 2:12 And the gold of that land is good: there is bdellium and the onyx stone.Gen 2:13 And the name of the second river
ok the man and put him in the garden of Eden to do work in it and take care of it.Gen 2:16 And the Lord God gave the man orders, saying, You may freely take of the fruit of every tree of th
It is not good for the man to be by himself: I will make one like himself as a help to himGen 2:19 And from the earth the Lord God made every beast of the field and every bird of the air, an
air and to every beast of the field: but Adam had no one like himself as a help.Gen 2:21 And the Lord God sent a deep sleep on the man, and took one of the bones from his side while he wa
is now bone of my bone and flesh of my flesh: let her name be Woman because she was taken out of Man.Gen 2:24 For this cause will a man go away from his father and his mother and b
which the Lord God had made. And he said to the woman, Has God truly said that you may not take of the fruit of any tree in the garden?Gen 3:2 And the woman said, We may take of th
Death will not certainly come to you:Gen 3:5 For God sees that on the day when you take of its fruit, your eyes will be open, and you will be as gods, having knowledge of good and evil.Ge
ere open and they were conscious that they had no clothing and they made themselves coats of leaves stitched together.Gen 3:8 And there came to them the sound of the Lord God walking i
ne man, saying, Where are you?Gen 3:10 And he said, Hearing your voice in the garden I was full of fear, because I was without clothing: and I kept myself from your eyes.Gen 3:11 And h
o be with me, she gave me the fruit of the tree and I took it.Gen 3:13 And the Lord God said to the woman, What have you done? And the woman said, I was tricked by the deceit of the snak
our food all the days of your life:Gen 3:15 And there will be war between you and the woman and between your seed and her seed: by him will your head be crushed and by you his foot wi
n 3:17 And to Adam he said, Because you gave ear to the voice of your wife and took of the fruit of the tree which I said you were not to take, the earth is cursed on your account; in pain yo
l till you go back to the earth from which you were taken: for dust you are and to the dust you will go back.Gen 3:20 And the man gave his wife the name of Eve because she was the mothe
owledge of good and evil: and now if he puts out his hand and takes of the fruit of the tree of life, he will go on living for ever.Gen 3:23 So the Lord God sent him out of the garden of Ede
ay to the tree of life.Gen 4:1 And the man had connection with Eve his wife, and she became with child and gave birth to Cain, and said, I have got a man from the Lord.Gen 4:2 Then agai
.Gen 4:4 And Abel gave an offering of the young lambs of his flock and of their fat. And the Lord was pleased with Abel's offering;Gen 4:5 But in Cain and his offering he had no pleasure
g, sin is waiting at the door, desiring to have you, but do not let it be your master.Gen 4:8 And Cain said to his brother, Let us go into the field: and when they were in the field, Cain made a
ave you done? the voice of your brother's blood is crying to me from the earth.Gen 4:11 And now you are cursed from the earth, whose mouth is open to take your brother's blood from you
gth.Gen 4:14 You have sent me out this day from the face of the earth and from before your face; I will be a wanderer in flight over the earth, and whoever sees me will put me to death.Ge
re the face of the Lord, and made his living-place in the land of Nod on the east of Eden.Gen 4:17 And Cain had connection with his wife and she became with child and gave birth to Enoch
and Methushael became the father of Lamech.Gen 4:19 And Lamech had two wives; the name of the one was Adah, and the name of the other Zillah.Gen 4:20 And Adah gave birth to Jabal
'ubal-cain, who is the father of every maker of cutting instruments of brass and iron: and the sister of Tubal-cain was Naamah.Gen 4:23 And Lamech said to his wives, Adah and Zillah, giv
Cain's death, seventy-seven will be taken for Lamech's.Gen 4:25 And Adam had connection with his wife again, and she gave birth to a son to whom she gave the name of Seth: for she said
worship.Gen 5:1 This is the book of the generations of Adam. In the day when God made man, he made him in the image of God;Gen 5:2 Male and female he made them, naming them Man
Seth:Gen 5:4 And after the birth of Seth, Adam went on living for eight hundred years, and had sons and daughters:Gen 5:5 And all the years of Adam's life were nine hundred and thirty: an
nd had sons and daughters:Gen 5:8 And all the years of Seth's life were nine hundred and twelve: and he came to his end.Gen 5:9 And Enosh was ninety years old when he became the fathe
: and he came to his end.Gen 5:12 And Kenan was seventy years old when he became the father of Mahalalel:Gen 5:13 And after the birth of Mahalalel, Kenan went on living for eight hun
n he became the father of Jared:Gen 5:16 And after the birth of Jared, Mahalalel went on living for eight hundred and thirty years, and had sons and daughters:Gen 5:17 And all the years o
on living after the birth of Enoch for eight hundred years, and had sons and daughters:Gen 5:20 And all the years of Jared's life were nine hundred and sixty-two: and he came to his end.Ge
d daughters:Gen 5:23 And all the years of Enoch's life were three hundred and sixty-five:Gen 5:24 And Enoch went on in God's ways: and he was not seen again, for God took him.Gen 5:2
years, and had sons and daughters:Gen 5:27 And all the years of Methuselah's life were nine hundred and sixty-nine: and he came to his end.Gen 5:28 And Lamech was a hundred and eighty
ed by God.Gen 5:30 And after the birth of Noah, Lamech went on living for five hundred and ninety-five years, and had sons and daughters:Gen 5:31 And all the years of Lamech's life were
en were increasing on the earth, and had daughters,Gen 6:2 The sons of God saw that the daughters of men were fair; and they took wives for themselves from those who were pleasing to
on the earth in those days; and after that, when the sons of God had connection with the daughters of men, they gave birth to children: these were the great men of old days, the men of grea
d grief was in his heart.Gen 6:7 And the Lord said, I will take away man, whom I have made, from the face of the earth, even man and beast and that which goes on the earth and every bir
n: he went in the ways of God.Gen 6:10 And Noah had three sons, Shem, Ham, and Japheth.Gen 6:11 And the earth was evil in God's eyes and full of violent ways.Gen 6:12 And God, look
ow I will put an end to them with the earth.Gen 6:14 Make for yourself an ark of gopher wood with rooms in it, and make it safe from the water inside and out.Gen 6:15 And this is the way
are to make it with a lower and second and third floors.Gen 6:17 For truly, I will send a great flow of waters over the earth, for the destruction from under the heaven of all flesh in which i
with you.Gen 6:19 And you will take with you into the ark two of every sort of living thing, and keep them safe with you; they will be male and female.Gen 6:20 Two of every sort of bir
And all these things Noah did; as God said, so he did.Gen 7:1 And the Lord said to Noah, Take all your family and go into the ark, for you only in this generation have I seen to be upright.Ge
emales, so that their seed may still be living on the face of the earth.Gen 7:4 For after seven days I will send rain on the earth for forty days and forty nights, for the destruction of every liv
er all the earth.Gen 7:7 And Noah, with his sons and his wife and his sons' wives, went into the ark because of the flowing of the waters.Gen 7:8 Of clean beasts, and of beasts which are no
over all the earth.Gen 7:11 In the six hundredth year of Noah's life, in the second month, on the seventeenth day of the month, all the fountains of the great deep came bursting through, and
d his sons' wives, went into the ark;Gen 7:14 And with them, every sort of beast and cattle, and every sort of thing which goes on the earth, and every sort of bird.Gen 7:15 They went wit
he waters were over all the earth; and the waters were increased so that the ark was lifted up high over the earth.Gen 7:18 And the waters overcame everything and were increased greatly o
een cubits higher, till all the mountains were covered.Gen 7:21 And destruction came on every living thing moving on the earth, birds and cattle and beasts and everything which went on th
n the face of the earth, and birds of the air, came to destruction; only Noah and those who were with him in the ark, were kept from death.Gen 7:24 And the waters were over the earth a
8:2 And the fountains of the deep and the windows of heaven were shut, and the rain from heaven was stopped.Gen 8:3 And the waters went slowly back from the earth, and at the end of
on the first day of the tenth month the tops of the mountains were see [illegible] h the open window of the ark which he had made.Gen 8:7 Noah sent out a raven
e for her foot, and came back to the ark, for the waters were still ov [illegible] and took her into the ark.Gen 8:10 And after waiting another seven days, he sen
n days more, he sent the dove out again, but she did not come back [illegible] and first year, on the first day of the first month, the waters were dry on the earth
6 Go out of the ark, you and your wife and your sons and your son [illegible] ry living thing which is with you, birds and cattle and everything which goes o
d every living thing of every sort which goes on the earth, went out of the ark.Gen 8:20 And Noah made an altar to the Lord, and from every clean beast and bird he made burned offering
st days: never again will I send destruction on all living things as I have done.Gen 8:22 While the earth goes on, seed time and the getting in of the grain, cold and heat, summer and winte

The Story of Christianity

Peter Partner

With Forewords by Melvyn Bragg

To Joyce, who made it possible

With thanks to Richard Thomson and Simon Cherry

This edition first published in 2005 by André Deutsch Limited,
20 Mortimer Street
London W1T 3JW

In association with Granada Media Group

First published in 1999 as two volumes:
2,000 Years: The First Millennium and
2,000 Years: The Second Millennium

A catalogue record for this book is available from the British Library.

ISBN 0 233 00127 1

Picture research by Sophie Seebohm
Book design © Design/Section

Printed and bound in Dubai

Contents

Part I

The First Millennium
The Birth of Christianity to the Crusades

FOREWORD

I owe Christianity a debt, and so, I believe, does the world we have lived in for the last 2000 years. Much of what is best in that duo-millennial span has been inspired by the man who inspired the faith which took his name.

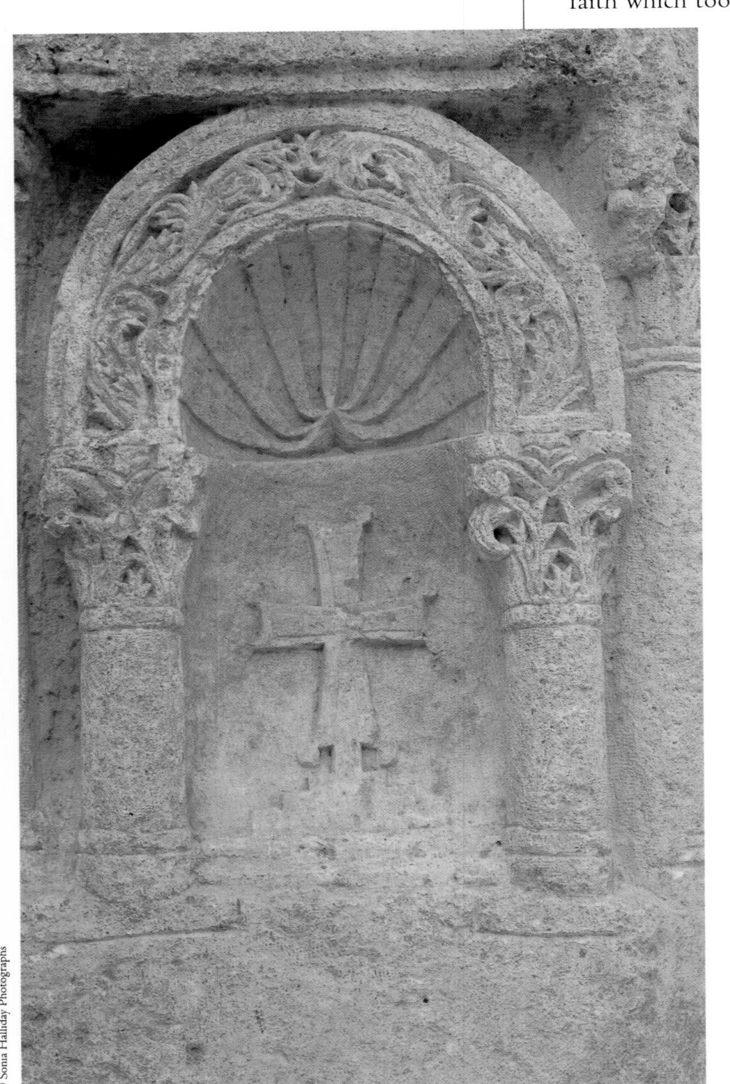

© Sonia Halliday Photographs

The Alaham Monastery, Turkey

But Christianity also owes me an explanation. As it does to so many others: for the bigotry, the wickedness, the inhumanity and the wilful ignorance which has also characterized much of its 'history'. Its force and extraordinary persistence have informed 'the best of times and the worst of times', from the manger in Bethlehem to the gas chambers of Auschwitz.

It has been the pivot of the argument in matters of morality as it has been in questions of immorality, divine intervention and the source and nature of truth. Music, architecture, art and society have risen to show off the powers of Christianity while states, monarchs, despots, villains and all the variety of the corrupt have used and abused its messages and its meanings throughout the centuries.

It has made secular wars more senseless by its involvement and hopeless conditions hopeful by its devotion. Literature has flourished under its example – indeed the Bible is probably the most influential of all books of literature – but literature has also been censored. Science was sent into outer darkness for centuries, clawing its way back despite persecution and terror. Yet science, despite seeming the ultimate challenge to Christianity, has recently presented it with the Big Bang theory, which appears to dovetail so happily with the Book of Genesis.

Over two thousand years, where there has been slavery, where there has been sacrifice, where there has been enlightenment, where there has been suppression, for richer and poorer until death and beyond Christianity has wedded itself to civilizations and through them it has flooded the world more forcefully and with more perseverence than any other religion.

In more pious days, all of a couple of generations ago, Hollywood called a film about Jesus Christ *The Greatest Story Ever Told*. We would not use that phrase now, but in their epic populist boldness, ironically the Jewish men who ran the world's dream factory knew what they were dealing with.

More sensitive or more politic or less Christ-struck today, we might tend to be apologetic about the Greatest Story. When I suggested we make twenty television programmes of one hour each on the history of Christianity century by century, coupled with discussions arising from some of the engrossing and vivid and perennially relevant issues engendered by the complex penetrations made into the minds and estates of humankind by Christianity, I was aware, almost at the same moment as the simple notion struck, that there would be questions raised on all sides – partly because other religions and other non-religions might feel affronted or even diminished by the implications of non-inclusion in what for British television is a huge commitment.

But this is the year which marks the 2000th anniversary of the birth of Jesus Christ, whose ministry and Church have marked the centuries indelibly and whose presence is still global, active and powerful. Of course there are similar series to be made about Judaism, about Islam, about Buddhism, Hinduism, Confucianism and about more secular beliefs and systems – Marxism, Capitalism, monarchism, tyranny, paganism, various shades of anthems and so they go on and on into the night of the twentieth century, arriving finally at its monstrous Gemini – Fascism and Communism and their nightmare progeny Hitler and Stalin, Mao, Pol Pot and all their ideological offspring. And some of this too is part of the Christian story, some of them drawing strength from Christianity, alas, and some of them using Christianity as a necessary opposition.

Maybe all the work we do is some form of paying debts. I began regular churchgoing – Church of England – in the early 1940s. In 1945 I joined the local choir of St Mary's in Wigton, Cumbria, and sang Sunday after Sunday, two or three times a day for twelve years.

I still know prayers and psalms, hymns and collects by heart, still hear the music, remember snatches of the sermons, can feel the crushing, holy silence, live with the guilt which if not engineered by religion was certainly stirred and spiced by it, still think the Sermon on the Mount is the most radical manifesto ever delivered, still clutch at God at unexpected moments and still have the fundamental doubts about His existence which I began to experience at the age of about sixteen or seventeen.

It is difficult perhaps for younger generations to imagine a place known so well and often hated so firmly by so many of us until recently. The place I speak of is Sunday. A place of suffocated silence and closures. A place where casual blasphemy outside the male workforce was absolutely forbidden; a place in which a small town such as my own in the north of England with a population of about 5,000, could support more than a dozen flourishing churches of different denominations. A place where the churches stood as pillars of the community and centres for the stern and innocent leisure which was most of our public ration of fun.

There is also personal anger. Did we have to be driven so unremittingly with that intransigent image of utter perfection which will never leave us and still haunts to torment us? The forgiveness of the Father could not really cancel that out because we were never good enough to earn it. Did guilt have to be so remorselessly cultivated until all pleasure became stolen – sweeter perhaps for that but also corroded by the sense of sin in which we became Olympic contenders? Were the contradictions never to be pointed out until we ourselves dared raise them, only to be pitied and dismissed? Simple questions never addressed until we had to shut them into the void. How did Cain and Abel get children? Why did Christianity support evil people? What does eternal life mean? Where exactly is the soul? Answers came there none.

The Borghese gladiator

So this twenty-hour enterprise for me has been one which has returned to open up old pathways to see where they now lead, wondering why and how they once dominated my life entirely, spiritually – if one can claim that – and intellectually – an even more tenuous claim for the religiously saturated boy I was then, fired to be a missionary and earnest beyond embarrassment even when a teenager kneeling by the bed, in prayers before sleep.

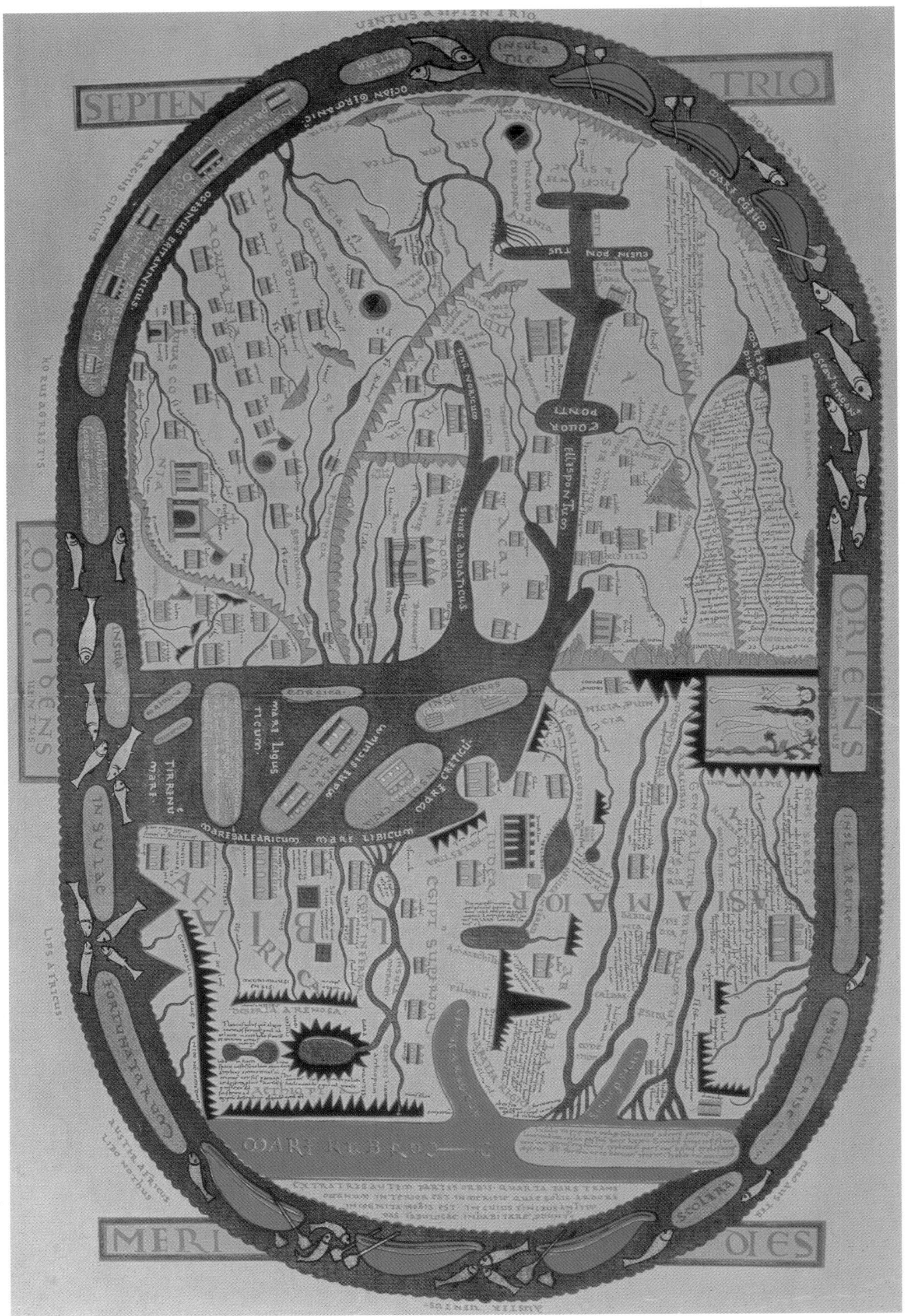

Beatus Mappamundi, c. eighth century

On the broadest level, what meets you when you return to the Gospels, which are the burning core of Christianity, and when you scan the history of two thousand Christian years, is the clamour of events, the violence of the arguments and the men, men, men whose furies drove them for and against the teaching of the gentle rabbi on the shores of Galilee.

The voice of Constantine is there with his earth-changing dream of victory in battle, which made him convert to Christianity. He took care not to do it until the very end of his life, but during the greater part of his reign he dismantled almost four centuries of persecution, slaughter and intolerance. By the end of the fourth century the Emperor Theodosius was forced to beg mercy from Bishop Ambrose of Milan, who had been appalled by the massacres at Thessalonika and excommunicated him. Though the State would use the Church whenever it could and abuse it and distort the teachings and the purpose of its founder, yet the journey of the outlawed sect which began in Judea and persisted for centuries, finally displacing all other gods in the greatest empire on earth, is an astounding tale.

So too is the story of Charlemagne, 400 years after Constantine, when, inspired by English missionaries, he conquered pagan tribes and forcibly converted them to Christianity, thus re-establishing but more emphatically, the empire. But this time it was not the Roman Empire but the Holy Roman Empire. He also took on the mantle of teacher, and book production and the invention of a new more legible system of writing thrived under his rule, which reached a climax on Christmas Day 800, when Pope Leo III crowned him as the first Holy Roman Emperor.

The success of Christianity in the worldly sphere was paralleled by its influence among the unworldly. In fact it scaled new pinnacles of self-abnegation – literally in the case of the hero of the desert coenobites, Simeon Stylites, who became a venerated figure by living on the top of a pillar for thirty-eight years. The Celtic saints emanating from Ireland – in which St Patrick, it was said, sowed seeds which yielded the rich harvest of holy men and women – spread across the islands of Britain and east on to the mainland of Europe, driven there by their emulation of the Acts of the Apostles.

Christianity produced the Gospels – the life and teachings of Christ – whose influence will bear comparison to anything written anywhere ever. It has inspired philosophers and commentators, the most dynamic of whom, Saint Augustine of Hippo, still speaks to the human and the spiritual condition today.

With its written Gospels, its moral system, its equal invitation to all to believe and so to join, its promise of eternal life and its remarkable tenacity, Christianity in its first thousand years came out of insignificance, through the most fearful oppression of centuries, to ride successive waves of barbarism and often equally worrying patronage, and in that first thousand years entered into every structure of life in the increasing number of people and tribes it embraced. It could be ludicrous as it showed in 897 at the Cadaver Synod, in which the corpse of Pope Formosus was put on trial, mutilated and hurled into the Tiber. It could be swept into the worst of millenarianism, as when Emperor Otto III had his ancestor Charlemagne disinterred and moved to his court in Rome to wait for the world to end in the year 1000.

But in those first thousand years, it had become a force which would capture emperors and captivate the humblest individual, be seen as salvation for the peasant and fulfilment for the ruler. The first millennium passed and the world did not come to an end – and neither did Christianity.

Melvyn Bragg, 1999

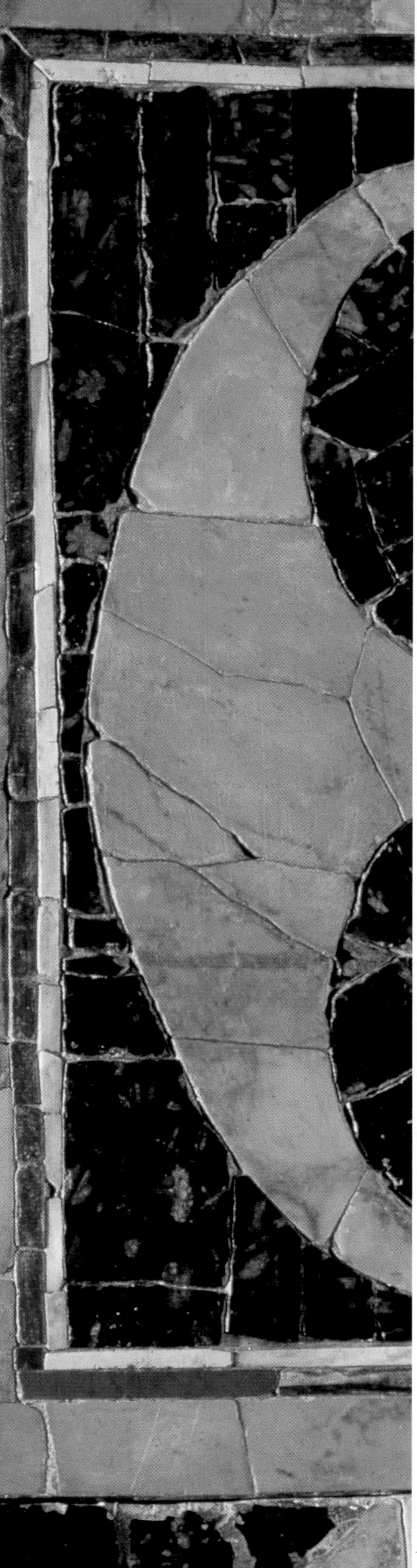

© AKG London / Erich Lessing

1

THE BIRTH OF CHRISTIANITY

Jesus of Nazareth was a Jewish charismatic healer, exorcist and religious teacher. That may be a bald statement, but reliable information about him is very scarce, and in human terms it must do. It is extremely hard to see what connections exist between this Jewish holy man of a remote past, and the complex stories of human desires, failures and ideals that fill the rest of this book. Some connections do exist, although they constantly slip out of the grasp of even the most learned. About human salvation, which has very little to do with history books, and perhaps not much to do with theology manuals, Jesus of Nazareth has in the reckoning of many wise persons a great deal, perhaps everything, to say to us.

Jesus was executed by the Roman government in Jerusalem, probably in or close to the year 36 of the Common Era, at the time of the Passover feast. He and his closest followers, along with large numbers of other Jews, had gone to sacrifice at the Temple prior to a private celebration of the appropriate religious acts. Jesus had perhaps made an earlier public entry into the city, which could have been understood as a form of political provocation. Before the feast he created a disorder in the Temple: whether his arrest by the Jewish Temple authorities was a result of his actions in the sacred area on this occasion, or whether they had already determined to arrest him at some earlier point, is not known.

Evidence about the life and career of Jesus is very patchy. This is not surprising, because we are dealing with someone whose political importance as a Jewish religious teacher was so slight in his lifetime that we would know hardly anything about him if we excluded the evidence contained in the writings of his early followers. Evidence about his last days is also obscured because those responsible for the main Gospel texts wished to avoid suggesting that he constituted a security risk for the Roman rulers. In exonerating him they were right in the sense that it is unlikely that Jesus belonged to one of the terrorist Zealot groups that conspired against Roman rule. But Jesus proclaimed a personal

Left: A coarse stone mosaic of Christ dating from the third century.

Above: A third-century Roman graffito caricatures the crucifixion. Christ is shown with the head of an ass; the inscription reads 'Alexamanos prays to his God'.

Below: Domitian, shown on a golden coin, became Roman Emperor in AD 81. He launched inquiries into Jesus' family, indicating that the Roman leadership had begun to take the new Christian sect seriously.

prophetic mission, referred to the early establishment of a 'kingdom', and violently denounced the priests (established by the Roman government) in charge of the holiest religious site. Such a person was bound to be thought an extremist who constituted an appreciable security risk, both for the priestly establishment and for the Roman authorities that stood behind it.

The high priest of Jerusalem must have brought grave religious charges against Jesus, although whether this was in a religious court with the legal jurisdiction to pronounce sentence is doubtful. If reports are accurate, Jesus rent his own priestly garments during the course of the examination, which would have been a drastic symbolic act. But the subsequent Roman capital condemnation of the accused man was on the political, not religious, grounds that he had claimed to be in some way 'King of the Jews'. This was what was written on the crime or charge sheet that was posted above him at the head of the cross. A comparable situation, due to a crisis of some other form of religious extremism, Jewish, Christian or Muslim, is quite conceivable in the Jerusalem of today.

Crucifixion, the terrible death inflicted in an almost casual way upon Jesus, was not in the least unusual – and before we condescendingly add 'for its time', it would be as well to remember that equally terrible forms of death have been imposed upon huge numbers of people within the lifetimes of persons alive today. But the demeaning, humiliating nature of a punishment used in the ancient world for the lowest criminals or the most despised political enemies has to be emphasized to modern people. Someone in the early period of Roman Christianity, who wanted to ridicule the Christians, made a cruel caricature of a crucified man with the head of an ass.

Jesus in History

One of the first people to inquire into the historical Jesus was the Emperor Domitian (AD 51–96), who is said to have sent police investigators to Galilee to interrogate his surviving family, about fifty years after Jesus' death. They were found to be hard-handed peasants getting subsistence from a smallholding, and were released without charge. However, if Domitian, who was worried about the refusal of the Jesus sect to acknowledge his own divinity and that of the other gods, sent a mission of this sort, it tells us that the sect was no longer totally obscure. If the imperial government bothered to pull in the great-nephews of Jesus for questioning so soon after his death, it shows how quickly judgements about his political significance had changed in the realist world of the Roman Empire.

Even the dates of the birth and death of Jesus are uncertain. It is unlikely that he was born almost exactly two thousand years ago, in the year commonly called the first year of Our Lord (AD 1). A rather rough-and-ready judgement was made, some five centuries after Jesus, concerning the date then chosen for the year to be treated as the first 'year of the Incarnation of Our Lord'. For reasons of convenience, this date for the beginning of the Christian (or Common) Era is the one that is still commonly used, although Jesus was probably born several years before it. The date of 4 'B[efore] C[hrist]' has often been put forward as that of the birth of Jesus. But some have argued for an even earlier date. The doubt about the birth date, which was certainly not at the time of the pagan feasts of the Winter Solstice, means that the Christian millennium has very probably already passed. This is a conclusion that may worry some people, and comfort others. The date of the death of Jesus is just as hard to establish. It probably (but not quite certainly) took place between AD 26 and AD 36, the period during which Pontius Pilate was Roman prefect of Judaea. Many scholars prefer the period between AD 30 and AD 36.

There is very little indication that Jesus expected anything like Christianity to happen. Nothing in his career or sayings, if we exclude things that seem to have been invented or changed to fit in with doctrines that followed his death, clearly authorizes us to think that he intended to challenge the whole fabric of Jewish practice and belief, in spite of his conviction that the orthodox Judaism of his time had failed. That Jesus thought that he stood in a special relationship to God is certain, and followed directly from his prophetic mission. That he thought of this relationship in terms comparable to those used about him in later Christian definitions of faith is very unlikely, especially if we accept the full humanity and the purely human consciousness that these same definitions assert.

But, in spite of later adjustments and additions to what was written about Jesus in the Gospels, a core of his reported teaching and action refers to a great Jewish teacher who had a clear idea of what he stood for and what he was doing. That cannot be explained by the needs of a later Christian community whose aims lay essentially among the Gentiles. Jesus' teaching was a subtle blend of rigorism, or strictly judged conduct (especially evident in the precepts about sexual relations) and flexible, humane advice (expressed very often in parables). Behind it lay a profound conviction of his own authority to proclaim his mission, and of an imminent, divine judgement on Jewish society (typically expressed in the eschatological prophecy of the overthrow of the Temple).

Above: An ivory carving dating from c. AD 420 shows the crucifixion of Christ. Crucifixion was considered a particularly demeaning form of execution, much favoured by the Romans.

Alexander's Legacy: Hellenization

For well over two centuries, Jewish society in Palestine had been subject to intense Greek, or subsequently Graeco-Roman, cultural pressure, a process known as Hellenization. Two Greek dynasties, the Ptolemaic and the Seleucid, had contested for rule in Palestine during the third century BC. After the Seleucid victory, the new rulers of Syria-Palestine had made a most determined effort to achieve a complete Hellenization of the elites of the area, even to the extent of changing, for a short time, the entire pattern of the worship in the Temple in Jerusalem. Worship of Zeus, the head of the Greek pantheon, was substituted for that of the Old Testament God, Yahweh, and circumcision was abandoned.

Nor was this only a local trend; the Hellenization of the Middle East was part of a drift that affected the whole huge area of Alexander the Great's conquests in the fourth century BC. Large numbers of Jews were dispersed over a vast Middle Eastern and Mediterranean zone, partly because of forced emigrations, partly because of economic pressures. Jewish culture and teaching continued to be marked by strong scripturalism, insistence on the fulfilment of precise dietary and ritualistic practices, of which circumcision of males was the most important, and the conviction that salvation history was to be worked out by and for the Jewish people alone. But the Jews went a long way towards interpreting their own religious tradition in Greek terms. The extent of their cultural acclimatization may be judged from the fact that the Greek 'Septuagint' – sacred writings made in Egypt in the third and second centuries BC – are thought to be guides as valuable to the various critical revisions of the texts as the existing (but largely later) Hebrew versions themselves, not excluding Biblical texts among the Dead Sea Scrolls.

There was fierce and successful resistance to the direct Hellenization of Jewish religion. It led to the liberation wars waged by the family of Judas Maccabaeus, and to the emergence from that family of the Hasmonean dynasty of which Herod the Great was a late and unpopular member. This did not achieve the triumph of Jewish separatism in Palestine: what had begun as a Jewish revolutionary movement became in the end a Roman satellite government. In spite of Roman protection of the

Above: Zeus, having adopted the form of a bull, abducts Europa. During the period of intense Hellenization, workship of Zeus, king of the Greek gods, replaced that of Yahweh in Jerusalem.

approved Jewish Temple worship, the predominance of Greek culture in Roman Imperial Asia was as undeniable in Jesus' day as the predominance of American electronic culture is in our own. Renewed Jewish resistance was manifested in Zealot terrorism, but their rebellion collapsed in AD 70, and was punished by the destruction of the Temple of Jerusalem by the Roman Emperor Titus (AD 39–81). These were the brutal facts of Roman political domination. However, Graeco-Roman cultural influence was more subtle and insidious than military might, and profoundly affected the Jewish religious elites. By the time of Jesus, it was an influence already centuries old.

Jesus in Context

Jesus came from Galilee, a rural though prosperous area of Palestine in which Greek cultural presence was at its lowest. It was not entirely absent in Capernaum, where Jesus is known to have taught and worked. But it was much stronger in Sepphoris. The city of Sepphoris was very near his home village of Nazareth, but his presence in the former place is not attested. This may have a sort of negative political significance: at the minimum it meant that he did not think the city a suitable place for the exercise of his ministry. Galilee was a notorious stronghold of Jewish, anti-Roman nationalism and – in Roman terms – terrorism. The Galilean reputation may have contributed to the feelings of political insecurity that marked the Jewish and Roman official response, when Jesus came to the attention of the authorities at the end of his life.

But whatever his tactics may have been in avoiding a city such as Sepphoris, Jesus' ministry was certainly directed to Hellenized or partly Hellenized Jews no less than to those who were not, as is evident from the Greek language of the Gospels themselves. At Ephesus, St Paul and his mission are said to have received into their congregation a highly educated Alexandrine Jew called Apollos. He was a trained Greek orator who had, years earlier, received the rite of baptism of the Evangelist John, most probably from Jesus himself.

Besides being a charismatic healer and exorcist, Jesus was also a prophet who denounced the sins and inadequacies of the leaders of the people. He preached, mostly through allusion and parable, 'the kingdom of heaven', which was something between an immediately available new moral order in which men and women could live in a quite new, God-inspired way, and an imminent

Left: A detail from the Arch of Titus, showing Romans removing the menorah – the Jewish seven-branched candlestick – from the Temple of Jerusalem.

divine judgement. In all these functions he had Jewish contemporaries or near-contemporaries whose paths were in some ways similar or comparable, although none who is known to have united with healing and prophecy, as he did, the gift of convincing all sorts of men and women how they ought to live their lives.

Above: Lake Genezareth, Galilee.
Below: Countryside around Nazareth. Little is known with certainty about Jesus, but he came from Galilee, a main centre of Judaism. His home village was Nazareth.

The Essene Sect

There was a kind of social openness, especially to Gentiles, about the way Jesus preached his message, that may have been characteristic of the wandering exorcist healers. He differed deeply from various inward-looking religious groups such as the contemporary one of the Essenes. This was a sect that emphasized above all the apartness of the chosen few of a chosen people, who lived in small, sequestered groups, and were convinced of their own exclusive God-given and race-conferred knowledge of Jewish salvation history.

There are no obvious points of contact between the kind of prophecies attributed to Jesus and those found in the writings of the Essenes. The central Essene doctrines relate to the unnamed 'Teacher of Righteousness', who was betrayed by 'the Liar' or 'the Wicked Priest', at some time before the Romans (the 'Kittim') came to Palestine. The historian Josephus (AD 37–?100) named some

Right: A stone relief showing Jesus raising from a death-like sleep the 12-year-old daughter of Jairus, a Jewish merchant. This was one of the miracles of healing performed by Jesus and described in the Gospels.

individual Essenes as prophets, but they seem rather to have been diviners. The Essenes, like Jesus, denounced the wickedness and the failings of the Jewish priestly class, the leaders of the people, but this is a characteristic of so much Jewish prophecy that it does not offer a real comparison. Jesus' prophecy of the catastrophic end of world order, as reported in Mark 13, makes an overt reference to the earlier prediction of such terrible events in the Book of Daniel.

The execution of Jesus did not have the effect of silencing his closest followers. It probably was not thought necessary to silence them, because none was arrested at the time. Understandably, their immediate reaction to the execution was one of bewilderment and defeat. But the strange discovery of his empty tomb, and their experiences of some sort of encounter with Jesus after his death, caused the faithful disciples, relatives and followers to cohere into a group that preserved belief in Jesus' messianic mission. Its centre was in Jerusalem, not in Galilee, from where the key figures in the movement came, and where some of them had initially returned after his death. Its focus seems to have been his disciple, Peter, and Jesus' own family. Among the family, the most important was James (Jacob), a brother of Jesus, who a generation later was tried and executed by the then Jewish high priest, Ananus. Before his death, James and Peter had had dealings with Paul of Tarsus that show the Jesus-followers in Jerusalem to have been conforming Jews, as Jesus had been.

But when ye shall see the abomination of desolation spoken of by Daniel the prophet, standing where it ought not (let him that readeth understand) then let them that be in Judaea flee to the mountains. (Mark 13:14)

Below: A stone slab from a sepulchre in Rome showing the apostles Peter and Paul. After the death of Jesus, his disciple Peter, members of his family, and later Paul of Tarsus, continued to carry and preach his message.

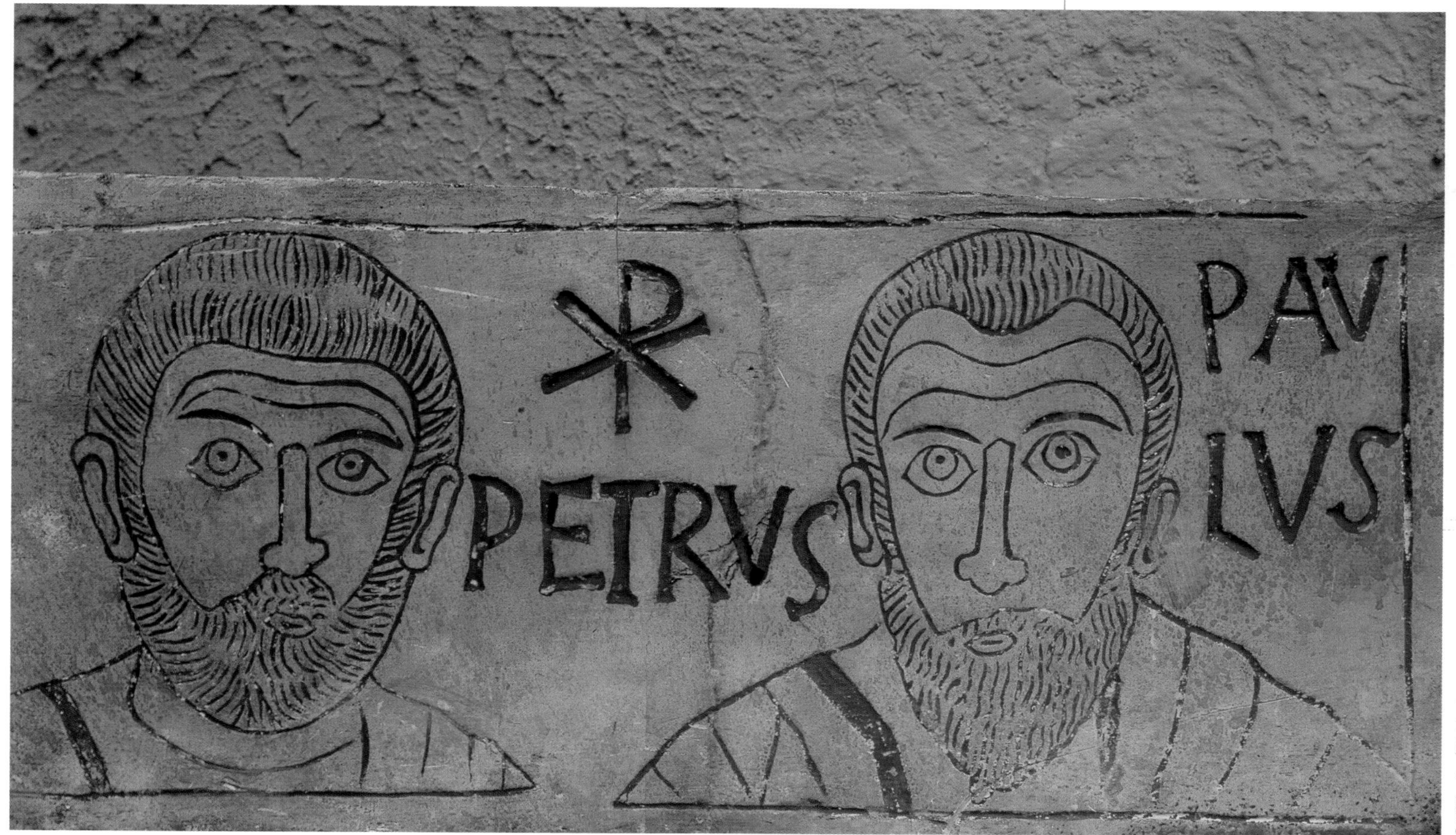

The Jerusalem group was critical for the transmission of the memory of Jesus' person and the content of his message. Without it, these would have become even less known to posterity than the doctrines of the Essenes. Its audience, to which the good news about Jesus the anointed one of God (the Messiah) was preached, remained essentially Jewish. Jesus was not, after all, the last Messiah to be proclaimed among the Jews: there are examples from sixteenth-century Palestine, and from times much closer to our own.

And I persecuted this way unto the death, binding and delivering into prisons both men and women.

As also the high priest doth bear me witness and all the estate of the elders: from whom also I received letters unto the brethren, and went to Damascus, to bring them which were there bound unto Jerusalem for to be punished. (Acts 22: 4-5)

St Paul and the Spreading of the Word

Where Gentiles were won over to accept Messiah-Jesus, as started to happen in Antioch as well as in Jerusalem, the males had to accept circumcision, and all the converts were subjected to Jewish dietary laws. It was not inconceivable that such a Jewish sub-cult might arrive, eventually, at a strong position within the Judaism of the Roman Empire. The Jews outside Palestine numbered several millions, and Jewish proselytism was far from new.

Because it was known that Jesus had not refused contact with Gentiles, and had even performed healings in their households, the question was bound to arise: might his message be preached differently to Gentiles and Jews? The question was eventually put, by Paul of Tarsus, in a manner that revealed extraordinary spiritual and moral gifts, besides a ruthless power of character. Paul's life as a follower of Jesus placed a clear boundary between the group of disciples and relatives who had experienced an encounter with Jesus after his death, and the 'churches' that subsequently became the main bearers of his message.

Paul was an articulate and educated Jew from a prosperous and populous city in the south-west of Asia Minor, whose family had obtained the envied privilege of Roman citizenship. He was literate in both Hebrew and Greek (although not necessarily highly competent in the latter), and passionately committed to the Jewish religion. His recent biographer, Jerome Murphy-O'Connor, thinks his birth year was not too distant from that of Jesus, shortly before the beginning of the Common Era. Paul's parents may have been Pharisees, an observant Jewish sect that had, in the past, played some political role but that in Paul's time was mostly a table-fellowship whose members had some influence in religious circles. Paul himself joined the sect, probably while living in Jerusalem, and later considered himself to have been, as a young man, learned in Jewish law. He was initially a vigorous enemy of the followers of Jesus.

It is argued that the apostle Luke overstated the legal authority Paul could have enjoyed as a Pharisee, even if he had belonged to the Jewish supreme religious court, to seek out the Jesus sect, and order their punishment [Acts: 22:4-5; 26:12]. There are particular doubts about the draconian legal powers attributed to him in Damascus, a Roman province far from Judaea, where it is unlikely that Jewish religious authorities in Jerusalem would have enjoyed any legal powers at all. At the least, Paul denounced the followers of Jesus ruthlessly whenever he could smell them out, and was loud in his condemnations. How long he behaved in this manner is unknown, it might have been for months, or years.

Paul refers to the circumstances of his conversion outside Damascus in a very elliptical way, in a context [I Cor.15] that prefaces his testimony by a short creed which asserts the resurrection of Jesus after his death, 'according to the scriptures'. Paul then relates his own version of the 'appearances' of Jesus after death, first to Peter and to the twelve disciples, then to 'over five hundred of our brothers at once, most of whom are still alive', then to James and the apostles, and finally to Paul himself. Paul's recognition of the manifestation of this risen Jesus to himself comes in a sense to finish the story, at the end of a series of earlier appearances of Jesus to others. And indeed, it should have been near the end of the story, given the belief by Paul's generation of Jesus-followers in a proximate coming of God's kingdom. From Paul's recognition of the risen Jesus came the power of his call to faith and apostolate, which endured through a long and often harsh life, until his martyrdom in Rome.

Below: The altar in St Peter's Church in Antioch, southern Turkey. Following his conversion to Christianity, Paul preached at Antioch and set off on his missionary journey from here.

© Sonia Halliday Photographs

Paul later attributed the manifestation of Jesus that he had experienced outside Damascus to a divine order that he should proclaim Jesus among the Gentiles. But this mission took years to assume a definite shape. It was three years before he fled Damascus – after an abortive and probably brief journey in the Nabataean kingdom south of Damascus – and visited Peter and the Jesus-fellowship in Jerusalem. In one way, the Jesus apparition was enough for Paul, but conventional information about Jesus must have been short. There may already have been writings, but perhaps not. If there was insufficient or no written tradition about his life, the surviving relatives and disciples had to be asked.

If the account in Acts (10) is correct – and some have thought it to be a fictitious interpolation made to justify the missionary opening to the Gentiles – the critical moment for the Jerusalem community must have followed Peter's conversion of the Roman officer, Cornelius, in the garrison town of Caesarea. This is said to have followed Peter's vision of a heavenly visitation that told him to cease making the distinctions, incumbent on any practising Jew, between 'clean' and 'unclean' objects (and, by implication, people). Peter is said to have baptized not only Cornelius himself, but also all those other Gentiles standing by who were equally accepting of Peter's message, and who were thought to have 'received the Holy Spirit' (and, according to Acts, the gift of ecstatic utterance) equally with Cornelius. On his return to Jerusalem, Peter is said to have convinced the Jewish Jesus-fellowship of the validity of the acceptance of Gentiles for baptism.

Paul had returned to his own area of Cilicia in Asia Minor, and to Antioch on the River Orontes, and preached the Gospel there alongside a Jesus-follower called Barnabas. He then carried his message to an area that must have presented him with a new kind of challenge: the predominantly rural, military and Celtic society of Galatia, in the central plateau of Asia Minor. Why he should have gone to this isolated area is a bit of a puzzle; he may have formed a resolution to take his mission there while he was preaching in Pisidian Antioch.

Eight years later, Paul's apostolate took him across the Bosphorus into Europe and Macedonia. There he spent two years in the cities of Thessalonica and Phillipi with predominantly Gentile converts, strengthening them in what may now be called the new religion. From there he went on to Athens and Corinth. How lacking in sharp definition this new religion still was, outside a few convictions about Jesus, and about the approaching end of all things, emerges from Paul's letters. His mission to these communities was not to legislate, but to

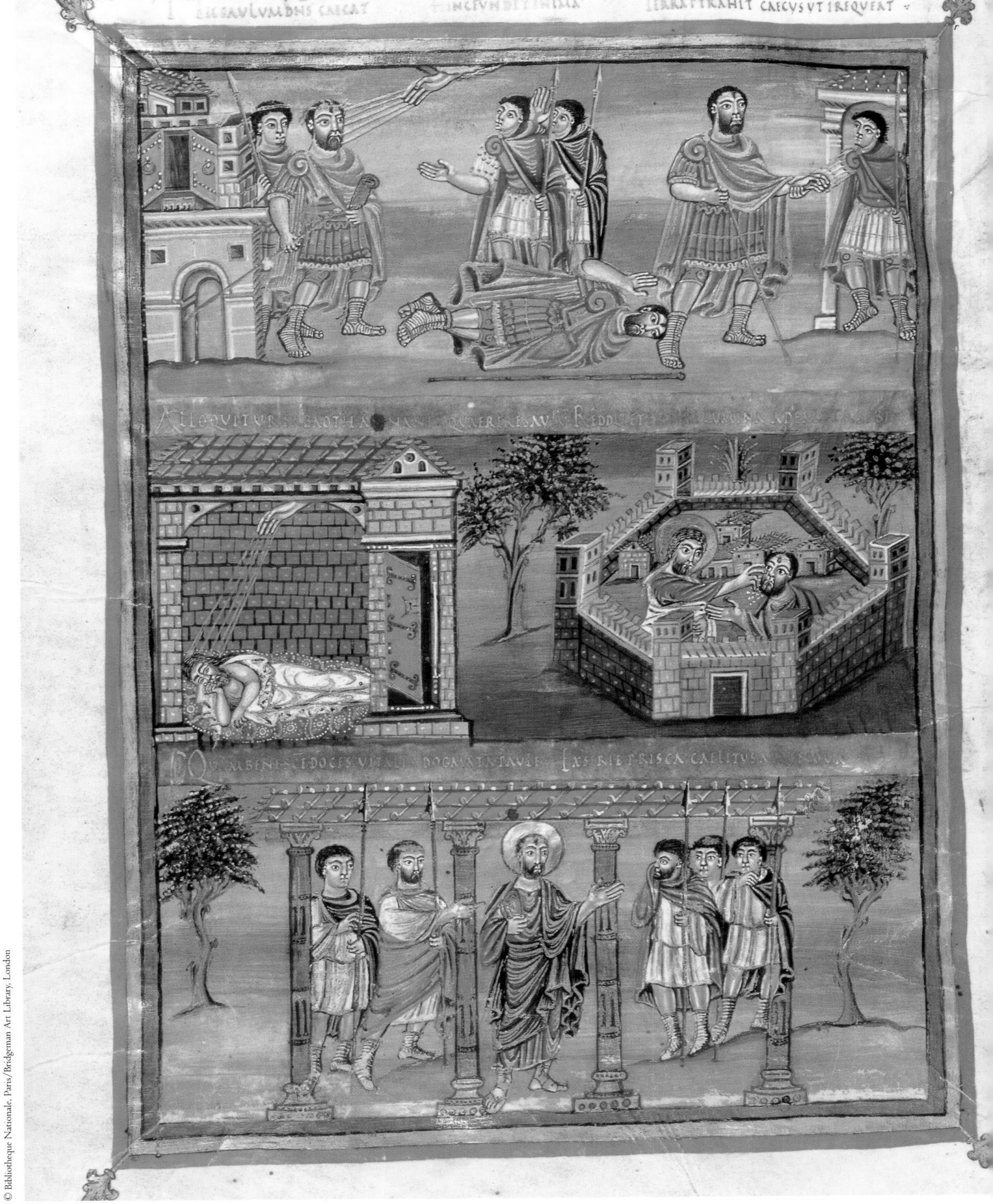

Right: The conversion of Paul and scenes of Paul preaching. The illustration comes from a ninth-century Bible made for Charles I of France, also known as Charles the Bald, emperor of the West (875–77).

strengthen their sense of identity and common moral purpose, and to 'pass on the tradition of the way we must live to please God.' The designation of 'Christians', from the messianic title of Jesus as Christos, the anointed one, was only one of several used to describe them.

In Athens and in Corinth Paul was in the geographical historic centre of Greek culture. In Luke's account of Paul at bay among the Athenian intellectuals in the Areopagus [Acts 17], there is a sharp sense of the historic clash between Jewish fideism and Greek scepticism that took place. It was a dispute that Paul clearly lost, because some of those present mocked him, and others prevaricated. Some were convinced, but there is no mention of an Athenian church. In Corinth he had better fortune, although the traditionally pleasure-loving society proved quite resistant to the severe way of life that Paul seems to have to some extent taken for granted among his converts.

Therefore disputed he in the synagogue with the Jews, and with the devout persons, and in the market daily with them that met with him.
Then certain philosophers of the Epicureans, and some of the Stoicks, encountered him. And some said, What will this babbler say? other some, He seemeth to be a setter forth of strange gods: because he preached unto them Jesus, and the resurrection.
And they took him, and brought him unto Areopagus, saying, May we know what this new doctrine whereof thou speakest, is?
(Acts: 17: 17, 18, 19)

In Galatia, Paul may have gone outside the towns, which would have been more modest and isolated than those in Cilicia, Palestine and Syria. The main thrust of Paul's missionary effort was not rustic; it was located where it might have been expected to take place in an ancient world entirely dominated by the power and privilege of the city. The theatres for his propagandist effort were the public places offered by the ancient city: the public square, the synagogue and the lecture hall. The house-churches – which were just rooms in dwelling houses – were the natural meeting places where the followers of the religion could meet, eat a communal meal, speak of their faith, and acquire a sense of communal identity. However, while potential converts could be introduced there singly, there could be no general outreach in the house-church to a pagan or a Jewish public.

The natural tendency for Paul was to speak in the Jewish synagogue, as Jesus had done. To Jesus-believing Jews it must have seemed that the synagogue was itself the natural meeting place, to be used by all when the process of convincing Jewry of the righteous cause of Jesus had been terminated – or abandoned when the proximate end of time and the proclamation of God's kingdom came. Neither expectation was fulfilled. The first Christian churches to be substantial public buildings were not to be built for another two centuries.

Paul, Peter and the Conversion of Gentiles

The question of leadership and direction in the new cult came up decisively in AD 51, when Paul and Barnabas visited Jerusalem, probably with a mandate from the Christians in Antioch, to decide whether Christian male converts ought to be circumcised and, by implication, submitted to the full requirements of Jewish traditional law and dietary custom. The problem did not only affect Antioch. It was common to all the missions in Europe and Asia Minor. At a meeting with the Jerusalem leaders, Paul claimed the issues of policy and status were decided in his favour. James, Peter and John accepted his claims (and those of Barnabas) to leadership of the mission to the Gentiles, and agreed not to press the issue of circumcision of Gentile converts. This was not only a theological issue, but also a practical one. Christianity became vastly more accessible the moment that its male converts no longer had to submit to a worrying and painful surgical operation from which they might take quite a long time to recover. At the same time that Paul made this momentous agreement, he agreed to forward charitable contributions from the diaspora Christians for the community in Jerusalem.

The matter was too delicate to be amicably settled at a stroke. Possibly after the Jerusalem agreement it reappeared in the form of a dispute over dietary laws between Paul and Peter, when the latter was in Antioch. Peter, influenced by pressure from James in Jerusalem and supported, to Paul's

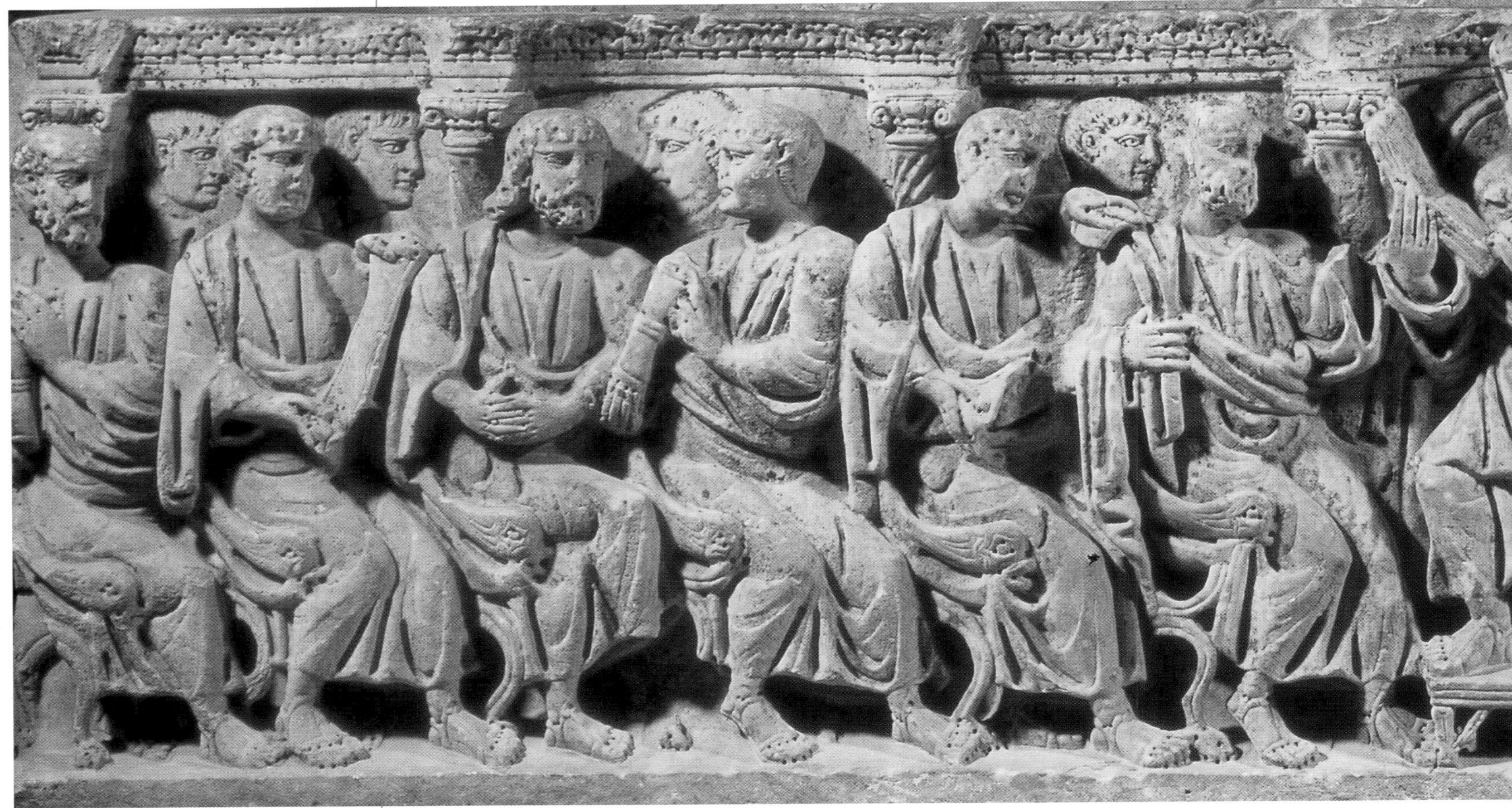

Above: Carved relief from a marble Christian sarcophagus dating from the end of the fourth century. It shows Christ with his apostles.

indignation, by Barnabas, refused to share meals with the Gentile Christians in Antioch. It may sound a magnification of trivia to modern Western ears, but it was not. Hospitality was a solemn matter in the ancient world and conferred a form of kinship, as it still does in the Middle East. So a refusal to participate in a non-kosher meal was not just peevish, but a denial of belonging to the same society. To an ex-Pharisee such as Paul, who had lived in a community where two-thirds of the special rules known to us concern diet, Peter's refusal to eat the common meal was extremely serious. Four or five years later, when he was again in Corinth, Paul was still conscious of the estrangement with Peter. At this point it is possible to speak of the churches of Asia and Europe. The Greek term for a church means those who are called to the assembly. The quarrel between Judaizers, who thought the Levitical laws in the Old Testament were still binding for Christians, and those who sided against them with Paul, continued. This was especially true in Galatia, where perhaps the strength of Greek culture with its assertion of natural law and morality was weaker than elsewhere and where, consequently, the novice Christians felt the need for the more comprehensive support of Judaism. Paul tended to assume the moral framework of Judaism without spelling it out. His dramatic assertion of the claims of the spirit over the law has tended to puzzle the more timid souls, up to our own time.

When Paul resumed his missionary journeys, he continued to target the great centres of population that he judged to be accessible to his efforts. A great prize was Ephesus, one of the great economic and cultural centres of Asia Minor, with a population of at least 150,000, and an ampitheatre judged by contemporaries to be one of the wonders of the world. It may be that his efforts in Ephesus cost Paul a period of imprisonment.

The hostility of the orthodox Jews of Jerusalem led to the troubled final period of Paul's life, during which he was moved about the Mediterranean at the behest of Roman justice. He had perhaps come to Jerusalem to bring the contributions from the Christians in the churches that he supervised, to the church in Jerusalem. After his arrival he was accused by the Asian Jews in Jerusalem of smuggling a Gentile into the forbidden sacred areas of the Temple, and they tried to lynch him. Roman troops intervened, and sent him under protective custody to their headquarters in Caesarea. Paul claimed Roman citizenship, but was still held in custody in Caesarea for two years or longer. Finally, a new governor sent him to Rome for trial. And in Rome, after a further unknown period of custody – perhaps for a time, only of house arrest – he was put to death during the anti-Christian measures of Emperor Nero, no later than AD 68. Peter was executed in Rome during the same period and for the same reason, although the history of Peter's presence in Rome is unknown.

Above: The great amphitheatre at Ephesus, which dates back to the first century AD. During Paul's time Ephesus was a wealthy cultural and economic centre. Paul visited the city and addressed an epistle to the Christians.

Some seventy years after the death of Jesus, the churches Peter and Paul had established, and those set up by other followers, were scattered over a vast area of the eastern Roman Empire and a good part of the western, including Rome itself. The numbers of Christians were still very modest, but their communities were so tenaciously and bravely supported that they became a new factor in the cultural and religious life of the Empire. The Christian congregations saw their obedience to Jesus as a prelude to the coming of God's kingdom, and not as some new chapter in the history of human power. Yet Christianity was still only a minor, novel cult. Power was to remain, for at least another century, something that Christians recognized in human relationships, but repudiated for themselves. However, the churches were already near a point where, if we look at them as part of human history and not as part of salvation history, power was to drift towards them whether they wanted it or not.

Right: The Roman Emperor Nero (AD 37–68). A virulent anti-Christian, Nero introduced a wave of persecutions during which both Paul and Peter were put to death.

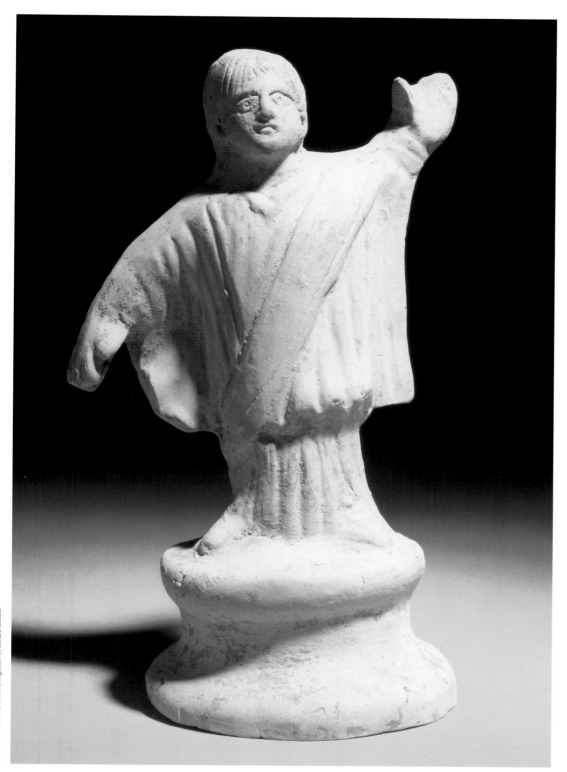

Left: A first-century terracotta statuette of a Christian priest. Within seventy years of Jesus' death, Christians still only numbered a few but their early churches and communities were established.

ΑΡΩΝ

2

Persecutors and Martyrs

It is hard to conceive of Christianity without the Roman Empire. No one who has written about it, from the authors of the Gospel of Luke onwards, has failed to make the connection, even if only in the negative context of persecution. Luke made a incorrect statement about a supposed census decree of the Emperor Augustus (63 BC–AD 14), which he made responsible for a fictional journey of Mary and Joseph to Bethlehem, so that the birth of the Messiah could be said to have taken place in the exact locality that the Jewish scriptures required. There was no such decree, and the Roman legate Quirinius, mentioned by Luke as being in office at the time, did not arrive in Syria until nine or ten years after the probable birth date of Jesus. These things are not important for the credibility of the historical Jesus. But they are important, in that the authors of one of the pillar texts of the religion chose to anchor the incarnate appearance of its founder in time by attaching two great figures of Roman power, the Emperor and the Legate.

Without the great grid of the Roman Empire, which established a common regime and ruling culture from the Parthian to the British and Moroccan frontiers, the followers of Jesus could never have taken the message of salvation to earth's farthest bounds, as first-century Hellenized Jews conceived those bounds. Nor could the ideas of the celestial and terrestrial cities of God have come into being. These inspired St Augustine, four centuries after Christ, to conceive a Christianity that, as it were, stood on the shoulders of the transformed Empire. To Augustine, God had given the Romans the arts and practice of dominion, and the imposition of a kind of peace, although the Romans had failed even to give effect to the ideals of justice that they served.

Was Christianity really a subversive force that proved hostile to the Roman Empire? A thousand years after the birth of Christ, a Roman Emperor still ruled a great Empire in the East, led great Roman armies, and ruled over a version of the Roman senatorial aristocracy. In the West at the same time a barbarian ruler sought recognition as a Roman Emperor, and presided over a version of the

Left: The synagogue at Dura-Europos, Syria.

Above: The apotheosis of Caesar in AD 161. In pre-Christianized Rome, the Emperor was welcomed into the pantheon of existing gods and worshipped as a living deity. This marble slab shows Marcus Aurelius, who ruled from AD 161–180, who renewed the persecutions of Christians.

Imperial Roman court. Today, two thousand years after the birth of Christ, a Christian bishop of Rome, wearing a costume reminiscent of that once worn by Roman Senators, flies all over the world to his flock. He speaks, when necessary, an inflected dialect of Latin, and the doctrines he preaches (many of which have been codified in the Latin tongue) are full of echoes of the supremely Roman principles of order and decorum, and of historical survivals of the religion's remote late-Roman past.

The Roman Empire was one of the greatest autocracies the world has known, supported by a large civil service, a huge army and a powerful secret police. It was perhaps not efficient in the modern sense, but terrifyingly effective when it felt it had really identified an enemy. Over the at-first obscure Jewish cult of Christianity, it hesitated for a very long time between bad-tempered proscription and

Left: Bacchanalian abandon on a sarcophagus fragment; Roman authority treated early Christianity with the same suspicion it had directed towards the pagan cult of Bacchus in the second century BC.

contemptuous quasi-toleration. It was made aware of the cult's existence at quite an early stage, because of the converts it had made in the capital, even in or near the Imperial Court.

Christianity was sometimes felt by the Roman ruling class to be subversive because, even more than that of its Jewish parent, its monotheism, or doctrine of one single god, cut at the basic social cohesive force of Roman religion, that was not so much a state religion as a religion of the state. In Japan there is a modern parallel in Shintoism, which makes certain shrines into imperial and national shrines. The many gods that were worshipped in the Empire were not incompatible with the official religion, which could also take the form of worship of the personal divinity of the Emperor.

However, in the past certain foreign pagan gods had awakened deep political disquiet in Rome. The accusation of 'depraved religion' had once been made against the new cult of the Greek god, Dionysus, known to the Romans as Bacchus, who was worshipped in secret, supposedly orgiastic rites. Fear of a Bacchanal secret society resembled later Roman suspicion of the Christians. The nearest modern equivalent is suspicion of the Freemasons. In 186 BC the Bacchanal scandal became a major political panic about possible treason in Rome, and led to the execution of a good many of its adepts.

Christians refused to make the libation of incense and wine before the Emperor's statue and the images of the gods, so demonstrating – though only on the occasions when specifically asked to conform – their impiety and disloyalty. As well as these acts of open dissidence, Christians were also sometimes noted to display a sort of obstinate and disparaging attitude towards the traditional religions, which did not make them friends.

Left: Trajan's Column, Rome, built in AD113. The Emperor Trajan left a permanent record of his achievements in the shape of a column with graphic depictions of his military and civil triumphs. His policy towards Christianity was a pragmatic one, designed to diffuse anti-Christian hysteria and civil unrest.

Above: A gold coin, or aureus, minted in the reign of the Emperor Hadrian (AD117–138). While not actively encouraging Christianity, he did not oppose it, reserving his intolerance for the Jews who were rebelling against Roman rule.

© Yale University Art Gallery, Dura Europos Archive

Right: The baptistry of a Christian house-church at Dura-Europos. Its simplicity was a marked contrast to the lavish and highly decorated synagogue in the same town.

Like many governing classes, that of the Roman Empire was prone to bouts of xenophobic suspicion. The Jews, with their single, exclusive god, their practice of circumcision and their recent participation in the Palestinian rebellions, were an obvious target. So too was their Christian offshoot, whose abandonment of circumcision could be seen as having rendered them even more socially dangerous. In the last decade of the first century the Emperor Domitian seems to have suffered an attack of acute insecurity. Not only did he proclaim his own divinity and require worship, but he also had members of his own family executed on the suspicion of 'atheism' and consorting with foreign religions. This atmosphere was dangerous to both Christians and Jews, especially in the east of the Empire where both groups were unpopular. Later, in the first half of the second century, the eastern Jews took part in two further major revolts. The repressions that followed were severe.

As the end of the first century of the Common Era approached, the tie with Judaism that had been vitally important in the first years after the death of Jesus, became subject first to a slow and then to a brusque estrangement, although a form of Judaic Christian church persisted in Palestine for a long period. The estrangement was mutual: formal denunciations of the Christians were pronounced in some synagogues. Quite separately from their mutual disagreements, and for different reasons, both Christians and Jews incurred government distrust and displeasure. St Ignatius of Antioch, who was martyred in the early years of the second century, wrote: 'It is absurd to talk of Jesus Christ and to practise Judaism. After all, Judaism believed in Christianity, not Christianity in Judaism'.

Perhaps a possible modern comparison would be the paranoid fear of Communism widespread in the United States from the late 1930s onwards, which produced the Congressional Un-American Activities Committee of 1938, and lay behind the McCarthyite persecutions of the 1950s. Once an issue is defined as the defence of a way of life, the advocates of a conspiracy theory have scope to demand arbitrary action against the hidden enemy. On the other hand, other establishment elites may be more confident about the resilience of official culture, and may resist the tendency to panic.

Trajan and the Beginnings of Toleration

In Imperial Rome very few people were prepared to say that members of a religion, which refused formal allegiance to the state gods, and who met in secret, were worthy of anything but severe punishment. But there were powerful people, sometimes including the Emperor himself, who were not disposed to make the refusal of some religious fanatics to conform to the letter of the observance of state ceremonies into a big issue. That seems to have been the upshot of the discussions between Pliny the Younger (AD 62–?114), the provincial governor of Pontus-Bithynia in Asia Minor, and the Emperor Trajan (AD 53–117), when the former asked the Emperor for guidance on how to treat Christians who were denounced for disloyalty.

The Emperor decided how denunciations were to be treated in future. Instead of encouraging people to inform against the Christians, he discouraged them by invoking the normal procedure in calumny cases. If charges could not be substantiated, the whole weight of the criminal penalty was visited on the accuser. Trajan also gave accused Christians the chance to renounce the religion, and so free themselves, after accusation. This was not toleration, but it was a policy of live and let live that discouraged anti-Christian fever, and gave Christianity many chances to continue to preach its mission. A decade later the Emperor Hadrian (AD 76–138) was to maintain a similar policy towards the Christians.

Above: A Christian martyred at the stake, as shown in a Byzantine manuscript. After a century or so of toleration, Christianity became a political target for the Emperor Marcus Aurelius and many of the faithful were martyred for their faith.

Left: The synagogue at Dura-Europos in Syria, an area sufficiently remote from the Emperor Hadrian's anti-Jewish policy. While the city of Jerusalem had lost even its name, large and richly decorated synagogues were built in and around the Near East. The frescoes show scenes from the Old Testament.

Right: A marble slab showing a public sacrificial procession with animals to be immolated for Mars. Roman people were suspicious of the privacy of Christian meetings. Christians refused to take part in the pagan rituals which would publicly show allegiance to the Roman gods and thus the Roman state.

Hadrian's policy towards the Jews, who had supported armed rebellions, and were to mount a further, final rebellion in AD 132–5, was far less favourable. Hadrian abolished even the name of Jerusalem: he renamed the city Aelia Capitolina, and by AD 310 the old name was so far forgotten that a Roman governor of the nearby city of Caesarea had no idea that a city called Jerusalem had ever existed. But this did not mean that Judaism was finished as a proselytizing force in the Graeco-Roman world, nor that it could not prosper. Synagogues continued to be built all over the Near East; in Dura-Europos, on the Euphrates, the synagogue expanded in size, wealth and decoration in a much more impressive way than the little house-church of the Christians in the same frontier town. While Christians still succeeded in converting Jews, Jews still quite often succeeded in converting Christians.

Persecution of Christians by the Roman authorities began with Nero's repression of AD 64. It was only sporadic after that until the great persecutions of AD 165–180, which included the terrible severities inflicted upon Christians of Lyons in AD 177. The temper of martyrdom was forged during that period.

The Secret of Christian Rituals

At the same time that Christianity finally fell away from Judaism, great cultural gaps between pagan and Christian began to appear. For a long period, the main problem that Christians faced was that of ignorance about their religion on the part of the pagans. The privacy of their meetings, and the known big variations in class and status of their members, meant that they were vulnerable to suspicion of unspeakable crime: of infant sacrifice, of incest, of cannibalism.

Right: The slab marking St Paul's tomb in the church of St Paul's Outside the Walls, Rome. It is marked with the letters PAULO APOSTOLO MART. Balsam was poured through the holes on to the saint's body. The faithful used to lower pieces of cloth to soak up the balsam, to be kept as holy relics.

Taken from *The Tombs of St Peter and St Paul*, E Kirschbaum S J, 1959.

The innocent truth about Christian meetings for worship, which at this point could only take place in rooms in Christian houses, and the equal innocence of their religious common meals, began after a long time to come to light. Even while Christians gradually ceased to be suspected of the most nefarious crimes, their other big differences from majority culture were noticed. For example, the reverence and familiar worship that Christians accorded to their martyred dead shocked the pagan world. It broke the taboo that in traditional culture an unbridgeable gulf separated the dead from the living. When Virgil's hero, Aeneas, descended to the underworld, he could speak to the pale spirits of the dead only across the blood of the sacrifices he had made. To the Christians, their dead only slept, to awake in the Lord on the Last Day.

By the third century the communion of the living Christians with their dead martyrs was achieved not only in the eucharistic feast, but also from the physical contact that they insisted on making with the tombs. In the slab that marks the tomb of St Paul, there are holes through which the faithful poured balsam. The openings served to let down small cloths. Once they had soaked up the perfumes poured into the tomb, they were recovered and regarded as precious relics. Allied to this (although more compatible with pagan custom) was the practice of a kind of funerary feasting at the tombs of the saints, a usage that St Augustine half excused, but, in the end, condemned, in his own mother.

The Concept of Charity

Christianity spread through the Mediterranean, including North Africa and Spain, and to the Near East. By the second half of the second century, it had spread to the Rhone valley. To what extent or in what areas the settled Jewish communities acted as springboards for this expansion is uncertain. It may be that Greek-speakers were the key transmitters. The expansion was probably still very modest. Socially it was notoriously a religion that took converts from every class of ancient society, from slaves to a sprinkling of members of big land-owning and merchant families. Artisans and freedmen supplied a good number of Christians, but firm evidence for numbers and proportions is scarce.

It is unlikely that slaves were disproportionately numerous in the Christian communities. There was no internal pressure on slave-owning Christians to free their slaves, and church leaders told slaves to obey their masters. It is even possible that manumissions of slaves by Christian slave-owners were less frequent than among pagans, because married male Christians were forbidden the sexual contact with female slaves that was normal to a pagan slave-owner. Such contact was one of the main stimuli to grant freedom to the slave mother and child. However, church funds were sometimes used to buy the freedom of Christian slaves of pagan masters.

One function of the churches was to act as friendly societies, whose charity looked after their members irrespective of social class. 'See, how these Christians love each other' was a frequent pagan comment. Not only the indigent, who among other things were helped with the decorous burial of their dead, but also members of classes above this were assisted. Help was given in particular to widows, whose remarriage was discouraged, and unmarried young women, who perhaps were unmarried because of their lack of a dowry, but who were helped to maintain their celibate state. Foundlings were often cared for by the churches. Sickness or imprisonment, above all imprisonment for religion, also attracted community assistance.

The churches could not have their own finances because Roman law did not recognize them as bodies capable of owning property. But the body of clergy that had grown up to supply leadership

Right: Mural painting from the sixth century in the catacombs of San Callisto, Rome. The saints Calixtus and Cyprian are shown together. St Calixtus, released from prison after the intercession of Marcia, a concubine of the Emperor Commodus, became pope in AD 218 but was martyred four years later. St Cyprian (c.AD 200–258), became Bishop of Carthage in AD 248, but was martyred a decade later during the reign of the Emperor Valerian.

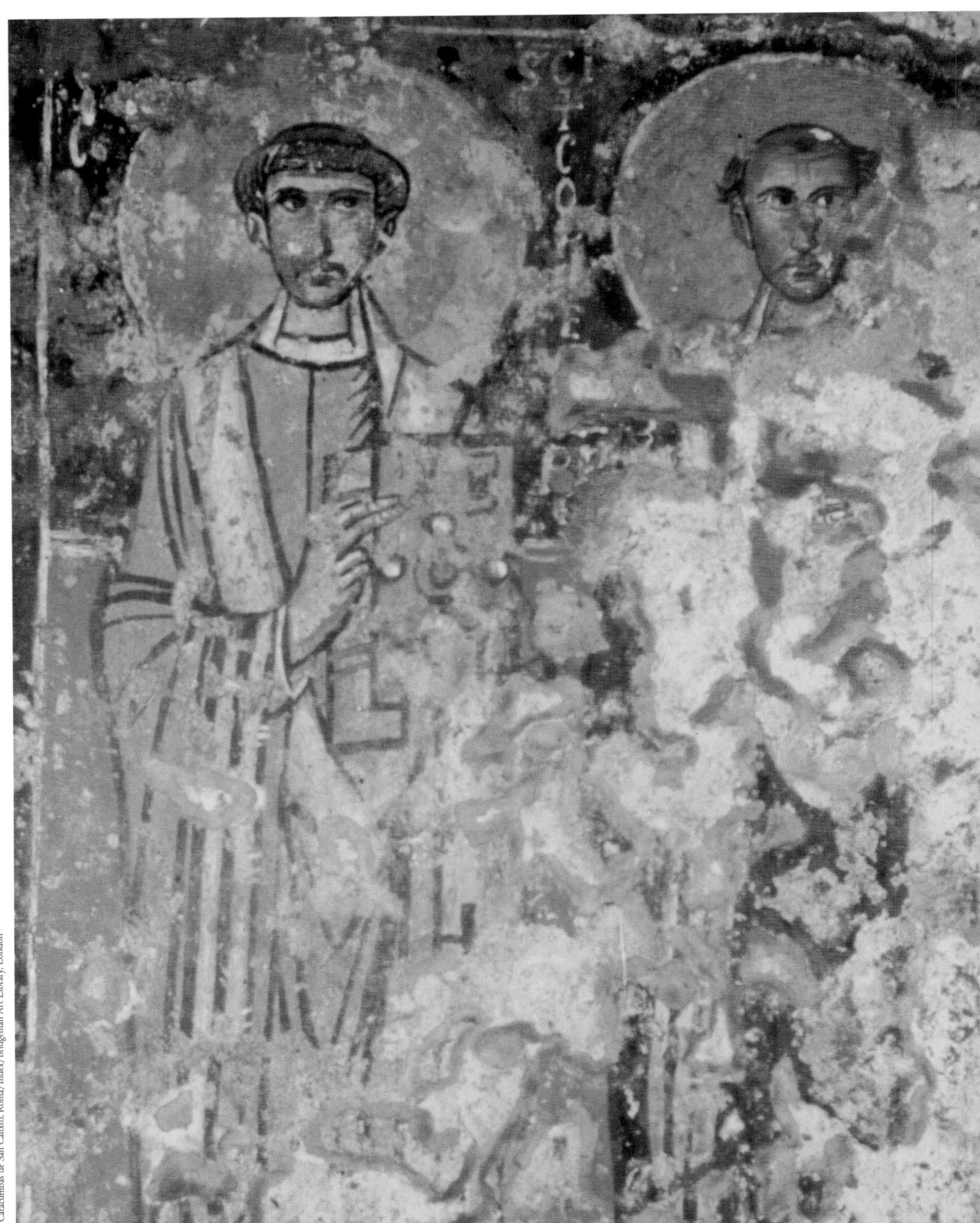

and to look after liturgical and practical needs was recognized to have a material claim on the local believers. From an early point the clergy, or at least its main members, were not expected to follow their own secular callings. In the larger churches an organized clergy included deacons in charge of social services, readers, acolytes, exorcists, doorkeepers.

Women and Celibacy

Women, although without clerical status, were extremely important in the Christian community. The prophetess was not unknown, nor without honour. Some Christian women were rich ladies, although not, during the first two centuries, from senatorial families. If women of such rank wanted unions with Christian men, they had to have them outside marriage, as there were no marriageable Christian men of their own class. Women could exercise political influence on behalf of the Church from unexpected places. Marcia, the concubine of the Emperor Commodus (AD180–92), was instrumental in securing the release of Christian prisoners from the mines. One of the released detainees was a certain Calixtus, later Bishop of Rome, who was the first of several popes to have been closely connected with the banking industry, although the later examples occurred only after a gap of many centuries.

Both men and women in the Christian congregations were affected by the emphasis on celibacy, which severely discouraged remarriage for either sex. Women were especially affected, too, by the social provision of funds to help them survive a long widowhood. Persuading young women to value an indefinite chastity had a very strong social effect. This had not always been so: at the beginning the lack of discrimination between the sexes in the Christian groups had been one of the things that caused most scandal among pagans. The growing emphasis on chastity as a virtue may have owed something to St Paul, but more to the wish of the priests to be distinguished from the other males in the community. Not that the married state was entirely forgotten: at the end of the second century St Clement of Alexandria devoted a lot of sympathetic attention to the moral problems of married Christians.

Part of the coherence and resilience of the Christian communities was due to the rigorous and often long apprenticeship imposed upon converts. The status of a catechumen, or Christian receiving instruction, meant that for a period of years – or, in the case of catechumens who deferred baptism until the last possible moment before death, for most of their lives – converts accepted a life in which they were in an important sense still outside the main body of believers. Together with the penitents who were deemed to have fallen from grace, they were offered bread that was not the bread given at the sacred communal meal, and restricted in how they participated in the communal life of the group. It was a subclass of believers still maintained, at least until times within living memory, in Ethiopia. In the ancient world, similar distinctions between the novices and the adepts would have been familiar to followers of other contemporary religions.

The Rite of Baptism

Baptism, in the Christian regime, was the rite that marked the passage of a man or a woman (or a child, for they also were provided for) from the profane to the sacred life.[1] The detailed prescriptions for the ceremony, dating from the early third century, are starkly explicit. Baptism was to take place at dawn on a Sunday, after an all-night vigil and administered, if possible, in running water. Witnesses were interrogated about the suitability of the candidates. According to the Roman priest Hippolytus,

Below: Roman mural painting of first to third century. Women played an important role in the spread and maintenance of Christianity. Many were martyred.

who wrote the tract, people from quite a long list of callings and moral categories were to be excluded from baptism. The list includes pimps, prostitutes, actors, homosexuals, gladiators, magicians and army officers who give orders to kill – the history of Christianity would have been very different if the last prohibition had been maintained. In the days leading up to baptism the candidate was given repeated exorcisms to reveal and excise impurity, and then, after a devotional night and a final exorcism-anointment, was led naked to the water: the women, at this point, took off their jewellery. There was a final interrogation about past moral conduct, and about the reasons for asking for baptism.

Then the liturgy took its course: the candidate renounced the Devil and his works, and pronounced the Creed, as the bishop gave the neophyte a triple immersion in the waters. No one who had experienced these sacramental solemnities, and the long apprenticeship leading up to them, was going to take the Christian commitment lightly.

1 P. Cramer, *Baptism and Change in the Early Middle Ages*, c.200–c.1150 (Cambridge,1993), pp.9–45

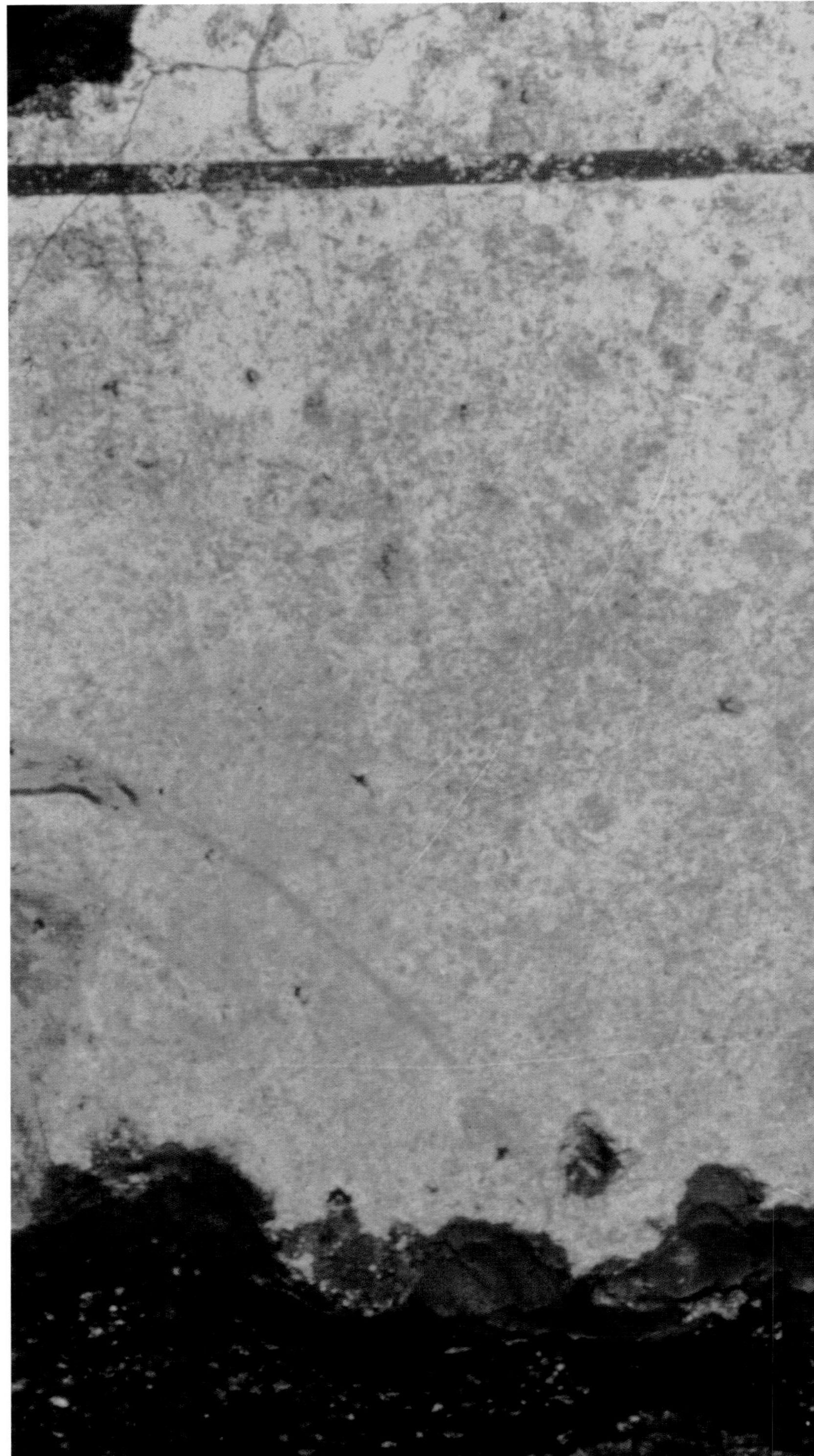

Left: Fresco from the catacombs of San Callisto, Rome. A baptism scene from the third century emphasizes how significant the ritual was in the new faith. Baptism was prefaced by long and elaborate preparation and was not lightly undertaken.

3

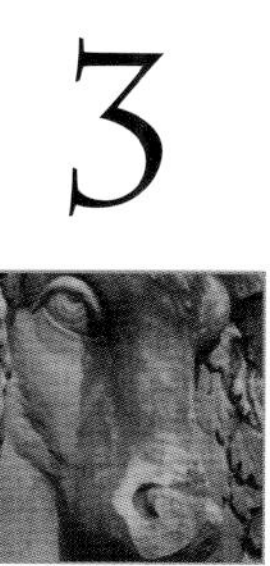

Christians in a Pagan World

Christian persecution resumed in the second half of the second century. The bishops were the leaders of the Christian communities and they did not refuse to bear witness. In Smyrna (Izmir) in Asia Minor, the bishop was the 86-year-old Polycarp, a leader well known as far as Rome and Lyons. He was also remembered as the one-time host of Ignatius, the Bishop of Antioch who was then being escorted to Rome for martyrdom, and he had known St John the Divine. Polycarp was known to and respected by the civic authorities in Smyrna, who nevertheless had to bring him before the Roman provincial governor. The proconsul was willing to allow him to address the pagan and Jewish mob in the stadium where he had been taken after his arrest, but Polycarp declined, perhaps knowing that it would only inflame passions further; he expressed himself willing to discuss his religion further with the governor, but not with the people. He could not be thrown to the beasts, as the governor had closed the so-called Games, but was forthwith burned in the stadium. Significantly, after his death, his remains were retained, to stop Christians from using them as sacred relics.

Hostility to Christians was not just the work of people who wanted more human bloodshed in the circus: it had a rational, conservative basis. By this point, the anti-Christian movement essentially rested on the widespread popular feeling that some corrupting internal force was at work to undermine traditional cultural values. That these were the feelings of 'the mob' does not mean that they were of the people and therefore to be disparaged: historians have analysed 'the mob' in the context of modern history, and found that it often included large numbers of very 'respectable' citizens.

One who put up a rational argument against the Christians was an intellectual called Celsus who wrote a polemic work against the Christians. His arguments have not survived in a complete form, but they were in general those of an enlightened stoic who saw the Roman Empire as the protector and defender of local gods and civic custom, and the guarantor of peace and justice. The Jews and the Christians, but particularly the latter, were the advocates of a pernicious and dangerous religious

Left: Detail showing Jonah and the whale from a fourth-century mosaic.

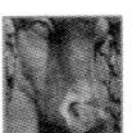

Right: A stone frieze showing a Roman butcher at work. Christianity welcomed people of all classes on an equal basis. For anti-Christians, such as Celsus, this represented a threat to traditional values.

Below: A bust of the Emperor Decius (c.AD 200–251). Under his rule, Christians were persecuted with great severity.

particularism, who both peddled versions of a divinely chosen people whose destiny excluded everyone else. The Christians, who had 'spread to become a multitude', were also dangerous because they threatened to impose the values of the ignorant upon the rest of the community.

> *'In private houses we see woolworkers, cobblers, laundry men, and the most illiterate and bucolic yokels, who would not dare say anything at all in front of their elders and their more intelligent masters. But whenever they get hold of children in private and some stupid women with them, they let out some astounding statements... They alone, they say, know the right way to live...'*

However, Celsus mocked Christian Messianism on account of its practical impotence. In the crises of the prosecution of Christian impiety, their God had singularly failed to intervene on behalf of any of them.

The heroism of Christians must be saluted. Their movement remains to this day the most important passive and peaceful resistance to an autocratic government to have occurred anywhere in

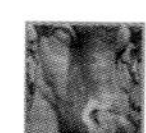

the western world. Not that the Christians rejected all Roman government; they protested their loyalty, and their refusal concerned only the submission they were told to make to demonic idols. Nor did they all with one accord choose martyrdom: on the contrary, in the persecution (AD 249–51), of the Emperor Decius, the apostasy of an overwhelming majority in a Christian congregation was not infrequent. But the strength and constancy of many Christian witnesses remained in the face of terrible punishments. A moving and probably genuine prison diary has survived from the persecutions of Carthage at the beginning of the third century, by a lady called Perpetua, who was martyred together with her slave, but who, while awaiting martyrdom, recorded her dreams and spiritual experiences.

Apostasy and Martyrdom

The heroism of the few inevitably meant judgement on the poltroonery of the many. There have always been those whose conviction in moments of great trial proves inferior to that of the strongest. Muhammad's attitude to such people, 'waverers' or 'hypocrites', was severe. The Christian attitude was less severe, but it did not exclude rigorism. If the lapsed Christians wanted to return to the communities of the faithful when the danger had passed, the attitude of the surviving confessors was not necessarily vindictive. But there was among them a very strong doubt that, after such a decisive apostasy, there was any authority in the Christian community to forgive such things. Or, if there was, many of them thought that the returned apostate could be absolved only when at the point of death.

The issue about the absolution of returned apostates was critical to the future of Christianity. If the penitent apostate could not be reintegrated into the community of the people of God, the Christian groups were destined to become a narrowed sect. The matter came to a head in Rome, where the rigorist position was led by a Roman priest called Novation (*fl.* third century), who eventually felt it his duty to seek election as Bishop of Rome, and in Carthage, where a severe but still not absolutely inflexible position was assumed by Bishop Cyprian (c.AD200–258). Novation was opposed in Rome by a party of leniency, whose candidate, the deacon Cornelius, got a majority vote. Cyprian hesitated over which candidate he should support for the Roman bishopric, because the issue so closely concerned his own church. Eventually he opted for Cornelius and so, implicitly, for a policy of mercy.

Tied up with the matter of receiving apostates back into the fold was the the question of the authority of bishops. If dealing with returned apostates was going to be left to the congregation, and so to the surviving confessors, rather than to the bishop, they were going to be harshly done by. If the bishop had the power of absolution, the community of Christians was going to be ready to compromise, and to pardon the lapsed believer. The debate in the end concerned the place of ordinary mortals in the Church.

Another hidden danger of the big persecutions was that Christians would come to see martyrdom as an end in itself. 'Do not look forward to dying in your bed, in childbirth or

Below: A mosaic pavement illustrates Jonah being spat out by the whale. Early Christians used the Old Testament story of Jonah being swallowed and spat out as an allegory for the Resurrection.

in the lassitude of fever, but in martyrdom so that he who has suffered for you may be glorified.' This doctrine of the Montanists, an extremist Christian wing that originated in Phrygia, in Asia Minor, is not entirely unfamiliar to our own generation, although in an Islamic, not Christian context, and in a warlike rather than a passive form.

Apologists for Christ

There was persecution of Christians not only in Asia, but at the other end of the Empire, at Lyons in the Rhone valley. But towards the end of the second century the persecutions died down again. The Roman Empire was experiencing a time of reduced internal and external tensions, and the big wars on the borders, though never entirely quietened, were for a time less exacting. The cities of the provinces reached a period of yet bigger public works. The intermittent civil wars were not over, but the army was still under firm central control. For the moment, the call for scapegoats died down. A moment of balance seemed to have arrived. This can only fill a generation like our own, which may be experiencing a similar moment, with interest and apprehension.

On the Christian side, the apologist Athenagoras, in the second century, addressed a pamphlet in the form of a 'supplication' to the Emperor. It was written in a conservative and placatory spirit that emphasized how the Christians were close to the best of the Stoic moral philosophers, and wished to further the pacific and harmonious operation of society. In some ways it was not too far from the anti-Christian writer, Celsus. Athenagoras was not alone in this deference to power: other Christian contemporaries shared it.

Below: A second-century Roman wedding ceremony. The social bonds of family and kinship were immensely important and a significant focus for early Jesus-followers.

Christians with good training in Greek oratory had appeared in the first generation of converts, though not among those responsible for writing of the Gospels. In the second century able Christian literary apologists, trained in philosophy as well in rhetoric, began to tackle the Jewish question from their own point of view. The main manner in which Jewish scriptures were related to Christ by the apologists was through the allegorical method. Adam foreshadowed Christ in a manner that could be described as his providing the 'type' of Christ. Where Old Testament prophecy did not directly predict Christ and his life and doctrine, it foreshadowed it in a general way similar to that in which the Jewish Exodus from Egypt prefigured the redemption brought by Christ the Messiah, or Jonah swallowed and disgorged by the fish became the symbol of the Resurrection.

This allegorical 'typology' has remained one of the main Christian ways of looking at the Jewish scriptures, as anyone may check who looks at the marginal notes of a King James or a Revised version of the Bible. Not unnaturally, the allegations by Christian writers that they understood the true meaning of Jewish scripture in a manner inaccessible to the Jews themselves, were not too kindly received by Jewish scholarship.

Marcion and the Old Testament

One route not followed by mainstream Christianity, but nonetheless important and widely received among second-century Christians, was that of total rejection of Jewish scripture. This was the position of Marcion (c.AD100–c.165), the son of a bishop from Asia Minor, although he preached in Rome. An enthusiast, in his own way, for the doctrines of

St Paul, Marcion saw inconsistency and weakness in the Old Testament accounts of Yahweh. The God of the Old Testament seemed to him a God utterly unacceptable, for the way he occasionally admitted ignorance about his own creation, for his having taken responsibility for the entrance into the world of evil, and for afterwards tolerating that it should continue. The Old Testament, Marcion concluded, should be entirely rejected. By his time, the acceptance of one category (or canon) of authoritative writings about Christian ways to salvation, and the elimination of others, had become a normal practice, although Marcion's wholesale repudiation of the main body of Jewish scripture did not find general favour.

Marcion was also repelled and disgusted by the sexual and reproductive processes that God had determined for men and women. For the numerous Marcionite communities he decreed that marriage and sexual contacts were to be avoided. Marcion emphasized all the elements of the Gospels that were most hostile to the ties of kinship: in ancient society, and also in most societies that followed, down to a comparatively recent time, this was a profoundly disruptive message. Most ancient men saw in kinship the most profound and meaningful of all social bonds. That this was so had already been demonstrated in Christianity in the way the earliest Jesus-follower assembled around the nucleus of his family.

Gnosticism

The desire to find a road to enlightenment and salvation was common to huge numbers of people in the ancient world at this time. It was so not merely for Christians and Jews and their sub-sects, but also for very many, principally mystically inclined, pagans. The Mithraic mysteries, in which ritual meals celebrated the slaying of a primal bull, had an enormous following throughout the Empire, and its adepts had included at least one emperor. The Christians had an idea of individual redemption and of its proximate achievement through God's kingdom that was shared by few; but the notion of enlightenment through revealed knowledge (gnosis) was common to many. The first sentence of the Gospel of John shows that the Christians also followed

Above: A detail from a sarcophagus showing Adam and Eve. For the Christian Gnostic Marcion, sexual activity was abhorrent even though it was a process determined by God for humans.

© Ronald Sheridan, Ancient Art & Architecture Collection

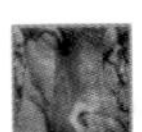

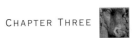

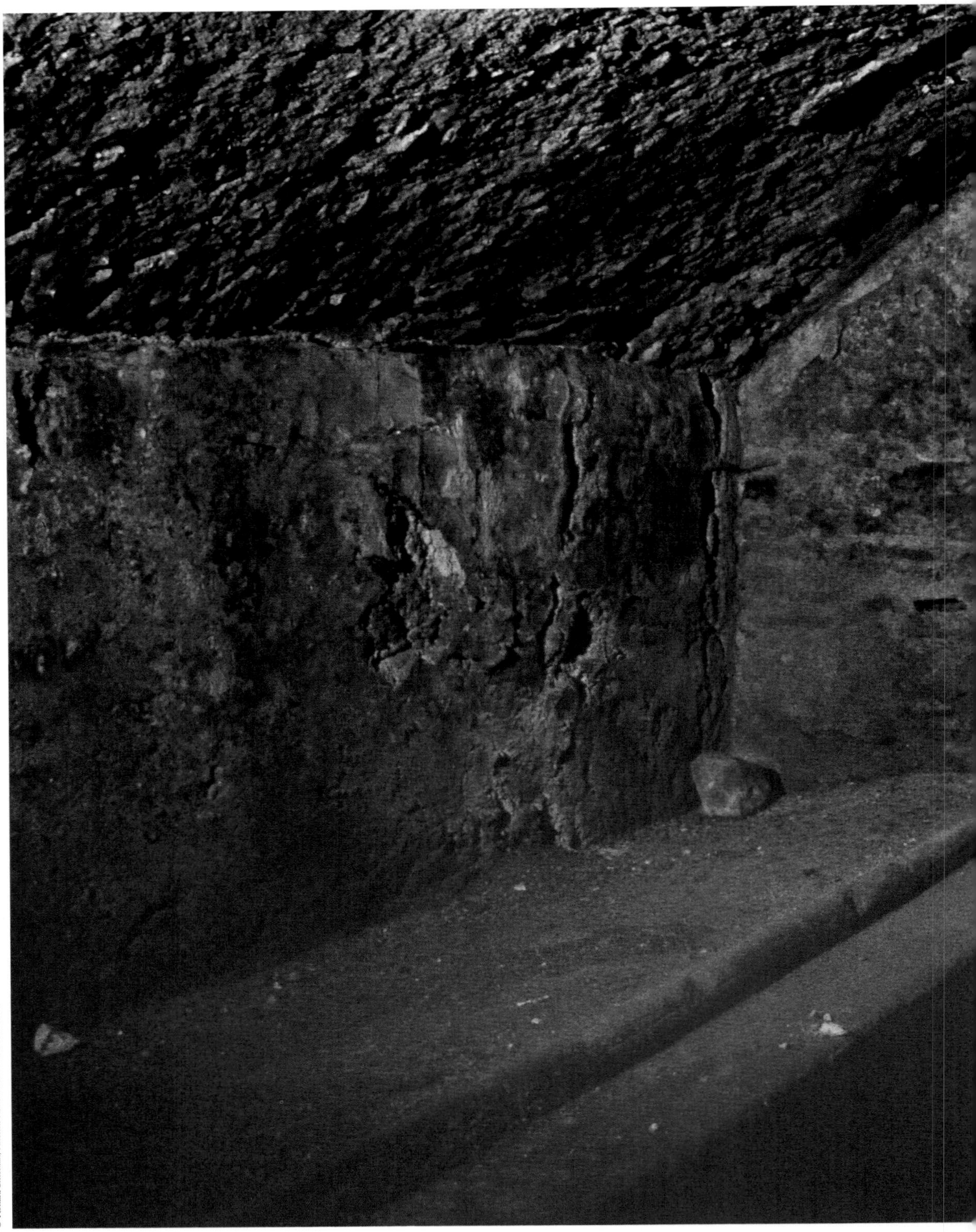

Right: Mithraeum or shrine to Mithras. In Persian mythology, Mithras was said to have slain a bull from whose blood all life sprang. The cult of Mithras was especially popular with the Roman army.

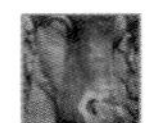

this path, and indeed, although 'Gnostic' became a term later applied to certain deviant Christians, it was earlier a designation that some orthodox Christians applied to themselves: a notable example was Clement, a learned and eloquent philosopher and theologian who lived and taught in Alexandria at the end of the second century. The way in which Clement discussed Gnosticism, in spite of the strictures he made concerning one or two individual Gnostic thinkers, showed admiration and respect.

Did Gnosticism exist before Christianity? The historian, Henry Chadwick, has posed the question as follows:

> *'Were the second-century heresies the consequence of trying to impose alien theosophical elements on the Christian substratum? OR systems which resulted from fitting bits of Christianity into a prior religious entity, which might take several different forms and could assimilate Mithras or Attis or Judaism with as little trouble as it accepted Jesus?'*[1]

Above: Fourth-century Gnostic writings inscribed on stone stele or slabs.

Gnostic tradition was a complicated mixture, in which the Platonic idea of the immortality of the soul was only one of a number of elements. Faith and wisdom inspired the Gnostic with knowledge of the origin and destiny of the world. Material things were of no concern to the deity, and the all-important element to the believer was the spark of the divine that he carried – if he was one of the enlightened – within him. Such views were ultimately fatal to the sacramental view of material things that lay behind most of the developing sacred drama of the Christian liturgy – one need only think of the prescriptions for baptism that are described above. They were bound, also, to impinge upon people's concepts of a Jesus who had been seen after his death, apparently restored to the condition of an approachable human being.

The Gnostics thought that people had become alienated from the all-informing divine spirit in some original, cosmic disaster, and that only a chosen few could now benefit from the knowledge of their true origin and from their relationship to the divine. Such views had been current in Palestine at the time of the first Jesus-followers; even at this stage there had been a current of Jewish Gnosticism.

In Samaria a preacher called Simon, who probably held Gnostic views, had represented himself as the voice of 'the Great Power'. Simon was given baptism by Philip the Jesus-evangelist, although his proffer of money for authority to 'lay on hands' caused Peter to eject him from the Jesus-community.

How the basic split between the material and the spiritual worlds should determine conduct was a question answered differently by the different Gnostic groups. A majority followed the path attributed to Marcion, and chose to lead extremely ascetic lives, and to refuse or drastically restrict sexual activity. But others decided that, because of the non-divine nature of the material world, as long as they were enlightened adepts of the divine way, it did not matter how their bodies were used; such views could lead to sexual libertinism. There may have been influence of this kind upon the Christian communities at a very early stage and within the lifetime of Paul: something of the kind seems to be hinted at in his letters to the Corinthians.

Zoroastrianism and Manichaeism

The cosmic dualism professed by the Gnostics may eventually have been rooted in Persian (Iranian) Zoroastrianism, which had already in the past influenced Judaism, and had probably been responsible for the belief in Satan and in demonic possession that had played a part in the life and ministry of Jesus. But after Zoroaster by far the most influential of the Persian dualisms that grew from Christianity, and proceeded to make inroads on Christians and non-Christians alike, from China through to Mesopotamia, Syria, Egypt, North Africa and Spain, was Manichaeism, the religion that grew from the visions of a Persian Baptist Christian called Mani, born in the province of Media in Mesopotamia. In the early third century Mani was granted a vision of his own Heavenly Twin, or guardian angel, a prelude to the revelations of divine wisdom that followed, one of which showed his opponents sinking for eternity into a black sea.

Mani claimed to be an apostle of Jesus and proclaimed him as a divine being who could not have suffered true incarnation or true death. Like him, Mani worked miraculous feats of exorcism and healing. Like the other Gnostics, Manichaeans supposed an eternal opposition of spiritual light and gross matter. Like them, they made the superior adepts into an God-chosen elite, who in the Manichae case practised severe asceticism, teetotalism and vegetarianism, and even felt it necessary to

Below: Breaking the Bread. Christians celebrating the Eucharist from the catacomb of Priscilla in Rome. The bread and wine symbolized the body and blood of Christ.

SCALA

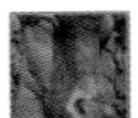

Right: Zoroastrian fire altar from Sassanian Persia. Zoroastrianism focused on the struggle between good and evil, predicting the ultimate triumph of good, in the form of the supreme god Ahura Mazdah, often represented as fire.

discourage gardening and silviculture, and to apologize to the bread they consumed – an attitude which has earned for them the contempt of a modern, garden-loving English historian, Robin Lane-Fox. The lesser believers were excused the obligations of chastity and asceticism, but had in compensation to suffer several incarnations before they could be purified to the necessary degree of enlightenment. Like many other Gnostics, the Manichaeans were willing to give women a prominent part in their ceremonies.

Manichaeism gave third- and fourth-century orthodox Christianity a powerful and widespread opposition to contend with, though it was then only one among many Gnostic oppositions. It was destined to endure in various forms for many centuries. Its last conspicuous manifestation in the West was perhaps the Cathar heresy of the twelfth and thirteenth centuries, bloodily put down by the centralized and authoritarian Roman Church of the time.

Orthodoxy, Rite and Ritual

The idea of orthodox Christianity, of a 'great Church' (or 'great assembly', a Jewish idea) that was the God-given custodian of right views about the faith, took root in the second century, in the climate created by the growth of what were seen as a perilous undergrowth of mistaken opinions and customs. Such reactions were already visible in the church of Peter and Paul, in apostolic and following times.

The assertion of right opinion was joined with the assertion of correct and traditional rites, which had been passed down faithfully from earlier times. The rite of baptism has already been described. In the mid-second century the apologist, Justin, described the eucharistic rite that in some ways resembled the order followed in the synagogue, but in others was entirely Christian.

'Bread and a cup of water and mixed wine are brought to the president of the brethren, and he, taking them...offers thanksgiving..'; the administration of the elements to the congregation by the deacons follows. 'This food we call Eucharist, of which no one is allowed to partake except one who believes that the things we teach are true, and has received the washing for forgiveness of sins and for rebirth, and who lives as Christ handed down to us.'

Orthodoxy (correct belief) stands out in every phrase of this account. Those who held these right opinions were the defenders of the great Church that was already widely defined as 'catholic', meaning universal. 'Catholic' was used to serve, as it were, as the Christian surname. When Pionius, a well-educated Christian of Smyrna, was interrogated by the magistrate during the Decian persecution, about what church he was, he replied: 'Of the catholic church, for Christ has no other.'

Irenaeus (AD130–200), the Greek-speaking Bishop of Lyons, the friend and disciple of Bishop Polycarp of Smyrna, was one of the main builders of intellectual defensive systems against what were seen as hostile opinions that threatened the truth of the Gospel messages transmitted to his generation by faithful believers. His main literary work was entitled *Against all Heresies*. In it he took the position that true Christian belief, whose best custodians he thought to be those churches founded by apostles (he cited Rome as a particularly authoritative example), was in effect revealed progressively to faithful persons. The hostility of Irenaeus to curiosity and innovation in religion may make him seem an authoritarian defender of a monolithic 'great Church', but this definition today contains overtones of power and authority that Irenaeus certainly did not possess.

The question of authority led inevitably to that of the authority of texts. It was a question that the Gnostics themselves had also raised, but their criteria were entirely unacceptable to Irenaeus. For example, some Gnostics had their own version of the Gospel, the so-called Gospel of Thomas, the doubting disciple, whose text has been rediscovered only in the present century. 'Gospels' of this kind were rejected by Irenaeus from what came gradually to be known as the canon of accepted sacred writings; some rejected works we still know in the form in which they were consigned to the Biblical Apocrypha. Irenaeus laid great stress upon the joint authority of the four Gospels that were from the following century onwards to be described as 'canonical'. The first systematic list of canonical books in the Old and New Testaments was given by a Council held in Rome in AD 382.

Quarrels started at the very beginnings of the Church, whose history, as the great historian Gibbon spitefully recorded over two centuries ago, is from one point of view one of ceaseless internal hostilities. That these negative elements are not the most basic facts of church history, does not make them go away. Like all scriptural religions, Christianity has its gatekeepers. But for this a price has to be paid. If we can only know about the faith through a tradition that requires interpreters, conflict among the gatekeepers is inevitable.

Persecutions began again in the first half of the third century. One of the triggers for the outbreak was the unsatisfactory Christian attitude to the celebration of Rome's millennium in AD 248, a moment in which loyalty to Roman tradition became politically very sensitive. There had already been a revival

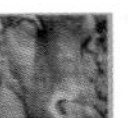

Right: The four tetrarchs: Diocletian, Maximian, Constantius and Galerius. Towards the end of his rule, Diocletian divided the Roman Empire into four political units, two eastern, two western. He and Maximian ruled the east as Augusti; Constantius and Galerius ruled the west as Caesars.

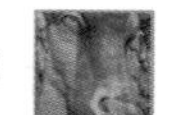

of persecution in AD 235–236, as a reaction against the Emperor Alexander Severus (AD 205–235), who had been seen as excessively pro-Christian. This outbreak may have stimulated the learned controversialist, Origen (AD185–254), to write an exhortation to martyrdom. Origen was an Alexandrian intellectual said to have made himself a eunuch to reduce sexual temptation in the course of giving mixed seminars, a procedure unlikely to recommend itself to modern academics. He was the son of a Christian martyr, and was himself to suffer torture and grievous imprisonment for the faith. However, his 'Exhortation', written before his own arrest and witness, contains a hint of divine threat to the torturers, when he says that the cry of the blood of the martyrs calls to God from the soil on which it fell.

Below: The dove of peace hovers above the heads of three youths enduring in the fiery furnace of Nebuchadnezzar (Daniel:3). Detail from fresco in the catacomb of Santa Priscilla, Rome.

Organization and Infrastructure

However, from AD 260 until the end of the century there was a very important lull in persecution. The Christians all over the Empire benefited from a *de facto* toleration. In spite of the shaky legal basis on which the churches were allowed to own property, many churches were built as public buildings to accommodate congregations. An elaborate organization of church officials was set up in the richer dioceses to administer charities and relief works. In AD 251 the Roman church had a staff of more than 250 persons, and looked after more than 1500 widows and poor people. Christians were allowed to occupy important public offices, and where these meant executing duties of deference to pagan gods, the authorities were often willing to turn a blind eye. A bishop such as Cyprian of Carthage – who eventually suffered martyrdom – had been a rich and powerful member of the civic magnate class. When toleration returned, many other bishops were accorded respect by the local government authorities.

Diocletian and the Great Persecution

The second half of the third century was, however, a bad time for the Empire. There was recession, inflation, and defeat in some of the great wars on the Roman frontiers. Great soldier-emperors again took control, above all Diocletian (reigned AD 284–305). Towards the end of his long reign, he became worried about the high positions held by Christians in the army. He and one of his junior co-Emperors were incited against them by the Oracle of Apollo at Didyma, near Miletus on the coast of Asia Minor. There had been a remarkable revival in the activities and popularity of the pagan oracles of Asia Minor in the second and third centuries, and Diocletian's visit to Didyma – on which Constantine, the future Christian emperor, may have accompanied him as a young staff officer – witnessed its last big manifestation. Pagan intellectuals were also calling for action against the Christians, notably Porphyry, a pupil of the great Platonist philosopher, Plotinus. The Christians had become vulnerable to official attack, not only for the old ideological and popular reasons, but also because the government had become worried by the power their members held.

On 23 February AD 303, the day of the gods of Boundaries (Terminalia), Diocletian launched one of the final, and perhaps the greatest, of the persecutions. Christians were not only required to submit and sacrifice, but, as in some previous persecutions, also to hand over their sacred books for destruction. This produced divisions among the Christians, because the consignment of the books by the traditores (whose description supplies the origin of the later words for 'traitor') created a new class of apostates whom some Western Christians refused to receive back into the fold when persecution ended. It had previously been accepted that only sacrifice to the pagan gods created an apostasy that was difficult to purge.

Diocletian's persecution was an extremely serious and bloody business, the more serious because the Christians were no longer insignificant scapegoats, but an influential minority, and in some parts of the Empire an influential majority. They no longer met only in poky back rooms, but in substantial churches. The cathedral of Nicomedia was clearly visible from the Emperor's palace. Because of the geographical division of power among the co-Emperors, the effect of the persecutions varied in different parts of the Empire. In the areas subject to Diocletian and Galerius, which included Rome, Syria, Egypt and Asia Minor, all places where the Christians were socially influential and demographically numerous, the persecution was most consistent. It was also savage in North Africa. The Christians were no longer, when suffering the final penalties, always subjected to the jeers of the mob as they had been a generation earlier, but their punishments were still very often ferocious.

Roman Emperor from AD 284–305, Diocletian launched one of the last and bloodiest of the Christian persecutions.

1 H. Chadwick, *The Early Church* (Harmondsworth, 1967), p. 35

4

The Christian Empire

Above: The head from the colossal statue of Constantine which once stood in his basilica in Rome.

In AD 312, Constantine, the joint ruler of the Roman Empire in the west, had a vision. Its impact on the development and spread of Christianity was immeasurable.

Constantine is one of the most difficult major figures in Christian history to assess. It is possible to think of Christian history up to his times in terms of men and women who almost all aspired to holiness, even if they did not all achieve it. But Constantine was a man of power, whose whole life was dedicated to defending and seizing power, who lived behind the mask that all men of power wear, never revealing his motives unless and until it was politically expedient to do so. There are many reasons to believe that he accepted the Christian faith more or less as it was presented to him by its exponents, and that he accepted a duty to serve its aims, especially in supporting its bishops. He accepted without demur the obligation to judge between the quarrelling and disputing members of its clergy. But certainty about his motives seems impossible to obtain.

Constantine had been proclaimed an Augustus in AD 306 at York in Britain, in succession to his father Constantius. Neither was a Christian, but Constantine inherited a tolerant policy towards the Christians from his father, and reinforced this tolerance immediately on his accession by restoring the rights and property Christians had enjoyed before the beginning of the recent persecutions. For another six years, there was no indication that Constantine was getting ready to make the Christian faith the fulcrum of his policies.

Left: Scenes from the Passion of Christ on a fourth-century Christian sarcophagus. On the left is the chi-rho symbol that inspired Constantine.

Even after a commitment to Christianity first appeared in AD 312, the translation of this commitment into coherent government policies could not take place until AD 324, when, after conquering his opponent Licinius, Constantine ruled the whole Roman world. To turn the religious policies of a world power upside-down, repudiating the whole former religious basis of the state, could not be effected until the ruler's legitimacy was unquestioned throughout his empire.

Constantine invaded Italy at the beginning of AD 312, and arrived outside Rome in the autumn to confront Maxentius, the other ruler of the western Empire, who was at this stage his main opponent. Maxentius, on his part, was too nervous of internal opposition in Rome to face a siege, and prepared to leave the city with his army, to battle with Constantine on the northern bank of the Tiber, on the Via Flaminia outside the Milvian Bridge.

Below: The Victory of Constantine at the Battle of the Milvian Bridge, a fresco by Piero della Francesca, probably painted in 1452–57. This is part of the True Cross Cycle in the Church of San Francesco, Arezzo, Italy.

A Dream and a Vision

A vision and a dream shortly before the battle determined Constantine on the more or less Christian symbolism to which he should entrust his fortunes. The vision was not his alone but that of his whole army. As they arrived outside Rome they saw a cross, or something very like it, in the noonday sky. The dream was the emperor's alone. In it he saw a sign that he ought to paint on the battle equipment of his troops, in sign of victory. It was not a recognized Christian symbol. The two Greek letters that seem to have composed it, *chi-rho*, could conceivably be understood as the initial letters of *chrestos*, for Christ, although that was a far from obvious interpretation. The sign was, nevertheless, duly inscribed on Constantine's own helmet and on the shields of his personal bodyguard, and in Constantine's view it brought him, together with the symbol of the cross in the sky, a great victory. Maxentius' army was crushingly defeated, and pushed into the Tiber, which flowed at its rear; Maxentius himself drowned with the rest, and Constantine entered Rome as senior Augustus.

What happened in October AD 312 was interpreted by Constantine as a divine dispensation of some kind in his favour. This would have been the conclusion of any earlier emperor; the difference lay in Constantine's decision that it was the God of the Christians who had supported him. He used the *chi-rho* symbol on a new dynastic battle-standard, the so-called 'labarum', which also bore the pictures of Constantine and his children. From that moment Constantine's religious policy was thrown entirely on the Christian side. Towards the official pagan symbolism of Rome he showed at best an ambiguously silent attitude, that after several years changed into outright public rejection. The triumphal arch built for him after he entered Rome still stands just outside the modern Forum area. It contains no central representation of a pagan god. The Senate's inscription on the arch refers to his victory having

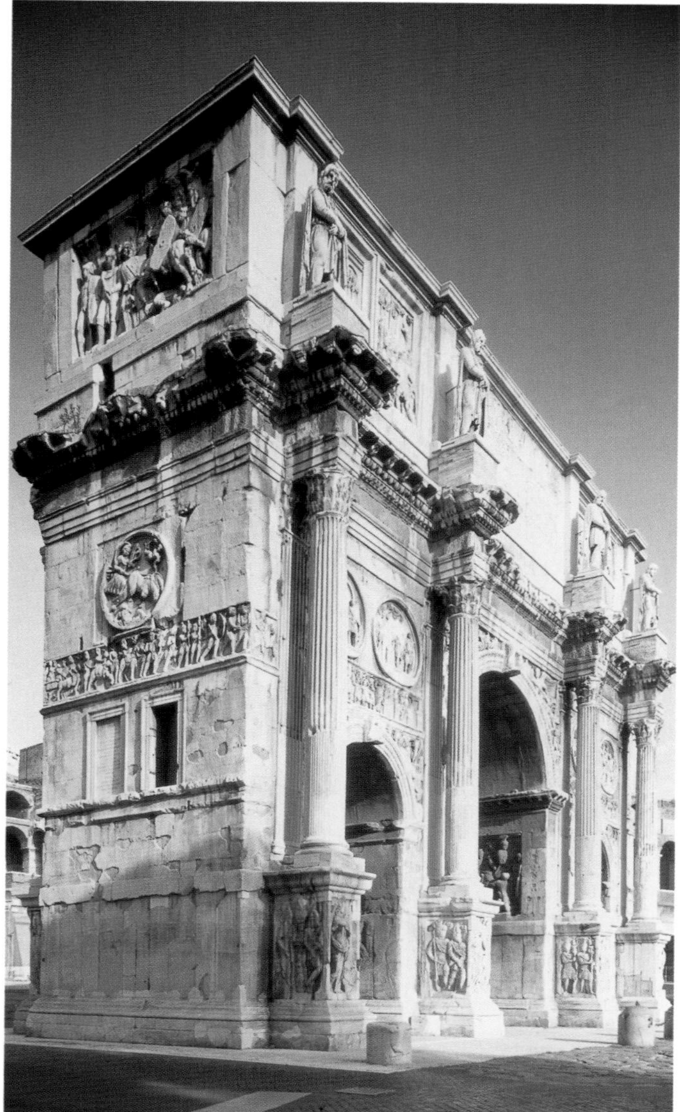

*'...at about midday, when the sun was beginning to decline, he saw with his own eyes the trophy of a cross of light in the heavens above the sun, and bearing the inscription Conquer by This (*Hoc Vince*). At this sight he himself was struck with amazement and his whole army also...' (Eusebius De VC)* 1,28

Left: The Arch of Constantine in Rome, built in AD 315 to celebrate the victory over Maxentius.

Below: A detail from Constantine's triumphal arch, showing the sun god Apollo. Diplomatically, Constantine continued to acknowledge the sun god, while transferring his beliefs to Christianity.

Right: A c. fourth-century mosaic of Christ as a manifestation of the sun god from the new 'basilica' church built by Constantine on the reputed site of St Peter's martyrdom in Rome.

SCALA

happened 'at the prompting of the deity', by which the sun god may be intended.

The public consequences for Christianity of the Battle of the Milvian Bridge followed quickly and were very favourable. Early in AD 313, Constantine met Licinius, the eastern Augustus, at Milan, and together the two declared a policy of religious tolerance in both parts of the Empire. They purported to think that freedom of worship and the right to care for sacred things according to free choice were individual rights, an unlikely statement of principle for two ruthless autocrats to issue, although one that would have made sense to people of late antiquity.

Constantine's father had been inclined to reverence the sun god, and in the preceding century richer Christians had already employed artists who showed Christ as a sort of manifestation of the sun god. In AD 310, according to a pagan panegyrist, Constantine had had a vision of the sun god Apollo, who offered him crowns to signify his future victories and rule. It is probable, however, that he had understood and accepted the main Christian doctrines soon after AD 312. The Christian Bishop Eusebius wrote of Constantine's talks with Christian apologists, which began immediately after the Battle of the Milvian Bridge. However the overall pagan majority in the Empire was so large that until the victory over Licinius in AD 324, he used the skills of a practised diplomatist and politician to blur the edges of his changes of belief. Continued emphasis on the sun god, which is visible on his coins, may have played a part in this.

Above: A gold coin from the reign of Constantine (c. AD 274–337). The labarum can be seen on top of the Imperial standard.

The Babylonians, the Assyrians, the Greeks, and especially the small tribe of the Israelites, had all believed that a ruler can owe victory in battle to a god, and in their imagination the divine leader had 'gone before' the warrior king in the battle. Such things can be found in the Old Testament, in Homer and in ancient Mesopotamian writings. If there was ever a religious conversion of Constantine to Christianity, the point of departure must have been something of this ancient nature. Subsequently, when he frequented and consulted Christian holy men, Constantine internalized the Christian moral universe to a high degree: whether this was exceptional among educated converts it is hard to say, but the political stakes for which he had chosen to play in accepting Christianity were extremely high. It is known that he possessed at least the sort of literary culture that would have been expected of a Roman aristocrat, which enabled him to make sense of the disputed Christian theologies of his day.

From his first accession to his father's dominions, Constantine had shown favour to Christians. Apart from having ended the persecution several years before the Battle of the Milvian Bridge, he had already had Christian bishops in his entourage before AD 312. The more bishops he met, the more he understood that skilled and useful propagandists and politicians could be found among them. The presence of numerous and powerful Christian populations in the east of the Empire was an important political factor, when the now aggressively Christian Constantine decided to dispute the Empire with the eastern Augustus.

The decisive year was AD 324. After his fleet had won a big naval battle, Constantine landed his army, achieved decisive victory outside Chalcedon (on the Asian shore of the Bosphorus) over Licinius, the eastern Augustus (and also Constantine's brother-in-law), and made himself sole Roman Emperor. The joint rule of several Augusti that Diocletian had set up, late in the preceding century, was finished, and a single autocrat once more governed the Empire. The new regime was stamped by an ideology of stunning novelty: a lame observance of some of the old rites of the Roman state persisted, but Christianity was to be its official religion.

Christianity Established

Constantine's decision to give preference to Christianity appears to have been taken very soon after the Battle of the Milvian Bridge. The first tax exemptions for Christian clergy were made in AD 313, and further ones followed after AD 325. The first of Constantine's huge grants of money for the rebuilding and finance of the major Roman churches also followed quite closely upon the battle. After AD 324, Constantine built a vast new 'basilica' church on the Vatican hill, the reputed site of St Peter's martyrdom. Inside the church he had a splendid monument or Memoria built, to replace the earlier one over the site venerated as that of Peter's tomb. The basilica was one of the standard architectural forms for a major public building in any city centre: the secular basilica built by Constantine in the Roman forum is still partly extant, as is a huge monumental head of Constantine that was probably sited within it.

So, within little more than two and a half centuries, the Emperor honoured in Rome the executed Galilean apostle, whose original tomb – possibly located in the street of late Roman tombs that still

Below: Mosaic pavement from the late fifth century showing a Christian basilica. The basilica design was originally used for secular buildings but was appropriated by Constantine and formed the template for later Christian churches.

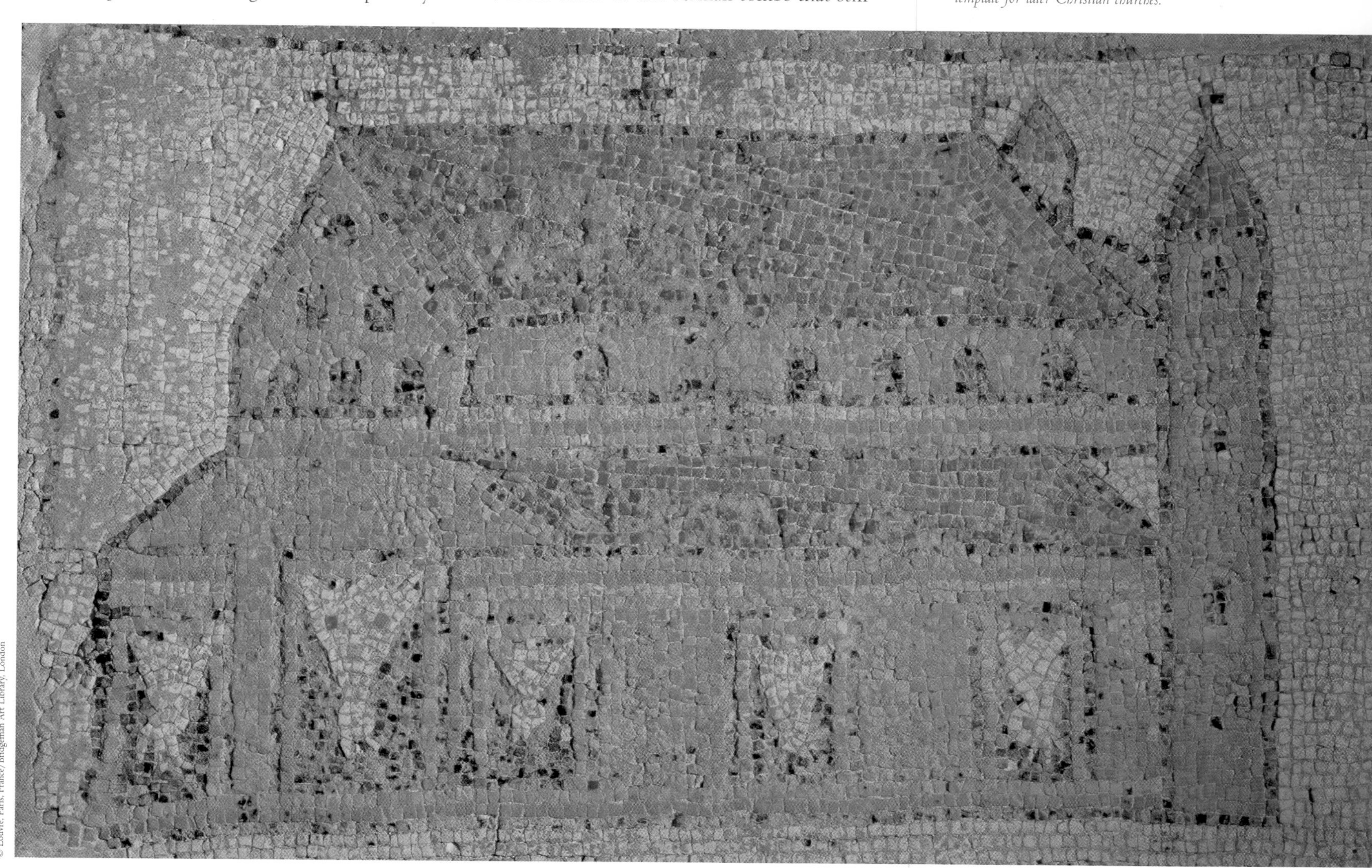

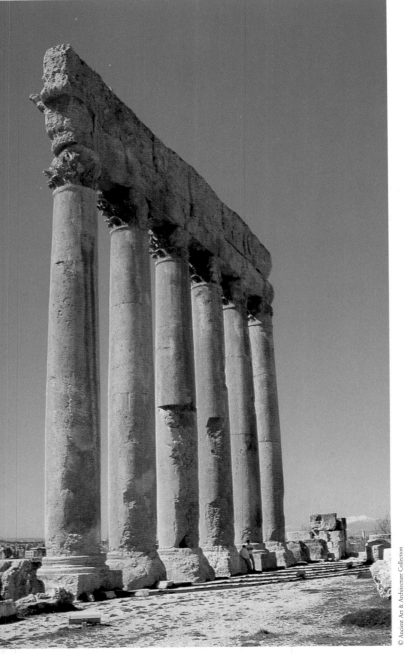

Below: A row of columns are all that remains of the Temple of Jupiter, supreme god of the Romans, in the Lebanon. After AD 324, Constantine waged war on pagan temples, describing them as 'groves of falsehood'.

exists under St Peter's – had been probably recorded by no more than a couple of bricks, if it had been marked at all. Other huge Christian basilicas were built by Constantine and his family in Rome and in Palestine. In Rome he built the great new church of St John Lateran, which was the parish church of Rome. It formed part of a huge complex that included a baptistery, a palatial residence for the bishop and appropriate charitable annexes.

Whether financed by the government or other means, churches that had been destroyed in the persecutions all over the Empire were rebuilt. The church in the old eastern capital city of Nicomedia, that had been destroyed at the orders and in the presence of Diocletian himself, was extravagantly reconstructed by Constantine. In Antioch he began to build another great church 'of concord' to replace the old – although, in spite of its title, its dedication in AD 341, four years after the death of Constantine, was accompanied by an almighty theological row among the clergy.

Constantine's hostility to paganism was now open; he described the temples as 'groves of falsehood'. Although pagan beliefs were not in themselves made illegal, many of the institutions that supported pagan worship were in effect proscribed, and sacrifice, the essence of the cults, was forbidden. The temples were not systematically destroyed, but their funds and valuable possessions were expropriated (with the exception of worship forming part of the state religion, which continued under the emperor who was its chief priest or *pontifex maximus*). A large part of the former resources of the pagan temples was in effect reallocated to Christian churches, and permanent government subsidies were set up for the latter. Certain sexually immoral cults were proscribed, such as that practised in the northern hills of Lebanon at Aphaca at the source of the river of Adonis (now Nahr Ibrahim), and the temples razed. Ferociously puritanical laws about conduct in sexual matters were enacted. Men guilty of rape or abduction were to be burned alive (as were consenting girl victims), and women servants who abetted abduction were to swallow boiling lead. This was not a gradualist emperor who was slowly educating the pagan people in a kinder way of life, but an autocrat of whom the modern mirror image would be the Communist Russian governments which imposed atheism after the Revolution. Like the Communists, Constantine allowed a semblance of the old religion to continue, and like them, he had paid lip service to religious toleration.

Constantine's savage laws reflected tendencies that were to be found, though in a much milder form, in the churches. The need to combat the 'encratic' or sex-renouncing doctrines of many Gnostic teachers had now declined, and the practice of virginity and widowhood dedicated to God was generally encouraged. The idea of 'brides of Christ' began to be spoken of. Women became hermits, undertook long pilgrimages, possessed a means of withdrawal to some extent from the closed world of the family. These were not all negative things. Holy women were privileged, and one of the ways they could use this privilege was to have close spiritual relationships with other holy women or men. Rich holy women could also set up convents that made them in effect into influential church dignitaries.

Left: An early Christian cleric from the Lullingstone fresco of the fourth century. As the officially recognized state religion, Christianity by this time had become formalized and ordered into bishoprics with a hierarchy of administrative staff.

Constantine did not become a Christian in the full sense until he was baptized on his death-bed in AD 337; in this he was only following a very common practice. This did not mean that the emperor, who was sometimes styled by his bishops as 'equal of the apostles' did not accept to the full his responsibility for the unity and discipline of the Christian Church he supported. Fourth-century church leaders quarrelled and bickered endlessly about the ways in which their faith ought to be defined: some of these disagreements were technical or linguistic, but others went to the core of the faith.

Right: The First Council of Nicaea, a fresco by Speranza dating from about 1600. At this momentous Council, called by Constantine himself in AD 325 to resolve the Arian controversy, the exact wording of the Creed was established. This defined what orthodox Christians believed to be the nature of the relationship between Jesus Christ and God.

Power to the Bishops

By the fourth century, church leadership was exercised without serious contest by the bishops. The antiquity and apostolic connections of the various bishoprics had an important influence on the authority and credit given their various incumbents. Each of the ancient sees felt itself particularly responsible for the transmission of authentic doctrine and practice. In the west, there was no serious competitor to Rome, although the status of Milan in Italy and Carthage in Africa was much respected. There was a group of prestigious eastern sees: Jerusalem, Antioch, Alexandria, Nicomedia, Ephesus

and Caesarea are the obvious ones. The inclusion of Nicomedia in this list shows that the Roman provincial system was not without influence on the way that churchmen thought of their bishops.

There was a persistent problem: under what circumstances could Christians who had compromised with the persecutors in order to survive be accepted back into communion after the storms had passed? In North Africa, these uncertainties had produced the 'Donatist' schism. In AD 314, when his engagement with Christianity was absolutely fresh, Constantine summoned a meeting of Christian bishops from the west of the Empire to Arles, near Vienne on the lower Rhone, to try to deal with the matter.

The Arian Controversy

More challenging to Constantine as an arbitrator were the disputes concerning the nature of Christ that were rocking the churches of the East, and that required early settlement after the victory over Licinius in AD 324. Arius, an Alexandrian priest of impressive ability, also had the gifts of a great popularizer: among other talents, he was able to set his theological verses as popular songs. Arius chose to take up a theological position about Christian definition of the nature of the Godhead that was, at least in appearance, relatively easy to comprehend, and that must be allowed to have raised

Right: A silver casket from the fourth century. This wedding present, from a Roman Christian named Secundus to his wife, indicates how the old pagan gods and the new religion rubbed along together. On the lid of the casket is a scene showing Venus.

legitimate doubts about some of the competing theories. He sustained that if God is one ultimate and self-sufficient principle, and at the same time also three separate beings, there are perhaps insuperable difficulties in saying that the Father and the Son are one indissoluble being, who as the incarnate (and therefore limited) son is nevertheless uncreated, as the father is.

The doctrine of Arius held that Christ must have been in some sense inferior to the Father, and must in some way have had a beginning in time. This was a doctrine entirely different from the types of doctrine professed by the Gnostics, and was a product of the reasoning of the Alexandrian church from which Arius came, particularly the reasoning of the great thinker Origen (that in itself could be sustained as orthodox). Plenty of very respectable Eastern clergy took Arianism, the doctrine of Arius, very seriously, including Constantine's later clerical adviser, Eusebius of Caesarea. However, a local church council in Alexandria condemned Arius, who left Egypt for Asia Minor.

The Solution of Nicaea

It may be that Constantine saw Arius and his doctrine as primarily an administrative problem, caused by a cleric who was unnecessarily rocking the boat. He certainly took his own responsibility to the Divinity for the welfare of the churches of the Empire extremely seriously. A Council of Bishops had been summoned in AD 325. Constantine had it transferred to Nicaea (Iznik), the site of an imperial palace. The peace and concord of the church were very important to the emperor, at a moment when he was launching new policies for a reunified Empire that used the Christian religion as their most important principle. The bishops, some two or three hundred of whom attended the council, used the imperial posting service to get to the conference, and their expenses were all government-funded. The bishops had not become part of the Roman civil service, nor were they to do so, but they had become part of the imperial organization in a wider sense.

'For my part, I hold any sedition within the Church of God as formidable as any war or battle, and more difficult still to bring to an end. I am consequently more opposed to it than anything else.' (Constantine's opening address at the Council of Nicaea.)

There had been at least one episode in the third century when bishops in dispute had appealed to the pagan emperor for settlement, but the dispute had not concerned doctrine. The part played by Constantine at Nicaea was an absolute novelty, because he himself formed an integral part of the Church Council, presiding over the opening sessions which took place in the imperial palace. At later sessions he was often present, and without doubt extremely influential. That a Christian still technically under instruction, a so-called catechumen, should be playing a major part in defining the faith, did not, in the imperial circumstances, seem odd. What may seem odd to those who think of the clergy as a learned profession is that a central tenet in the Creed still recited in Christian churches is perhaps the work of an amateur theologian.

This central tenet concerned the description to be used of the common nature of God the Father and God the Son. The relationship was defined by the Council as one of 'identity in being' (*homoousios*, 'of one substance', a suggestion that Eusebius said was due specifically to Constantine himself). To the learned professionals that some of the bishops were, this definition was still somewhat ambiguous, and the ambiguity may well have been apparent to Constantine. But it was a formula of which any diplomat might have been proud, as all but two of the bishops present felt able to adhere to it, and the Council was also able to anathematize Arius – not that this entirely silenced him, or removed his party for ever from the scene. The two bishops who refused to adhere to the anathema against Arius incurred the civil penalty of exile. No one knows what the informal reactions of the bishops to the Council of Nicaea were. But to some of the eldest among them, who a generation earlier had experienced contact with the imperial government in the torture chamber, sitting down with Constantine in the imperial palace at the final state banquet must have been a strange experience.

Nicaea showed that Christian rulers were not going to be neutral in the major disputes of the clergy, and this has remained true to the present day. The peace of the church was far too important for Constantine to leave it entirely to the decisions of a lot of bickering bishops, who had filled his lap with petitions denouncing one another for this cause or that on the very first day of the Council. That he was present merely as an interested Christian observer strains all credulity. The subsequent history of church councils is against it. An early instance of the emperor's direct intervention is that

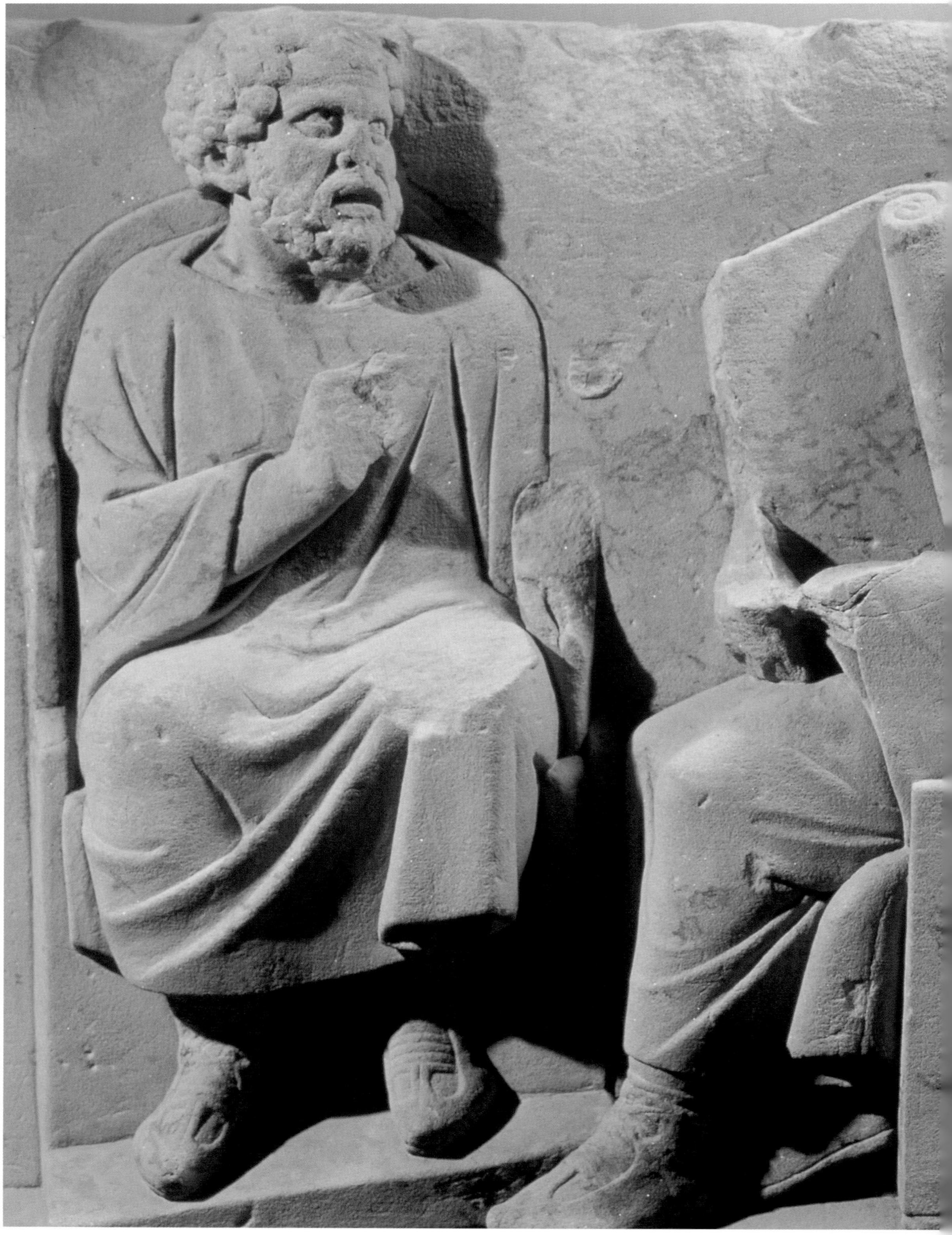

Right: Detail from a stone block from the Neumagen School Pillar, dating from second to third century AD. When the apostate Emperor Julian reinstated paganism, Christian schoolteachers, who were supposed by Julian to know nothing of the old religion, found themselves redundant.

© AKG London / Erich Lessing

of AD 359 by Constantine's successor Constantius. He had the bishops meet in two separate councils of East and West in order to get the decision (more or less in favour of Arianism) he wanted over vexed questions that were to some extent a rerun of those discussed at Nicaea. This kind of thing became permanent; if we look forward to the later Roman ('Byzantine') Empire, and then forward again to relatively modern times, say to the sixteenth-century Council of Trent, we find the same phenomenon of lay powers straining every diplomatic nerve to influence theological decisions.

Constantine saw the bishops as leaders of their congregations, whom the imperial autocracy should support, subsidize, revere, and who were formally independent of the state in matters of church discipline, even though he had no hesitation in exercising political pressure to obtain the church policies he wanted. There was both paradox and ambiguity in this relationship. The Christian dialogue with power, which had experienced some periods of calm in the preceding century, but all too often had been one of fear and terror, had entered upon a new phase, one that was wonderfully favourable to the spread of the good news of the Gospel in many respects, but that held dangers of a new kind for the believers.

From AD 324 onwards Christianity became to some extent a prerequisite of imperial favour, though pagan favourites and panegyrists were still not entirely obsolete. The old social and religious structure of the Empire still told against the new religion in many ways. In every city there were dignitaries such as the flamines, urban notables, whose civic functions were inseparable from their pagan religious ones. The entire framework of civic decorum and tradition had a pagan basis and vocabulary that could not disappear overnight.

Julian the Apostate

The concepts of what we would now call high culture were still in some respects foreign to the majority of Christians. The traditional vocabulary of Christian teaching, from the Greek Gospels outwards, was based on what was called in the law courts the *sermo humilis*, meaning that it was expressed in popular idiom. At first, it made only a marginal difference that for a long time the religion had been attracting people of good literary and intellectual attainments, who sometimes had claimed all sorts of pagan literary precedents for Christian ideas, finding them in the pronouncements of the sibyls and the works of Virgil – as Constantine himself had done, in his only known literary composition. But a new Christian Empire was not long in producing a new Christian political vocabulary. Imperial panegyrists emerged who swiftly adapted Biblical concepts of royalty and majesty to the new Roman situation.

The term 'pagan' to describe a non-Christian was unknown to the literate people of classical antiquity until quite a late date. Its primary meaning was to indicate someone who was a civilian as opposed to a soldier: whether this meant, not a 'soldier of Christ', is uncertain. It also had a quite separate meaning of 'rustic' or countryman, which came sometimes to be applied to non-Christians of a rather later date.

By AD 361 Christianity had so far become the dominating orthodoxy of the dynasty of Constantine that the idealistic young Julian, Constantine's great-nephew, who had escaped the massacre of males of the half-blood in AD 337 because of his infancy, could profess paganism and a passionate faith in the old high culture of Rome, particularly in Platonism, as a mark of adolescent rebellion against the tyranny of the elders. When he became emperor in AD 361 Julian formally threw off Christianity, thus gaining for himself the later title of 'Apostate'. That Julian had the political ability and the force to reverse the religious and social revolution due to Constantine seems unlikely.

He failed to see that by his day, if the Empire had a social cement, it was already Christianity. In the event his policy got no further than a declaration of general toleration, followed by the reopening of the temples and the encouragement of pagan cult rites, and a sharp cut in state subsidies to the churches. Schoolteachers, as sometimes occurs in ideological quarrels, were among the innocent victims. Julian argued that people should not teach things, such as pagan literature, of which they did not approve, and so Christian schoolmasters lost their jobs. In general, although he preferred pagans for promotion, Julian consciously avoided anything that could be interpreted as a renewal of the persecutions of Christians.

In the East the Christian mob lost little time in replying with riots, and with the vandalization of the restored temples, but there was never time for a general reckoning, because of Julian's early death in a skirmish on the Persian frontier, in AD 363. Outside a few elitist and culturally conservative circles, particularly in Rome, there seems to have been general relief that the Empire could return to what had become traditional dynastic religious policies, and to observing the latest moves in the theological struggles about Arianism.

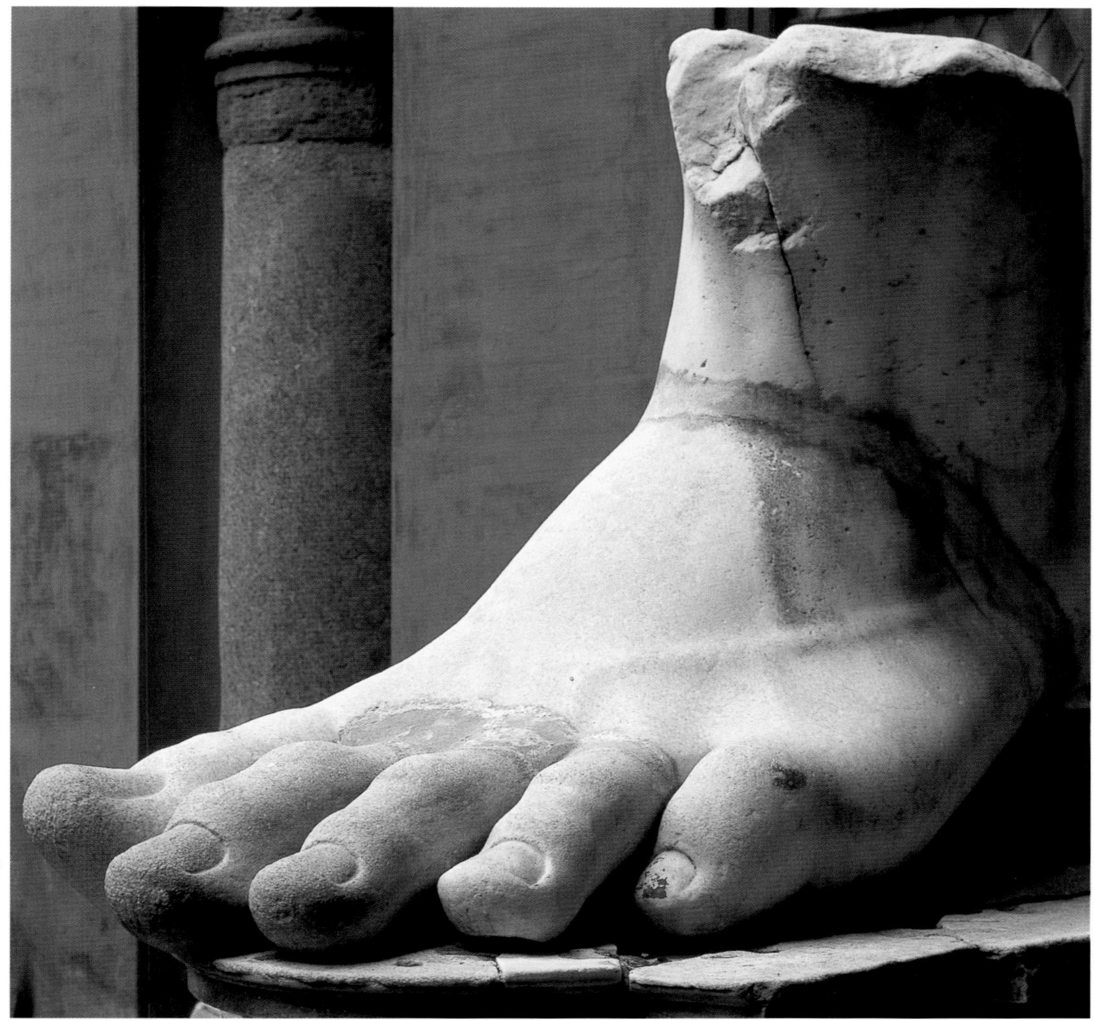

Left: The massive left foot from the larger than life statue of Constantine symbolizes the power and autocracy of the man. His vision and adoption of the cross marked a turning point in the fortunes of Christianity.

5

BISHOPS AND HERMITS

The bishops had become minor political players on the imperial board. The annual cost of the Church to the Empire had come to exceed the cost of the imperial civil service. The ideological results of this degree of commitment by the state can sometimes seem bizarre. The disputes between the clergy concerning the definition of the divine natures was a serious matter for all Christians, but it could be only be expressed in terms that come easier to philosophers than to holy men. The situation was rather as if all today's Western governments had for the past thirty years been compelled, as a part of their main political objectives, to have a policy on structuralism and post-structuralism. Constantinian and post-Constantinian bishops whose policies were later to come to be seen as having been orthodox, could incur severe government displeasure.

For example, under Constantine, Athanasius, the bad-tempered and violent but nevertheless orthodox Bishop of Alexandria, was a fervent and influential supporter of the Nicaean solution of the controversy about the divine natures. Yet he was condemned unjustly for supposedly mistaken doctrines by a packed church council in Tyre in AD 335; he might have secured imperial support, had he not rashly used his position as bishop to threaten to organize a dock strike in Alexandria. He was exiled to Trier on the Rhine frontier and, after Constantine's death, he fled to Rome, where the Roman bishop received him in AD 340. The doctrines of Athanasius were unacceptable at that time to most of the eastern clergy, and also to the imperial court, but he was supported by the popes of the time.

The Athanasius affair was the first of the serious squabbles between Latin west and Greek east: they were to continue spasmodically for another millennium. The disunity of the east and west made Arian influence on the imperial court even more powerful, and Arianism was not finally defeated in the East until a church council held in Constantinople in AD 381. At the same council, a deeply divisive decision was made that the Bishop of Constantinople should rank after the Bishop of Rome, 'because

Left: Renaissance polyptych illustrating, from left to right, Bishops Gregory, Ambrose, Augustine and Jerome.

Above: Relief showing Theodosius I (AD 347–395) and his family. Theodosius was the first emperor to submit to the moral superiority of the Church, when he did public penance before Ambrose in AD 390.

it is new Rome.' The promotion openly placed the politics of the Empire above the traditions of the Church, which gave bishoprics more or less weight and prestige according to their apostolic history.

The Church and the State

Fourth-century bishops lived in a world in which religion had become one of the most powerful, if not the most powerful, agent of social change. From AD 363, under the Emperor Julian's successors, the drift towards Christian conformism gathered momentum. In AD 380 Theodosius (AD 339–97) made Christianity the official religion of the state, and began to initiate severe punitive measures against religious dissidents such as the Manichees. The Church began to be a career for the educated classes. The magnate-bishop had not been unknown – the martyred Cyprian of Carthage was a third-century example – but he began to be a very common phenomenon. Ambrose of Milan, one of the greatest bishops of the period, a man with the power and independence to put the emperor into a penitent's habit, was the son of a praetorian prefect (who was a Christian), and at the time of his election was himself the governor of Aemilia-Liguria, with his seat at Milan. In AD 374 Ambrose, although still unbaptized, was acclaimed bishop. He resisted nomination, and tried to fend it off by immediately having some suspects tortured in a way he hoped would disqualify him for a bishop's office.

Unable to refuse the bishopric, Ambrose became the first bishop to bring the administrative experience of the top echelons of the Empire to the governance of the Church. His influence over the emperors was of major political importance. He was instrumental in securing laws and policies that virtually eliminated Arianism in the Balkans, and that made paganism into something quite close to a proscribed religious attitude. His major clash with the government did not concern his own diocese, but distant Thessalonica, where the Emperor Theodosius in AD 390 had massacred 7,000 innocent persons in the stadium, to punish the city for riots against the government. Ambrose required and obtained that Theodosius should accept excommunication and do penance for the deed. The event did not inaugurate some sort of quasi-theocratic rule: the Empire was too hardy a plant for that. But it showed that the moral order of the Church could now challenge the moral order of the Empire in ways hitherto undreamed of.

Ambrose was the ideal type of the patrician bishop, and with this he united some of the charismatic qualities of the holy man, including an alarming capacity, on occasion, to strike the wicked dead on the spot. The holy-man bishop was not extinct by any means, but he was not welcomed as he might have been a century earlier. In AD 370 neighbouring bishops had objected to the future St Martin of Tours, a Pannonian ex-soldier, as Bishop of Tours on the grounds that he was dirty and unkempt.

Where bishops were not themselves great men, they tended to pay court to the great. This, again, was far from new, but in this period it became far more widespread than hitherto. In Rome, these things had been so for a long time, but the fourth century, a period of immense enrichment of church treasures and possessions, and of the construction of many of the city's greatest churches, saw some quite worldly Roman bishops. When Pope Liberius, whose Roman basilica is still the greatest Roman treasure house of fifth-century art, was exiled as a result of his siding with Athanasius in the Arian dispute, the smart society ladies of Rome petitioned the Emperor for his return.

Above: Illuminated manuscript from the fifteenth century, made for the Duke of Burgundy, showing St Martin of Tours.

The Nature of Christ

The early fifth century was a time of ferocious theological quarrels about the elements of man and God in the person of Jesus. The disputes were politicized because of the involvement of the emperors and their families, and they aroused the passions of whole populations in the eastern part of the Empire. Because of the interest of the Empire in compelling some sort of settlement, in 451 the main

© Catacombs of Priscilla, Rome, Italy/Bridgeman Art Library, London

Above: Detail from a third-century fresco from the catacombs of Priscilla, in Rome, showing the Virgin Mary as Theotokos, or God-bearer.

theological questions were compromised in the Council of Chalcedon (situated on the Bosphorus). The Council said that Jesus was fully God and fully man in both his natures, consubstantial with God the Father as regards his deity, and of the same substance as men, as regards his humanity.

About the theological disputes of this 'sad century', a wise church historian of an earlier generation may be quoted:

> *'Since... ...the unwisdom of the theologians kept upon the dissecting table the Sweet Saviour who offered Himself for our love and our imitation far more than for our philosophical investigations, at the least it was requisite that these should be conducted in a peaceable manner by men of acknowledged competence and distinction, far aloof from the crowd and its bickerings. It was the contrary that happened.'*[1]

There remained after Chalcedon a contested distinction between those who said that Christ was in two natures, and those said he was from two natures. The dispute became a clash of cultures between the Egyptian-Syrian part of the Empire and Constantinople, that was finally to be rendered obsolete by the Arab generals of Muhammad in the mid-seventh century. Theological hates therefore still flourished: only six years later a Patriarch of Alexandria was lynched and murdered by the populace in order to let in a bishop who satisfied the local dislike of the theologians of Constantinople.

The controversies about the divine and human in the person of Christ had results that may not all be obvious to modern people. One of the most passionate opponents of Arius, Apollinaris of Laodicea (d. AD 390), emphasized the incarnation of the divine word in Christ to such a point that Jesus appears not to have had, in his view, a mind that was truly human, but rather one that was divine. Mary was thus literally Theotokos, God-bearer or mother of God. A very popular devotion to Mary already existed, but her status as Virgin Mother was enormously increased by this new theological twist, that attributed the most basic of all ties of kinship to the deity himself.

© Sonia Halliday Photographs

Right: The remains of the baptistry in the church of the Virgin Mary at Ephesus, southern Turkey. It was here that the third Ecumenical Council was held in 431.

Above: A sixth-century mosaic from Carthage, showing a Vandal on horseback, leaving his villa. Having invaded north Africa, the Vandals set up their capital at Carthage where they adopted a Roman lifestyle.

The orthodox theologians on the whole repudiated Apollinaris, but they could not stop the drift towards the veneration of Mary, who had accepted the invitation to bear the Christ-child, which had been offered her by the angel of God. Another theologian suspected of rationalism was the Patriarch of Constantinople, Nestorius, who had created scandal by remarking that 'God is not a baby two or three months old.' Nestorius was judged at the Council of Ephesus in 431, his condemnation took place in one of the first Christian churches to be dedicated to Mary, and the final statement of the Council referred to the union of two natures in Christ, 'on which ground we confess Christ to be one, and Mary to be the mother of God.' In Rome, too, the great basilica built by Pope Liberius in the preceding century was dedicated to Mary (the basilica of St Mary Major), and Pope Sixtus III (432–440) decorated it lavishly with mosaics, some of which are still in place, that honour Mary the God-bearer.

Sin, Guilt and St Augustine

One of the greatest of the fifth-century bishops, Augustine, Bishop of Hippo (Bône in Algeria; he had been born in Thagaste, in the interior, now Souk Ahras, in AD 354), was great in his own times,

VICTOR

Left: The Vision of St Augustine painted by the Venetian artist Vittore Carpaccio (c. 1450–1522). Initially a Manichaean, Augustine was baptized in AD 387 and became Bishop of Hippo in Algeria.

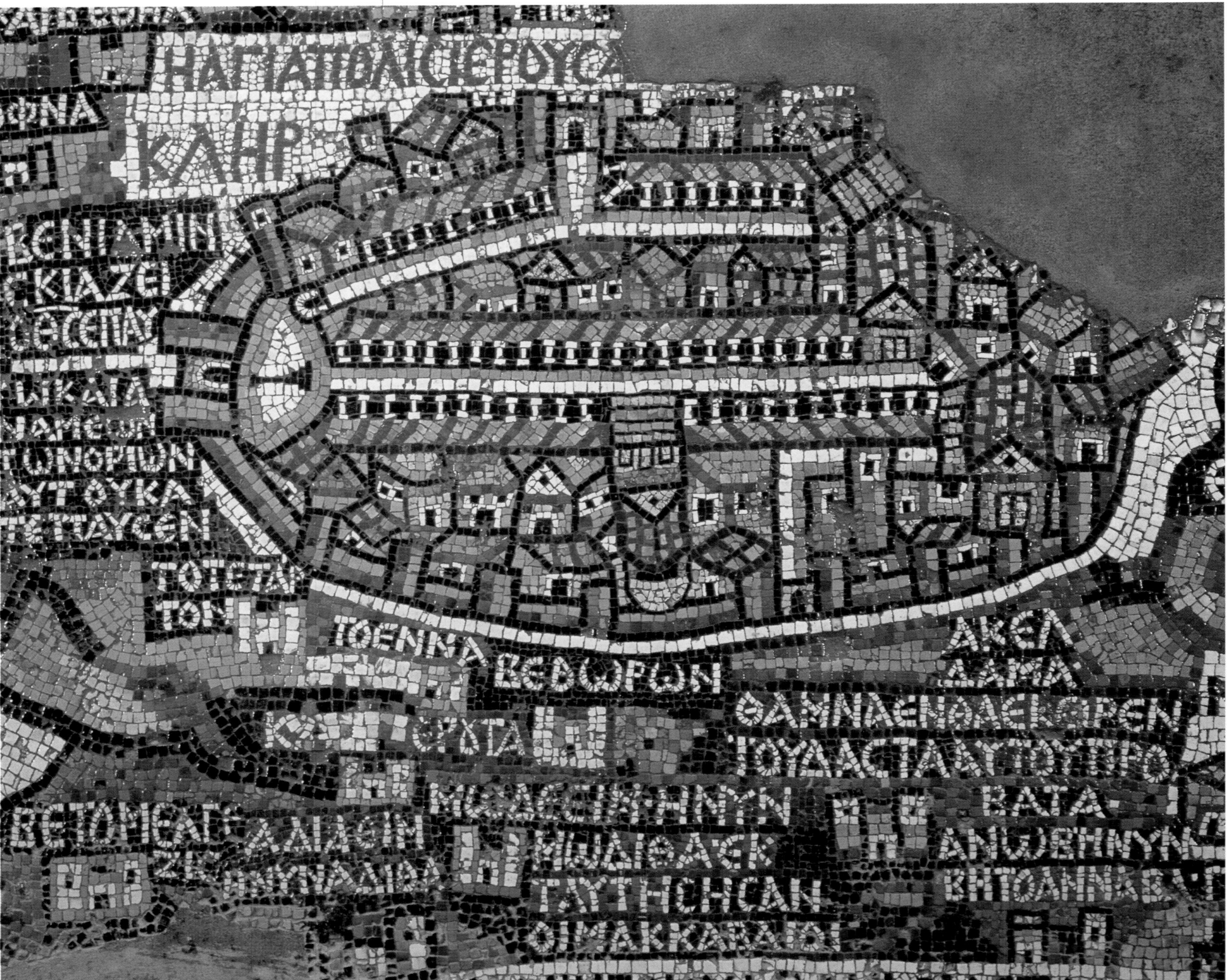

Above: Detail from a sixth-century mosaic map of Palestine and Egypt, built into a modern church in Madaba, Jordan, and showing Jerusalem with its Constantinian buildings.

but even more remarkable for the immense influence that he exerted on later times. Augustine was not a patrician bishop: he was, on the contrary, an example of the promotion that skilful men of letters could still obtain in late antiquity, coming from modest families quite outside the official world. Tragically, he who had lived through so many of the dramas of his times, survived to die in his own cathedral city, while it was under under siege from the Vandal armies (Christian, but heretical and Arian) that were sweeping through North Africa. Hippo was to fall in 431, a year after his death, and the rest of Roman Africa with it.

In the rustic outpost of Thagaste, and later in Carthage, the young Augustine learned enough of the classics to lay the basis for a later literary career, though not enough to give him a good knowledge of Greek. This was a limiting factor, because the big theological debates in Augustine's lifetime over doctrines of the divine natures were almost all conducted in Greek. As a bishop, Augustine was the correspondent of a few of the great Christian figures of his period, such as St Jerome, the Jerusalem-based author of the Latin 'Vulgate' translation of the Bible, and Paulinus of Nola, but he had no direct contact with the theologians of the east.

The great originality of Augustine was to understand the historical situation of Christianity, at a moment when a large part of the political and social structure of the western Empire was collapsing. The Roman army, on which the Empire depended to remain in being, did not entirely disappear. But in the south, the north and the west of the Empire, and also for a long time in Rome and the Italian peninsula, the capacity of the army to defend the interior was so diminished that the basic Roman administrative structures became hardly recognizable. The towns, which had been the core of the protected Roman area, and had frequently been based on the great military camps, suffered severely. In Gaul, in Spain, Roman culture was to a considerable extent taken over by barbarian, sometimes heretic nobilities, who then co-existed with the survivors of the old, provincial elites. At the peripheries, in Roman Britain, on the Danube, and in Africa outside Egypt, recognizable Roman rule ceased to exist.

The responsibility that fell upon the Church tended to dominate Augustine's life as a bishop in a practical as well as in a general way. Ever since the Christianization of the Empire, bishops had become part of the system of patronage and favour that governed all late Roman elites. They sat in judgement upon endless lawsuits, and were endlessly asked to favour the promotion of this person or that, or beseeched to influence the outcome of lawsuits in which they were not judges. These things would have been so whether Roman administration was being transformed under 'barbarian' pressure or not. But behind all this, especially after the signals conveyed by the temporary but destructive occupation of Rome by the barbarian Alaric's troops in 410, lay the rapid deterioration of the whole political system. Such things inspired Augustine to remark that:

> *'We (the Church) are having to conduct the affairs of a whole people – not of the Roman people on earth, but of the citizens of the Heavenly Jerusalem.'* [2]

St Augustine marks the point at which the Church ceased to be the gathered church of the faithful few: the people who by temperament wanted to belong to such groups were in his time creating new locations and vocations within the Church, where they might feel more at home. In his book, *The City of God* (413–26), Augustine took a considered, deliberate look backwards at the long history of the pagan Empire of Rome, and at the relatively short history of the Christian Empire. As he did so, he not only passed moral judgement on the old Empire, but also formed new theories of political and social life that were consciously adapted to the imperatives of the world in which he lived. The expression 'catholic' meaning universal or all-embracing had been in use since the end of

Right: A scene from the school of Plato, from Pompeii. St Augustine had been a keen student of Platonic thought.

the first Christian century, especially to describe the 'great' or universal Church of orthodox belief, in opposition to mistaken, heretical belief. With Augustine, the expression becomes a decisive way of including the right-thinking, and excluding the rest.

St Augustine was able to look at the pagan Roman Empire with a cold scepticism that had never before been publicly available, to condemn its ruthless *Realpolitik*, and to remark that 'kingdoms are great robberies'. In him the rhetoric of earlier Christian publicists about the providential nature of the pagan Empire, which had provided such a great peaceful field for the sowing of the Gospel, had vanished. But his appreciation of the positive values of pagan thought and culture, and particularly of the Platonism that he had so eagerly studied, was undimmed. It could not have been otherwise, since it was to this culture that he owed the literary sensibility that was the foundation of his being. Nor had Augustine in the least abandoned the typically Roman values of peace and order, which remained at the top of his moral hierarchy. Peace was the one aim that the earthly city and the heavenly city pursued in common, and order was in either case the guarantor of peace.

There is a sort of political dualism in Augustine, which was to endure throughout the Middle Ages in the clerical mentality. The Christian had a kind of double membership of society. In so far as the Christian was a sort of resident alien in the earthly city, he or she accepted its rules so long as they did not go against divine 'eternal' law. But there is only one republic of all Christians, and this land of the heavenly Jerusalem could in one sense be located in this life. It was a concept destined to grow into that of 'Christianity' or 'Christendom'.

Augustine went along with earlier clerical leaders, in asking the state to enforce Church discipline. The African 'Donatists', who had refused to receive back into the Church the 'traditores', who handed over holy books during the persecutions, had for the preceding century run a nonconformist church, electing their own bishops. In 411 there was a conference in Carthage of Catholic and Donatist bishops, in which both sides spoke under the presidency of the imperial commissioner. After a number of sessions the good manners with which the conference had begun ceased, and the meeting turned into a trial in which the commissioner delivered judgement. Relying on the precedent of the appeal of both sides to the Emperor Constantine in AD 314, he gave the Catholic bishops what they asked, and in Augustine's words, 'compelled them to come in'. There was a thorough repression of the Donatists, which dissolved their organization and visited individual membership of their church with penalties. It was an invocation of the secular arm to compel and punish dissent, of a sort that persisted in the Latin Catholic Church until modern times.

Below: A fourth- or fifth-century image of the 'lady of Carthage', believed to be an African Donatist. She is thought to have instigated Donatism by falling out with the Bishop of Carthage and electing a rival bishopric.

The Desert Hermits

St Augustine's world included the African desert, but his sphere of action was essentially urban. In many respects Christianity had, from the beginning, followed the ways of the ancient pagan world, which led from one city to another. But faith could have a very different setting. In the Mediterranean and African lands that gave harbour to the Jewish sects and to early Christianity, there was unplanted wilderness outside the settled and cultivated land. The shepherds of the pastoral folk might wander in the wilderness, but to the cultivators this was a hostile world. The indigent, or those banished for crimes or fleeing punishment, might find themselves there. So also might the holy. In the stories of St John the Baptist and Jesus, of the Essenes, or six centuries later in that of Muhammad, the desert was present as well as the sown land. The holy man, or the man who aspired to holiness, could not always achieve the self-mastery and the communion with God that he sought, through the life of the towns and villages. The claims of kinship alone would impede him, as Jesus himself had complained. In the wilderness the fasting and self-denial that led to holiness had a different meaning than they had in the towns.

There was no theological room in Christianity for people to wander into the desert to seek a new revelation, although the Gnostic initiates may sometimes have pointed in this direction. But in the middle Nile valley, south of Memphis, a pious Christian youth named Antony had found his way to the desert in the late third century AD to escape from the family and other pressures that impeded him from seeking God. Sexual problems may have played a part, although they did not loom as large in his ascetic enterprise as the visual fantasies of Hieronymous Bosch and the

Left: The Mother Figure on the Altar of Peace in Rome, a pagan representation that influenced the imagery of the Madonna. During the fourth century, the status of Mary as Virgin Mother increased enormously.

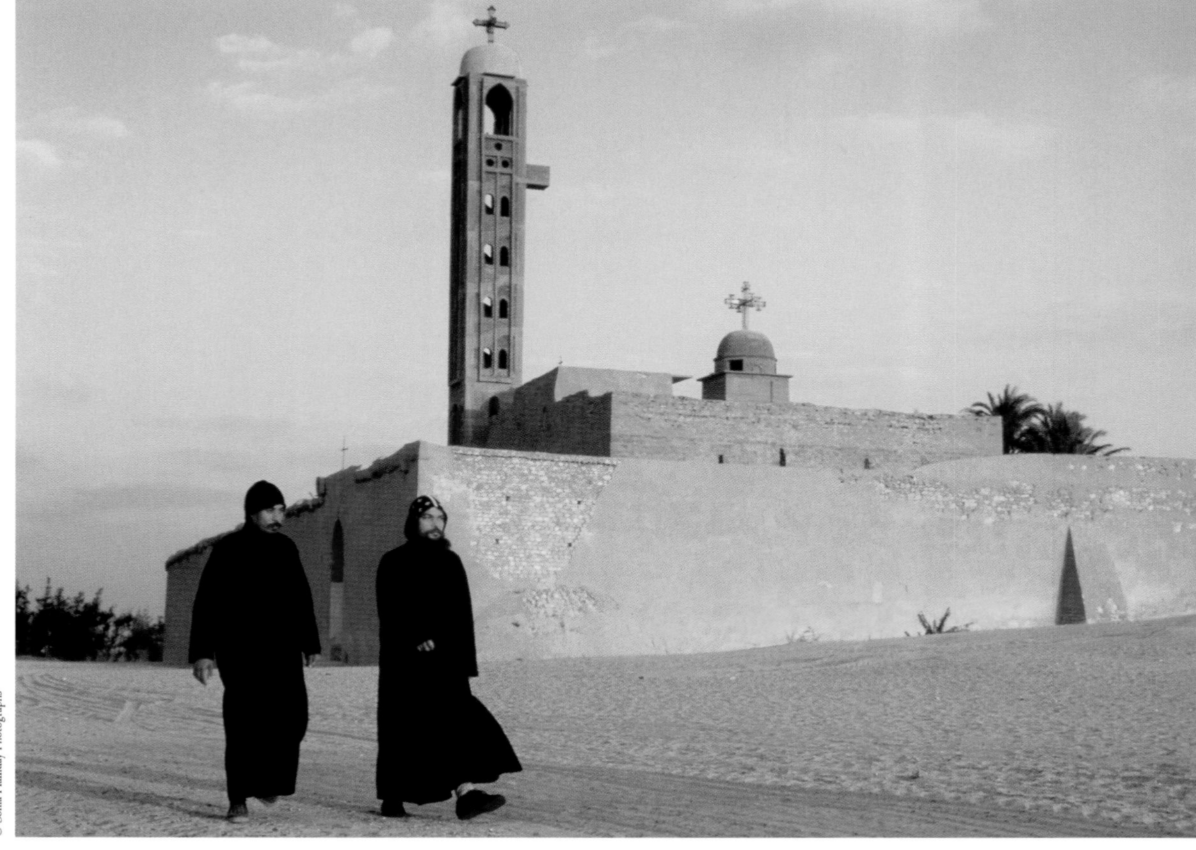

© Sonia Halliday Photographs

Right: Present-day Coptic monks at the monastery of St Bishoi, Wadi El Natrun, in the western desert. Monasticism began in the Egyptian desert.

literary fantasies of Gustave Flaubert have made them. For much of his long life (he died in AD 356) he was a conspicuous representative of a wide Christian trend. After spending twenty or thirty years as a hermit, Antony moved his life to the eastern desert; by this time his refuges were surrounded by the refuges of other hermit followers. In the same period great new migrations into the desert took place further north, in the Nile Delta at Scetis (Wadi Natrun) and Nitria. Coptic monks still live in or near these places.

John the Baptist had lived in the wilderness dressed in a coat of camel's hair and a leather belt, and had fed there on locusts and wild honey. By the standards of fourth century Egyptian and Syrian asceticism, he had all but feasted. The fasts and vigils of the desert fathers, and their continuous exposure to sun, thirst, cold and all the hazards of a starkly hostile environment, made them into heroes of a new sort. They voluntarily undertook the semi-starvation and privations that were the worst fears of the rustic poor. They sometimes imposed penances upon themselves which appear superfluous, such as loading themselves with heavy chains.

The hermits were privileged in their exemption from the awful responsibilities of maintaining families through times of fear and famine. For these gains, and for the privilege of finding their own way to salvation, they often paid a truly dreadful price. Most were publicly anonymous, although all were treated with reverence by the laity, who judged an audience with one of them a kind of physical

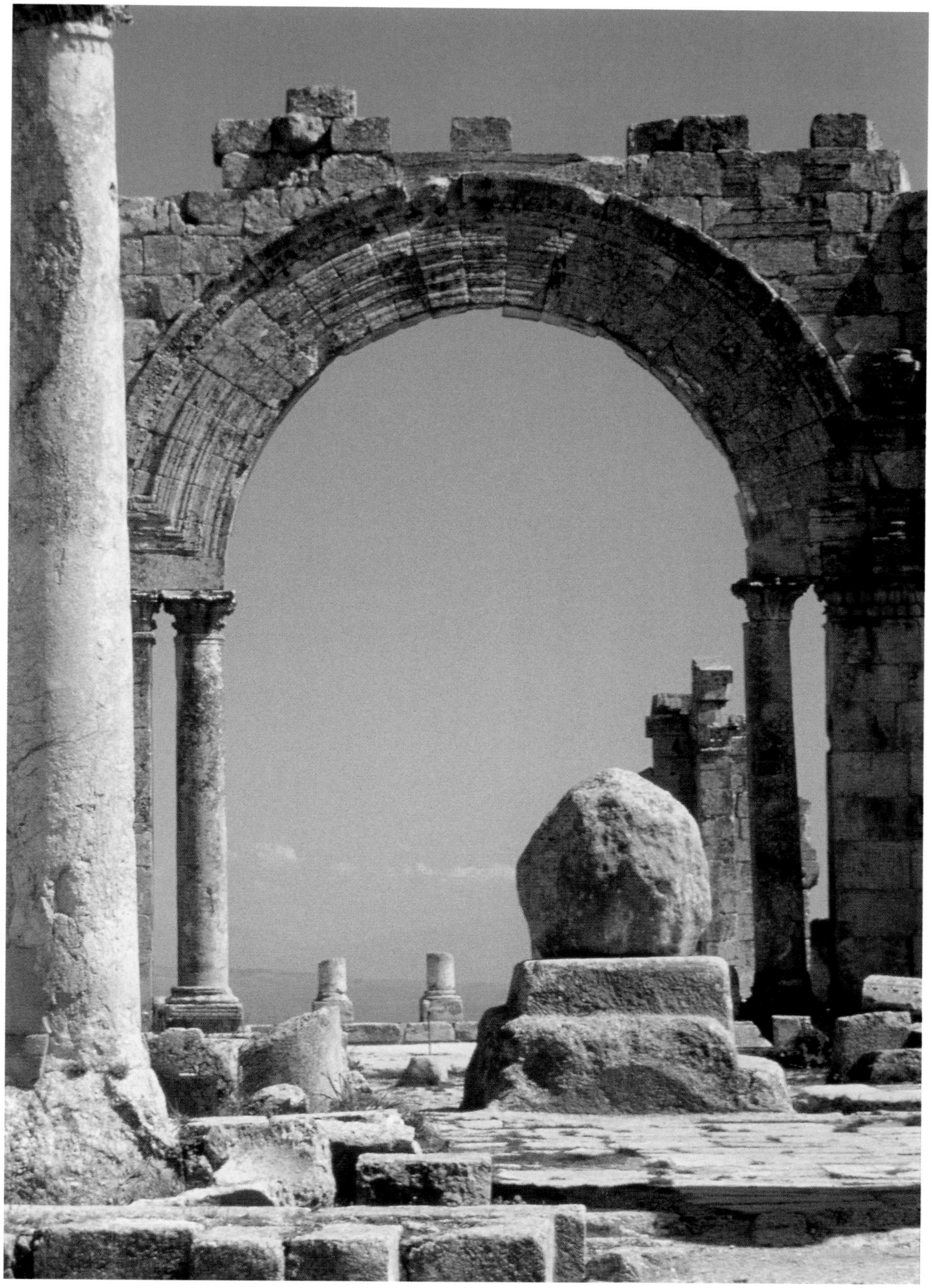

Left: The base of the column of St Simeon the Stylite (AD 390–459) in the courtyard of St Simeon Monastery, Qalat Sim'an.

touching of the eternal. Those who were widely known as holy men lived the same life of austerity, but they were also public figures, who were called upon to adjudicate quarrels and lawsuits, to forward petitions to the government, and to act as consulting pyschiatrists. Their austerities were often trimmed to their public needs. It was to flee the press of suitors and pilgrims that continually surrounded him that Simeon 'Stylites' lived for years at a time perched at the summit of tall stone pillars. His pillars, now contained within the great ruined church of Qalat Sim'an in Syria, were not situated far out in the desert, but a few miles off the main Roman road (a long tract of which still exists) from Antioch to Chalcis.

Below: A sixth-century representation of Simeon Stylites on his pillar. The Devil in serpent form attacks him in an attempt to dislodge the saint.

From a conforming Christian point of view, one objection to the desert was the entire absence of churches, and the practical impossibility of attending the liturgy, and taking part in the communal life of the congregation, except in the most occasional manner. The bishops were leaders of urban communities: there was already difficulty in finding ways of evangelizing the countryside, and the problems of controlling disorderly hermits in a wilderness were not always welcome to them. The Church had already experienced intractable problems in rural areas. For example, the schismatic Donatists in Africa had been far harder to cope with because of their having been supported by wandering rural bands of supporters. One thinks of the recent history during the 1990s of the Taliban movement in Afghanistan, the supreme recent example of the religious dictatorship of country lads.

In one way the development of a sort of communal ascetic life in the desert was inevitable, because the hermits tended to cluster round leaders, and also because of the purely practical advantages of mitigating the rigours of desert life by some sort of loose association. In the fourth century, much further south in the Nile valley, in the Thebais north of Luxor (Tabennisi near present Qina), there emerged a different, more tightly organized kind of community, under a superior called Pachomius. He organized the desert-dwellers into a labouring semi-military organization, something between a modern kibbutz and a medieval monastery.

The movement of the hermits pointed to the permanent tension in Christianity between the solitary seeker after God and the life of the believing community. To what extent was the solitary to be allowed to place the needs of his own spiritual devotion and quest before the needs of others in the fellowship of religion? He made few material demands on the other believers, it is true, but he made moral ones. There were also supposed hermits in the desert who created problems of a quite different sort – bankrupts, people on the run from justice, bandits, who might all claim to shelter under the cloak of religion.

The Roots of Monasticism

A kind of answer to these problems was offered by an eastern intellectual bishop, St Basil, Bishop of Caesarea in Cappadocia (d. c. AD 379). Basil encouraged the growth of communities that were in essence what would later be called monasteries (coenobia) in which religious men lived under a set of accepted rules, worshipped in the context of a common life, and were firmly placed within the control of the local bishop. The bishop occasionally abused his position by using the monks as auxiliary troops or gangs in theological rows with other churchmen. But on the whole Basil's new arrangements, where they were adopted, worked in the direction of peace and order.

A western alternative to the ideas of Basil was produced by a monk from the Danube frontier called Cassian, trained in the eastern Empire, who set up monastic communities of both men and women in Gaul, near Marseilles. The western attitude to these things was on the whole more disciplined than that of the the East. Cassian's regime was essentially one of communal prayer, organized into five daily 'offices' that the monks or nuns executed together. The regime of prayer was supplemented by a regime of labour, either intellectual or physical. The moral control was strict, and the sequestered community was given a kind of programme to try to overcome the sins that monastic management carefully indicated to them. It was the beginning of monastic life organized for the praise of God, to be carried out by ordinary (but dedicated) persons rather than by spiritual heroes.

1 Mons. L. Duchesne, *Early History of the Christian Church*, trs. C. Jenkins, vol. 3 (London, 1924), p. 226

2 Quoted by Peter Brown, *Augustine of Hippo: a biography* (London, 1967), p. 287

6

Barbarians, Missionaries and Saints

The barbarians who entered the Roman Empire in late antiquity were far from alien savages. Most had been within the frontiers of the Empire for a considerable period, either as allies or as troops actually serving in the Roman army. A considerable number of the late Roman generals were barbarians, and by the sixth century Roman armies were in most ways like barbarian ones. When barbarians settled within the frontiers, they were usually qualified as 'guests' and the law applied to their presence, making a fictional assumption that it was acceptable to their Roman hosts, was Roman billeting law. Their numbers were not so great that they completely swamped existing local society. In modern terms, most of them could be described as 'assimilated' Romans, even when their tribal law and customs continued to apply in some respects at least. Barbarian notables became part of the same society as the Roman provincial nobility.

However, religion did not fit tidily into this pattern. The Arian missionaries had been extremely active on the northern borders, especially on the Danube frontier, and some of the most important tribes – Vandals, Goths – were Arians. There was no western emperor after 476. At the end of the fifth century Theodoric, the Gothic king, entered Italy bearing Roman official titles, and set up a regime in Ravenna that controlled Rome and imperial Italy. Arian heretic as he was, he brought with him a complete Arian clergy, that had nothing to do with the Catholic clergy.

The conversion of the barbarians to Christianity was often initiated by the wholesale submission of whole tribes. But it did not sweep away pagan culture in a few moments, as we are reminded every year by the feasts of Christmas, the Winter Solstice celebration of the northerners for which the nativity of Christ is a cheeky Christian misnomer, and of the New Year, in Roman usage the great

Left: A detail from Trajan's Column showing the Emperor Trajan greeting barbarians.

pagan feast of the Lupercalia. In Rome the ancient fertility rites of Cornomania were still celebrated annually, in the presence of the pope, as late as the eleventh century. Such pagan customs could persist obstinately in the heart of Christianity, and at the periphery there was often an interim in which the new religion sat uncomfortably with or above the old.

Above: Detail from the late fourteenth-century Grandes Chroniques de France showing St Remigius Bishop of Rheims anointing Clovis I, King of the Franks.

The overlap of Christianity and paganism can be glimpsed in two of the great heroic poems of north-west Europe: the Anglo-Saxon Beowulf, first written down around 700, and the Irish epic of the warrior-king Sweeney, of which the modern Irish writer, Seamus Heaney, has made an English version (*Sweeney Astray*) that is in its own right a great poem. Sweeney threw the psalter of the priest, Ronan, into the lake and killed his clerk. He was punished by being turned into a sort of half-bird, made to live on berries and to flit from one part of Ireland to another for the rest of his life, in a grotesque parody of the life of a Christian ascetic. In Beowulf the clash between the religions is not direct: the Danish pagan lords suffering from the depredations of the monster, Grendel, are pitied for their heathen sacrifice, and the Christian King of Glory is given recognition by the poet and his hero at various points, but the Christian deity makes no visible impact on the story.

Clovis the Catholic

The conversion to Catholicism of the Frankish King Clovis (c. 465–511) had important consequences both in his own and in the other barbarian kingdoms, including those of southern Britain. Clovis' wife was a Burgundian Catholic, although Burgundy was largely Arian at that time. The king's conversion was almost certainly due to what would now be called *raison d'état*. Clovis found his way to the south-west blocked by the Arian Visigoths. Either he decided that a holy war against them would be more successful than any other, or he may have become genuinely convinced, in the course of a successful campaign against another tribe, that the Christian God would favour him in battle. At all events, 'like some new Constantine', in the last years of the fifth century or very early in the sixth, he and his whole army were baptized by the Catholic Bishop of Rheims.

Clovis was at that point exceptional among the barbarian princes in preferring Catholicism to Arianism. The Bishop of Rheims was unlikely to make difficulties about receiving him, in spite of Clovis' bloodstained past, and of the bloodstained future that might reasonably have been expected of him. Clovis' war against the Arians was well stage-managed. Like any Roman king consulting the oracles, he went to the shrine of St Martin at Tours, laden with appropriate gifts, to ask for a sign. An appropriately military quotation from the Psalms was found for him, and according to Gregory of Tours, a divinely summoned pillar of fire led him to the decisive, successful battle with the Visigoths near Poitiers. He had fought the first holy war of the western barbarians. His baptism had neither dampened his aggressive ardour, nor blunted his cunning.

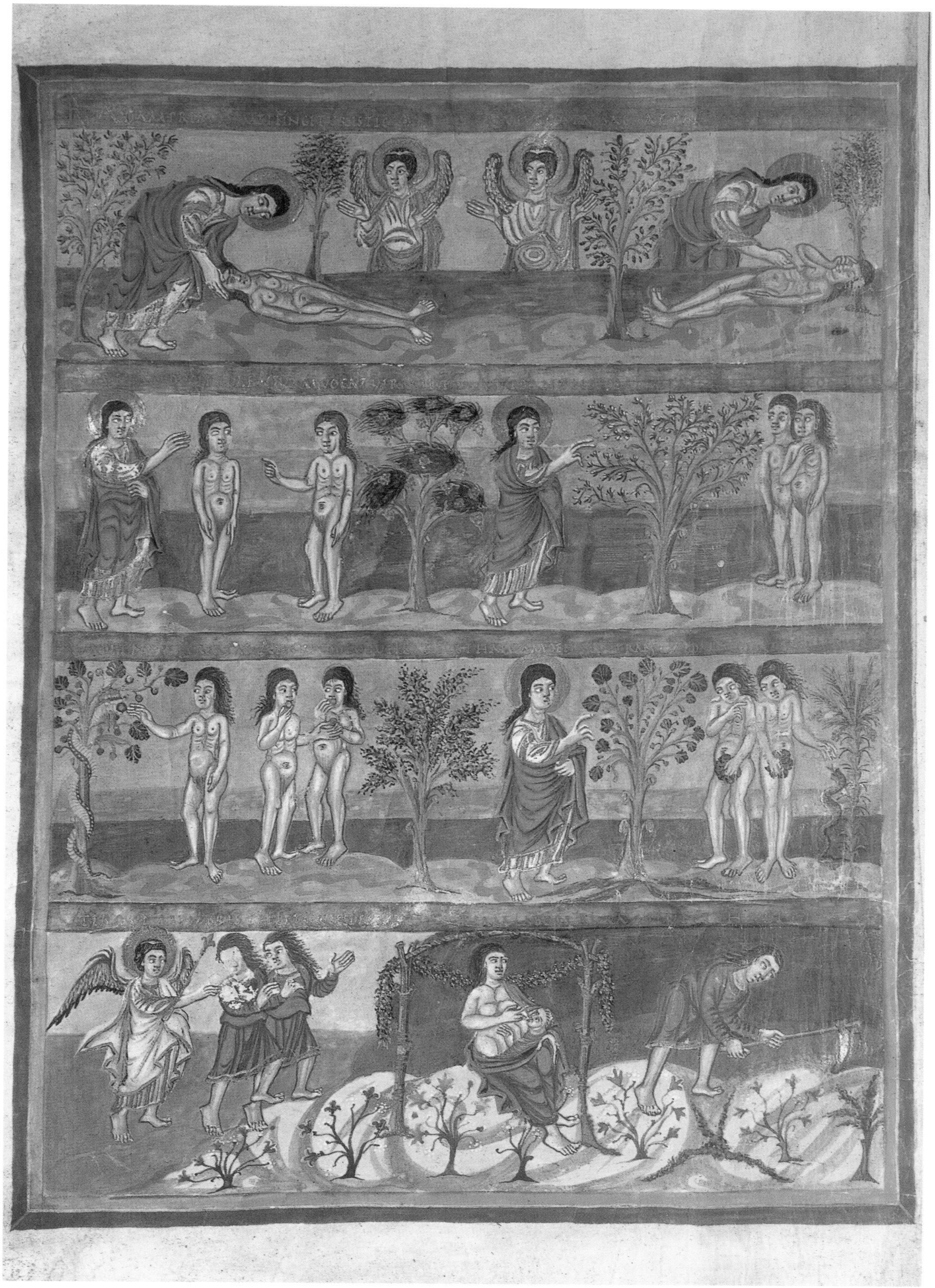

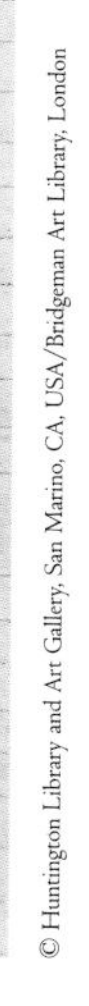

Above: Detail from the Golden Legend of Jacopo da Voragine, illustrating St Patrick greeting a king, an indication of the rising influence of the Christian Church on secular matters.

Left: The story of Adam and Eve as illustrated in the ninth-century Moutier-Grandval Bible, in the Carolingian Abbey of St Martin, Tours.

Patrick and Columbanus

In Ireland, which had never formed part of the Roman Empire, the history of the conversions was different from elsewhere in north-west Europe. The faith was brought to Ireland by a fifth-century Briton called Patrick, who began a very gradual and piecemeal conversion of the tribes that was far from complete by the end of the century. Patrick also had effects upon the place of Latin and Greek in Irish culture. As a result of his mission and of the communities that he set up, Irish learning was lively and productive for some four or five centuries after him.

In 590, roughly a century after Patrick's death, a Northern Irish monk called Columbanus (543–615) came with his followers to north-eastern Francia. To Frankish monasticism, and later to the monasteries of northern Italy, Columbanus brought Irish learning and peculiarly Irish penitential practices, which allowed a much more individual approach to sin and penance. The earlier Western Christian approach to the erring had been that they should ask the Christian community for forgiveness. The tradition brought by Columbanus, which also had its parallels in the Eastern Christianity of the time, was that the troubled soul could discuss the sinner's plight with a holy person who was a sort of spiritual doctor but also a friend; from this discussion the appropriate penance and restoration could take place.

Below: Seventh-century high cross and uncapped round tower at Clonmacnoise, County Offaly, Ireland. Monastic settlements arose in Ireland as monks integrated their secluded, devotional lifestyles into the surrounding communities, thus making their spiritual influence communal rather than individual.

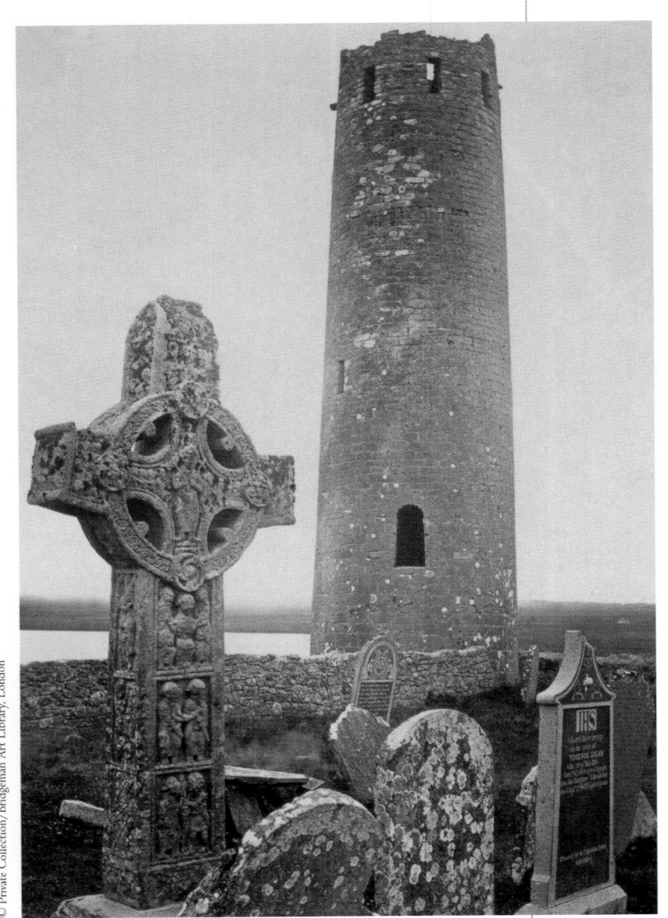

Monastic Rules

The sixth century was a critical time for the way men and women followed a dedicated and secluded coenobitic, or monastic, life in the monasteries and hermitages. Withdrawal from the world to live in the manner followed in the Egyptian desert, in cells located outside the ordinary commerce of the world, often in frighteningly inhospitable localities, was a pattern that needed an ordered society to back it up, and a certain level of general economic prosperity. For example, very large numbers of the Egyptian desert coenobites – up to several thousand at a time – would finance their charitable activities by offering themselves on the labour market in the harvest season. When social disorder prevailed, such things were more difficult, and the monks could themselves be a destabilizing influence, if they were not subject to proper controls.

There had been many attempts in East and West to stabilize monastic life around some simple and workable principles. The variety of this way of life was very great, as were the delicacy and complexity of the spiritual and collective issues. Particularly influential over a very long period were the anonymous 'Rule of the Master', and the 'Rule of Benedict of Nursia', both composed in central Italy in the first part of the sixth century. Both were drawn up for particular communities, and not as some sort of code of general application.

The distinguishing characteristic of the Rule of St Benedict is its assumption of a sheltered community of celibate males dedicated to a life of prayer, which to a large extent is to be prayer carried out in common. The spiritual aims are those of the community rather than those of the individual. Why this rule, which was intended for the governance of the communities headed by Benedict and none other, imposed itself over such an enormously wide area of the Western church, is almost certainly a consequence of the wisdom and moderation of the advice that Benedict gives for leadership. He is not prescribing for heroes of the spiritual life, nor for great mystics, but for honest people who want to give of their

Left: The ruins of St Catherine's monastery in the Sinai desert. In the sixth century, the template for monastic settlements was forged in inhospitable regions.

best in a calling that is quite certainly very difficult to describe. Anyone who has ever had anything to do with pastoral care will recognize the moral world of which he speaks, and would be prepared to value what he says about it.

Of the abbot the Rule says:

> *'The abbot should remember always what he is and what name [sc., father] he bears, and know that to whom more is committed, more is demanded. Let him realise also what a hard and difficult task he has undertaken, to rule souls and to adapt himself to many different characters. This one he must praise, that one rebuke, another persuade, and according to each one's character and understanding he must adapt himself in sympathy so that he may not only not suffer loss in the flock entrusted to him, but may rejoice in their increase. Above all things let him not give his principal care to fleeting earthly things and so neglect or undervalue the salvation of the souls committed to him... Let him study to be loved rather than feared. Let him not be impetuous or anxious, autocratic or obstinate, jealous or suspicious, for so he will never be at rest... and let him so temper all things that the strong may wish to follow, and the weak may not draw back.'*

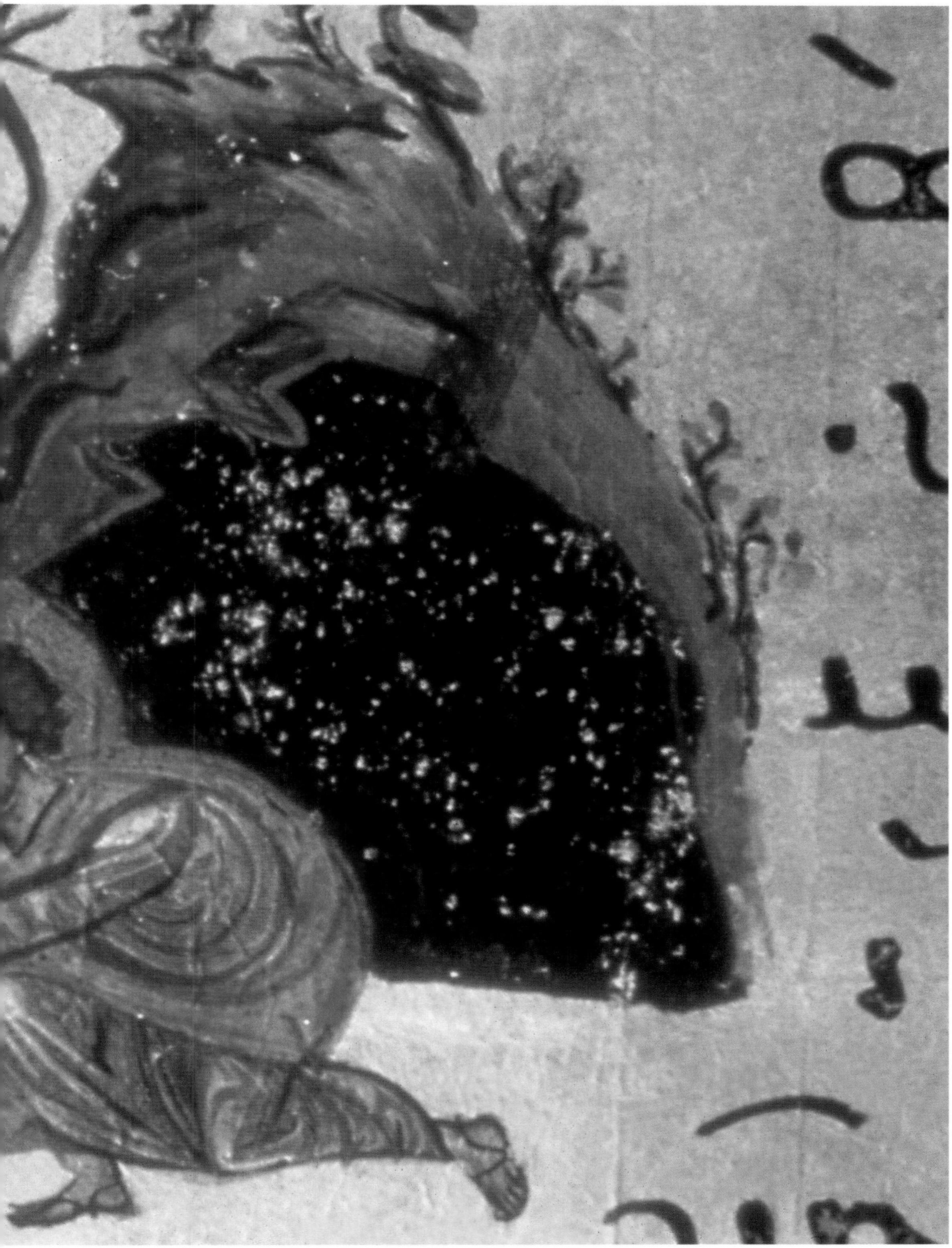

Left: A monk milking a goat from a sixth-century fresco in the Monastery of Saint Catherine, Mount Sinai. The coenobite monks could not survive in isolation without some interaction with society, such as offering themselves for work during the harvest.

St Benedict's work took place in dioceses of central Italy that were controlled or strongly influenced by the Roman Church, and this is reflected, as Dom David Knowles, a Cambridge professor who had lived under it, said[3], in the simple, strong outline of government prescribed in the Rule. The just use of authority, and submission to it, on the implied model of the Roman household, are the core of the Rule. Authority in the monastery had not merely to be present, but to be audible, visible, articulate. The aim was to serve and praise God in a common life separated from the world. The means to achieve this end were the liturgical life of common prayer, the private life of meditation, prayer and study and the domestic life of manual or artisan labour, in the house, the garden, or the workshop.

The social assumptions made in the Rule are widely different from those of Eastern or Irish monasticism. It presupposed a social organization that would be disposed to support the coenobite community through the gift of quite substantial estates; when it makes no reference, for example, to the harvesting of produce, it assumes that the monastery will be supplied by a late Roman large country estate or latifundium. The Rule sees the monk only in the house or in its immediate vicinity; it does not see him labouring in distant fields, or carting produce far from the home grange. Nor was the monk to be in the slightest degree a wandering holy man. He could not even become the spiritual friend and counsellor of the laity, save under the strictest of controls. St Benedict chose for his two most important monasteries sites that were hard of access: Subiaco in the valley of the Aniene south-east of Rome, and Monte Cassino, astride the main line of communications between Rome and Naples. Neither foundation was by any means in the desert.

The Rule was perfectly suited to a Western Roman world in which provincialism and regionalism prevailed everywhere, where the local landowners and the rulers above them were quite willing to subsidize coenobitic life by the gift of estates. In return, the monastery educated some of their male children, perhaps also taking others that were indisposed to, or unsuitable for, the military life, and retaining them in the community. They were also very willing to support nunneries (for whom the Benedictine Rule could be easily adopted) which would retain their surplus females. Beyond the transactions in children that were involved, there were questions of the honour that accrued to a family from supporting works of holiness that led to salvation, and of the holy men who remembered families and local principates in prayer.

The monasteries were not private schools filled with aristocrats. They took recruits from every walk of life, just as the coenobite communities had from the outset. But the role of the noble families in financing, building and endowing the monasteries was bound to be reflected in the way they were run. In a world where government authority was precarious at least, they were in a privileged position that was open to abuse, and the austere precepts of the Rule did not always protect them.

Above: A Benedictine monk painting a statue of the Virgin and Child. The detail comes from the Lambeth Apocalypse c. 1260.

Gregory the Great

At the end of the sixth century, the monastic tendency and the clerical leadership of the upper nobility were well represented by Gregory (c. 540–604), the grandson of a former Roman bishop, but a great aristocrat who occupied the office of Prefect of Rome. This was some half a century after the armies of the eastern Emperor Justinian had carried out a precarious reoccupation of the Italian peninsula, the north of which had been swiftly lost again to the heretical Arian Lombards. Gregory founded a monastery on the Aventine hill, not far from the Roman Forum, but he was not at first its abbot. Gregory joined the Roman clergy reluctantly. He was a gifted and tireless writer, whose work

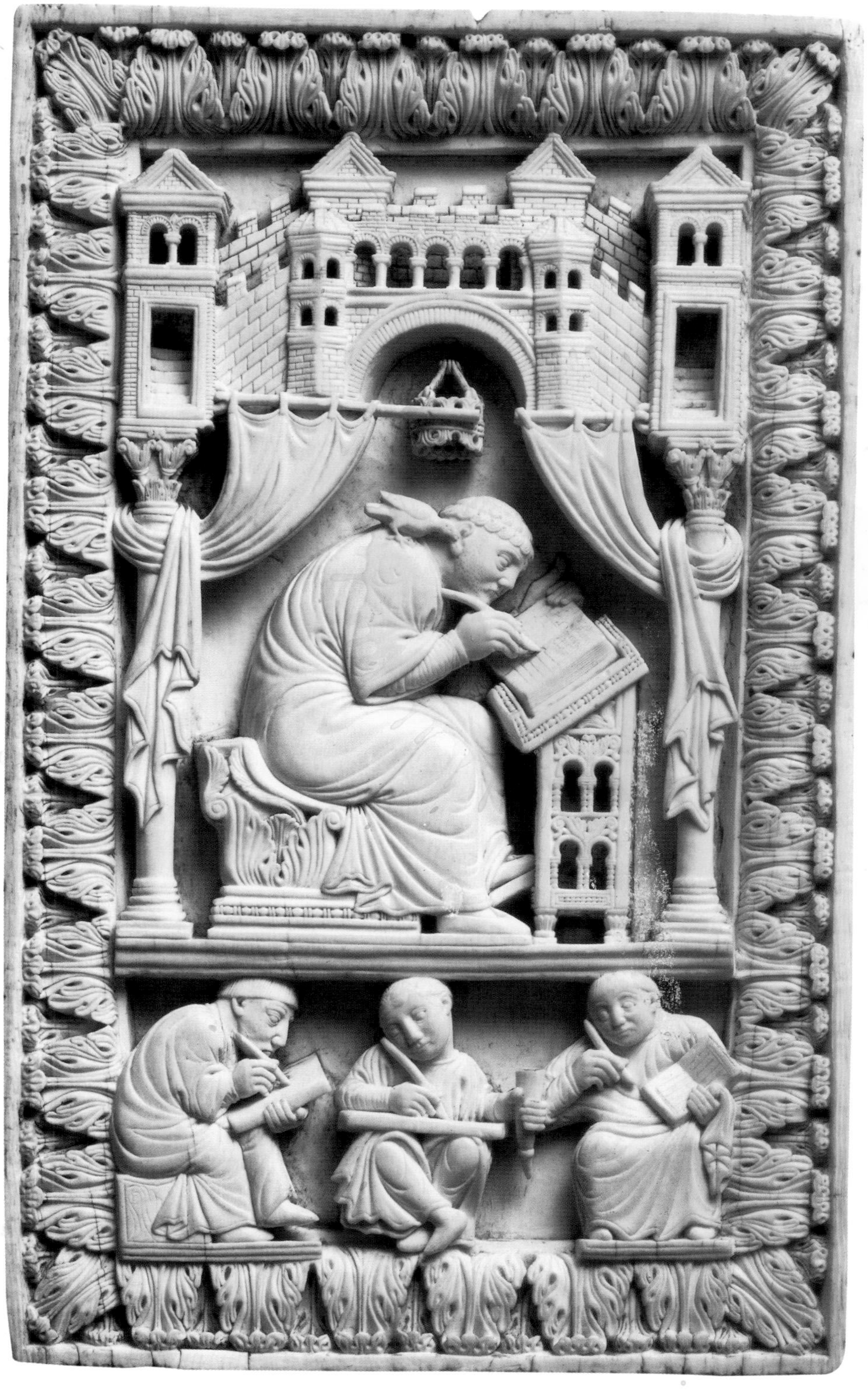

© Kunsthistorisches Museum, Vienna, Austria/Bridgeman Art Library, London

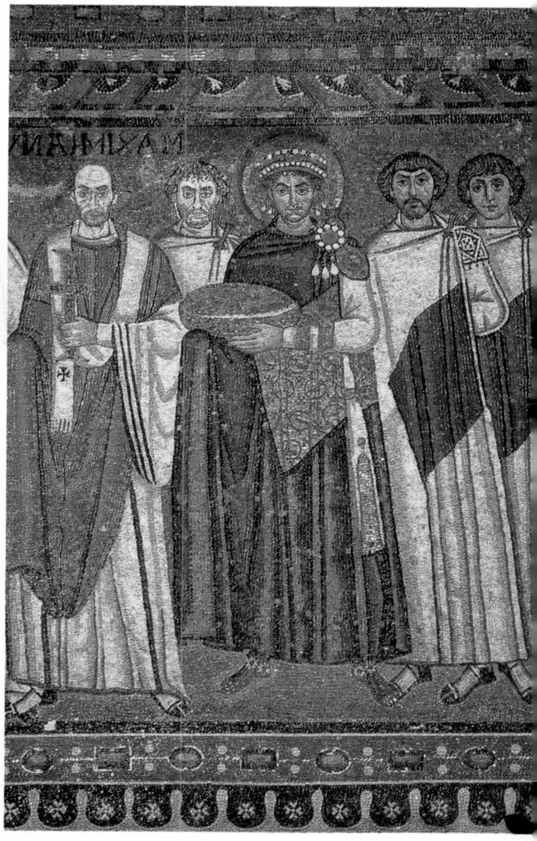

© San Vitale, Ravenna, Italy/Bridgeman Art Library, London

Above: A sixth-century mosaic showing Justinian I and his retinue. A learned man, Justinian was emperor of the East Roman Empire from 527 to 565.

Left: St Gregory writing with scribes below. Gregory was a gifted and tireless writer. His Pastoral Care became one of the great medieval handbooks.

Pastoral Care was to become one of the great handbooks of the Middle Ages. (Two centuries later, it was translated into English by King Alfred.) Even more reluctantly, in 590 he became Pope.

Gregory's career was a classic example of the way in which government often devolved upon the Church at this point of the early Middle Ages, because no one else was competent to assume it. The Roman Church was by his time the greatest landowner in western Europe, with lands located not only all over Italy and its islands, but in Gaul and as far to the east as Asia Minor. Its land management was modelled on that for the imperial domain. It had taken over the provisioning of the city of Rome, and had become something between a huge soup kitchen – that looked after thousands of refugees from barbarian incursion elsewhere – and a public ministry of supply. The imperial palaces and the ancient public buildings, lacking all maintenance, were literally falling down; the aqueducts and walls (the walls measured some 20 km/12 miles) were now looked after by the Church. It fell to Gregory to negotiate with the Lombard armies who were pressing down upon the 'Roman' (or Byzantine) lands from the north.

Above: A silver penny minted during the reign of the Anglo-Saxon King Ethelbert of Kent.

Right: A reliquary surmounted by the head of Oswald the Holy, King of Northumbria. The crown is made of gold, enamel, and decorated with precious stones and pearls.

From Gregory's Rome, an advance missionary venture set out in 596 for England; the second, effective missionary party left two years later. It was headed by the monk, Augustine, who brought Roman monasticism to England at the same time as Christianity. His mission was not initially addressed to the Anglo-Saxons. The invitation to send Roman priests had come from Ethelbert, the King of Kent, the formerly Jutish south-eastern province of England. Ethelbert had a Frankish, Catholic wife. Gregory had jumped at the chance of bypassing the usual missionary ventures that departed from the Catholic periphery; instead he despatched evangelists direct from Rome, which he regarded, in an entirely excusable way, as the centre.

Gregory was a subject of the Byzantine Emperor; south of Rome lay the solidly Byzantine provinces ruled from Naples, and north-east was located the real Byzantine seat of government in Italy, that of the Exarch in Ravenna. Gregory had recently protested the Patriarch of Constantinople's assumption of the title of 'universal patriarch'. But in the barbarian north-west of Europe, the eastern Emperor's writ did not run.

The English mission occupies a special place in the development of medieval papalism, because no other ecclesiastical province among the barbarians came to have the same dependent relation on the Roman see. The missionary leader, Augustine, after a short period received the Kentish king as a Christian, and baptized also large numbers of his subjects. King Ethelbert was said to have understood that Christianity must be freely accepted, and so the mass baptisms were perhaps not so indiscriminate as some of those that took place on the Continent. But the king was still said to have favoured those who converted more than those who did not, which was not without effect on his nobles. After his consecration as bishop, Augustine sent back to his principal in Rome for guidance on a number of topics. The correspondence at once made Gregory into a lawgiver for the bishops in Britain.

The English conversion, like the Frankish conversion, depended on the evolution of barbarian princely politics. For reasons that are hard to penetrate, the most powerful king in the island, who exercised some sort of hegemony over the rest, Edwin, King of the Northumbrians, decided to take a Kentish wife and subsequently to accept Christianity. The second decision was only taken after much hesitation. Edwin adhered to it, and so, after some disputes over the succession, did his successor Oswald. The eventual conversion of the Anglo-Saxons was thus assured. Oswald finally imposed Catholicism on his own dominions, and made its eventual victory only a matter of time in the areas south of the Humber. The victory that established Oswald's position was achieved not over the pagan Mercians (who were converted at a later point after being defeated by Oswald's son Oswy), but over the British King Cadwalla.

The Roman mission of Augustine to Britain imposed a Roman pattern of Catholicism upon the country, which might under different circumstances have accepted Christianity from the Celtic

Above: St Cuthbert shown both praying in the sea and having his feet licked dry by sea otters. A monk looks on. The image comes from Bede's Life and Miracles of St Cuthbert.

Left: The ruins of Whitby Abbey, Yorkshire. The original abbey was founded in the seventh century and was the site of the Synod of Whitby called in 663.

church, which had already converted most of Scotland by the time the Roman missionaries reached Northumbria, and that had quite a body of adherents in the south of the country. The triumph of Roman Catholicism in Northumbria was not automatic, because Oswald, the key figure in the conversion of the North and the Midlands, had already made contact with the Celtic monks among the southern Picts, and been converted by the Celtic monks of Iona, before he came to power there. Scottish, Celtic-trained bishops were called to fill sees in the Northumbrian church.

Right: An illuminated manuscript – the Codex Amiatinus – which was produced in Jarrow, Northumberland. It shows Christ in majesty with angels and the four Evangelists.

The Synod of Whitby

But a reckoning between Roman and Celtic traditions in Britain came with sharp disputes about the mode of tonsuring clerics, which differed between Celtic and Roman practices, and about the system for fixing dates for the annual celebration of Easter. The Synod of Whitby, held in 664 under the presidency of the Northumbrian king to decide the matter, ended in the victory of the Roman observance. The Celtic monastic tradition continued to influence strongly the Northumbrian church, particularly through St Cuthbert, at a time when the Celtic influence of Columbanus was very much alive on the Continent in the Frankish church. But the essential discipline of the English church continued to be Roman, more so than was the case in Francia.

Especially because of the way in which they had combined Roman and Celtic monastic and cultural traditions, the Northumbrian monks at Jarrow were among the most vigorous and flourishing monastic communities in western Europe by the early seventh century The Venerable Bede (c. 673–735) was at this time a towering figure, the most cultivated monastic historian of his time, a master of the difficult science of chronology, and the biographer of the far-off contemporary Roman popes.

The art of the illustrated book was practised there and in Ireland in a manner to make their manuscripts the envy of Europe.

By the early seventh century, the barbarians who had settled in the western Empire and its former possessions were virtually all Christian. Some had secured their position in the Empire as Arian Christians but they, with the rest, had virtually all become Catholic. Franks, Anglo-Saxons, Visigoths, Burgundians, Ostrogoths, even the Lombards, who had been the especially violent enemies of the Catholic 'Romans' in central Italy, had all accepted the Catholic traditions. Only in Anglo-Saxon England was there an organic historic root in the faith that had actually been sent to them from Rome. On the lower Rhine, there were still substantial pockets of paganism, such as that of the Frisians, and in many other areas outside the old Roman frontiers, such as the territories of the Saxons, the still huge areas of the pagan German hinterland remained. In much of southern Italy and Sicily, in Rome, and in the enclave of Ravenna in eastern Italy, the Byzantine emperor remained in rather precarious control. But the more or less assimilated barbarian tribes of the western Empire, although no longer subject to any real form of temporal control by a Roman emperor, were in one sense culturally Roman through their Catholic belief, and through the Latin culture of the clerical class.

Patronage and Privilege

In their conviction of the conquest of death through holiness, and the accessibility of the martyred and saintly dead to the living through the frequentation of their tombs and the veneration of their relics, late Antique Christians had introduced a new form of sociability. Social privilege was not indifferent in the pursuit of the holy. Networks of influential families undertook to uncover and conserve holy relics, and to move them to new locations where the patronage systems could influence the bishops to have them displayed in the way the patrons wanted. Under popes such as Damasus, the Roman catacombs became great museums to illustrate holiness and martyrdom. In Rome, the great shrines such as those of St Peter, St Paul, St Lawrence, and the churches dedicated to the other martyr-popes, became places to lodge petitions with these influential denizens of eternity. In Christendom the healing of the sick, which paganism had assigned to innumerable divine shrines, was transferred as a duty to the shrines of the Christian holy ones. A shrine such as that of St Martin of Tours benefited from a long series of miracles, and became one of the great shrines of north-west Europe.

A process of extending the patronage networks of the powerful to the halls of eternity took place in the monasteries of the barbarian kingdoms. Not only did the princely barbarian families place their own members in the monasteries they founded and provided with huge landed endowments, but their kinsfolk in the monasteries also set up for them a most elaborate system of commemorating family members for ever in the prayers of the monks. Books of remembrance were produced, specifying who was to be remembered in the liturgy and on which days. These books became a sort of Almanac de Gotha that recorded all the appropriate members of the princely families who had endowed the foundations.

The universal charitable aims of the churches were by no means forgotten in this rush to commemorate the rich and powerful. Both in the eastern and western Empire, and within its western successor-states, the redistribution of wealth to the poor and destitute was one of the main functions of the bishops and the monasteries. Dealing with the huge influxes of refugees that occurred in the disturbances of the barbarian invasions was the duty of the Church; no other authority even attempted

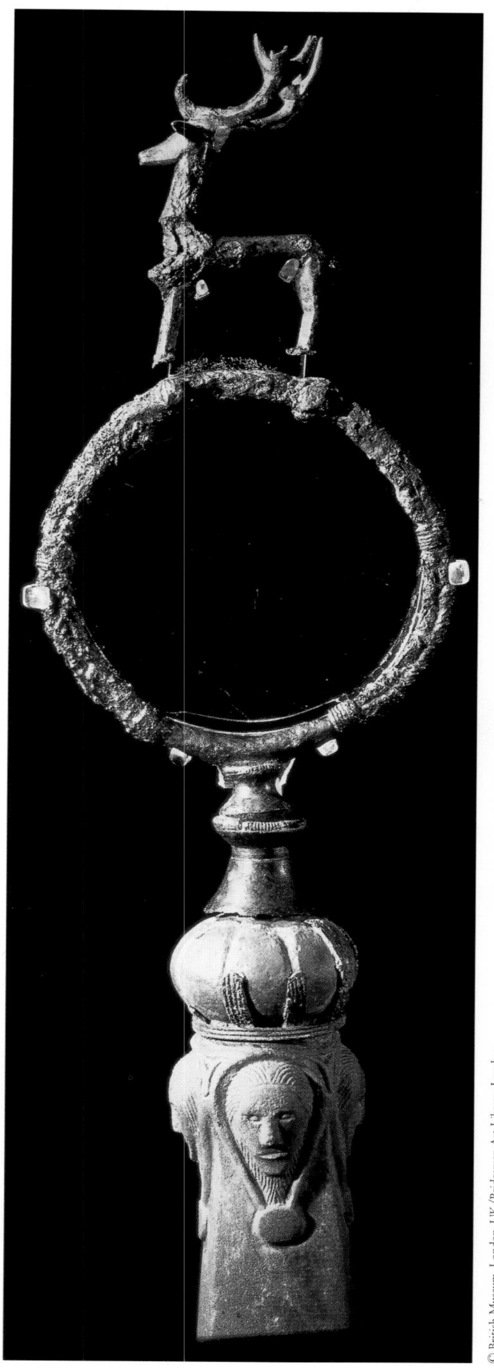

Above: Detail of ceremonial sceptre surmounted by a bronze stag, from the seventh-century Sutton Hoo Treasure.

to cope with it. The penetration of the holy into most aspects of life continued, as it had in pagan antiquity. But in Christianity the holy men had assumed new functions that allowed their ideas of the holy to penetrate the social fabric of noble barbarian society. Later in the Middle Ages the Church was to take upon itself many of the former functions of the state. A few of these transfers have been astonishingly long-lived. Despite the religious upheavals of modern times, the bureaucracy of the late Roman Empire continues today to pursue a shadowy existence in the bureaucracy of the Roman Church.

1. Mons.L. Duchesne, *Early History of the Christian Church*, trs. C. Jenkins, vol.3 (London, 1924), p.226.
2. Quoted by Peter Brown, *Augustine of Hippo: a biography* (London, 1967), p. 287.
3. *The Monastic Order in England* (Cambridge, 1941), p.9. The quotation from the Rule of St Benedict is from D. Knowles, *Christian Monasticism* (London, 1969), pp.34–35.

Left: Tenth-century German book illustration. At the top St Boniface meets his martyrdom at the swords of the Frisians.

7

Christianity and the Rise of Islam

In the early seventh century Christianity continued to inhabit the space and the time of the Roman Empire, its domicile since its beginnings. Here and there it had slipped outside the Roman frontiers, as it had done in Ireland at one end of the Roman world, in Armenia at the other. In India it had made a tentative minority appearance, in Persia and Mesopotamia a more tenacious one, one of whose manifestations – Christian Nestorianism – had penetrated as far as China. In Arabia it had reached some areas in the west of the peninsula, although Judaism was probably better known there. But although there were a few great Christian centres that lay outside the territories of the Roman Empire at its fullest extent, Christianity continued to be firmly based in the lands of the old Empire, which contained all the bishoprics of its apostolic and heroic periods, from Alexandria and Carthage in North Africa to Jerusalem, Antioch and Rome.

At the beginning of the seventh century it started to become apparent just how precarious was the hold of Byzantium on its south-eastern lands. The Sassanian Persian armies had secured the upper hand in Mesopotamia and Armenia during the last part of the sixth century, and had had to be bought off. In 607 the Persians started to overrun Syria, and in 614 they occupied Palestine – where they carried out great massacres, and seized the relic of the true cross from Jerusalem – and subsequently Egypt. It looked as though Christian rule in a huge area might be finished.

Left: The Dome of the Rock (built 688–91) in Jerusalem.

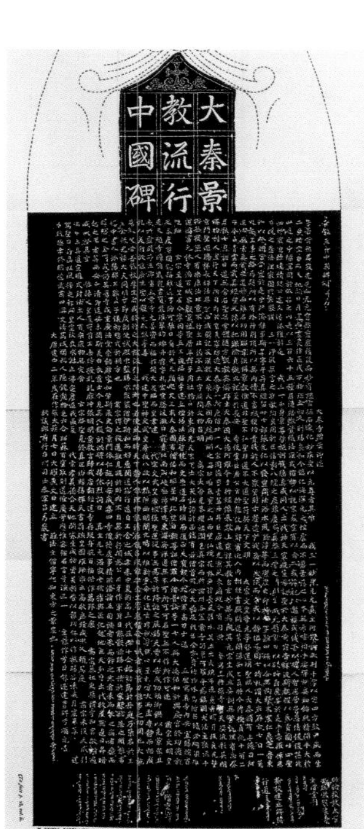

Above: Stone inscribed with Chinese and Syriac characters from Singanfu in China. In the seventh century, Singanfu was the site of a flourishing Christian church.

Above: A detail from Piero della Francesca's The Legend of the True Cross. In 629, Emperor Heraclius forced the Persians to return the relic of the true cross. He himself walked up the Via Dolorosa carrying the relic.

There was a Byzantine reaction under the Emperor Heraclius (575–641) that looked for a time to have succeeded. In 622 he launched a daring strategy that aimed to recover the lost provinces by a direct major attack on the Iranian part of the Sassanian Empire. In executing this plan he showed the utmost coolness, keeping his main army in the field even when the Avar tribes from the Danube besieged Constantinople in 626. The defence of the capital was conducted by the Patriarch and the Emperor's son with desperate gallantry, and its success was attributed to the intercession of the Virgin. It was on this occasion that the Patriarch Sergius composed the great Acathistos hymn to the God-bearer, the mother of Christ. Heraclius engaged the main Sassanian army in 628 in the mountains near the ruins of Nineveh, and destroyed it. The Persians were compelled in the following year to return the lost provinces, the Christian prisoners, and the relic of the cross.

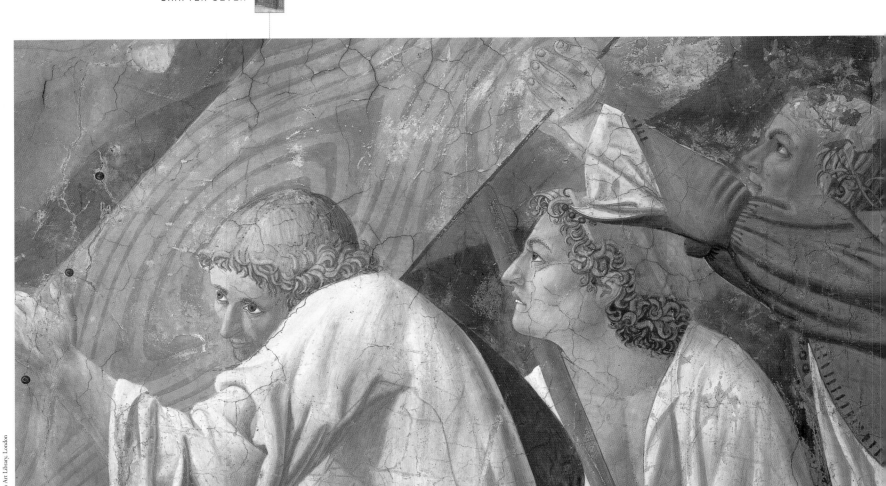

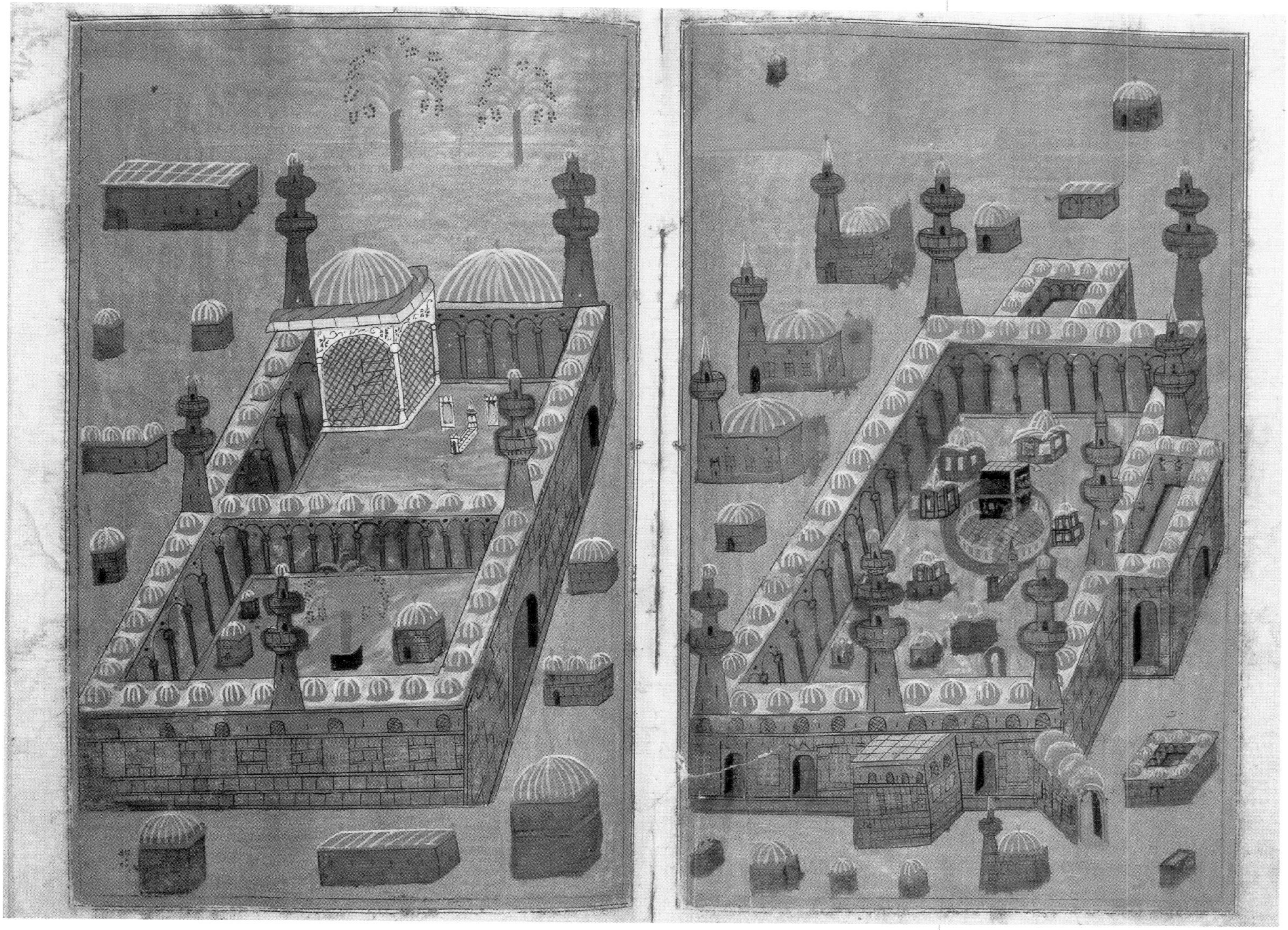

Above: Persian illustration from Reasons for Charity by Mustafa al-Shukri showing the mosques at Medina and Mecca, the centre of the Islamic world.

In the Christian western Empire, no one took orders from the Emperor in Constantinople any more, outside the strongpoints of Byzantine Italy. One of those strongpoints was Rome, which was the only bishopric in the west to have apostolic origins. When it began in apostolic times, the language of the Roman Church had been Greek, and in the early seventh century Greek was still the official language used by the imperial government in Rome, although Latin had become the language of the western church. The Roman pope was still a bishop inside the political life of the eastern Empire, although the relations of the western with the eastern church and its Emperors were often poor: in 653 Pope Martin was arrested for treason, flogged, and sent to die in exile in the Crimea.

The western church thus remained in contact with the east through its Roman leadership, and the western barbarian kingdoms remained in trading and other relations with the eastern Empire. However,

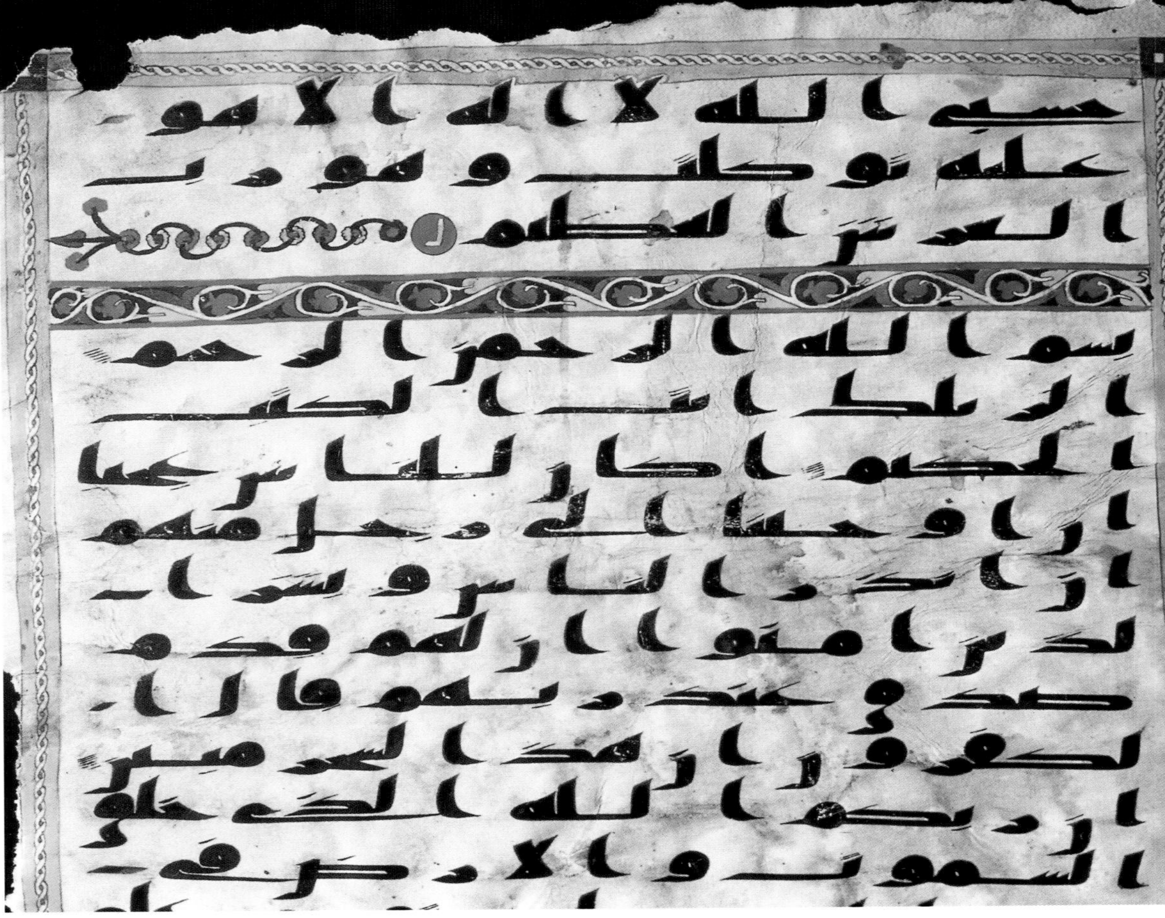

Right: Page from a handwritten version of the Qur'an, possibly eighth century. The fragment is from the Great Mosque in San'a, Yemen.

these things took place against the background of a deterioration of almost all the late Roman towns in the west, and very sharp declines in population and production, with consequent changes in settlement patterns, that far preceded the seventh century. The prolongation of the Christian space of the ancient Roman Empire into that of the barbarian kingdoms was in that century to be cut by the irruption of a new political order into the Near East and the southern Mediterranean.

Muhammad, the Messenger of God

The new Islamic order was to place new barriers between Christendom and its historic origins. The bishoprics of the barbarian West had for a very long time been drifting apart from the ancient patriarchates of the East. But Islamic supremacy in the East meant, in spite of their common Christian roots, that they ceased finally to share a common cultural world. In one sense the barrier has never been completely lifted, even in periods like those of the early crusades, or the times of modern Anglo-French hegemony in the Near East and North Africa. In another sense, however, the Mediterranean Sea was never totally closed either to the West or to the East: in spite of pirates, holy warriors and war fleets, there remained a certain porosity that for centuries allowed merchant ventures to leak from one culture to another, whether Islamic, Byzantine, or Latin.

In the early seventh century a member of a pagan merchant family in Mecca in the region of the west-Arabian Hijaz began to have intimations, as though from behind a veil (Qur'an, 53.1-8; 2.97-98), from divine spiritual beings, that he ought to carry out certain actions, and to say certain things to those around him. The Hijaz was the economic and cultural centre of Arabia, linked by commercial ties with Syria and Palestine, and so a main point tied indirectly with the Mediterranean. Christian monks and Jewish rabbis walked the roads of Arabia, and their doctrines were far from unknown in Hijaz.

The subject of the visitations, Muhammad (570–632), thought of himself as God's messenger.[1] In the Qur'an (42.51) he is reported to have said that 'it is not fitting for any human being that God should speak to him except by revelation or from behind a veil, or by sending a messenger to reveal by his permission what he will.' Some of the suggestions that reached him from on high were connected with the revelations he knew to have been made in the past to earlier prophets. He was thus guided to follow the religion of Abraham, the breaker of idols and the worshipper of Allah, although this did not mean that he was to follow the Jewish religion as understood by some of the tribes in the Hijaz. From the beginning the spoken word seems to have figured as a sort of future scripture. In one of Muhammad's earliest revelations, in which he was told to 'recite', a part of the revelation is of what the Lord 'taught men by the pen'. The verb for 'recite' can also mean 'to read' (Qur'an, 96.1-5).

The history of the text of the Qur'an is as obscure as that of the Christian Gospels. After Muhammad (whose literacy is still disputed) went to Medina he is known to have employed secretaries, and tradition records his having dictated a particular passage (sura) to a scribe. But the writing down of the revelations was only partial, and at the time of the prophet's death large numbers of the revelations were 'in the hearts of men', known only through their having been memorized by his companions. The first written collections are thought to date from the time of the caliph 'Uthman, probably between 650 and 656. But at this stage knowledge of the Qur'an was still based on memory more than on writing: the emergence of something pointing towards a canonical text did not begin for another half-century.

Mecca was the city of many important gods as well as a trading centre, and Muhammad's messages were received by most of the merchant rulers, including some members of his own tribe, with derision. He was described as a teller of old wives' tales. The close relation of his revelations both to Judaism and to Christianity would have come as no surprise to his hearers, since some tribes within the mercantile orbit of Mecca had been converted to one or another of the two faiths. His assertion of a single god, Allah, and his denunciation of the polytheists, or worshippers of many gods (who came for him to include the Christians, whom he defined as Trinitarian) were commercially and politically inconvenient, because they threatened the benefits that Mecca obtained from being the resort of many polytheist traders and worshippers.

By 622 the position of Muhammad in Mecca had become untenable, because his kinsfolk had become unwilling to protect him further against his enemies. His adherents helped him in his flight (*hijra*) to the oasis of Yathrib (that later became Medina, the town of the prophet, or messenger), some 200 miles distant, and took an oath of support. The community that joined him in submission to his divine messages became the nucleus of a political and religious organization. Submission to the will of Allah that had been intimated by Allah to his messenger was the core of the new religion.

Above: Points of pilgrimage at Mecca and Medina, from a sixteenth-century manuscript by Futuh al-Haramain. Muhammad was born in Mecca but by 622, his position there had become untenable and he was forced to flee to Medina, the 'city of the prophet'. His flight is known as the hijra.

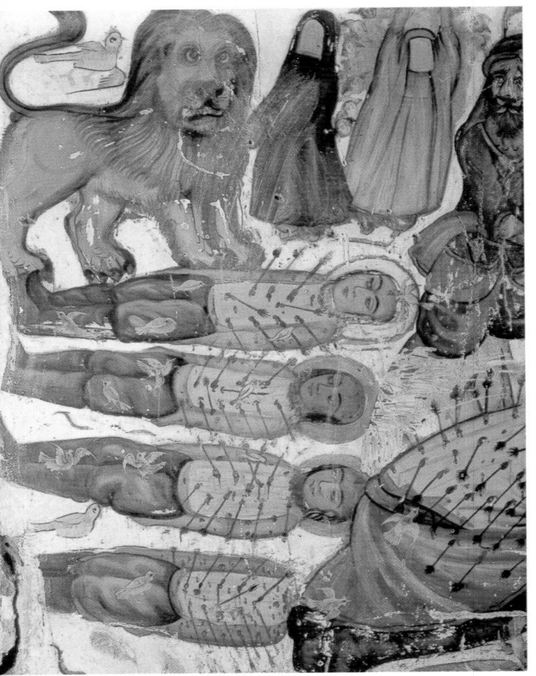

Above: Mural painting in the Imam Zahdah Chah Zaid Mosque, Isfahan, Iran, showing martyrs of the Shi'ite faith fallen in war.

The 'submitters' were called Muslims, and the community of Muslims was called (from the same root, *salima*) Islam (Qur'an, 3.19, the true religion with Allah is submission [Islam]).

Muhammad received many divine messages at Medina. Their complexity and often very practical nature have frequently given the impression that he was fundamentally a lawgiver who set up a written code of behaviour. But this is to do a grave injustice to a man who came to announce and warn, and to convey a moral message that was just as much directed to the heart as had been the teachings of Jesus. Muhammad told people that they must face God's judgement for their works on earth, on a last day when all created things will be rocked by earthquake, and men and women will be sentenced to heaven or hell for their behaviour in this life, receiving credit for their acts of kindness and mercy, and perdition for their misdeeds.

The believers who seceded with Muhammad formed what can in modern terms be described as a political society, that lived, fought and prayed together. It was in a sense tribal, although beyond tribes. His position was without parallel in the Arabian society of his time. He called his supporters the party of God (*hizbullah*): it was their duty to struggle in the way of God (the verb is *jahada*, hence the noun, holy struggle, *jihad*) with all those who scoffed at, derided or impeded God's messenger. This opposition to Muhammad and his cause was deemed *fitna* (persecution), referring to acts of disintegration or dissolution of the community; the implication is political in this case as well as religious. Muhammad said that slaughter is an evil thing, but that fitna is worse, implying quite clearly that sacred war was the duty of the community when such sacrilege was otherwise unavoidable. To struggle in the way of God preserved, however, its primary general meaning of spiritual and moral effort. The armed struggle was only a single aspect of this general moral struggle. For an individual Muslim, jihad can include all acts of worship, and other acts associated with belief.

However wars of secession from the Meccan community were duly fought, and they formed a pattern that served to define a part of the duties of the believer. When they ended with his victorious return to Mecca in 630 of the Christian era, Muhammad had become an Arab sovereign as well as a divine messenger. Those who from the start had been his faithful helpers (*ansar*) enjoyed a specially privileged position in the regime. That there were others whose position had at one time or another been ambiguous, or who had become hostile to him, is obvious from the names he attached to classes of followers described as 'hypocrite' or 'hesitant'. The families of Meccan notables who had opposed him down to the very last moment, nevertheless became the great, rich princes of the Arab Empire that formed after Muhammad's death.

His troops crossed the Byzantine frontiers in 631, and were bloodily repulsed. The following year he himself led a great military expedition to northern Hijaz and as far as the Syrian-Byzantine border at Tabuk. The campaign of Tabuk ended without any major engagement; Muhammad marched back to the Hijaz, and in 632 made his last pilgrimage to Mecca. The sermon he gave on this occasion represents his last thoughts on what is called in the modern West the expansion of Islam. He gave four months' grace to those non-Muslims who were not protected by previous treaties. At the end of this period of grace the unbelievers were to be slain wherever the Muslims could find them (Qur'an, 9.29). Quite whom among the unbelievers Muhammad had in mind when he gave this sermon is uncertain: there were at that time still many unconverted tribes among the desert Arabs, of whom we know that Muhammad entertained a very poor opinion. But he may, equally, have been thinking of the 'Roman' (i.e. Byzantine) Christians, or even of the Sassanian Persians. Shortly after the 'farewell' pilgrimage, Muhammad died in 632 at the age of 62.

By the time of his death Muhammad had come to be a divinely inspired model of human conduct for many thousands of men and women. His courtesy, kindness and patience, his moderation in every aspect of behaviour, including food and drink, his ability to combine firm leadership, including leadership in war, with generous and charitable actions, produced a style of life that ordinary people could reasonably hope to imitate, and that his followers managed to transmit to succeeding generations by recording their memories of him. He had rejected cruel and destructive things such as infanticide and blood feud, although he had not managed to impose his way of life upon the wider Meccan community without armed combat. His leadership had shown remarkable political adroitness. He had avoided the ascetic excesses of many holy men, but he still brought to the world glimpses of his experience of things that to him and subsequently to others seemed to have transcended the merely human.

When Muhammad is compared with the other great prophet of the same ancient world, the contrast with Jesus is not as sharp as Christians have made it in the past. A dissimilarity has traditionally been seen between a celibate Jesus and a Muhammad whose uxorious disposition was allowed to dominate the society he made and the paradise he promised. The contrast is false: Muhammad regulated the law of marriage in a way that was undoubtedly reformist and humane, and no less rigorist than the comparable views of Jesus. His use of sexual imagery in religious contexts is considerably more restrained than what is to be found in the Song of Songs.

The other traditional Christian reproach, that Christianity is a religion of love and Islam a religion of power, points to great differences in the lives and teachings of the two prophets, but when put in this stark way is really no more than ancient holy-war propaganda. The teachings of both Muhammad and Jesus place the love and mercy of God at the front of the models of life that they propose. Because as Muhammad saw it he could not carry out the divine commands that were transmitted to him without resort to arms, the resort to arms was incorporated in the society that he founded, although only as a last resort against moral impiety (fitna). In Christian terms the result was as though the Emperor Domitian had adopted Christianity at the end

Above: Seventeenth-century mural painting from the Imam Zahdah Chah Zaid Mosque, Isfahan, Iran, depicting the fourth caliph of Islam, Ali-ibn-abi-Talib (602–661), murdered on his way to the mosque at al-Khufah.

Right: An illustration from the Persian Makamat (Literary Gatherings), a collection of rhyming adventure stories by Abu Mohammed al Kasim ibn Ali (1054–1122). It shows the Caliph's guard.

of the first Christian century, instead of the Emperor Constantine having done so in the fourth. The society inspired by Jesus was unarmed for almost three centuries, and subsequently armed. The society inspired by Muhammad was armed almost from the beginning. There is a distinction, but it is perhaps finer than many Christians would like to think.

Muhammad had promised the believers in his last sermon that Islam as a religion would prevail over all other religions, that their enemies would be destroyed, and that they would (like Moses) be masters and God's deputies in the land (Qur'an, 9.33; 7.129). This was the political vocabulary of expansionism, but it would have remained a dead letter if the natural tendency of the Arab tribes to scatter in confused blood feuds had broken the quite frail basis of the Islamic community. That this did not occur after his death was owed to the religious piety, and also to the political and military ability of the small group of Islamic leaders (by no means all of them early 'companions' of the prophet), who chose to accept one of their number, Abu Bakr, the father of Muhammad's favoured wife, 'A'isha, as caliph or successor of the messenger of God.

The Caliphs and the Rise of Empire

The caliph made no claim to be the chosen recipient of further divine revelations, nor did those who came after him. He was in one sense no more than the prayer leader of the Muslims. But in effect the political leadership and the ultimate military command devolved upon him. The first task of the new caliph, without whose accomplishment there could have been no Islamic Empire, was to force the Arabian tribes that were scattering as was the natural tendency after the death of the big leader, to return to the discipline of Islam. In modern times this might be called a war against counter-revolutionaries, but it was understood in religious terms as a war against apostasy (the wars of the ridda).

Once victory in the wars of the ridda had given back to the Islamic community its obedient armies of religion, they could follow the injunction in the farewell sermon of Muhammad that the Muslims are brothers one to another, and are forbidden civil strife, and that they should fight all men who associate others with Allah in his divinity. The political results came practically as fast as the armies could move. Islamic holy war was in a very short time taken out of Arabia, first to Syria-Palestine, then Iraq, to Byzantine Egypt, and then to what remained of the Sassanian Persian Empire. No doubt, the armies of the caliphs of the second and subsequent waves of conquest were largely composed of non-Arabs.

How far the wars of conquest were genuinely wars of religion is hard to determine. A distinguished scholar, Bernard Lewis, observed that the army commanders were not particularly religious men, and that the truly converted and the pietists played little part in the creation of the Arab Empire. On the other hand, 'Umar (caliph during a critical period of the conquests, from 634–44) was clearly not indifferent to the military struggles. He made a special journey from Arabia to receive the submission of Jerusalem (see below), and he is also said to have incited the Muslim Arab armies to unite with those of a doubtfully Islamic Bedouin chief to attack the Persians in Iraq.

The consequences for the eastern Roman Empire were disastrous both politically and economically. The earlier victories of the Emperor Heraclius over the Persians were revealed as empty; all they had done was to weaken the Sassanian Empire so that the Muslims could conquer it. Egypt had been the granary of the Empire, and the maritime base for a large part of its sea power: both disappeared overnight. The territories controlled by the eastern Empire were halved. Both Alexandria and Jerusalem,

Below: The lavishly decorated interior of the Dome of the Rock. The Dome of the Rock was built on the site of Solomon's Temple in Jerusalem.

two of the historic deposits of the Christian faith and of its central theological traditions, became the local centres of a Christian religion that was still important in the eastern territories and which still had numerous adherents there, but that was now subject to political Islamic control, while its adherents had to pay the poll tax that was exacted from subject Christians and Jews.

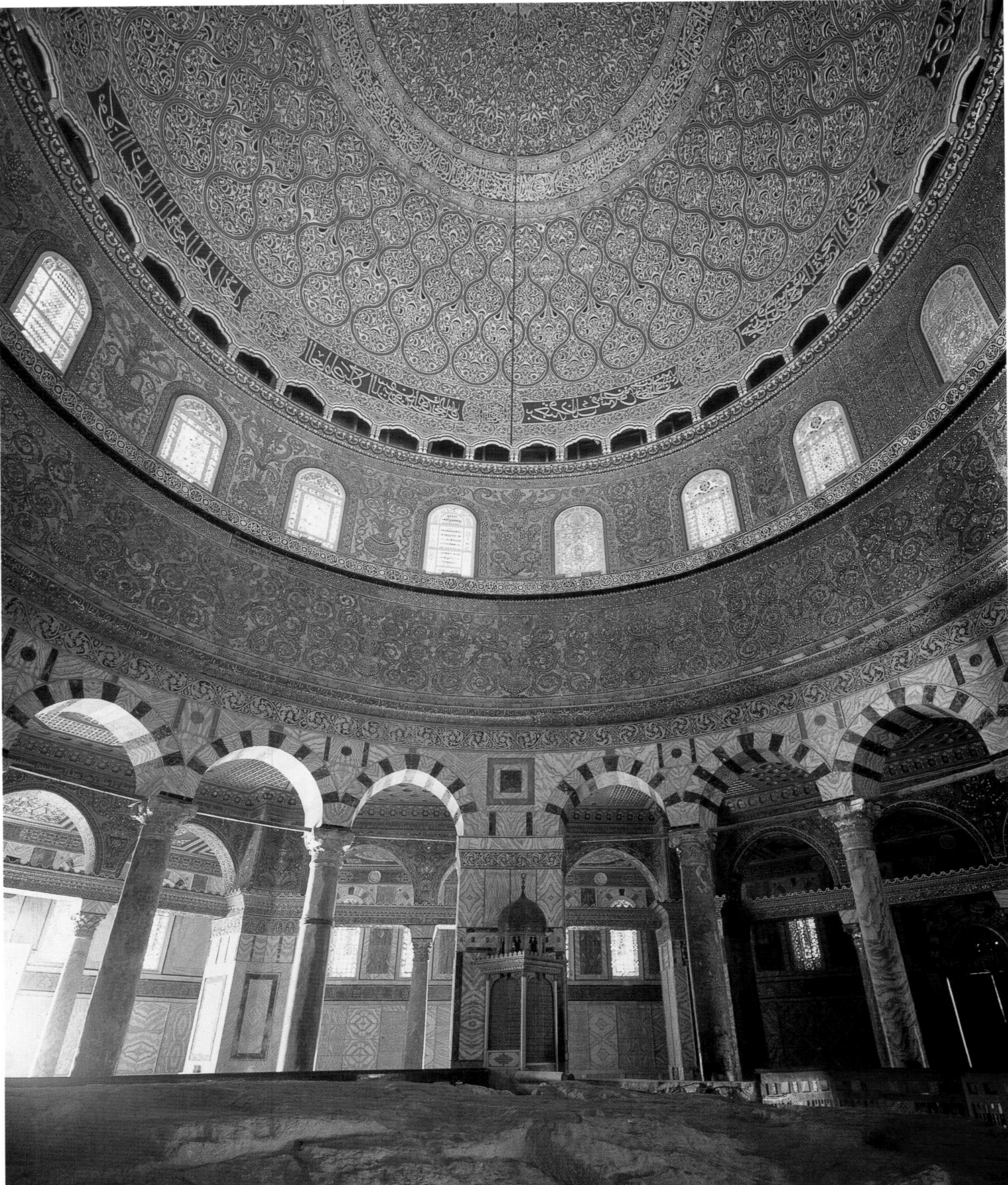

The differences that Muhammad had had with both Christianity and Judaism had been profound. And since the core of his revelation was its independence of other revelations and its superiority over them, or at all events over the way their adherents had understood them, he often tended to lump them together as hostile, hypocritical elements. He told Muslims to 'take neither Jews nor Christians for your helpers' (Qur'an, 5.57). The followers of both religions had, he felt, sinned in a way that he felt to be more hurtful to him than any other: they had mocked and ridiculed him. So he told believers that they were not to allow Christians or Jews to turn them back to unbelief 'from envy'.

To Muhammad the Christians, but even more so the Jews, were not distant, unseen people whose religious texts he had read, or had had read to him, but people who played a part in the normal course of his life and of the lives of those to whom he preached. With the Jews he had had a working alliance for the first part of his stay in Medina, and they had impinged upon a central part of his religious practice in the first mosques. The first arrangement of the believers at prayer in the mosque had been to turn in the direction of Jerusalem to pray. Then, after a couple of years, Muhammad experienced a revelation that impelled him to change the direction in which his people turned to pray to that of Mecca, and also to abandon the observance of the Jewish Day of Atonement in favour of the fast of the month of Ramadan.

Neither of these changes was made without considerable hesitation, and it is probable that they were connected with political changes in his alliances in Medina. But, as had occurred some five and a half centuries earlier in Christianity, the results had been to remove any tendency the new religion might have experienced to become a Judaizing sect, and to open its path towards a new, universal mission. However, the first Islamic connection with Judaism had been profound, and it has been noted by a modern historian that, while the polemic of Muhammad in his lifetime with Christianity as recorded in the Qur'an was rather fragmentary and inconsistent, that with Judaism was coherent and intense.[2]

Muhammad's approach to Jesus was deeply positive, his approach to Christianity much less so. He made Jesus himself, although a miracle-worker, deny his own divinity (Qur'an, 5.116). He said of Jesus: 'It does not benefit Allah to take unto himself a son.' (Qur'an, 19.35). On the other hand, Jesus was to Muhammad the prophet and messenger of God, as he himself was to become. The purity and holiness of Mary were fully recognized by Muhammad. But the death of Jesus was treated very differently by Muhammad than by orthodox Christians. In the Qur'an Jesus is said to have been neither slain nor crucified; but Allah 'raised him to himself' (Qur'an, 4.157–158). The same goes for the first generation of Islamic religious tradition after the Prophet's death.

O you People of the Book, overstep not bounds in your religion, and of God speak only the truth. The Messiah, Jesus Son of Mary, is only an apostle of God, and his Word which he conveyed unto Mary, and a Spirit proceeding from him. Believe therefore in God and his apostles and say not Three. It will be better for you. God is only one God. Far be it from his glory that he should have a son.
(Translation of inscription in the Dome of the Rock)

Christians in a Muslim Context

The position of the Christians and Jews in the huge areas newly conquered by the armies of Islam was a particular one. As 'people of the Book', understood as the Bible, they were not treated as pagans. Socially, also, it has to be remembered that the Muslims settled outside Arabia in the new Empire were nothing like so numerous as to constitute a majority, even if the first generation of Muslim converts is taken into account. Christians and Jews were not on that account over-privileged. They had to pay a poll tax (*jizya*) that Muslims did not pay and they could not marry Muslim women. In the later stages of the Islamic Empires they were subject to other restrictions that concerned their churches and synagogues, their dress, and other matters. But in the first stage of the conquests they still lived peacefully alongside the Muslims. There was no instant conversion of whole populations to Islam in Egypt or Syria, if only because people could only become Muslims by the acceptance of the Arabic language, sometimes also by a fictitious incorporation as clients of an Arab tribe. For quite a long time the situation in the newly Islamic lands resembled in some respects that in the West, where a foreign barbarian elite of a comparable but different religion cohabited with an anciently Christian population. But the ideological claims of Islam were too powerful to allow this to persist indefinitely.

The Muslims made huge borrowings from Byzantine culture, as may be seen by anyone who enters the Dome of the Rock in Jerusalem, with its rich mosaic splendours. Jerusalem occupied a special place in the sacred geography of Muhammad, because of its connection with the prophet Abraham. In later Muslim tradition, but probably not yet at the time of the construction of the first

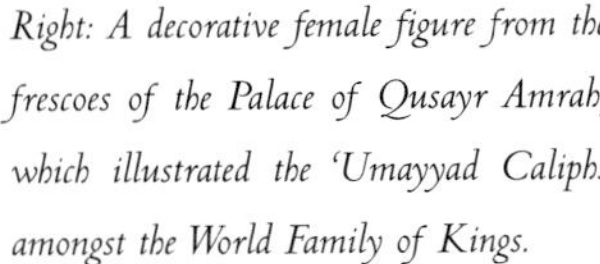

Right: A decorative female figure from the frescoes of the Palace of Qusayr Amrah, which illustrated the 'Umayyad Caliphs amongst the World Family of Kings.

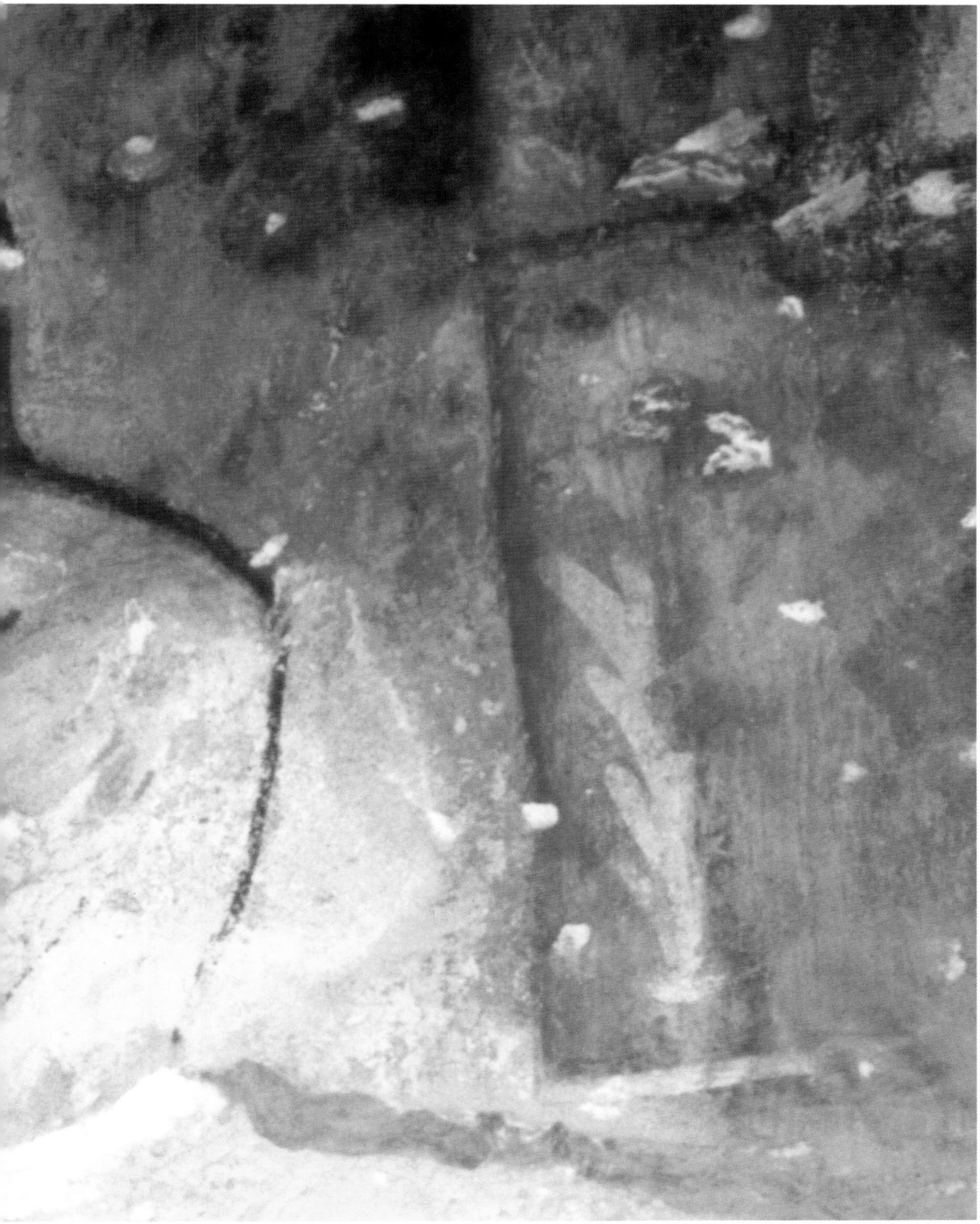

Muslim sanctuary, the Temple platform was said to have been the arrival point of the miraculous 'night journey' of Muhammad from Mecca to the 'further mosque' (al masjid al-aqsa, Qur'an, 17.1). The second Islamic Caliph, 'Umar, made a special journey to receive the submission of Jerusalem after its fall to Muslim forces, within only seven or eight years of the Prophet's death in 632. 'Umar would not pray with the Christian patriarch of Jerusalem in his church, although invited to do so, because such an act would have sanctified the place to Muslims, and so made it inaccessible to Christians. Instead, he went to the platform of the Temple Mount to pray, where the Dome of the Rock and the al-Aqsa mosque were subsequently built within the Muslim holy area. The Qur'anic inscriptions that were at the end of the seventh century placed round the inside of the Dome of the Rock, assert the oneness of God. They also ask for a divine blessing upon Muhammad and equally upon Jesus, emphasizing the position of Jesus in Islam as prophet and messenger. In this city sacred to both religions, the anti-Christian polemic of the Qur'an is still present in the inscriptions, but muted.

By the early eighth century the Islamic Empire extended from Visigothic Spain and Morocco in the west to the Indus valley in the south-east and to Transoxiana in the north-east: North Africa including Egypt, Syria-Palestine, Iraq, the whole Persian Empire had been swallowed up. In the 'Umayyad desert palace of Qusayr Amrah there was placed in the caliphal baths a fresco that was intended (against several Islamic precepts) to represent the 'Umayyad caliphs as part of the world family of kings. The eastern Emperor, the last Visigothic ruler of Spain before the Muslim conquest, the Negus of Ethiopia, the Sassanian Emperor of Iran (who had been displaced permanently by the 'Umayyads) and, probably, the Chinese Emperor were all illustrated.

The caliphate, which remained united until 750, had become one of the great civilizations, and had entered into a close relationship with the cultures of both Hellenism and Iran. But towards the end of that period the aims and nature of the caliphate suffered a further change. The close emulation of the Byzantine Empire that had marked many of the policies of the earlier 'Umayyad caliphs was practically abandoned after the failure of the last great medieval Islamic siege of Constantinople in 718. The brief Islamic flirtation with political Hellenism had ended.

The period between the first and the last siege of Constantinople by the Arabs, between 673 and 717, was a time of great peril for eastern Christianity. It is true that the internal dissension in Islam imposed a form of peace for a long time after the lifting of the first Muslim siege in 677. The great quarrel with Islam had results on the internal religious quarrels about the divine and human natures of Christ that had been splitting the Byzantine Empire for over a century, and that had contributed to rendering imperial rule precarious when the Muslim attack came in Palestine-Syria and Egypt. In 681 the areas of the Empire that had most strongly supported the doctrine of a single divine will in Christ, 'the one incarnate nature of the Word', had passed under Muslim control, and their bishops were no longer in a political position to influence imperial policy.

Rome and Constantinople Reconciled

At the Council of Constantinople in 680-1 the doctrine about the divine nature of Christ that had been expressed at the Council of Chalcedon in 451, was reasserted in a manner on the whole acceptable to the Roman see, whose legates were chosen to preside, after the Emperor, over the conciliar sittings in the imperial palace. The doctrine of two natural wills and two energies co-existing in Christ, that was unacceptable in Alexandria and Jerusalem, was reasserted. The Emperor's

Above: The Little Palace of 'Amrah, in Jordan, which was built during the reign of Caliph Walid I (705–15).

attempt to satisfy the Roman see was manifest; the conciliar decisions quoted both the 'tome' or written opinions on the matter of Pope Leo I (pope from 440–61), and the opinions of the choleric Athanasius, who in his life had never found much favour in the imperial court.

The papal legates at Constantinople were satisfied. The doctrines that were now proclaimed, under authority of the Council and the eastern Emperor, were the same as those whose profession only a generation earlier had caused Pope Martin to be driven by imperial persecution and exile to his death in the Crimea. On the other hand, the Emperor preserved his imperial dignity in 681 by insisting on the condemnation of Pope Honorius (pope from 625–38) for heretical views on the same matter. The topic of Honorius was still found to be embarrassing to the strong papalist cause when it was raised in opposition to the thesis of papal infallibility, during the sittings of the Vatican Council in 1870.

The entente between Rome and Constantinople lasted only a very few years. In 692 the Emperor Constantine IV held a council in Constantinople (the 'Quinisext') that issued disciplinary provisions for the clergy entirely unacceptable in Rome. When the Emperor instructed the imperial official in Rome, Zacharias, to arrest Pope Sergius and to dispatch him for trial in Constantinople as Pope Martin had been dispatched in 653, the regional troops mutinied, and Zacharias had to escape their wrath by hiding under the papal bed. The order of arrest was never executed.

Behind the theology of the Council of Constantinople in 681 the clash of Muslim arms can be heard in the background. In Italy the pressure of the Lombards had been severe for over a century. Significantly, in the same year that the Council of Constantinople was called to conciliate the bishops in the western part of the Empire, a peace was signed by the Empire with the Lombard barbarian intruders, which recognized most of the conquests in northern and central Italy that they had made at Byzantine expense during the preceding century. The huge pressures that were operating

Above: The Third Council of Constantinople, which was held in 680–81 under Pope Agatho and Emperor Constantine. The image is an engraving taken from a fresco in the Vatican.

on the Empire everywhere from the borders of Syria and the Euphrates to the garrisons remaining in North Africa, meant that the frontiers in Italy – which included Rome, now only fifty or so miles from the nearest Lombard forces – were increasingly going to be left to their own devices. The story was already familiar from the experiences in the north-west of the Roman Empire in the fifth and sixth centuries. Like those experiences, it was going to have consequences for the Christian religion in the West.

1 Albert Hourani, *A History of the Arab Peoples* (London, 1991)

2 J. Wansbrough, *The Sectarian Milieu: Content and Composition of Islamic Salvation History* (Oxford, 1978), pp. 40-1

Left: Constantinople under siege. The city was besieged many times and was taken on different occasions by both Christians and Muslims. In 1453, Constantinople finally fell to the Muslims.

© AKG London / Erich Lessing

8

THE BOOK AND THE SWORD

At the beginning of the eighth century, Constantinople was still one of the wonders of the world, and still the centre of a large, powerful, militarily active Empire. It had remained the great Christian, Roman capital that Constantine had intended when he inaugurated the city in AD 330. Although the urban population had much declined after the first Arab assaults, until they began, it had been the greatest and most populous city west of the Chinese Empire. During the 40-year rule of Emperor Justinian (527–65) it had been the centre of the biggest and most concerted military and administrative effort made by the Roman Empire since the third century, and had sent armies to recover lost provinces in Italy, in Sicily, in Dalmatia, in Africa, in Spain. The armies were smaller than the old armies, but still very effective.

The huge churches and imperial palaces of the capital had been marvelled at since Constantine, but Justinian added new wonders, most notably the great church of the Holy Wisdom (Haghia Sophia) that he had constructed after the destruction wrought by the Nike riots in 532. Building activity was not confined by Justinian to the east. Much of his construction in the west was military, but some, as in Ravenna, was of splendid churches and palaces. Byzantine culture, which had become more and more ecclesiastical in nature, nevertheless retained its basis in late Greek language, literature and philosophy.

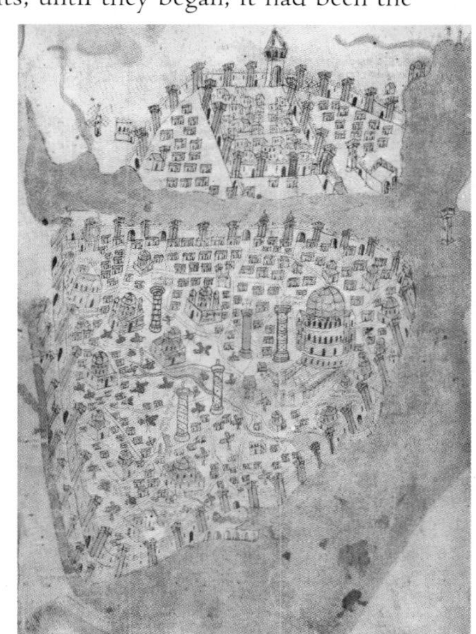

© British Library, London, UK/Bridgeman Art Library, London

Above: Map of Constantinople dating from 1422. Haghia Sophia is visible.

Left: Haghia Sophia, Constantinople. It was originally built as a church but has been a mosque since 1453.

Above: Mosaic from the south vestibule of Haghia Sophia. The Virgin Mary and Child are enthroned between Emperors Justinian and Constantine.

Justinian lived too long; the great plagues, and the Persian military revival that started to take place before his death, announced the numerous cracks in a logistically overstretched and (in both senses) overtaxed system. But the apparatus of taxation that was the big engine of the military power and central organization of the state, and that had long since vanished in the barbarian west, remained in being long after Justinian. Politics remained essentially court politics, as they had been since Augustus.

The Arab invasions, and the consequent removal from the Byzantine world of Syria-Palestine, Egypt and what had been left elsewhere in Africa, profoundly disrupted an economic and military system that had been in place since the beginning of the Roman Empire. The last Arab siege of Constantinople in 717–18 had put the entire existence and ideology of the eastern Empire in question. Although the siege was lifted, and the chanting of the great hymn to the Virgin on the city walls appeared to have been heard on high, the culture had experienced a trauma from which it was not to recover easily. Not unsurprisingly, a culture so profoundly religious in character exhibited its shock in a religious form.

Leo the Iconoclast

At this critical moment, leadership was seized in 716 by Emperor Leo III, the 'Isaurian', whose dynasty took its name from their tribal home in the Cilician Taurus mountains, in south-west Asia Minor. Leo adopted a radical religious tendency that objected strongly to the veneration of the images of the incarnate saviour and of other saintly persons, beginning with the Virgin Mary. For at least three centuries these objections had been swamped by the almost universal devotion accorded to such images, to which the faithful sometimes attributed quasi-magical powers of healing and intercession. Some religious images were credited as having been 'not made with hands'. In a religion that was by now so imbued by the sacramental principle which endowed the physical symbol with holy qualities, this was perhaps almost inevitable. But in a culture that had a long tradition of rational theology, as well as one of sentimental devotion, there was bound to be a reaction. There was certainly some scriptural basis for objection to religious images, not only in the Old Testament (Exod. 20: 4), but in the New Testament (Acts 17:29). The whole question was to resurface powerfully in Protestantism during the sixteenth century.

Until this time the only audible objectors in the eastern church to the cult of images had been small dissenting groups such as the Paulicians, who had originated in the Upper Euphrates area, and who refused the veneration of Mary as well as that of images. But Leo III, perhaps feeling his way towards a radical religious view that would unite and energize the Empire (as Constantine had done in the fourth century), decided to turn the whole Church within the Empire towards an 'iconoclast' or image-breaking policy: venerated images were to be condemned and avoided, perhaps destroyed, following an edict issued in 726. Perhaps Leo was also somewhat influenced by his resentment of the scant military input of the great tax-exempt religious persons and bodies at a time of military emergency.

Leo III's iconoclasm gained wide popular support in the eastern areas of the Empire, particularly among the Armenians, but not in the western; it was particularly abhorred in Rome, which continued formally to be a part of the eastern Empire. Leo III was also criticized in the east as being 'Saracen-minded', since Muslim objections to visual representations of the human form were well known.

Below: A Saracen is converted to Christianity by the power of the image of the Virgin Mary. The detail comes from a thirteenth-century French manuscript.

There were no specific prohibitions of images (as opposed to altars or idols) in the Qur'an, but the Muslim fear of depicting anything that might remotely be understood as associating something or someone else with Allah in his divinity had led to an avoidance of them.

Left: St Nicephorus the Patriarch and the Holy Father looking on while iconoclasts break images.

There was no doubt about the military effectiveness of Leo III and his immediate successors. Faced by the prospect of extinction, the Empire pulled itself together and recovered much of its military muscle. There was a military reorganization of the army, based on big military regional divisions known as themes. The constant pressure from Muslim armies in Asia Minor was resisted much more successfully than before, for this reason and also because the trend to withdraw first-line troops to the capital had been reduced with the final breaking of the siege in 718. Asia Minor was not, of course, the only battle front. The Bulgarians were emerging as a formidable pagan fighting force south of the Danube, a danger to important grain-growing areas. The Slavs had begun their capillary penetration southwards into the Balkans.

Slowly, the military crisis of the Empire ended. The Islamic caliphate split for the first time in 750, and the far western lands in Iberia (Andalus) went their own way under 'Umayyad leadership, while the usurping 'Abbasid caliphs transferred the seat of power to the new capital of Baghdad. The centre of Islam was no longer in Syria, so close to the Byzantine border, but in Iraq. There were still big Muslim fleets, especially in Alexandria, but they were no longer subject to immediate control by caliphs. As they began to reform their armies with Turkish slave troops, 'Abbasid military concentrations became based in distant Khurasan and Transoxiana.

The war of the frontiers was not over, and to some extent it was a permanent holy war on both sides, conducted on the Muslim side by the mujahidin, on the Christian side by frontier levies called akritai. But the great conflicts of main armies became very infrequent, and big naval engagements ceased. The eastern imperial court remained rich and powerful, able to dazzle western barbarians with its pompous ceremony, on which much of the 'Abbasid caliphate court's ritual state protocol was to be based. But the economic power and heavy population of the old Byzantium had been sapped. Byzantine revenues were dwarfed by those of the caliphate, and the most flourishing and opulent urban life was henceforth to be found in the great Muslim cities.

In the western part of the Byzantine Empire the results of the setbacks of the seventh and early eighth centuries made themselves felt in a falling away from former imperial loyalties, which had repercussions all over the western barbarian world. The process began in the 720s with tax strikes in the Italian provinces in protest against the iconoclast measures of Leo III. The leaders of the resistance were the Roman popes. They got full support from the central Italian provincials, who had received no effective imperial protection against Lombard oppression.

In Francia the late Merovingian kings, feeble descendants of Clovis, had been unable to exert full royal power, and had been superseded in its exercise by the so-called mayors of the palace, of the noble line of the Arnulfings. Five years earlier, in 749, the Arnulfing Pippin III, 'the Short', had sent an envoy to Pope Stephen's predecessor, Zacharias, to discover 'whether it was good or not' that the infant Merovingian King of the Franks, on whose behalf he purported to rule, did not exercise royal power. In a classic statement of *Realpolitik*, Pope Zacharias had replied that it was better that he who had real power should be king, rather than he who did not. The result had been an assembly of the Frankish magnates at Soissons, which hailed Pippin as king, and saw him anointed with holy oil (a Biblical procedure entirely unfamiliar in either barbarian or Roman political life), probably by the Anglo-Saxon Bishop Boniface, who had first visited Rome in 719, and was in effect a papal agent. It was a momentous political intervention by the Roman popes in the affairs of a Frankish church and nation with which papal contact had until that time been polite rather than close.

The Popes and the Franks

In 753, when the main iconoclast council was held in Constantinople, Pope Stephen II made a revolutionary diplomatic move that had the effect of shifting the main political ties of the Roman bishop from the legal ruler of the Roman Empire to a Frankish nobleman who held effective but only doubtfully legal royal power in the Frankish kingdom. Pope Stephen took advantage of the presence of a special Byzantine envoy in Italy to accompany him on a mission to the hostile Lombard King Aistulf, in the Lombard capital, Pavia, in northern Italy. When the conference broke up without result, instead of returning with the imperial representative to Byzantine territory, Pope Stephen set off alone from Pavia to Francia.

Having made this unheard-of papal journey, Stephen was welcomed at the beginning of 754 by King Pippin at Ponthion in Champagne. He had come, in effect, to claim the political reward due to the pope and to the formerly Byzantine population of central Italy, for the support given by his predecessor Zacharias to Pippin's crowning and anointing as Frankish king. The pope fell before the king in sackcloth, and asked, with ashes on his head, if he would support the suit of 'St Peter and of the republic of the Romans' for the restoration of their rights in Italy by the Lombards. The promise was made, and formally ratified the following spring in the presence of the Frankish magnates. Pope Stephen had been asking for a Frankish invasion of Italy, and he obtained two Frankish military interventions, in 755 and 756, which damped down Lombard aggression, and which also foreshadowed the establishment of what in modern times came to be called the papal state. More important than that, he had established a link between the Roman bishops and the Frankish kings that was to have momentous consequences for Christian Europe.

The Frankish kingdom had, by the mid-eighth century, become the most powerful of all the

Below: In the eighth century the Roman papacy forged strong links with the Frankish kings.

fut decoste le maistre autel en un riche ser
queux dalebastre · Ci commencent les fais
& croniques du roy pepin filz charlemartel
Coment lui & son frere charles departirent
le roiaume apres comment cellui charles
devint moyne en un moustier quil fonda
en lonneur saint silvestre et apres coment
pepin fut couronne en roy a soissons

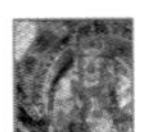

barbarian realms. When Pippin III died in 768 it stretched from the Pyrenees and the Mediterranean coast in the south, to the lower Rhineland and Frisia on the Atlantic coast in the north. On the east it included Thuringia and reached as far as the borders of Bavaria; to the south-east it included most of present-day Switzerland west of the Allgäu and the Brenner. When Pippin's son Charles became undisputed king of this huge conglomeration of tribal groups in 771, he had the military means to become the most important barbarian leader since Theodoric the Ostrogoth, at the turn of the fifth and sixth centuries. He was at a later period known as Charles the Great, or Charlemagne. Unlike Theodoric, if Charlemagne chose to intervene in the Roman province, he had the additional advantage that he was no Arian heretic, but ruler of a nation that had been Catholic for over a century and a half, and that had been linked with Rome by Charles's father, who had established a close treaty connection with the Roman bishop.

The Frankish kings had already been, earlier in the eighth century, the sponsors of a huge work of Christian evangelization on their eastern and northern borders, in Frisia and Saxony. It had mostly been carried out by Irish and Anglo-Saxon missionaries, to whom it had seemed natural to obtain papal as well as Frankish patronage. Those clerics, of whom Boniface was the most important as an intermediary, were sometimes to die as martyrs, but they had established a position at the Frankish court that played its part in setting up the Roman-Frankish alliance.

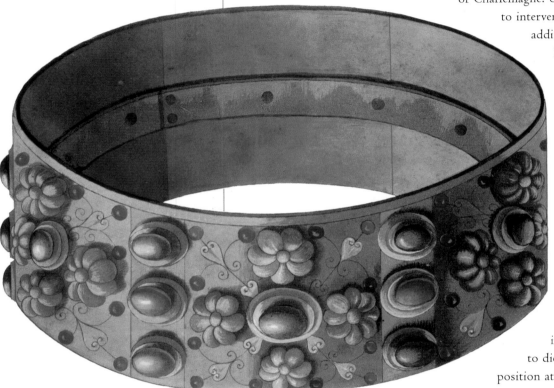

Above: The Iron Crown of Lombardy with which Charlemagne was crowned King of Lombardy in 774. Much later, in 1805, Napoleon insisted on the same crown for his coronation.

Charlemagne and Military Expansion

A man of immense energy and ambition, Charlemagne seems to have had an extraordinary awareness about the huge geographical and cultural realms in which he was able to move. Though illiterate until late in life, he attached great value to learning, and somehow seized fiercely on the huge possibilities for power that lay in the imposition of clerical social discipline in a centralized way. To most modern men and women who live in Charlemagne's old lands or their neighbours, the church liturgy probably looks like an optional extra in the religious life; to an eighth-century person, it could appear to be a way to regulate the lives of hundreds of thousands of people who had no other binding union but a vague allegiance to a distant tribal superior.

To Charlemagne it seemed that hegemony, the aim of all barbarian kings, had to be accompanied by religious conformity that was sponsored by the hegemonial monarch. When he started the huge

Left: A side panel from an altar showing the adoration of the Magi. It was commissioned by Ratchis, Duke of Spoleto. It is a fine example of Carolingian art.

wars on his northern and eastern borders, which lasted almost until his death in 814, his aim was conversion, and forcible conversion if necessary. While he was never going to change the tribal nature of barbarian society, he realized that the nearest thing to imposing what we would call assimilation upon conquered or recently subject areas, was a form of Christianity that was subject to some sort of

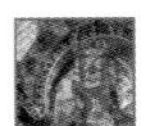

Right: Carpet page preceding St Mark's Gospel with circles of interlacing design linked with angular interlacing, from the Book of Durrow (c. 650–700). The art and literature of Christian Ireland would not be unknown to a man of Charlemagne's cultural stature.

Above: Charlemagne and his army fighting the Saracens in Spain in 778.

central control. For this reason the great wars on the eastern borders across the Rhine with the Saxons, that were fought for 33 years 'with immense hatred on both sides', and accompanied by transportations of populations and atrocious group punishments imposed on the Saxons at various times, ended in mass baptisms. After 785, evasion of baptism was to be punished by death. This policy did not meet with the entire approval of the missionaries working in Germany, and Charlemagne later modified it.

Early in the reign, in 773, Charlemagne marched into northern Italy and finally suppressed the old Lombard kingdom, of which he later assumed formal kingship. In the following year he went south, arrived in Rome on Easter Saturday, 774, and proceeded to guarantee to Pope Hadrian the control of the main areas of so-called Roman settlement in central Italy, probably according to the peace treaties the Lombard kings had made with the Byzantines at the end of the previous century. In effect, north Italy, with some of the south-lying Lombard dependencies, had been annexed by the Frankish king, and the rest of central Italy, including Rome and the former Byzantine exarchate of Ravenna, made into a Frankish protectorate under the Roman bishop. South Italy continued to be a part of the Byzantine Empire, which was powerless to affect these proceedings.

The territorial alliance with the Roman see was only a part of Charles's designs. These aimed at making the Roman see into the pivot of far-reaching ecclesiastical and even cultural policies, which would have further political results. The onset of the new Frankish order was due to the political misfortunes of Hadrian's successor as pope, Leo III, who was a Roman cleric of no great family, unlike his aristocratic predecessor. Four years after his election in 795 some Roman nobles rebelled, accused Leo of serious misdemeanours, and tried to have him blinded without trial. He was lucky enough to escape, and to travel into Saxony to find Charlemagne, whom he had earlier greeted as 'the new Constantine', and to ask him for assistance.

Pope Leo was sent back to Rome with a Frankish escort, honourably, but in fact to await some kind of legal procedure that would clear his name. His labouring under such a severe political disadvantage meant that he was unlikely to reject any procedure named by the Frankish king that would have the effect of releasing him from suspicion. Charlemagne himself came to Rome at the end of 800 with the intention of settling the matter. What occurred in 800 has continued to have effects on the political and cultural shape of Europe into our own times.

Above: Image of the Byzantine Empress Irene, a fervent anti-iconoclast. The mosaic is in the Haghia Sophia.

Right: The coronation of Charlemagne on Christmas Day 800, at St Peter's in Rome. Charlemagne was crowned emperor by Pope Leo III. This marked the beginning of the Holy Roman Empire.

The Origins of the Holy Roman Empire

Two days before Christmas, before a council of bishops, the pope was allowed to clear himself from the charges made against him, by the procedure of declaring his innocence under oath, one that had some precedent in papal history, and also happened to be a standard barbarian legal procedure. On Christmas Day 800 Charles went to mass in St Peter's dressed not as a Frank, but in the official Roman costume (the Greek *chlamys*) of a Roman patrician, a high office which had been bestowed on him by a previous pope. At the end of prayer Pope Leo placed a crown on Charles's head, and the Romans in the basilica acclaimed him as emperor. The ceremonial acclamatory hymns proper to the greeting of the (previously Greek) emperor in Rome were sung, and Pope Leo ceremonially prostrated himself in the Greek fashion.

As far as the Byzantine government was concerned, this was a meaningless, illegal pantomime. Unfortunately for that government, not only was it without military or practical power to intervene in Italy, but it was itself experiencing an awkward interregnum. The problem had grown from a series of intrigues that had to do with the opposition to iconoclasm of Irene, the former empress of Leo IV (who had died in 780). Having been regent during the minority of her son Constantine VI, Irene carried out a coup against him after he had assumed personal rule in 790; in 797 she had had her son blinded and imprisoned, and herself resumed the government. It became arguable that, as a woman was legally incapable of ruling it, in 800 the Roman Empire was vacant; it was an argument unlikely to convince anyone in the East.

Charlemagne's assumption of the imperial title had been canvassed in court circles for some time before 800, and can probably be seen quite as much as a result of barbarian ideas about recognizing hegemonial kingship, as an acceptance of concepts that genuinely sprang from late Roman tradition. Charles certainly had not needed the imperial title to execute his church policies so far as they touched the Roman bishops, who continued to be, as they had been before, the chief and most honoured bishops of the Frankish realm, worthy to receive gifts appropriate to their status. But the assumption of 'empire' was to have consequences that Charlemagne almost certainly did not anticipate, particularly for the protocol that later had to be followed for a Frankish – or other western – king who wanted to assume the title.

Above: Gold sword and scabbard, set with precious stones, said to belong to Charlemagne.

For what can from 800 onwards be called without qualification the Western Latin Church, the reign of Charlemagne had absolutely decisive results. The split from iconoclasm was no longer the only reason for the distance at which the western bishops held themselves from the eastern. In 787 Irene had succeeded in holding an eastern church council against iconoclasm in Nicaea, which had been attended by two papal legates from Rome, who assented to its proceedings. Charlemagne had himself entered some cavils against Nicaea, or rather, his theologians had done so for him, and he held his own western church council that looked at the matter, in Frankfurt in 794. From the eighth century onwards, and particularly from the imperial coronation of 800, the real differences between the Western and Eastern churches centred on their contrasting allegiances to different political masters. The independence of the Roman see from the Frankish ruler, or of the dynasties that followed the Franks, had subsequently to be worked out in centuries of tortuous and often painful political and religious experience.

Charlemagne's religious, educational and cultural policies were achieved partly through the elitist means of the influence and leadership provided by the small group of clerics attached to the court,

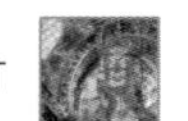

Right: An illuminated manuscript from Kaernten, Austria, from the eighth or ninth century. It shows Charlemagne and his wife.

and also through the insertion of many requirements regarding religious matters into the general instructions ('capitularies') that were circulated throughout the various areas of the Frankish realms by the imperial envoys ('missi'). The new monasteries that were being established, especially in the newly-annexed areas, became the centres that received, protected and diffused this new court-inspired religious culture. In this respect the new Frankish nobility, preferred by the ruler, and granted huge lands and offices everywhere in the new Empire, became an integral part of the official religious culture by their endowment and patronage of the new monastic centres.

Below: Charlemagne was very keen to foster education throughout his realm. This is an early ninth-century illustration of The Fountain of Life from the Court School of Charlemagne.

Literacy and Liturgy

Charlemagne insisted that the court bishops and literary and clerical figures around them collected and to some extent distributed Christian and also pagan texts that not only reached a high standard of calligraphy and book production, but of grammatical and textual competence. Even the laymen around the court were encouraged and, up to a point required, to reach a good standard of literacy. In a sense the regime attained its cultural aims through the holy books, whether of the Scriptures themselves, or of the liturgy, or of theology. 'Carolingian minuscule' script has exerted an influence that reaches as far as the modern printed book. The court literati also created new kinds of court panegyric of the ruler, comparable in type to those of the post-Constantinian period, although always written in Latin and not in Greek. And some of them had to be capable of sustained theological argument, up to a level that would bear some comparison with the theologians of the contemporary Eastern church.

Probably the most influential and formative of all Charlemagne's church measures was the insistence on a degree of general conformity of the liturgies that were to be followed in the churches. There were areas where local and ancient church custom had to prevail, as in the proud dioceses of Milan and Ravenna, and in some dioceses of Francia, but in the rest of Francia and in the newly converted areas the Roman Rite, known as the Gregorian Sacramentary, was followed everywhere.

There is a contrast between the enormous geographical and political extent of Charlemagne's Empire, and the relatively modest size of the cadres that he employed to govern and serve it. The contrast exists, too, in the modesty of the physical proportions of much of what he built. His conquests

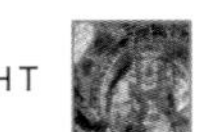

Right: Charlemagne divided his kingdom between his three sons, Pepin, Charles and Louis in 806. After his death, his Empire disintegrated.

of Saxony and Bavaria, his pushes beyond the Elbe into lands of Slav tribes such as the Wilzi, his subjection of many of the Danes, his thrusts into what became the Frankish county of Barcelona, added up to give him a degree of control over a great part of western Europe. But in spite of this, in comparison with the old empires his tax base was tiny, and his military control spasmodic. Charlemagne's palace at Aachen was not huge, nor was its church. Nonetheless, Charlemagne's imprint still lies heavily upon the mentalities of the churches of Europe, and influences the ways in which they define themselves relative to the Eastern Christian and the Muslim worlds.

Below: The throne of Charlemagne in his chapel at Aachen.

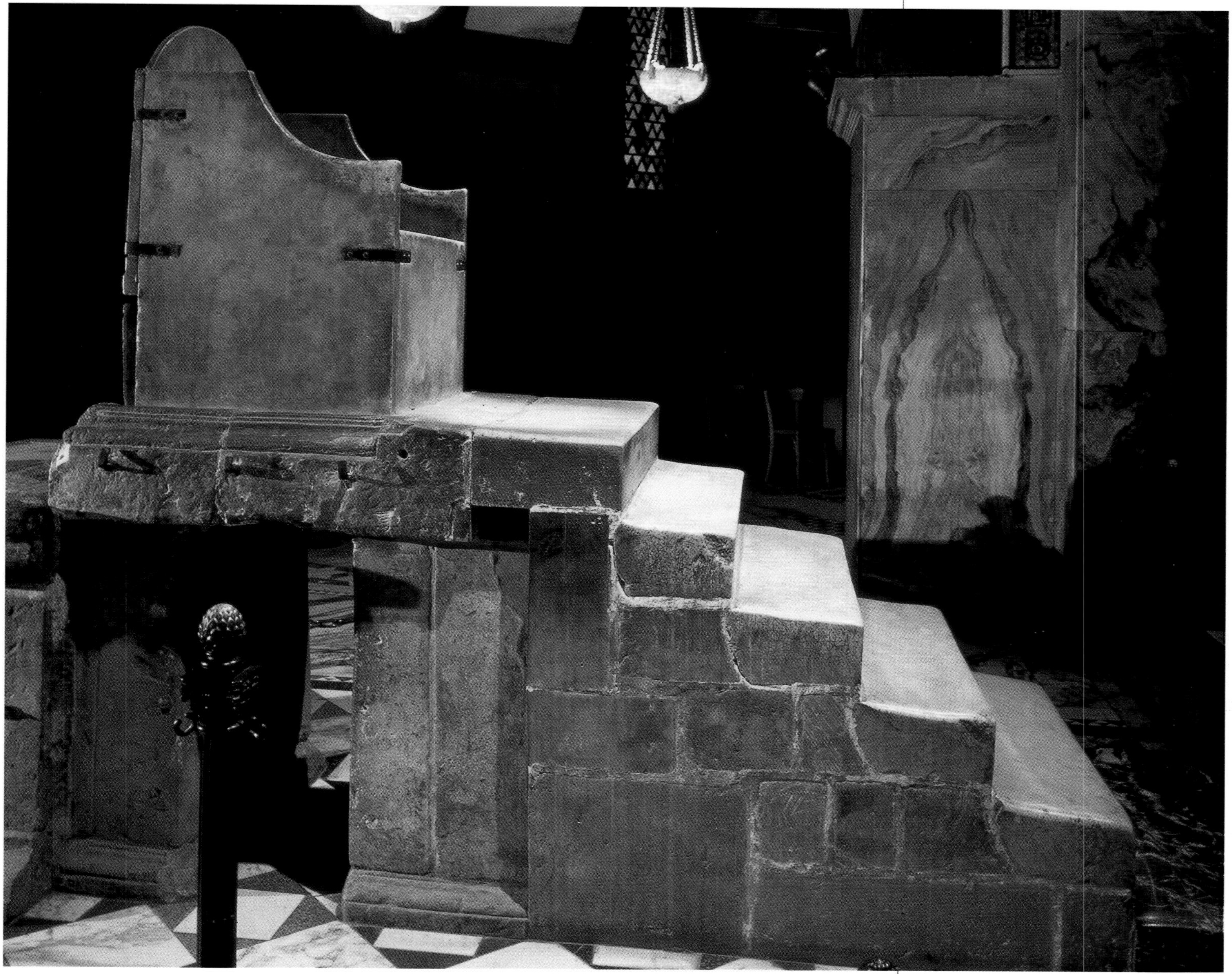

© AKG London/Erich Lessing

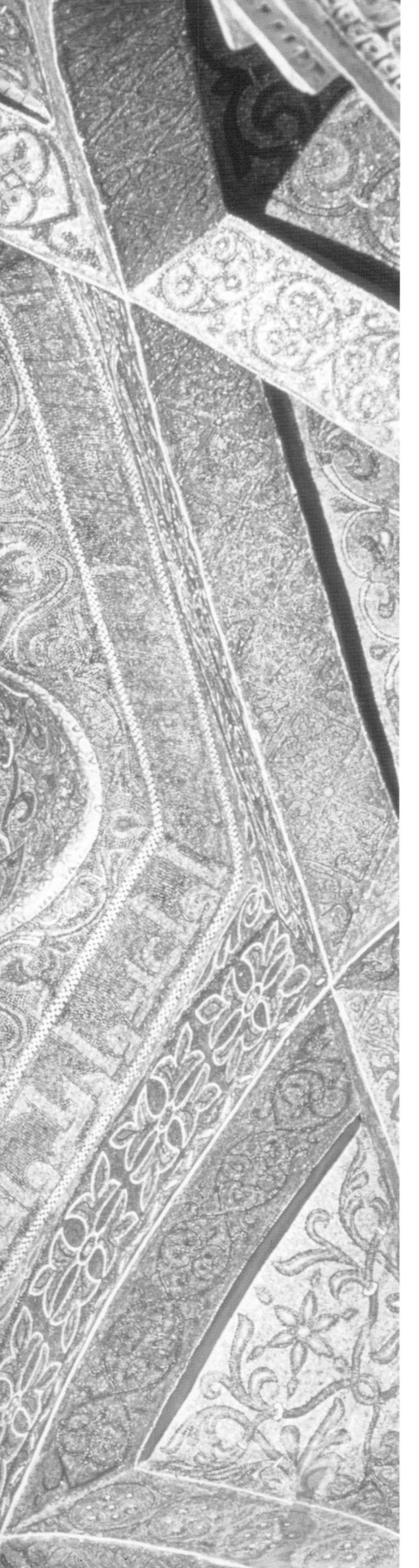

9

EAST AND WEST

The last half of the eighth century was the period of the maximum flowering of early Muslim urban life and culture. The Muslim world had become a huge market for goods and human resources (including slaves) that stretched from the North African cities to central Asia and the Indus, and through the Indian Ocean to south-west India. The eastern Caliphs, having built a splendid new capital at Baghdad, presided over a genuine successor-state to the old empires of the Iranian Sassanians and the Hellenistic and east Roman rulers of the Near East and North Africa. The caliphal armies were at this point centrally controlled and tax-financed through the central diwan, and in this respect were probably nearer the late Roman imperial troops than were the Byzantine ones of the same period.

Above: Medallion of the Caliph of Baghdad.

Islamic buildings drew on a range of historical reference that was just as widely based as Islam itself.[1] The basilica (in its non-ecclesiastical, Roman urban form), the Christian church, the Iranian palaces, the ziggurat, the Zoroastrian temples, all left their mark. The pattern of late Roman urban design in the Near East was enormously important for Islam, although a lot of the public spaces of the Hellenistic town were rejected, and filled by rather haphazard Muslim inner-urban sprawl. The needs of the mosque were very simple: they could be met by almost any large enclosed space that would accommodate the adult male population for Friday prayer. Such spaces could be large enough to hold an army, as in Samarra, Cairo (Fustat), or Qairawan. The liturgical needs were simple: a recessed niche (mihrab) to indicate the direction of prayer was the minimum. Neither the minaret nor the pulpit-like minbar, which was usually of wood, was essential.

Left: Interior of the dome over the mihrab – a recessed niche indicating direction of prayer – in the Great Mosque in Cordoba, Spain.

Right: View of the city of Cairo with the Fustat mosque in the foreground.

Greek culture, or at any event the Greek culture of philosophy, mathematics, and medicine, was assimilated by a new Arabic-speaking intelligentsia, or in some areas by an Arabic and Persian-speaking intelligentsia. There was, for a time, some attempt to conciliate Muslim theological ideas with Greek philosophical concepts, which was a sort of parallel to the great theological debates in Christendom. It was, however, a relatively short-lived debate in the Muslim world, which ended in the victory of the fideistic thinker, Al-Ghazali (1058–1111), and the subsequent rejection of the Greek philosophical forms as a normal language for theology. The severely scriptural basis of Islam triumphed easily over abstract speculation, especially after the development of a clerical class that had acquired a big body of traditional religious learning. If there was a Muslim religious world that could speak to the Christian religious experience, it was probably to be found in the mystical discourse of the Sufis. Yet there was also a world (overlapping with Sufism) of the popular appreciation of holy men and holy objects, in which Christians and Muslims venerated the same local saints and relics without much distinction.

Christianity within Islam did not die. By the end of the third century after Muhammad, the society of the Islamic zone had become for something like a majority Islamic society. For the first time the majority of the population would contrast the *dar al-Islam,* the peaceful house of the Muslims, with

Right: A ninth-century astrolabe from Iraq. Islamic science flourished at a time when European culture was at a nadir.

Left: The Council of Abelda in Toledo, Moorish Spain. It was held to establish a peaceful means of incorporating Christian religion into a totally Muslim culture.

Right: The shadow falling on the intricate tracery of this Byzantine basket capital forebodes the fall of the eastern Empire.

the *dar al-harb*, the house of war of the infidel. Not that this meant the persistence of endless great wars with all the Christian powers; on the contrary, even if war was endemic on the frontiers, the more usual relationship between Muslim and Christian powers was one of truce.

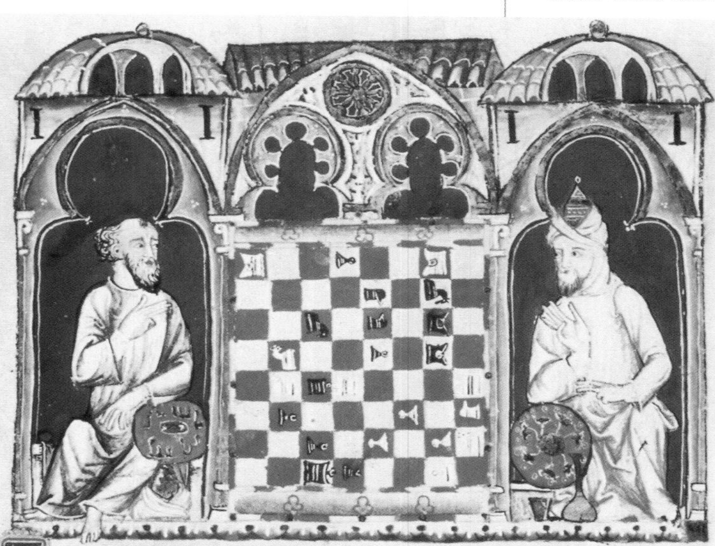

Above: A Christian and Muslim play a game of chess, symbolizing the wary truce between the two religions.

The Christian sects within Islam were, at least, no longer troubled by persecuting Christian governments. The Armenians, whose kingdom was for a long time subject to the 'Abbasids, although on occasion it escaped; the majority Egyptian Christians ('Copts'); the Syrian or Jacobite church; the so-called Nestorians (whose sphere of influence stretched to China) were all groups that had objected to the definitions of Christ's nature made by the Council of Chalcedon. They are all groups whose religious affiliation has survived into our own times.

So long as the caliphate was controlled, outside Andalus, by a single caliphal succession, Byzantium could hope for nothing better than to hang on. In 782 an 'Abbasid force reached the Bosphorus and exacted tribute from the Empress-regent, Irene. In 806 the Caliph Haroun al-Rashid himself led a big army that crossed the Cilician Taurus to take the main city of Cappadocia, Tyana (Kalesihisar) and marched on into the Anatolian heartland to ravage Ancyra (Ankara). Muslim sea power returned in great strength in both the eastern and western Mediterranean: Crete fell in 825, and two years later a great force embarked from Tunis under a Persian mujahid leader, and got a toehold in Sicily (still Byzantine at this point), which led to the eventual Muslim occupation of the island.

Fortunately for Byzantium, the 'Abbasid caliphate was undermined, something like a century after its foundation in 750, by centrifugal forces that were both religious and regional. The last great caliphal expedition marched in 838 through western Anatolia to take Amorium in Phrygia, on the western edge of the Lycaonian highlands, where it captured an entire Byzantine army. But this turned out to be the last great Muslim success in Anatolia before the Seljuk conquests of the eleventh century.

Caliphs in Control

The most fundamental of the splits in Islam had occurred only a generation after the death of the Prophet, in 656–61. The legitimacy of the election of the fourth Caliph, 'Ali, the cousin of Muhammad and the husband of the Prophet's daughter, Fatima, had been challenged unsuccessfully by a coalition that included the Prophet's former most favoured wife, 'A'isha. Subsequently a second opposition movement headed by the discontented 'Umayyad governor, Mu'awiya, again challenged 'Ali's right to rule. Mu'awiya outwitted 'Ali, so that when the latter died in 661, his right to the caliphal title was still in some doubt. The second round of the dispute between Mu'awiya, proclaimed Caliph after the death of 'Ali, and 'Ali's family, was fought in 680, when 'Ali's son Husayn contested Mu'awiya's right to the caliphal title, and was killed by an 'Umayyad army at Karbala, in Iraq. The 'Umayyad dynasty was henceforth unchallenged until 750, but from Husayn's death sprang the religious party of the adherents of 'Ali (shi 'at 'Ali or Shi'as), which has remained in Islam until the present day, and was the moving force behind the Iranian revolution of the Ayatollah Khomeini in 1979.

In the ninth century, the 'Abbasid dynasty was challenged on two levels, the dynastic and the religious. In Iran, in Khurasan, in Egypt, and inTunisia, it found itself in the second half of the century displaced from effective power by local dynasties or rebellious governors whom it could not dislodge. Other dissident movements surfaced. By far the most important was that of the Shi'a, who initially organized successful movements in Arabia and North Africa (the Maghrib), and then, in 969, eventually put into place in Egypt an anti-'Abassid caliphate of 'Fatimids' (i.e. supposed descendants of 'Ali and of the Prophet's daughter, Fatima). But throughout the ninth century there had also been lesser dissident movements of various sorts, which all contributed to weaken the caliphate of Baghdad. There had been a half-century in which the caliphs emigrated to Samarra, near the ethnically Turkish centres of their military recruitment programmes, but their return to Baghdad in 892 had not re-established their power.

Byzantium Fights Back

This Muslim disunity enabled a strong Byzantine comeback during the ninth century. The Byzantines had recovered sufficiently to survive a strong attack on Constantinople by the Russians of Kiev in 860, to make the Anatolian

Above: Muslim soldiers recruiting for the armies of the faithful.

Below: This foundation stone carries an inscription in ornamental Kufic script. It mentions the construction of the grand palace of Monastir in 966 and the exodus from Magrib to Cairo on the order of the Fatimid Caliph al-Mu'izz, King of Egypt from 969.

Left: A Coptic funerary stela. The Copts were an Egyptian Christian sect who survived within an Islamic context.

borders and the Aegean seas safer than they had been for a generation, and then to take the war south into the heart of Syria for the first time since the period of the first Islamic conquests, reoccupying Damascus for a brief while. This did not mean a return of Byzantium to the huge armies and permanent garrisons of its heyday, but it meant that a fragmentation of power had taken place in the Islamic world, which allowed a freedom of manoeuvre to the Byzantines that they had not enjoyed for a couple of centuries.

The respite in the East was of particular value to Byzantines, first, because they had to endure further dangerous aggression south of the Danube from the Bulgars, who in 811 had destroyed an imperial army, and had made the skull of the Emperor Nicephorus into a drinking cup for their khan. The Slavs had already occupied most of Greece, including northern Thrace. Secondly, because the model of the sixth and seventh centuries still obtained, and the semi-assimilated barbarian tribes on the borders became disposed towards Christian conversion. The eastern Empire had to be capable of responding to these challenges, in case either another Christian sect or another religion – notably Islam, but Buddhism and Judaism were other competitors – was received by the pagan barbarians before Orthodox Christianity.

Above: A lustre bowl from the 'Abassid period. The image of Buddha indicates the extent to which Islamic pilgrims travelled.

The Danish Angle: Alfred and Cnut

All over the Christian borders, the situation was approximately the same. Islam remained a powerful, aggressive counter-culture that still possessed the capacity (although, perhaps, no longer the will) to win the religious and political battle with both the East and the West of Christianity. But in the fragmented world of the frontier tribes, the more military and cultural advances the outer tribes made, the more they became inner tribes, disposed to receive the religion of their hosts. An English pattern is provided by the reception and baptism of the victorious Danish King, Guthrum, by his Anglo-Saxon opponent, King Alfred, at Wedmore. Within a century and a half of that baptism, Cnut, the grandson of the Danish king, Harald Gormsson, who had converted to Christianity in 960 or thereabouts, became not only the Danish but also the English king. Cnut was a pious Catholic ruler. He made a pilgrimage to Rome, but also built a palace at Winchester whose iconography celebrated the pagan origins of the dynasty.

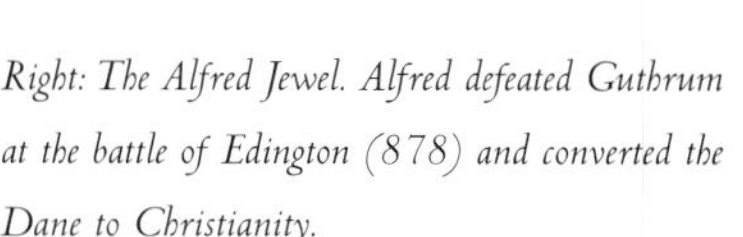

Right: The Alfred Jewel. Alfred defeated Guthrum at the battle of Edington (878) and converted the Dane to Christianity.

Left: Cnut and his first wife, Aelfgifu, at the Palace of Winchester. A pious Christian, Cnut became King of England in 1016.

In the West, the Frankish Empire half a century after Charlemagne's death in 814 split into a western, a 'middle' and an eastern kingdom. In the same period the Christian West had been subjected to severe external pressures, everywhere from Iberia and the western Mediterranean to the North Sea, the Channel, the Danube and even the Rhine. The Arab maritime attacks on Italy and the islands of the western Mediterranean were part of a pattern that stretched from Crete to Bari and Barcelona.

Above: An Arab trading ship. The skills of seamanship perfected in more peaceful times meant that Arabian sea power posed a particular threat to Christians in the Mediterranean.

Christianity under Siege

An especially disastrous attack for the Roman bishopric that was now one of the two or three chief centres of the Frankish Empire took place in 846, when an Arab army from Aghlabid Tunis landed at Ostia, brushed aside the defence forces of Anglo-Saxon pilgrim troops, and sacked Rome on the north bank of the Tiber. The two great apostolic shrines of St Paul and St Peter, both full of piously donated treasures, were plundered, and the tombs of the apostles wantonly smashed. In the next few years St Benedict's monasteries at Subiaco and Monte Cassino were also sacked. Modern archaeology has found the Muslim hammer marks on the old Petrine memorial stones under St Peter's, and has found the prostrate doors of the great southern monastery of San Vincenzo al Volturno, lying where

Right: King Sven Forkbeard, father of Cnut, drowns in 1014. He had led the Northmen on various successful raids along the eastern English coast.

they were thrown by the Muslim despoilers of the same years. Big Muslim 'pirate' bases appeared at Bari (that became for a time a Muslim emirate), and at the mouths of the Rhone and of the Tyrrhenian Garigliano.

Islam was only one of the areas – although the largest – from which attacks on the Christian kingdoms were launched. The sea power of the Scandinavian and Danish tribes, or Northmen, enabled them to raid a huge area, which stretched from the north of Ireland over much of the English coastline and interior, to the Rhine estuary and to the area of north-west Francia, later named Normandy after them. They also raided south as far as the southern Rhineland. The Hungarians raided the entire course of the middle and upper Danube, until they virtually met the limits of Northmen depredation on the Rhine. All over Europe the population retreated to defensible 'castle' or 'burgh' sites. Although the Frankish Empire had come into being through huge, occasionally mobilized armies, it did not possess the kind of taxation and type of central administrative basis that had allowed the late Roman and the subsequent Byzantine Empires to keep armies in being that were large and effective enough to defend enormous lengths of frontier. The 'Marches' that the Franks created on their borders were not militarily strong enough to support this degree of pressure.

The Avars, a Turcic people, had been contained in Pannonia between the Drava and the Danube by the last great military effort of Charlemagne. Behind them to the east and the north were the Slavic peoples of various branches, who pressed upon both Eastern and Western Christianity. Like the rest, they were a challenge to both the soldiers and the missionaries. A century earlier, St Boniface had thought the conversion of the Slavs a task not worth undertaking. His successors had to think differently.

The troubled relationship between East and West was exacerbated not only by the Roman-Frankish fusion, but by Eastern iconoclasm, which was revived by each fresh Byzantine military disaster. Gradually, the split between Roman (or in the terminology we now use, Byzantine) East and barbarian West had led to a great cultural and political divide, that had been consecrated in 800 by the creation of what became the 'Holy Roman Empire' of the West.

In the ninth century, moreover, the Roman bishops began to develop what had at the beginning been a claim for seniority of apostolic tradition into a principle of legal jurisdiction. There had never been any question of the authority of the Roman bishopric as the bearer of doctrinal tradition that was connected with the apostles, Peter and Paul. To this was added the pope's importance as the guardian of the pilgrimage to the holiest of the churches and tombs of the Roman martyrs. In earlier centuries this authority and prestige were shared with those of the great apostolic eastern sees, to which had been added (by the agreement of church councils) the imperial see of Constantinople. The Muslim conquests made this balance of the ancient churches obsolete. Alexandria, Antioch and Jerusalem, and the now ancient cultural heritage of the Egyptian and Syrian churches (not to mention some of the other churches further to the east), had been as it were excised by a surgical operation.

The Pope and the Patriarch

Nicholas I (pope from 858–67) was also responsible for two critical episodes in the history of Roman relations with the East. The Byzantine Empire had by this time reorganized its military and administrative systems, and found ways, within its reduced boundaries, of more or less containing Muslim expansion. In 843, it had also at last settled the critical issue of iconoclasm in favour of restoring the veneration of the images. In principle, the way was open to a restoration of pacific

Below: A Carolingian ivory panel from c. 875 showing an archbishop amongst his choir.

Left: A pen, ink, wash and chalk drawing from the studio of Cesare Nebbia (1536–1613), called The Burning of Photius's Books and the Verdict on the Patriarch Photius. A former soldier and secretary, Photius became something of a pawn in the complex politics of Constantinople. He was twice made Patriarch but was finally exiled by Pope Leo in 886.

relations with the Western churches. But in practice this was not the direction things were to take. On the one hand, both Eastern and Western churches were sending missionaries to the Balkans and central Europe. On the other, the political distrust between the Franks and the Byzantines was very much alive.

The issue came to a head with the imposition by the Emperor (or more exactly, by his minister, the Emperor Michael III's uncle, Bardas) of a new Patriarch of Constantinople. This was because the existing Patriarch, the former learned layman and civil servant, Photius, himself the son of a former Emperor, had become unacceptable to the government. When the ousted Patriarch refused to accept exile and defeat, the Byzantine government called upon Pope Nicholas in Rome for support. This turned out to have been a bad political error. Nicholas sent legates to Constantinople, who recognized Photius as Patriarch, but were then repudiated by the pope who had sent them. Instead, Nicholas, on his own authority, removed Photius as Patriarch and restored the former incumbent, Ignatius. Photius replied by holding a council in Constantinople that anathematized and deposed Pope Nicholas in 867. The affair had turned into a direct confrontation between Eastern and Western churches.

The affair of Photius had direct consequence in the missionary field of Bulgaria. The khan of the Bulgarians had just accepted Christianity from Eastern Orthodox missionaries, but had subsequently become worried about the political consequences of his actions as they concerned the Byzantine Empire. He sent envoys to Rome, and offered acceptance of Western, Latin Christianity as an alternative. Pope Nicholas I agreed to the new arrangement with enthusiasm, although it did not lead in the end to the imposition of Western church allegiance on Bulgaria.

Rome and Byzantium Drift Apart

The missionary field in eastern Europe was not always dominated by a spirit of unthinking competition between Byzantium and Rome. The missionary brothers Cyril and Methodios, who more than anyone else were responsible for the conversion of the Slavs and their coming into possession of a written language for the transmission of the Gospel, were sent among the Slavs from Byzantium, but backed by Rome. Methodios was consecrated Archbishop of Pannonia by Pope Hadrian II, although political changes caused him to end (he died in 885) as Archbishop of Moravia. He was still in touch with Byzantium, and he has been called the last great figure of the universal church[2].

After the death of Methodios, relations between Rome and Byzantium were still not broken, especially as Byzantine rule in south Italy was vital to the defence of the peninsula against the Muslims. A change of dynasty in Constantinople, and the assembly in 869 of a council of Eastern bishops that endorsed the deposition of Photius desired by the popes, smoothed the way back to more normal relations between East and West. But the gap between the clergy of Rome and that of Constantinople grew wider every year. In Rome, a doctrine of papal primacy over other bishops that emphasized the magisterial jurisdiction of the Roman see was being formulated. The wholesale forgery of early church laws that backed up this sort of view (the 'Pseudo-Isidore' decretals, after a Spanish collection of church laws that had been wrongly attributed to the seventh-century clerk of that name) was carried out, not in Rome during this period, but in Francia.

The doctrine of Roman magisterial primacy supposed Roman supremacy over the Greek churches. Rome was very far, on this account, from forgetting that the Christian East existed. In the late ninth century, Greek ecclesiastical culture was still studied in Rome, and knowledge about it there was not

Left: The imperial crown of Charlemagne. It was used to crown Otto of Saxony in 960. As Holy Roman Emperor, Otto I based his rule on the pattern set by Charlemagne.

confined to a few Greek monasteries. The popes still wrote their letters on papyrus imported from the Greek-speaking world. There were learned men in the papal court such as Anastasius (once for a short time pope, but more important as the adviser of Pope Nicholas I) and his son Arsenius, who understood the theology and politics of the Eastern Church.

Papal Problems

The late ninth to the mid-tenth centuries were a particularly dark age for the Italian peninsula. The Frankish emperors, who made only occasional expeditions to Italy, were unable to protect the civilization of great churches and monasteries that their predecessors had set up there. Arab and 'wicked Christian' plunderers wandered in Italy where they willed. In Rome the military and political situation became desperate. The military aristocracy controlled and exploited the churches and their lands in Rome and elsewhere. The last great pope of the century, John VIII (872–82), was unable to stop them. The clerical leader of the one of the groups of powerful Roman nobles was Bishop Formosus of Porto, whose ambitions split Roman society in two, and caused anarchy in the city over a period of about thirty years. In 891 Formosus appeared to have triumphed by securing his own election as pope, and he died as pope in 896.

Such was the hatred he had occasioned that after his death his papal successor had the nine-month-old corpse of Formosus taken from the grave to be 'judged' by a synod of bishops. The corpse of the former pope was condemned, and his tenure of the papal office pronounced invalid. The fingers that had expressed benedictions were torn from the body, which was thrown into the Tiber.

Matters did not improve for the papacy after this sad scene. The factions of Roman nobles continued to control the papacy; in the first half of the tenth century the dominating family was that of the senator Theophylact. His daughter, Marozia, is second only to Lucrezia Borgia among the fabled bad women of papal history. It was claimed, perhaps falsely, that she was the mistress of Pope Sergius III (904–11), and the mother by him of the future Pope John XI (931–5). The 'prince and senator' Alberic, her son by her third marriage to a great prince of the Middle Kingdom, was certainly the ruler of Rome from 932 to his death in 954. Alberic's son, a worldly young cleric whose recreations were women, gambling and hunting, became Pope John XII in 955.

The Restoration of the Empire

In the tenth century the various Frankish dynasties that had succeeded to the regional supremacies of the former Frankish Empire became unrecognizable or extinct. The Frankish Empire was resurrected by a new German dynasty, that of the former Dukes of Saxony. The agent of this rebirth of an ancient concept was Otto of Saxony, who by marching to Italy in 960, and securing his coronation as emperor at the hands of Pope John XII, launched a new imperial rule that relied on the legal and tribal framework set up by Charlemagne over a century and a half earlier. Otto I had John XII deprived of the papal office in 963, after defeating the pope and his army.

In the East at this time, the Byzantine army was also undergoing one of its many rebirths, and was for the first time since the seventh century trying seriously, while still holding the Bulgarians at bay, to regain some of the frontiers lost to Islam. Under Otto I's immediate successors, an alliance of the Ottonian and the Byzantine Empires began to oppose the Muslims in southern Italy. But these military alliances did nothing for the cultural gap that now yawned between East and West. By the late tenth century the mental division had proceeded to a point where Liutprand of Cremona, a Lombard bishop of a north Italian see, sent as an envoy of the Emperor Otto I to Constantinople, found himself on arrival in the Byzantine capital – in spite of his supposedly privileged diplomatic position – an excluded and inferior foreigner, trying to move in an alien and hardly comprehensible world.

Otto I's grandson, Otto III, son of Otto II and of the Byzantine princess Theophanu, became Emperor on reaching so-called majority in 995; he was, however, still a youth of fifteen. He proved to be an antiquarian imperialist, who wanted to revive the Empire of Charlemagne, although in a form that resembled Byzantium more than Germany. He was the pupil of the Italian-born Greek teacher, Philagothos, and of the Frankish philosopher, Gerbert, the greatest clerical intellectual of his age, whom Otto made pope under the title of Silvester II (999–1003). The young Otto was deeply religious and deeply idealistic. He may have acquired from Gerbert some kind of eschatological premonition of the approaching end of the world, which may even have been connected with the millennium year through which he lived. He dreamed of the 'restoration of the Roman Empire'. He had the body of Charlemagne (who had died in 814) exhumed in Aachen, and took relics from the tomb. He took up residence in Rome, built a new palace on the Aventine hill, and lived there in the style of a Byzantine Emperor, with court officials who boasted sonorous Greek titles. When he returned to Rome for the last time in July of the year 1000, he was greeted not by the approaching horsemen of the apocalypse, but by the cavalry of Italian rebels, whom he had failed to subdue before his death near Rome in 1002.

1 Robert Hillenbrand, *Islamic Architecture: Form, Function and Meaning* (Edinburgh, 1994)

2 A. P. Vlasto, *The Entry of the Slavs into Christendom: an Introduction to the History of the Medieval Slavs* (Cambridge, 1970), p. 80

10

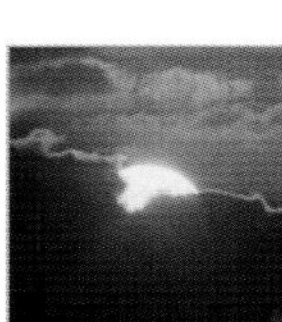

From Peacekeeping to Holy War

There had never been, during the first thousand years of the existence of the religion, any real question of making the Christian society into a pacifist society. That Christians wanted a pacific society was another, and a quite different question: there have been difficulties in obtaining such a society, which continue to plague us today. Christianity had taken shape in a Roman Empire whose military principles the Christians had from the beginning avoided calling into question.

The absorption of Christianity by barbarian societies revived the military questions in a different form. These societies were run by military aristocracies that in many cases attributed their ancestry to pagan war gods. Similar claims had been made by Roman Emperors; such things could be concealed or glossed over. But, because of the wide diffusion of power among the barbarian magnates, their military aristocracies were never controlled by the central authority in the way that the army was controlled in the Roman Empire.

Like the Christian Empire, the barbarian kingdoms were quite willing to exempt the ordained clergy from personal military service. But, because of the devolution of landed power in the early medieval West, it was going to be hard to separate the Church in a definite manner from the military organization of the kingdoms. The endowment of bishoprics and monasteries with huge grants of lands, inevitable in a gift-giving society, took the church lands out of the direct control of the nobles, but it did not remove them from noble influence entirely. The great nobles remained linked to the churches endowed by their families by a system of patronage that did not amount to ownership, but retained strong proprietorial characteristics. Nor did the king renounce his military rights over church lands.

The military crises of the ninth and tenth centuries, when Christian rulers were trying desperately to respond to the external threats of pagan raiders, much increased the pressure on the churches to use their resources for the defence of the kingdoms. In the former east Frankish kingdom, now ruled by a line of Saxon kings, the problem was solved in a particularly definite way, assigning to

Left: Crusaders take Jerusalem.

each bishopric a large military quota that the churchmen had to fill in time of war. There had been changes in military methods, and the most effective fighting unit had become the heavily armed cavalryman, who used expensive armour, weaponry and transport and was highly trained. By the middle of the tenth century the Saxon royal army depended on the heavy cavalry supplied by the bishops, as the nucleus of its main fighting force. The 'knight', as he later came to be called, had come to dominate Western warfare, and the Church was intimately concerned in the way he was financed and organized. That did not make the clergy the only employers of the knights, far from it: the great nobles were all surrounded by followings of heavily-armed retainers whose numbers corresponded to their rank and resources.

Above: Offa, King of Mercia (757–796), founder of St Albans, which he is holding in his hand. Charlemagne considered Offa to be an equal.

Church Militant

The manner in which the Church was involved with the military system varied from one region to another. In Anglo-Saxon England the bishops did not normally supply troops on the same basis as happened in Germany, but they often had to contribute large sums to buying off the raiders. In west Francia the clergy sometimes raised troops, but not in the same way, nor in the same proportions, as in the Eastern Kingdom. It was a long-lived system, especially in Germany, where in the twelfth century each of the great bishops still headed retinues of up to several hundred knights, which the king could call out for the army. By that time a similar system obtained in Anglo-Norman England, although the proportion of church knights in the royal army was much lower. In central Italy, when an abbot of the monastery of St Benedict's foundation of Subiaco died in 1145, the monastery's chronicler recorded that he left the monastery 'in great prosperity, and full of well-equipped troops.'

In western Europe the military calling was a precarious and competitive one that did not encourage orderly behaviour. In the ninth-century German romance *Ruodlieb* the hero is advised not to ride down the standing corn of the peasants more than is necessary, and is told to billet himself on peasants who have old and ugly wives: the story of a fellow warrior who murdered his host to have his young wife follows. This kind of bullying by troops billeted on the local people was as old as military history. But the early medieval knightly class was guilty also of extorting and stealing goods and money wherever they could find them. Churches were not in the least exempt for their depredations.

From the tenth century onwards the clergy tried to react, especially in south and north-west Francia, against this kind of lawlessness and oppression. On the one hand, big meetings of repentance were organized by the clergy, in which unlawful bloodshed and violence against unarmed persons were renounced by those who attended, and penance done or promised for what had occurred. At the same time the clergy began to sponsor what was in effect collective action to discourage bloodshed and

Left: A detail from the twelfth-century Westminster Psalter shows a crusading knight kneeling in prayer.

Right: Monks encouraging crusaders as they set off. The Church faced a dilemma in reconciling pacific principles with warfare but defined the Crusades as a holy war.

Above: A detail from the Bayeux Tapestry. In the centre Bishop Odo wields a club. The clergy were not allowed to be armed but a club was not defined as a weapon.

disorder, by taking new spaces of time into the realm of the holy. In the 'truces of God' the local warrior class undertook to renounce warfare on specified days and church feasts. From Wednesday evening until Monday morning, for example, could be a period during which they swore to abstain from violence, either for the purpose of extortion – even to seize pledges given under contract – or for that of taking vengeance. The 'truces of God' were enforceable by armed action on the part of the community, led by its church leaders, and this sometimes occurred. Such peacekeeping action could be viewed now as a species of 'holy war', although it was not so termed at the time.

The churchmen were not going to repudiate the huge property donations that gave them control of a very large part of the social and economic resources of north-west Europe. Nor, in spite of the moral ambiguities involved in giving bishops the administrative control and financial responsibility for keeping troops on permanent standby, were they going to repudiate this partial militarization of the Church. What they objected to was the political control exercised by kings and great nobles, that enabled them to use secular legal forms for 'investing' churchmen with their benefices. Even more, they objected to the possibility that these powerful laymen could actually sell the benefices. This is, after all, a situation perfectly familiar to attentive readers of Jane Austen's *Pride and Prejudice*, although Lady Catherine de Burgh did not require Mr Collins to keep troops in the parsonage.

Despite this, the upper clergy were not all obsessed by their own wealth, or if they were, they also reacted against it. There was in the eleventh century a drift towards the hermit life, but it was not

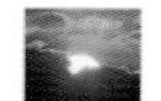

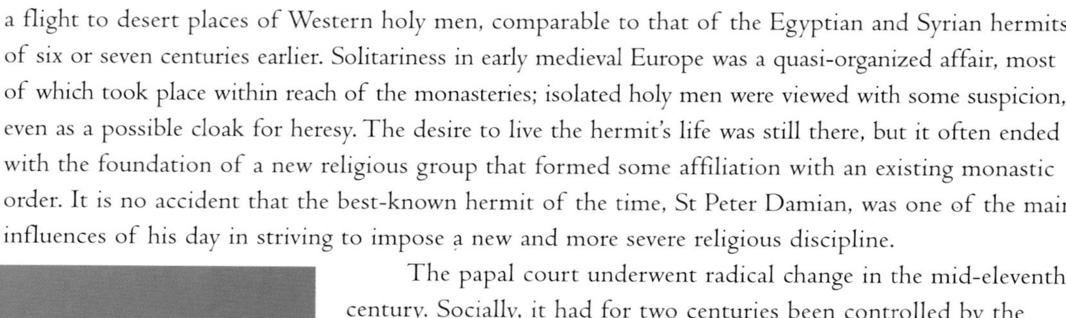

a flight to desert places of Western holy men, comparable to that of the Egyptian and Syrian hermits of six or seven centuries earlier. Solitariness in early medieval Europe was a quasi-organized affair, most of which took place within reach of the monasteries; isolated holy men were viewed with some suspicion, even as a possible cloak for heresy. The desire to live the hermit's life was still there, but it often ended with the foundation of a new religious group that formed some affiliation with an existing monastic order. It is no accident that the best-known hermit of the time, St Peter Damian, was one of the main influences of his day in striving to impose a new and more severe religious discipline.

Below: The reliquary of Henry II (973–1024). Henry was crowned Holy Roman Emperor in 1014. He donated lavish rewards to the Church to ensure that he kept political control in both secular and spiritual matters.

The papal court underwent radical change in the mid-eleventh century. Socially, it had for two centuries been controlled by the Roman aristocracy: the efforts of the Ottonian Emperors to change this, in the second half of the tenth century, had been in vain. But in the mid-eleventh century the Emperors again intervened in the affairs of the Roman clergy, this time more effectively, although to their own ultimate detriment. In 1046 the Emperor Henry III deposed Italian claimants to the papacy whom he deemed corrupt, and replaced them by a series of German bishops, who occupied the papacy until 1058. The most important of these was Bishop Bruno of Toul, who occupied the papal throne as Pope Leo IX from 1049–54. His pontificate proved a central one, both in defining the new papal policy of reform, and in its effect on relations with the Eastern Church. Leo IX appointed reforming cardinals to the Roman court from the Middle Kingdom, including a clerk from Lorraine called Humbert of Moyenmoutier.

Schism

At this period theological difference between the Eastern and Western churches was perhaps more to do with cultural and linguistic matters, than with critical differences in the ways that either church thought about the divinity. In the Western Latin liturgy it had very gradually became customary to recite the Creed in a form that referred to the Holy Spirit as 'proceeding from the Father and the Son', instead of using the earlier form, used at Chalcedon in 451, that restricts itself to saying that the Spirit 'proceeds from the Father'. Behind this difference of usage there do not seem to have lain the long years of highly articulate theological dispute that lay behind the ancient differences of opinion about the divine and the human in the person of Christ. The difference about the 'filioque' ('[from the father'] and from the son') may reflect a diversity of mentality, but it seems to have owed its existence much more to liturgical habit than to anything else, and in any case its use only became universal in the West in the eleventh century.

The Patriarch of Constantinople at the time of Leo IX of Rome was Michael Cerularius, an active character who seems to have decided to open some of the long-standing questions about the unsatisfactory practices and beliefs of the Latin Church. His most provocative act, which would have had economic and political results, was to close the Latin churches in Constantinople. It was unfortunate that this period of activism in Constantinople should have coincided with a quite unconnected period of activism in Rome. In 1054 Humbert of Moyenmoutier, who was particularly interested in theories of papal supremacy in the Church, was dispatched to Constantinople at the head of a small mission of like-minded clerks, to protest against the actions of Cerularius. The papal envoys were German noblemen of great power and influence, and the attitudes of these insolent barbarians to the upper Byzantine clergy, who were themselves conscious of a cultural superiority that needed no discussion, were judged by the Patriarch to be extremely unsatisfactory. It was a situation that Westerners were one day to encounter in the imperial Chinese court.

Humbert of Moyenmoutier and his colleagues met with the refusal of the Byzantine clergy to give any hearing to their complaints, which were not restricted to the matter of the closed churches, but complained of hostile Byzantine propaganda against the Latins. They stated the basic papal jurisdictional claims, which were totally unacceptable to the Patriarch. The reply of the Western delegation was to enter the church of Haghia Sophia without warning, and to solemnly deposit on the high altar a bull of excommunication of the Patriarch of Constantinople: they then hurriedly left the city. The Emperor Constantine was worried by this turn of events, and not particularly pleased that Cerularius had allowed it to occur. However, he was unable either to moderate the Patriarch's attitude or conduct, or to stop him from holding, a short time later, a synod that anathematized the Roman see on account of the conduct of its legates. The mutual anathemas were not finally withdrawn until 1965, although many attempts were made to reach an accommodation in the later Middle Ages.

The 'Schism of 1054' was not a turning point of church history. Its precedents stretched back for many centuries, and it was far less decisive for the relations of Eastern and Western churches than things that were later to occur during the course of the Latin Crusades, above all the sack of Constantinople by the Latins in 1204. But it was, nevertheless, a flashpoint that cannot be ignored. It demonstrated the extent to which the Western churches were tending to become one Church under papal leadership, and that showed also the unacceptability of this phenomenon to the Church of the East.

Below: The Palace of the Normans in Palermo, Sicily. The Nomans took over the city in 1072 after more than 200 years of Arab rule.

The Reform Papacy

The aim of the main church movement of the eleventh century was institutional reform that sought to preserve existing church institutions, while purifying and sanctifying them. As it happened, the attainment of these aims was to cause the transformation of many of the chief clerical institutions of the time, notably the Roman bishopric itself. But the reformers had it most to heart that church offices, which existed to serve the people of God, should no longer be bought and sold, and that the hands of laymen, hands that had often been stained with blood, should no longer transmit to the clergy the tangible symbols of their office.

The clerical group that more than any other understood these things was that of the German clerks introduced into the Roman bishopric by the Emperor Henry III from 1046 onwards. They knew about them because they themselves belonged to the uppermost levels of the German nobility, and to the court circles that had hitherto profited by them. The struggle against 'simony', the sale of holy things (Acts 8:18) was to be the main concern of the Roman Church for the following half-century.

The contested symbolism of the feudal 'investiture' with his benefice of a clerk by a layman (usually by the handing over of a staff or of some other sign of property) gave the struggle its modern name of 'Investiture Contest'.

The main figure in the stand-off with the German monarchy that the Roman popes led in the last three decades of the eleventh century was an Italian clerk called Hildebrand who on election took the title of Pope Gregory VII (1073–85). To oppose armed resistance to the Salian King Henry IV (reigned 1056–1105) was a practically impossible task for a Roman bishop, who in spite of the great prestige of his see was materially no more than the first bishop of the Empire. Gregory's assets did not lie in his armies, which melted away whenever he really needed them, but in his moral stature and diplomatic skills. In 1077, at their meeting at Canossa in north-central Italy, where he forced the king to appear before him as a penitent, Gregory came near to success. But the understanding with Henry at Canossa proved illusory. At the end of his life Gregory saw Rome taken by Henry's army (and subsequently much more thoroughly sacked, by his own), while he himself went off to die in exile. However, he may be said to have gained his essential aims, even if the German monarchy only acknowledged this some thirty-seven years after his death.

Right: Seljuk raqqa bowl showing two Seljuk horsemen.

The wars of the Investiture Contest, even if unsuccessful, changed the outlook and status of the Roman papacy in a decisive way. To achieve their aims the popes had had to mobilize armies to fight in holy wars: there had been an attempt to create a new 'militia of St Peter'. The popes were already the feudal sovereigns of the Normans of southern Italy, on whose support they had depended in the later stages of the contest. In one sense the popes were fighting to avoid finding themselves in the situation of the German bishops, who were also the army generals of the German king, but in another sense they had themselves accepted a sort of full militarization. The preceding transformations had been detectable in the social history of the papacy since

the early tenth century, but from the close of the Investiture Contest the papal monarchy may be said to have become a feudal monarchy among the other feudal monarchies. It was, of course, many other things besides.

The consequences of that militarization were worked out in a most unexpected way at the end of the eleventh century. The Roman bishops were not disposed to revoke the anathema of 1054, any more than the Greeks were to revoke theirs. Equally, they were indisposed to forget a Byzantium that had been the legal sovereign of the Roman bishops for at least two and a half centuries, and an Eastern Church that theological memory could not disregard. Politically, although the Byzantines had been finally expelled from southern Italy by their mutinous mercenaries, the Normans, Byzantium continued to be a very important factor in the seapower and political balance of the Mediterranean and Adriatic Seas. Rome could not afford to neglect any of these things.

In the same decade that Gregory VII was confronting the German king at Canossa, the balance of power had turned against the Byzantines in Asia Minor in a manner that was in the end to prove decisive. The Turks had for two centuries been the most important element in Muslim military power, but until this point they had featured as slave military levies rather than as independent actors. The intake of Turkish military slaves was to continue for the rest of the Middle Ages, but in the eleventh Christian century the Turks were to acquire an independent dynasty that played a major role in the Muslim world.

Seljuk attack

The Seljuk branch of the Turks, led by Tughril Beg, conquered Baghdad. In 1056 Tughril was made Sultan and King of the East and West by the Caliph. Tughril, and after him his son Alp Arslan, led the Seljuks in a series of holy wars against Byzantium in Asia Minor. They found very little determined resistance, and raiding armies were able to march far into the the interior of Cappadocia. The Byzantine Emperor Romanus Diogenes took his main army into Armenia to challenge Alp Arslan, and met him in 1071 near Lake Van, at the Battle of Manzikert. It was a last, desperate throw; the Byzantine army had for years been starved of men and resources. At this battle the Emperor was taken, and the Byzantine army destroyed. The result was to open most of Asia Minor to Seljuk attack, and to lead to the occupation of huge areas in Anatolia (not to mention the Aegean coast) by Turkish leaders; in 1085 Antioch also fell.

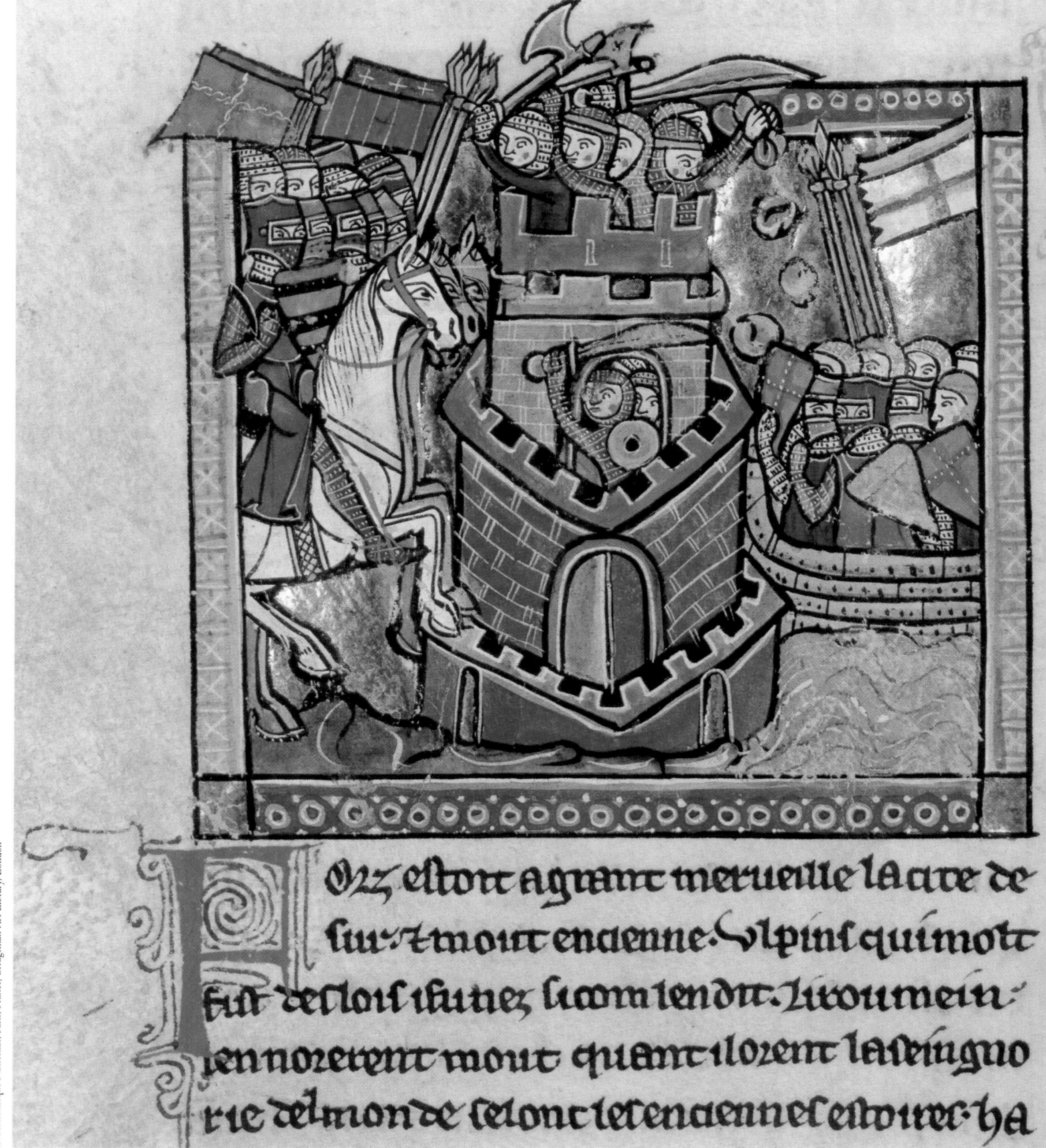

Right: The siege of Antioch from an illuminated manuscript. Antioch changed hands several times but in 1098 it was captured by the crusaders after a siege lasting six months.

The Byzantine experience with Norman mercenaries had been deeply disillusioning, and had ended, after the Battle of Manzikert, with the Normans themselves trying to set up their own principality in Asia Minor, but the Byzantines persisted in thinking that their own military incapacity might be offset by finding new sources of mercenary troops in western Europe. After 1081

Byzantium once more had an Emperor with a good military record and great talents as a diplomatist – Alexius Comnenus.

The sensitivity of the Roman bishop to what was happening in Eastern Christendom is known from a letter written by Gregory VII to a Burgundian noble in 1074, three years after Manzikert, in which the pope refers to the plight of the Eastern Christians in face of Saracen aggression. He says, very mysteriously, that if he resolves his own current military problems with the rebellion of his Norman feudatories, he may himself go to Constantinople to give armed aid to the Byzantines. Presumably, as he knew that Normans were already serving as Byzantine mercenaries in Asia Minor, he hoped either to bring those already in Byzantine territory back to obedience, or to take fresh contingents. The letter is interesting because it seems to show that armed voyages to the East which sound merely fanciful, were actually being contemplated in some way by the pope.

It is always tempting to modern people to think that because of their poor communications, medieval people were necessarily ignorant of what was happening in other cultures and at very great distances. The medieval poor were poorly informed, not surprisingly. But the Roman bishopric, recently energized by reforming zeal, also had traditional knowledge, and live diplomatic contacts that made it

Below: Peter the Hermit gives out crosses in support of the first Crusade. The image is taken from The History of Jerusalem from 1095 to its capture by the Christians, by the monk Robert. It was from the wearing of the cross that the Crusaders took their name.

Right: The first Crusade. Crusaders consisted both of organized armies and loose groups of peasants.

the best observatory in western Europe of the Muslim and Byzantine Mediterranean. Over half a century earlier, another pope (Sergius IV) was said to have declared his wish to proceed himself to Palestine to succour the Christians there, after he had heard of the anti-Christian policies of the then Fatimid caliph. And in the very early years of the new reforming papacy, in 1064, the pope had specifically approved of the mustering of French warriors to fight against the Muslims in northern Spain.

There was another factor that made Western Christians of all sorts aware of the inner Islamic world. The pilgrimage to Jerusalem was one of the most persistent phenomena of the time. Pilgrims left from all over Christian Europe, from as far north as Scandinavia and Iceland, and from all over the north-west and the south, to make the risky and arduous voyage to Palestine. They made the voyage in groups that varied in size from a few dozen to several hundreds. Such pilgrimages were perfectly practicable throughout the century, except in exceptional circumstances of local wars or of anti-Christian riots. The pilgrims often included knights, even feudal rulers, who hoped to gain some more substantial hope of salvation, in spite of the constant bloodshed that marked their careers. The Muslim rulers of Palestine received them peaceably, partly because this was a profitable early-medieval version of long-distance tourism, but also because Islamic custom approved the grant of protected status to Christians or Jews who were thought not to harbour intentions of hurting Islam.

The Christian eleventh century also had its own versions of the expectation of the end of time. These have been present in the religion from the beginning. Prodigies, such as comets and reports of monsters, and disasters, such as plagues and famines, could affect such fears, and so also could the locally destructive results of wars. Reported happenings in Palestine and the East could also affect eschatological consciousness. The most important was the report of the 'destruction' of the church of the Holy Sepulchre in Jerusalem by the anti-Christian caliph, Hakim, that had been supposed to have disturbed Pope Sergius himself, in 1009. News of the Battle of Manzikert in 1071 must also have been disturbing. That unlearned people had much information of a political sort is unlikely. But some of the knightly class may have known such things.

There is also a kind of strange, but in appearance precise, geographical frame of reference in the Book of Revelation, that can make a no less powerful impression on the Christian consciousness than the strongly local Palestinian contexts of the Gospels. It must have been strange for anyone in the West to hear of the infidel seizure of Ephesus, Laodicaea, Philadelphia, Smyrna, that all figure in Revelation's geography.

Pope Urban II was elected in 1088, three years after the death of Gregory VII. At the time of his accession there was still a Church schism in force, that had resulted from the quarrels of the Investiture Contest. King Henry IV of Germany was still excommunicated, and most of his kingdom was in consequence outside the direct influence of the Gregorian obedience. Urban II was a Burgundian monk, from the great monastery of Cluny, which had been a formative influence on Church practice and thinking ever since its foundation in the early tenth century. He called a church council in the north-Italian city of Piacenza in 1095, that was attended by the ambassadors of the Byzantine Emperor Alexius. Almost certainly, the ambassadors asked for military help from the Western Christians against the Seljuk Turks in Anatolia, and emphasized the common cause of the Eastern and Western churches in the matter.

In Rome, Pope Urban II was still afflicted by the civil war that the schism had occasioned. He therefore did not return there, but from Piacenza travelled in the autumn of 1095 to Clermont, in the duchy of Aquitaine, in the south-east of Francia, to hold another church council. He perhaps

Above: Armed knights and soldiers set sail for the first Crusade. Crusaders encompassed Christians of all ranks, including knights, many of whom hoped for material gain as well as eternal salvation.

preferred this area of Francia because King Philip I of France, whose lands lay elsewhere, was at the time under a cloud, as a result of his irregular relationship with Bertrade de Montfort. When the reform business of the council at Clermont was finished, Urban took advantage of the presence of so many of the bishops and nobles of southern France to go outside the walls of the town, where he could address a largely lay audience, and to make a statement and an appeal concerning the situation of Christians in the East.

The First Crusade

To a modern public accustomed to statesmen who address their audiences about events that have appeared on the television screens in the past few hours, the content of Urban's appeal may seem quite odd. The most recent event that he referred to was that of the fall of Antioch to the Muslims, which had happened ten years previously. He spoke of the desecration and defilement of other places by the infidel, although the events of which he spoke had started to occur after the Battle of Manzikert, twenty-eight years earlier.

Urban was the head of the Western Church at a time when the distinction between the lay and the clerical orders in Christianity was being emphasized by the reform party that he also headed. But he had just left the closed church council of bishops to talk to a gathering of laymen, some of them great noblemen, but for the most part knights. To these men, who were most of them soldiers, he talked without making distinctions of rank. He asked them, whether rich or poor, to put aside their quarrels (which he knew to be many) and to relent from their 'lawless persecutions', and to march to the East to the help of their fellow Christians. Urban offered his military ambience in 1095 a sort of battle cry: 'Deus le volt, it is the will of God.'

Urban had preached the first Crusade, though it had no name of that sort. The armed future pilgrims whom he wanted to send to the East had at Clermont torn up fabrics and marked them roughly with a cross to wear, hence *croisé* or cross-wearer. His argument for their departure contained, in fact, an implied judgement about feudal society. If he referred to their 'lawless persecutions' and their quarrels, he was repeating the protests that bishops in the middle and western kingdoms had been making for the past century, about the lawlessness and gangsterism of the knightly class. In wanting to despatch the lawbreakers across the eastern frontiers, he was trying to persuade them to voluntarily make a most arduous pilgrimage, a sort of holy exile. And, against all probability, the appeal worked. The probability was that he was despatching them to a harsh and terrible end in the unknown wilds of Anatolia and northern Syria.

There was, of course, a very large element of hard-headed political calculation in Urban's actions. The enterprise might have been conceived at Piacenza, while he was talking to the Byzantine envoys. He had probably at some stage entered into discussions with the leaders of the southern French nobility, who themselves had had some experience of fighting the Muslims south of the Pyrenees.

Above: Contemporary images portray the Jew as money lender in league with the Devil. Anti-Semitism flared during the period of the Crusades, giving rise to virulent propaganda.

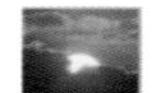

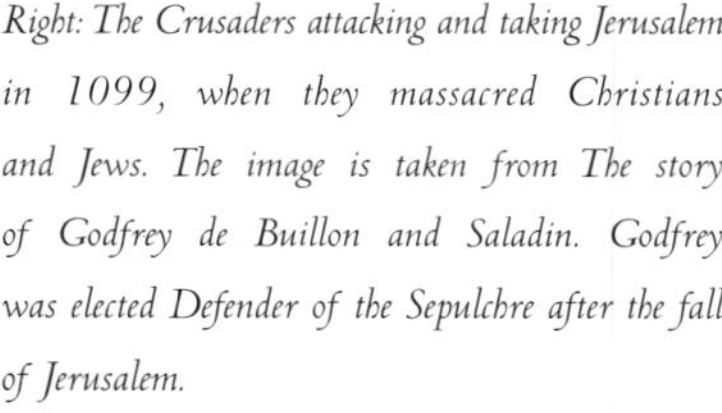

Right: The Crusaders attacking and taking Jerusalem in 1099, when they massacred Christians and Jews. The image is taken from The story of Godfrey de Buillon and Saladin. Godfrey was elected Defender of the Sepulchre after the fall of Jerusalem.

In sponsoring a new holy war, Urban was not making a fresh theological departure that affected the theories of either Western or Eastern churchmen. For centuries, both Eastern and Western Christians had been encouraged to think that the faith could be either spread or defended by force of arms, and that God would look kindly upon those who died for the faith, even though in the East the clergy continued to look upon killing as sinful, no matter what the occasion. Where he was breaking fresh ground, was in supposing that a priest, acting as the minister of God, could propose and preach, and even (as subsequently became evident) to a limited extent control a holy war. He also incorporated in his actions at Clermont a statement that whoever went to Jerusalem on wholly religious grounds, not attracted by honour or money, but only to free God's Church, would have his whole pilgrimage accredited to him for forgiveness of sin, and would be free of all further penance. By this he invented what was in effect a new way to gain merit towards salvation. He also fixed Jerusalem as the object of the armed pilgrims.

It took two and a half years to assemble the forces that Urban had had in mind, for the expedition to Jerusalem. In the interim, two abortive popular expeditions had taken place, and it had also already become clear that one inevitable result of the preaching of the cross against the Muslims, was to stir up savage anti-Semitic riots and pogroms. The connection between Jerusalem and perfidious Jewry was too close in the Christian mind to avoid: even when, much earlier in the century, the Shi'a Caliph Hakim had come down upon the Christians of Jerusalem, his actions had been attributed in the West to Jewish machinations.

The political disillusion that awaited the Byzantines, when the Western levies that they had asked for began to appear in Constantinople, was acute. It was not that the Byzantines were in the least ignorant about the Normans, who had, after all, stolen all the Byzantine possessions in Italy, and had attempted to set up their own dominion in Asia Minor, after the disaster of Manzikert. But, besides the perfidious Normans, the Western armies that arrived in Constantinople in 1097 included many of the greatest families of western Francia and the Middle Kingdom. They at first refused full feudal homage to Alexius, but oaths were found that satisfied both parties. The military co-operation that followed was real, and both sides were also conscious of the need for Christian unity. But distrust on both sides was real, too, and while the Westerners tended to think of the Easterners as other, barely acceptable Christians, the Easterners, following centuries-old habit, thought of the crusaders as barbarian auxiliaries.

Hardly any of the pilgrims in the Western armies that fought their way across Asia Minor in 1097 and 1098, in bitter and sometimes terrible conditions of exposure and hunger, had at the beginning any clear idea of what they were fighting for, beyond clearing their path to Jerusalem. But, like all holy warriors, they soon adopted the idea of armed martyrdom and holy vengeance. At one of the earliest battles, at Nicaea, their casualties 'all alike entered heaven in the robes of martyrdom, calling upon the blood shed in his name.' As the army marched on ruined roads over the anti-Taurus mountains in the

Left: A Islamic reliquary of the precious blood looted from the East.

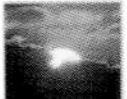

Below: Pieces from the shroud of St Josse acquired after the first Crusade. Many of the surviving Byzantine silk textiles were used in western graves to wrap the bones of a saint, revered ruler or bishop.

autumn rains, many troops and whole baggage trains slipped over precipices, and the knights threw a lot of their heavy equipment after them. At the siege of Antioch (1097–8), an especially severe and terrible experience, accompanied by famine and ending in the religious frenzy that accompanied the finding of the Holy Lance, their determination was forged into a terrible instrument of war. The awful massacre of almost all the surviving combatants and non-combatants of either sex that ended the siege of Jerusalem in the summer of 1099 could have surprised no one who had accompanied the army. The Christian troops walked ankle-deep in blood in the streets, some of it Christian blood.

The establishment of the Kingdom of Jerusalem in 1100 went against the probable plans of Urban II (who by that time was dead). The earlier arrangement, under which Godfrey of Lorraine had been 'Advocate of the Holy Sepulchre' was much nearer to clerical desires, but almost certainly a clerical or papal patrimony of Palestine would have been impossible to run, and in the long perspective a grave embarrassment to the popes. This new frontier at the extreme edge of Christendom could only be given to feudal frontiersmen to defend, and the feudal Kingdom of Jerusalem, while in some respects a sickly plant, was probably about as healthy as any feudal kingdom set up under those desperate circumstances could have been expected to be.

Below: A contemporary manuscript shows tormented souls locked in the jaws of Hell. It illustrates powerfully the fear of the apocalypse at the turn of the first Millennium.

Rather paradoxically, although the Latin Kingdom of Jerusalem had been the indirect result of the desire of the clergy to control the unruly and destructive feudal nobles, all it had really done was to transfer to Palestine many of those nobles, no less unruly and destructive than before, and to shift the moral and material burden of their finance, reinforcement and supply to the Western Church as a whole. This first experiment in Western collegiate colonialism, which is no surprise now to a West that has much experience in United Nations enterprises, was to have many unforeseen results for the Western Church, and particularly for the papacy.

The first Crusade was deeply significant both in the realm of faith and in the realm of power. The Eastern Church, in spite of any promises that had been made in Constantinople, was not restored in any part of the new Latin dominions: it was tolerated only under Latin control. Far from emerging as a great gesture of Christian solidarity, the Crusade had proved to be only one more act of betrayal of the eastern Empire by its Western mercenaries. In the domain of power politics, the Crusade was to herald a new period in the eastern Mediterranean in which Western seapower, mercantile and military interests were to be placed in a position in which they permanently retained the capacity to intervene. This was to continue even after the Crusader States had been pushed out of Syria-Palestine at the end of the thirteenth century. From the point of view of Byzantium and the Eastern Church, the Latin Crusade was a political death sentence, although one that took over a century to execute. From the point of view of the Roman papacy, the Crusade was the greatest political opportunity ever offered it in the high Middle Ages.

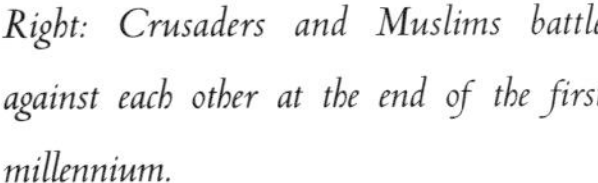

Right: Crusaders and Muslims battle against each other at the end of the first millennium.

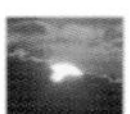

The Story of Christianity

Part II

Part II

The Second Millennium
From Medieval Christendom to Global Christianity

FOREWORD

It would not be difficult to present the second millennium of Christianity in terms just as melodramatic, bombastic and astonishing as the first.

This after all was the millennium that was soon riding into battle with one of its oldest enemies, Judaism, which itself was the ally of the biggest new threat to Christianity – Islam. Tension between these religions was matched by the tension between Rome and Constantinople within Christianity itself, their virulent feuds expressed in terms of theology which now seem bled of all passion (what was the status of the Holy Ghost?) but at that time carried the power of the sword. The Christian city of Constantinople (Byzantium), which had feared destruction from the armies of Islam, was ransacked by fellow Christians who had been launched on the Fourth Crusade from Venice.

And being the great sponge which has been one of its characteristics (just as being the great stone, impervious, has been another) Christianity absorbed learning – mathematics, medicine and many of the arts – from the Muslims, learning which was to transform the Western societies in which Christianity was now an integral and most essential part.

The massive divergent uses to which Christianity was put and the circumstances it inspired, continued on their spectacular way. In the thirteenth century for instance, wealthy, even opulent cathedral-building on a dazzling scale began to sweep through Christian countries resulting in works in stone and glass which still today have a grandeur scarcely matched since. Yet in the same century, the Cathars in southern France were preaching a stern unworldliness and found many converts, as did the wandering friars who continued in unbroken line from the apostles to preach 'leave all that thou hath and follow me'.

Below: Danse Macabre

The Crusades, like many other wars, were wars more often inspired and blessed by Christianity than averted or condemned. State Christianity had begun because Constantine gained victory in battle, a result he attributed to a visionary dream, and the association with battle continues up to the present century. In the fifteenth century the Western Church was divided against itself with two rival Popes – one in Rome and one in Avignon – and as the sailor warriors of the Western seaboard took the faith to new continents, the cross gave its blessing to guns and swords and conquests time and again. Christianity was a reinforcer of military power. Although, as always, many fine souls did good when most around them were evil, the alliance between the Church militant positioned to save souls at whatever cost, and the advanced European countries on the rampage for land, gold, loot of all kinds, yoked together a faith and colonialism that many thought more a pact made by Satan than any Jesus of Nazareth.

Intolerance was another unmistakable feature of this empire-serving, empire-building religion. Whether it was Luther's intolerance of the Jews and the Roman Catholics, or the Church's intolerance for science, or Christian rejection of the Enlightenment, Christianity fed the very worst in opposing the intellectual development of humankind. It commanded zealously in the name of the All-Powerful, All-Demanding, All-Knowing Invisible God to whom nothing was hidden. The only key was the life and teachings and texts that Christians alone held and believed should be held by everyone else.

Yet if nothing was too bad to do in the name of the Christian Father, the Son and the Holy Ghost, nothing was too good either. Christianity did indeed kow-tow to the European slavers who worked with the African slavers to provide the cheap labour for the New World. But Christianity was also the moral force that brought it to an end. Wilberforce and his friends have a place in history obscured by current understandable bruises and furies over slavery and ransom, but the fact that slavery was ended was due to the power of those carrying out the teachings of Christ.

Nor is it permissible to talk of Christianity without mention of a sect such as the Quakers, whose pacification and tolerance were a beacon difficult to see lit unless fuelled by the ethical commands of Christ. And individual lives, by the million, small unnoticed lives of kindness and goodness as well as ambitious philanthropic gestures, were again and again inspired by the wish to live up to the expectations set by the Christ of the Gospels and the Acts of the Apostles.

The works of art which owed Christianity everything from their existence and their execution to their force and persistence in the culture are literally countless. The cathedrals themselves, the stained glass of Chartres, the awesome simplicity of Durham Cathedral, the waves of stone from Notre Dame to the Sagrada Familia, these alone for some would vindicate the faith. But of course they are not alone; there are also the Passions and the Masses composed by musicians of genius, the story of Christ painted so often and so majestically. It is unnecessary to make a list. For 2,000 years, much of what has been, and remains, culture in various Western countries and civilizations and in the global Diaspora of the West can be related to the teachings and credo, the visible and invisible dynamism developed in bewildering variety from that one root planted by the Sea of Galilee.

It has had its opponents. Not only in Roman classical times and in the eighteenth-century Enlightenment, not only from Judaism and Islam and all the many faces of fanatical non-religious and pacific aetheistical positions, but also, again and again, from individuals who have dispersed and railed against its messages and its impact. Friedrick Nietzche for instance, famously announced that 'God is dead'. He detested its other-worldliness and found resentment at the heart of the religion: resentment of the world, of the body, of sex, of the vital intelligence, of everything strong and

Above: Quarrelling Cardinals

healthy. Even the Christians' love for their enemies, according to Nietzche, was only a tactic to ensure a quicker passage to eternal life.

But despite Voltaire, Nietzche, Darwin, Marx, Freud and thousands of dissenting voices gathering volume and power over the last 200 years in particular, Christianity still flourishes, though not in some of the countries it once did. But it is still a palpable force not least in the one remaining world empire – an empire as powerful as Constantine's Rome in the fourth century – in the United States of America. There the God of the New Testament and the God of Abraham still lives and the great Satan was seen until recently in Communism, itself inspired by another Jew, another rabbinical figure.

Nor is Christianity, even today when doubt is to be the new faith, bereft of intellectual defenders. An Oxford professor of philosophy, Lesjek Kolakowski, for instance, was recently described as one who 'belongs to the peaceful tradition of Christian thinkers who find in Christianity not a political or social programme or system of government but a way of life springing from two beliefs . . . the belief that Jesus the Redeemer appeared on earth in historic times in order to free us from evil from which we could not free ourselves, and the ability to remove hatred which follows from this belief'. Kolakowski himself has said, 'If God is dead, nothing remains but an indifferent void which engulfs and annihilates us'.

Above: The Sermon

At present Darwinians argue most persuasively against the Christian philosophers and teachers of the past and of the present, but the Christian agenda is still part of the lives we lead in this century. What part did Christianity play in the anti-Semitism that led to the Holocaust? Has Christianity helped to organize and enable the state, even the modern state, to become a machine for crushing individuals or has Christian faith fortified individuals against the juggernauts of state? Is wealth and its pursuit wholly inimical to a just society and where does the wealth of the Church fit in with the Sermon on the Mount? Will Darwin finally kill off the idea of the quest for a perfect society which we can see from Plato's *Republic* to Karl Marx's *Das Capital,* but most ferociously and relentlessly and often delightfully pursued in Christianity? And if science neither needs nor knows of a religious sense, where does the 'why' question, the spiritual need, the religious temperament, come from?

Christianity over this 2,000 years has magnetized history, thought and art; it has made coalitions out of contrary forces and yet bred and even cultivated centralism in itself. Its source and its power lie in resurrection even today. Witness the way it is absorbing the new discoveries of cosmology. It continues to strive to resurrect itself. It has never been afraid to preach and rely on the miraculous and its survival alone over 2,000 years must surely rank as some sort of miracle.

Melvyn Bragg, 1999

Above: Franciscan monks

Left: The masons of St Etienne, Bourges

11

Medieval Christendom

How was the preaching of the Christian message to the Gentiles being accomplished, a thousand years after the death of Jesus? Many times, sometimes within the Roman world, sometimes crossing its frontiers, the missionaries had left to fulfil Christ's command: 'Go forth therefore and make all nations my disciples; baptize everywhere in the name of the Father, the Son and the Holy Spirit, and teach them to observe all that I have commanded.' So long as the Roman Empire endured in the form that the human Christ had known it, the command could be kept by following models that went back to apostolic times. But as the ancient Roman Empire disintegrated, new patterns had to be found.

There was in the early medieval Western world a post-apostolic model for the propagation of the Gospel to the heathen; it was that set by Pope Gregory the Great (c.540–604), in the despatch of the Roman mission to the Anglo-Saxons. From the Anglo-Saxon mission field St Augustine of Canterbury sent (as later happened also with the missions of St Boniface in Germany and of the followers of St Methodios in Bulgaria), requests to Rome for law-making decisions about the problems they encountered. The missions were often not able to follow such tidy precedents: the realities of persuading unwilling pagans to give up their way of life were untidy, fragmentary, full of compromise, sometimes marked by the backsliding of the converts and by the martyrdom of the missionaries. But the principle of Roman supervision and control, though not observed in detail, remained intact.

No one speculated in that world about a moral need to distinguish between the preaching of the Gospel message and the imposition of cultural patterns. The biggest moral question occasionally discussed, was whether people should be baptized under the threat of force. But there was also a question, full of meaning for the integrity of cultures, whether the liturgy could be allowed in a language other than Latin. The need to preach in a vernacular the people could understand was not disputed. But the theological dangers of allowing a liturgy to be performed in a barbarian tongue were starkly obvious

Left: A map of the known Christian world at the turn of the first millennium. Jerusalem is at the centre.

to the legislators, and allowed by the popes only in the single instance of the Slav liturgy, probably translated by a Greek speaker from the Latin original used by Constantine and Methodios.

Conversions and Christendom

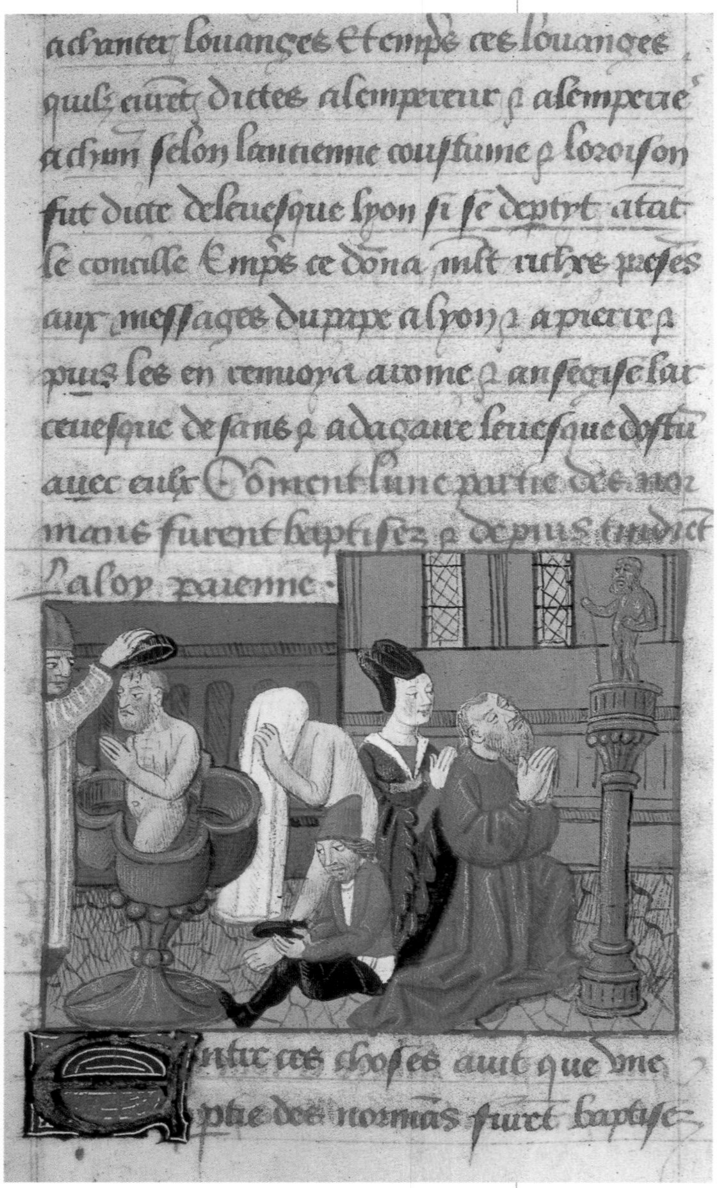

The statements attributed to Jesus about preaching the news of salvation to all nations and making them his disciples (Matt. 28: 19; Mark. 16: 15) may seem unambiguous, even though the proclamation of the Gospel was also related to his second coming and to the end of the age (Matt. 24). Equally definite, or so it seemed to St Augustine of Hippo, was St Paul's rhetorical question to the Romans about the salvation of the Jews (Rom. 10: 14–15): how could they be saved without someone to spread the good news to them, who had been sent with that purpose? But, as has recently been emphasized,[1] the missionary impulse was not something built into Christianity that operated, as it were, automatically. By the early Middle Ages, Christianity was becoming a closed society. St Boniface's reluctance to launch the conversion of the Slavs from an east Frankish base was not an isolated phenomenon. It was axiomatic with the majority of learned Christians that Christ did not die for every man, but for the elect alone. It was not for many centuries, and after much hesitation, that mainstream Christianity emerged from that position.

Nor was there anything easily predictable about the manner of effecting the conversion, either as to its duration or as to its practical effect. In the long term, the converted peoples were to become part of a cultural entity that was by the eleventh century called Christendom, and which for clarity scholarship calls 'Latin' Christendom. The common liturgical language was not in every single case Latin, and religious changes in modern and relatively modern times have meant that 'Latin' refers to the historical origins of national churches, and not to the religious practice of today, which may be Catholic or Protestant. Yet the matter can be politically relevant today; for example, states now wanting to join the European Union have on occasion referred to a cultural inheritance that includes their former membership of medieval Latin Christendom.

There was also to be a further question, first tested in the crusading states set up in the Holy Land in the late eleventh and early twelfth centuries, about the missionary principles to be followed in new colonies established among the infidels, which followed the established Roman Catholic pattern. In Palestine there was, in fact, a great deal of hesitation about trying to convert the Muslims, and in the end nothing resembling a missionary church was established there. In Spain there were many conversions from Islam, but it may be questioned whether the Iberian Christians ever established anything that could be called a missionary church among the conquered Muslims. The question of missionary doctrine and practice in colonies to be established after navigation of the Atlantic and other far-off seas remained in a far-distant future. In the eleventh and twelfth centuries it would have been impossible for people to know that both in Europe and in Palestine they could be setting precedents that would, centuries later, influence the ways in which Christ was brought to very distant, to them unimaginable, lands.

Above: The early fifteenth-century Chroniques des Bois *shows a Norman being baptized, apparently of his own free will. There was debate at the time about the advisability of baptism by force.*

Left: In the thirteenth century, Christianity began to regain its power base in Spain, with many conversions from Islam. The story of such a conversion is shown in pictures in the Cantigas de Santa Maria, *a musical narrative of the life of the Virgin made for Alfonso X of León and Castile, known as 'the Wise', who had made important conquests over the Moors of southern Spain.*

Below: Tripoli is captured by the Sultan of Egypt in 1288, from the Tractatum de Septem Vitiis. *The Muslim reconquest of Syria–Palestine marked the end of the Crusader state in the Holy Land.*

In the Western world, the tenth and early eleventh centuries had seen the conversion of the Scandinavian peoples, and of important branches of the Slavs, notably the Poles and the Bohemians. Outside the Slav world, the Hungarians accepted Latin Christianity under King Stephen (d.1038) at the turn of the tenth century. In quite a short time, the Christian Hungarian dynasty was absorbed into the mainstream of Western European politics by marriage alliances that associated it not only with the German royal house, but also with other Christian dynasties, notably with that of the Anglo-Saxons. The resistance of the pagan tribes on the eastern borders of the Holy Roman Empire to Christianization was stiffened by the avid colonialism of the German imperial dynasty. The Wends held out for a long time, and yet further east, the Lithuanians were to remain recalcitrant pagans for another two centuries and more.

To the south-west, the boundaries of Christendom were being extended by the gradual *reconquista* of many of the Islamic lands in Iberia, by the northern Iberian Christian princes. After the death of the last effective successor-ruler to the Iberian 'Umayyad caliphs, 'Abd al-Malik (1008), the Islamic lands in Spain tended to fragment in the hands of minor Muslim warlords, the so-called muluk al-tawa'if or kings of the factions. This enabled the northern Spanish rulers to press steadily southwards into Islamic territories until, after the fall of Toledo in 1085, there was a big military intervention from North Africa by the Almoravid holy-war dynasty of Morocco. This led to the defeat of King Alfonso VI of León-Castile in 1086, and to the re-imposition of a Muslim barrier against Christian reconquest that endured for at least a further twenty years.

Thus, by the time of the fall of Jerusalem to the First Crusade in 1099, the profile of a new Western Christendom could be seen, which in many respects survived for a further three centuries, and lived on in other ways to influence the Europe in which we live today. The religious colonialism that inspired the Crusader state in the Holy Land ended, it is true, with the Muslim reconquest of Syria–Palestine at the end of the thirteenth century, although a kind of Western political expansionism into the eastern Mediterranean persisted through the Middle Ages, and survived into modern times. The pattern of Christian reconquest in Spain led to a rather different solution to the problem of the cohabitation of Islam and Christianity, when the dominant faith became Christian instead of Islamic. For much of the rest of the Middle Ages, the Muslims in the reoccupied areas of the Iberian peninsula were allowed a sort of limited religious freedom, which tapered off towards the end of the period.

The religious framework that held together this whole ramshackle collection of Christian lands in Europe and the Near East in some sense, was the authority of the Roman bishopric, reinforced and reinvigorated by the efforts of the 'Reform' popes of the late eleventh and early twelfth centuries. It was an authority destined to grow in a spectacular manner. The papacy was to become an entirely different organization from the dignified, but in material terms very modest, bishopric that had protected and provided for the pilgrims who came to pray at the sacred Roman sanctuaries, and that had financed itself from modest contributions of 'Peter's Pence' from a few northern countries.

Papacy and Empire

At this period of the high Middle Ages the Christian countries of north-west Europe were on the edge of a great cultural, demographic and economic movement that was to transform their strength in the Mediterranean and western Atlantic lands, as well as in central continental Europe. At this critical moment of Western European development, the papacy was destined to play a key part not only in the religious but also in the political leadership of Western Christendom. Its role could in the latter respect perhaps be said to have been, if looked at over a long period, roughly comparable with that of the secretariat of the United Nations.

How did these things come about? The key lay in the persistent, obstinate assertion by the Roman bishops, over a period of many centuries, of claims to authority and jurisdiction over all the other churches. The critical political element was the integral link between the 'Roman Empire', which had been reinvented for Charlemagne in 800, and the Roman bishops who had the exclusive privilege of crowning the 'emperor'. That for a long time the 'Reform' popes of the high Middle Ages were hostile to the German emperors made no difference to the symbiotic relationship that existed between the two institutions.

But the Crusades represented a new, independent political venture on a European and extra-European scale by the papacy, in whose establishment the Empire had played no part. The principle behind the Crusades, of a papacy with supra-tribal, quasi-military powers, lost no time in influencing events with the Empire. That the lords of the Saxon marches, and the Hohenstaufen German kings behind them, should have turned to the popes in the mid-twelfth century for authority to launch a Crusade against the Wends on their borders, while at the same time a new Crusade against the Muslims was approved by the popes for the Castilian king in Spain, showed the emergence of an ideologically changed Europe.

The Holy Roman Empire, subject to German dynasties and ceremonially connected with the popes, was the other important link in the chain that tied 'Christendom' together. The territorial extent of the Empire, great as it was, was never vast enough to correspond even remotely with the lands of Christendom. The Empire was, however, especially important for the recognition it usually managed to obtain from the Slav lands in the east, as well as from some non-Slavs such as the Hungarians. Its advocates were not shy about vaunting the power of the Holy Roman Empire. The German courtier-bishop, Otto of Freising (?1111–58), wrote a *History of Two Cities* (i.e. the City of God and the Earthly City) that was in effect a world history brought down to his own times. As he was the uncle of the Holy Roman Emperor Frederick I, his comments on the politics of the time are especially valuable. He observed in the mid-twelfth century that the Roman Empire, in so far as it assumed the form of the Greek (i.e. Byzantine) Empire, was a mere shadow of former greatness. 'From Rome power passed to the Greeks, from the Greeks to the Franks, from the Franks to the

Below: Otto of Freising, the German bishop and historian, was a significant enough figure in his own time to be featured in a stained-glass window at the church at Heiligenkreuz (Holy Cross) in Lower Austria.

Lombards, from the Lombards back to the Germans (who can also be considered Franks).' In other words, in Otto's eyes the power of ancient Rome no longer had anything to do with Byzantine 'Rome', but with the Holy Roman Empire of the German house of Hohenstaufen.

In the West, the west Frankish kingdom was evolving into the kingdom of 'France', which owed no allegiance to the Holy Roman Empire, and which, after 1066, was linked through Normandy with the English State. The old Middle Kingdom of Burgundy and the lands north and south of it remained in an ambiguous position. The Iberian kingdoms and principates remained in a separate world of frontiersmen on the borders of Mediterranean and Atlantic Islam. The Scandinavian, Scottish and Irish kings and princes dwelt upon other, largely maritime frontiers. 'Europe' is to a modern European just recognizable in this Western Christian conglomerate.

Right: Fifth Italian Expedition of Emperor Frederick I (1174). A thorn in the side of the papacy, the powerful Hohenstaufen Emperor Frederick I (Barbarossa) dominated proceedings at the Papal Imperial Negotiations in Venice.

The Foundation of Cluny

The faith was the unifying factor, not only through the medium of the Roman Church as an organization, but also through other powerful Church movements that penetrated many kingdoms and regions. The reforming Benedictine abbey of Cluny, in Burgundy, founded early in the tenth century and supported by a Roman papacy that in other respects is supposed to have been at that time corrupt, was the most powerful monastic model of the high Middle Ages. The time of the greatest influence and renown of Cluny was in the second half of the eleventh century, when the great church was built, whose battered and reordered remains can still be seen and admired. Cluniac houses were to be found all over Europe, beginning with the big nucleus in all the lands watered by the Rhine from its source to the sea, but stretching east to Bavaria, west to Normandy and the Loire, south-west through Provence and across the Pyrenees to Navarre and Aragon, and south-east to northern and central Italy. Cluniac priories reached England rather later, but were eventually established from Lewes in the South to Pontefract in the North.

Cluny represented an aristocratic model of piety, it is true, but a noble one, which asserted silence, abstinence, and the dignity and beauty of liturgical worship, and particularly of liturgical music. The Clunaics were less tied to the support and pursuit of learning than earlier Benedictines, perhaps partly because the great social need for the basic texts had for the time been satisfied. A fine sculptured set of capitals that have survived from the choir of the great church of Cluny, show figures representing the eight keys of the plainchant octave.

In these Cluniac monasteries, the descendants of the great Carolingian foundations of the eighth and ninth centuries, medieval monasticism reached its most extravagant manifestation as at once a refuge from the world, and as the holy pattern put forth for the world to admire. Huge foundations, like Cluny itself, such as Fleury on the Loire, Gorze in Lorraine, Lorsch, St Gallen, Fulda further to the east, were endowed or re-endowed with enormous estates, built or rebuilt on a very big scale, existing as little self-contained, walled clerical towns with all the services a civilized community needed. In areas where all almost all other human habitations were built of wood, they were constructed in stone. The portals of some of these great churches were literally the gates of heaven, decorated on the outside with great sculptural allegories that told the faithful the stories of divine judgement, of prophecy, of salvation.

Above: The Sounds of Music. A twelfth-century capital from the choir at the abbey church of Cluny, one of eight, each showing a key of the plainchant octave.

The Cluniac movement was powerful and effective, but its social objectives were too narrow to continue to fill the needs of a rapidly changing Church. In the twelfth century the Reform Church found a new ideal in a great complex of new monastic houses spreading out – also, like Cluny, from an original base in Burgundy – from the monastery of Cîteaux, the monastic house of the great reforming abbot, St Bernard (1090–1153).

Right: The great tympanum over the west door of the cathedral of St Etienne at Bourges, built 1192–1275, carved in elaborate detail to show exactly what will happen at the Last Judgement. Many worshippers did not read and the graphic use of sculpture and stained-glass imagery helped to convey the Christian message.

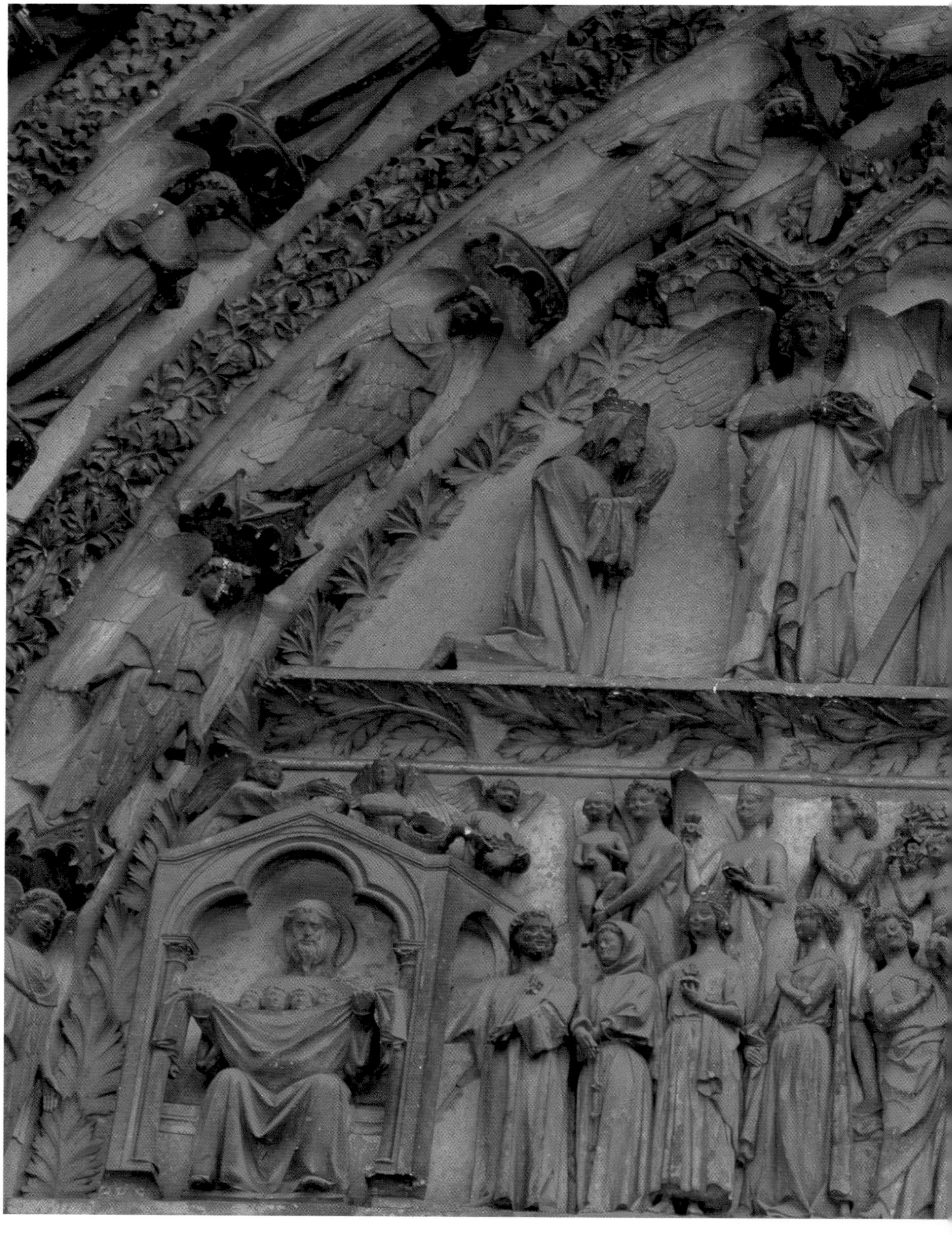

Right: St Bernard, co-founder of the Church militant in the form of the Templar Knights, preaches the Second Crusade before the King of France at Vézelay.

On the one hand St Bernard represented the intense activism of the Gregorian reform (so-called after Pope Gregory VII) and its political will to intervene in almost every phase of public life where it saw a moral principle at stake. From that point of view his life is almost a history of the Western European kingdoms of the first four decades of the twelfth century. His correspondence is an address book full of kings, princes, and popes. In the most political of all the Church activities of the time, the Crusade, St Bernard intervened twice in a most decisive way: first he collaborated in the foundation of the first major 'military' order of fighting monks, the Templars, and secondly he played a principal role in the recruitment and organization of the Second Crusade (1146–9), which he launched with a great sermon before the King Louis VII of France and his nobles, in the great church of Vézelay (Yonne), in eastern Burgundy. At this peak point of St Bernard's career, he had been asked by the French king himself to preach the Crusade, and he was so influential that he later managed to persuade the German King Conrad to support it alongside the French.

Above: St Bernard with his demon chained firmly at his side.
Below: The ruins of Rievaulx Abbey, Yorkshire, established in 1131 as the second Cistercian monastery in England.

Cistercian Reform

But from a different point of view St Bernard can be seen as the leader of a great mass movement of penance. He became a great figure in Europe, not from his political fame, but from the immense influence of the monastic reform that he initiated, called 'Cistercian', after the name of the abbey of Cîteaux. The new monasteries founded from Cîteaux swiftly found immense noble and royal support, so that, like the Cluniac houses of two centuries earlier, they grew up all over Europe. More than three hundred had been founded by the time of Bernard's death in 1153. In England their 'bare, ruined choirs' may be seen at Fountains and at Rievaulx in Yorkshire.

The Cistercian movement was based on the desire to praise God and to repent in poverty for sin, in a communal life whose austerity had nothing in common with the liturgical extravagance of the Cluniacs, and which, like the early hermit movements of Eastern Christianity, desired isolation from the world: the public were not admitted to the early Cistercian monasteries. Perhaps, no less than among the Cluniacs of long before, the core members of the Cistercians were penitent noblemen, although, like the Benedictines, the Cistercians did not restrict their recruitment to nobles. Cistercian churches austerely avoided decoration, in the same way as their worship eschewed elaborate music and ritual. Their monastic lives were not so strictly cloistered as those of the Cluniacs, in that they were expected to go outside the monastery into the fields, to work alongside the lay brothers, the conversi. There were economic reasons why this new system worked. Because land had become scarce, Cistercian houses were very often endowed with estates that were only marginally productive, and therefore labour-intensive.

St Bernard was the leader of a great movement of renunciation among the knightly class from which he came. It is not at all surprising that he sponsored the monastic order of Templar Knights, which he saw as another instrument of salvation for the secular knights whose bloodstained lives were otherwise irredeemably condemned by divine judgement. In this way they could continue to give battle, but 'The soldier of Christ kills safely [without peril to his soul]; he dies the more safely. He serves his own interests in dying, and Christ's interests in killing.' Translated into Arabic and given Islamic terminology, these sentiments would be perfectly understood today by the soldiers of Hizbullah.

One of St Bernard's Cistercian monks became pope in 1145 as Pope Eugenius III (pope 1145–53), and he issued the papal summons to the Crusade in the following year, after which St Bernard himself

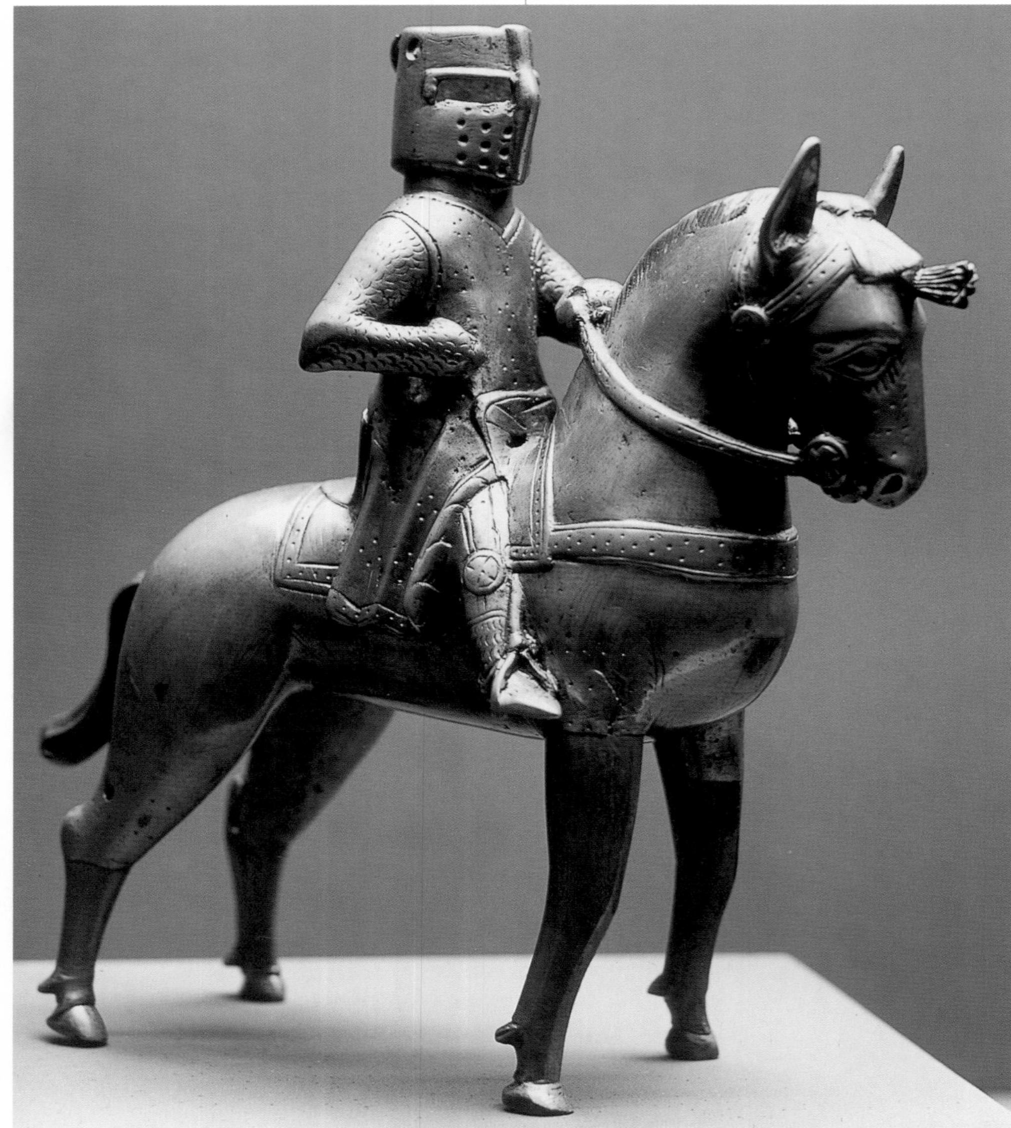

Above: A thirteenth-century French bronze sculpture of an armoured knight on horseback. Christian knights could claim salvation, and any killing they had done be forgiven, if they went to war in the name of Christ.

preached it at Vézelay. It was a time when the language and concepts of military feudalism had to some extent taken over the Church. To Bernard and his pupil Pope Eugenius, the infidel had stolen the 'patrimony of the crucified one'. As Bernard put it: 'The earth has been shaken: it trembles because the lord of Heaven has begun to lose his land – the land in which, for more than thirty years, he lived as a man among men.' The soldiers, the men of war, could fight in this cause without endangering their souls. The indulgence for sin that followed the taking of the cross to become a fighter for Christ, Bernard represented – ironically, it is true, when he addressed his audience at this point as 'merchants' – as being a splendid bargain, and a great opportunity.

Preaching ideally required good learning as well as godliness. By the sixth century the language of the Western Church had become Latin. Its message could survive without a knowledge of the Greek in which its creeds had originally been formulated, but by this time it was working and preaching in the midst of a babel of barbarian vernacular tongues. For a very long period, from the sixth century until the twelfth, there was no social system in Western Europe that trained fully literate cadres in the way they had been trained in the late Roman Empire. Able, articulate, learned churchmen existed, who very occasionally had some knowledge of Greek as well as of Latin, but their numbers were small. A competent standard of literacy in the Latin tongue could be acquired only in major monasteries, or in certain cathedral schools, or in certain nurseries of courtier-priests attached to royal courts.

The Scholar Class

When in the early twelfth century a growing number of clever young people sought training in rhetoric and philosophy in the schools of north-west France, and particularly in Paris, the consequences were to be important, firstly to the Church, but afterwards to secular society. A member of this intellectually and socially ambitious new class was the thrusting and innovative scholar, Peter Abelard (1079–1142). Having trained himself in logic and debate in the schools of Paris in the first years of the twelfth century, Abelard later extended his studies to theology, and began to teach a rigorous logical method that was applied to divine subjects as well as to philosophy. His book *Sic et non* began: 'Here begin sentences from the holy scriptures which seem opposed to each other...' Abelard's dialectic method did not

commend itself to St Bernard, nor, no doubt, did reports of his love affair with Héloïse, who ended as abbess of the nunnery of the community of the Paraclete that Abelard had set up in Champagne. A confrontation with St Bernard in 1140 ended badly for Abelard, who was condemned in Rome, and ended his life two years later as a monk in Cluny.

No such scholarly class as Abelard represented had existed in the Western world since the decay of the Roman Empire. Abelard was predominantly a logician, but as the twelfth century advanced, increasingly such people sought knowledge of Roman law, which was particularly important in the schools of northern Italy, and especially in Bologna. The revival of Roman law was to be very useful to government; immediately it was most useful to Church government. At the end of the Middle Ages, the revival of Roman law was to be one of the main engines behind the creation of the early modern state.

Twelfth-Century Renaissance

Knowledge of Greek began to creep back, although to a very limited extent that was, paradoxically, checked by the organization, in the early thirteenth century, of corporate teaching bodies which turned into 'universities'. The medieval universities developed no satisfactory way of dealing with Greek culture, either in its pagan form, or in its manifestation in the writings of the Greek 'fathers of the Church'. Many of the rediscovered Greek texts, especially those relating to science and philosophy, had been first translated into

Left: Diligent students study logic in a French school. From the twelfth century onwards, there was a growth in secular learning and universities were established all over Europe.

Below: The fourteenth-century statutes of the College of Hubant or the Blessed Virgin, Paris, graphically displayed by its students.

Above: The blighted lovers Abelard and Héloïse, illustrated in the fourteenth-century Le Roman de la Rose, *a French allegorical romance by Guillaume de Lorris and Jean de Meung, and the classic textual expression of the concept of courtly love.*

Arabic, and thence to Latin. The eastern Crusades, however, played little part in encouraging this sort of cultural linkage. Arabo-Greek texts usually reached the West either from importation through the semi-Arabized Norman kingdom of Sicily, or through the Christian kingdoms in Spain.

However, the gains of what has become known as the twelfth-century Renaissance were substantial, both in an intellectual way, and through the social gains of the creation of a new learned class. By the end of the eleventh century a new corpus of knowledge was available, which included quite a large part of the recovered culture of the late Latin Roman world, as well as additional knowledge and speculation that had come from the Arabs. It has been said that one of the great aims of the new intellectual movement was to achieve definitions and to specify boundaries and functions, and that one of the results of such a movement was to exclude whole categories of things and people from the privileged areas of society. This is arguable, although it can also be said that scholastic method enabled people to recognize the legitimacy of diversity. Whether increasingly excluded categories included those of women and homosexuals is a question much discussed, although still not answered.

The Second Crusade, summoned as a result of the Christian loss of the great Syrian fortress of Edessa in 1144, was one of the great medieval examples of international thinking in the politically (or rather, religiously) correct terms of the times. The great medieval rulers, most notably Louis VII of France and – after some hesitation – Emperor Conrad of Germany, embraced the project as mentioned above, and the armies started to march to the East in 1147. Not altogether surprisingly, the whole enterprise ran into political difficulties that rendered it a military failure. European military co-operation on the grand scale has never been easy, and in this case it suffered the more because the relief forces had not put too much effort into finding out what the Christian kingdom of Jerusalem actually wanted or needed. When the two Western sovereigns reached Palestine in 1148, their forces were not strong enough to launch the enterprise in northern Syria that the situation really required. Instead they launched an attack on Damascus, a city ruled by the one Muslim power that was reasonably well disposed towards the Christians. The affair reached a humiliating military conclusion, entirely useless to the Christian cause.

In the long history of the relations between Western and Eastern Christianity, the Second Crusade played a negative part. Its failure was somewhat implausibly blamed upon the Byzantine Empire by some westerners, and no less an authority than St Bernard is thought, towards the end of his life, to have recommended an attack on Byzantium as a preliminary to resuming the attack on Islam. Perhaps others felt as he did, but no action in this direction was to be taken until half a century after St Bernard's death.

The disastrous defeat of the Christian kingdom of Jerusalem at the Battle of Hattin in 1187 was immediately followed by the loss of Jerusalem to the great Muslim leader, Saladin. These traumatic events produced a sharp reaction in the West, which led to the summoning of a new crusading relief force.

The Third Crusade is often seen as the romantic Crusade *par excellence*, and it was certainly seen in this light by Sir Walter Scott when he wrote *Ivanhoe*. But in many respects it was the least sentimental of the earlier Crusades, and was conducted in a spirit of harsh political realism. King Philip Augustus of France and his vassal, King Richard of England, who accepted the challenge on behalf of the feudal West, were a great deal more able in both a political and a military sense, than had been the leaders of the Second Crusade. The Third Crusade began in Palestine in 1191, and the fall of Acre to the Christians in the same year was a severe blow to Saladin.

The victory of Acre was achieved by Christian leaders who no longer seriously thought of total victory in the East, and who, although they often used the language of passionate committment to holy war, recognized that the recapture of Jerusalem was probably unattainable. When they withdrew, it was under a system of truces with the Ayubid successors of which Saladin, was to serve more or less as a model for the Christian political presence in Palestine as long as it endured.

Above: An illustration of the Council of the Kings at Acre from The Council of Acre and the Siege of Damascus *by William of Tyre. The Siege of Acre was a pivotal event in the Second Crusade.*

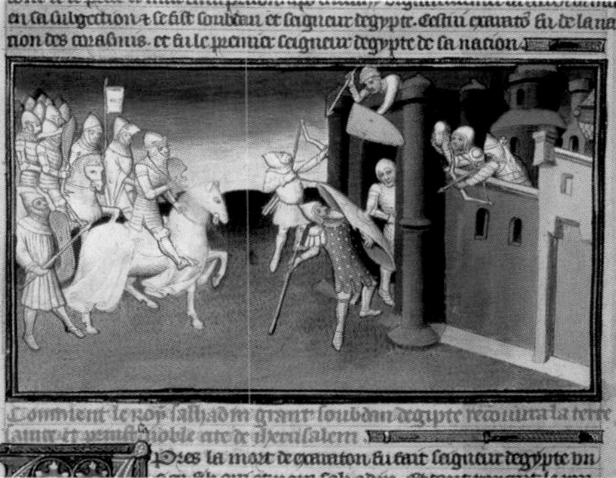

Above: The Saracen leader Saladin captures Jerusalem in 1187.

Left: King Richard I of England tilting at Saladin. From the Luttrell Psalter (prior to 1340).

In people's minds the Crusade dwelt on that boundary between power politics and fantasy that is one of the most treacherous and dangerous zones of human consciousness. Because the Jerusalem envisaged in Christian imagery was not a real city, but one whose bulwarks were strong with salvation, and whose streets were of shining gold, the humble details of Palestinian politics were – as they almost certainly still are – irrelevant to what was thought about the city. Nothing could eliminate Jerusalem from Christian imagination. The recapture of Jerusalem by the Christians was something that, three centuries later, Christopher Columbus thought might be accomplished by his voyages: in that kind of perspective, local truces made by Crusaders with Muslim emirs do not loom very large. Concretely, if the crusading state was to survive at all in Palestine, it had to do so through a system of diplomatic deals with the local Arab rulers, and that was the way in which the Crusaders managed to remain in an ever-shrinking Christian enclave, almost until the end of the thirteenth century. But this was the stuff of humdrum politics, not that of religious dreams.

I. R. Fletcher, *The Conversion of Europe: From Paganism to Christianity 371–1386 AD* (London, 1997), pp. 1-33

Right: A pilgrim contemplates an abandoned suit of armour on the road to Jerusalem. The dream of recapturing the city for eternal Christendom was never fulfilled.

Left: Jerusalem, from the Book of Hours *of Duke René of Anjou (1409–80). René claimed the thrones of both Naples and Jerusalem, although he occupied neither.*

SECVRI
TA

12

Popes, Cathedrals and Crusades

Behind the revival of learning and the building of the great cathedrals and castles in north-west Europe lay the economic and demographic revival that enabled medieval society to pay for them. The twelfth century had been the great age of forest clearance ('assarts' as the English called them), which added huge areas of arable land and pasture everywhere between lowland Scotland and eastern Germany, and that led, also, to the more intensive exploitation of the now-destroyed, but in its day immensely important, resource of the forest. On the back of increased agricultural production, population climbed. In northern and coastal Italy, northern France, England and Flanders, the towns expanded their economic and commercial activities, perhaps modestly in single instances, but collectively, an advance was made on a huge scale.

Everywhere kings, nobles and bishops supported the foundation of urban-style settlements, often at first small, in order to tax them to finance their own lifestyles and their warfare. The burgess, or burgher, or bourgeois, became an important economic and social factor. Great new centres of mercantile and monetary exchange, markets and 'fairs', came into existence in areas such as Champagne. The art of war attracted big investments in skilled warriors and their mounts, in better equipment, in improved fortifications. Crusading lords learned new techniques of fortification in Syria, and returned to build great castles in Normandy, England and elsewhere that set entirely new

Above: As administration costs rose, more taxes were levied.

Left: Detail from the fresco entitled Allegory of Good Government *by Ambrogio Lorenzetti (Palazzo Pubblico, Siena), illustrating a well-run and thriving town, protected by stout walls and served by neatly kept fields and farms. At this time, towns began to expand their economic and commercial activities.*

Above: A battle scene on a town wall in Syria. Many of the taxes raised paid for armaments and military techniques copied from the Syrian example.

standards of siege warfare. The castles constructed by Henry II (1139–89) and Richard I of England, particularly, in the valleys of the Loire and the Seine, were vast, expensive war machines of a kind never seen before in Europe. The seas were ploughed by new mercantile routes, and carried new bulk trades such as those in dried fish and wine; inland, new trading routes across Germany and the Alps opened great markets for salt, for textiles, for weapons.

In northern Italy especially, the urban settlements acquired their own style of government and an independence that was at first circumscribed. However, by the late twelfth century the 'communes' of northern and central Italy had outgrown a lot of the irksome controls and taxes imposed on them by bishops and German emperors, and organized themselves into groups such as the 'Lombard League', which possessed real military and political clout. The maritime Italian cities, especially Genoa, Pisa and Venice, profited from the general revival of trade, and from specific privileges in Eastern commerce that their stake in the crusading kingdom in Palestine gave them, to gain European political importance. Small colonial trading counters of this kind were the model for much of the later penetration of the Italian merchants into the eastern Mediterranean.

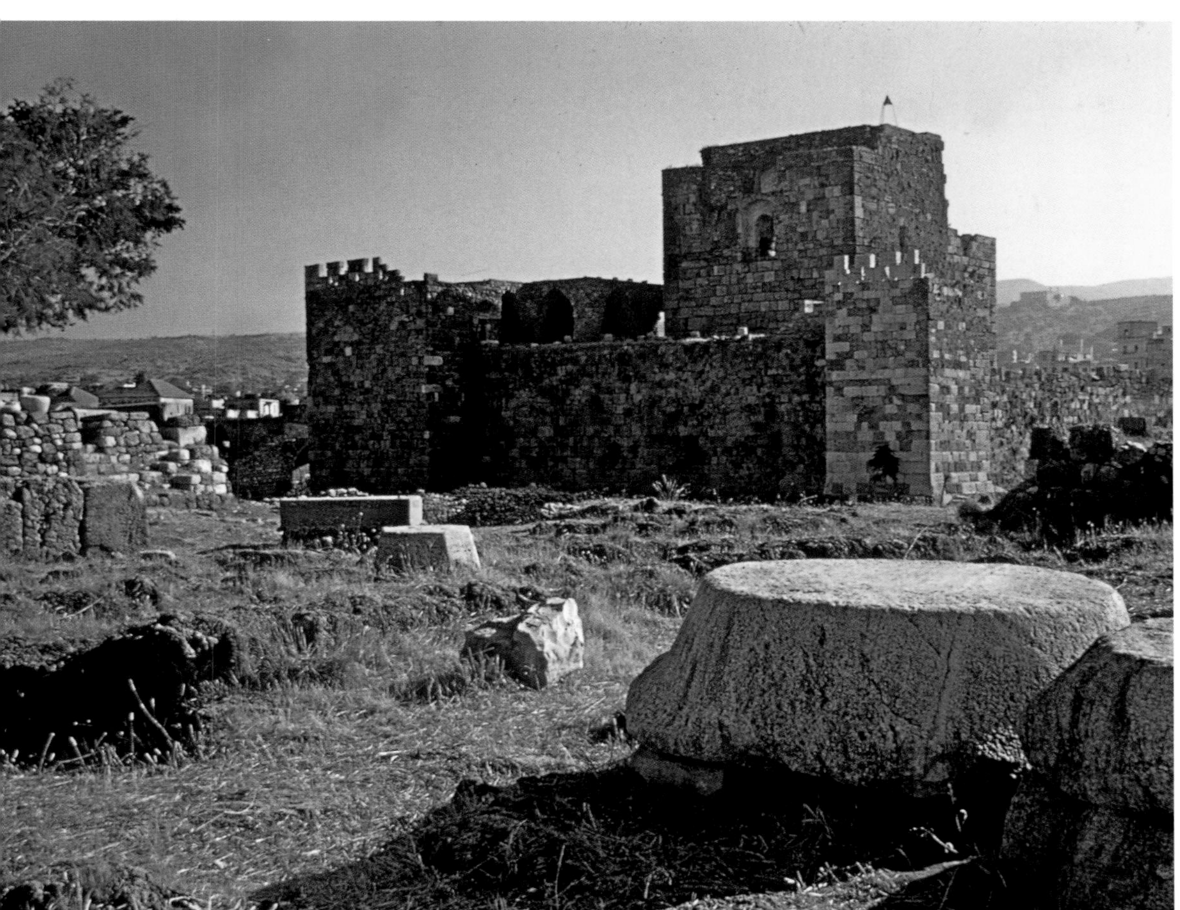

Left: The remains of a Crusader castle at Byblos, in the Lebanon. Such castles were considered state-of-the-art fortifications and inspired castle design in England, for example.

Below: Henry II built many chateaux in France, particularly along the Loire. This is the castle at Saumur, illustrating the month of September in the Très Riches Heures of the Duc de Berry.

In this great economic and cultural movement the Church played a leading part, because of its existing wealth and power, and control of scarce investment resources, because of its enormous advantages in disposing of very scarce trained personnel, and perhaps most of all because it controlled most of the main channels of cultural advance.

The Great Churches

However, the clergy could not exclude the laity from profiting from social developments that looked clerical, but were not always entirely so in their results. Huge social investments were made in great churches and monasteries, whose functions were not only to proclaim and teach the faith, but also to propagate the images of the power and religious zeal of the noble families, and even more of the new monarchies. Through church coronations and crown-wearing ceremonies, in which the kings were in effect worshipped by their subjects, the Church legitimized and honoured the monarchs who were in many respects its rivals. In England for example, the great cathedrals particularly linked with the crown were those at Westminster, Winchester and Gloucester, all places where William the

Below: The interior of Durham Cathedral, the masterpiece of Romanesque architecture that symbolized the Norman power in England in the twelfth and thirteenth centuries.

Conqueror had worn his crown on the great feasts. The huge cathedrals of Durham and York had also been symbolic of Norman power, in the earlier years of the Norman conquest, and they remained symbolic of royal power in the north at least until the time of Queen Elizabeth I.

The clergy, who were directly responsible for commissioning and financing the great churches, built them to serve the demands of the holy liturgy, and to provide an architectural setting for it which responded to the very practical requirements of the holy ceremonies and their adjuncts (such as saints' shrines), and also in its own language of stone, offered a worthy praise to God. The programmes of church decoration, including those of the new art of the stained-glass windows, were also huge manifestations of the elaborate symbolism that underlaid all sacramental Catholicism: this had aspects that were not only directly symbolic, such as the great visions of heaven and hell in the sculpture of the cathedral portals, but also mathematical, produced by a sort of science of holy numbers. The revival of learning and the changes in theological emphasis in the twelfth century had direct results on the decorative programmes, so that the great visions of Christ the Judge that inspired the earlier cathedrals were later changed to envisage a Christ who was the object of tender adoration by his human mother.

The Power of Rome

At the heart of the clerical transformations of the twelfth and thirteenth centuries lay the Roman bishopric, the papacy. The whole thrust of the Gregorian Reform movement, of the struggle against simony, of the foundation of new monastic orders and their authorization, of the astonishing innovation of the Crusade and the Christian settlement in the Holy Land, came from Rome. The Roman Court, which before 1046 had been run by a little-known group of Roman clerks, had by the late twelfth century become an elite European institution, which drew for its personnel on all the main feudal kingdoms of Europe, but especially upon the Holy Roman Empire, upon the French monarchy, and occasionally upon England.

The inevitable result of giving place in a court to any kin group, whether that court was lay or clerical, was that other members of the kinship and the region from which it came followed them to court preferment. When the Englishman, Robert Pullen, a former Oxford lecturer on theology, was made Papal Chancellor in 1144 he used his influence to prefer several Englishmen to office in the papal court. One, Nicholas Breakspear, became pope ten years later as Hadrian IV (pope 1154–9), the only English pope ever to be chosen. As pope, he organized a further development of the papal state as a feudal organization with the military power that it needed to protect the

Left: The stunning rose window in the north transept of Chartres Cathedral. The Virgin and Child are in the centre encircled by figures from the Old Testament. The decoration of churches was at once a way to praise God and an educational device for the illiterate. Stained-glass production was at the time the cutting edge of technology.

pilgrim roads to Rome; to do this he used techniques he had learned in the centralized feudal society of contemporary England. He also had to cope with Arnold of Brescia (c. 1100–55), an anti-clerical preacher who had been welcomed by the Romans in order to give some ideological colour to their attempt to assert independence from their bishop, the pope, on the north Italian 'communal' model. Hadrian, with a brusqueness of which Henry II of England must have been proud, had Arnold executed. Pope Hadrian also obliged Henry by recognizing his lordship of Ireland.

The cardinals in Rome, were in principle the priests of the main Roman churches and the heads of the various diaconates that had carried out charitable functions in Rome. Together with the bishops of a few churches located just outside Rome, they became the chief figures of a new papal civil service, and the privileged principals of a new clerical aristocracy, which elected the bishop of Rome, the pope.

The papacy was far bigger than any of its servants. Its position rested above all on scripture, and the twelfth and thirteenth centuries were the golden age of scriptural interpretation in an allegorical sense, in which the holy writings could be used as a topical basis for conferring authority on certain privileged clergy in modern situations. The power conferred upon Peter by Jesus to bind and to loose both on earth and in heaven (Matt. 16: 19–20) was the basic text, that may today be seen girding the interior of the great dome of St Peter's in Rome. But scripture as a whole was deemed to stand behind the bishops who succeeded Peter at Rome. Pope Innocent I (401–17) had addressed a letter to the bishop of Rouen, according to which any major church lawsuit ought to be referred for decision to the Roman bishop. Pope Innocent alleged as his reason that in the Bible Moses was advised by God to set up judge over the people (Exodus 18:22), but to reserve great matters for himself. In the words of a great and trenchant scholar:

Above: A posthumous engraving of Hadrian IV, the only Englishman (so far) to become pope.

Right: The royal seal of Henry II – a Norman king in full Norman armour.

'The standpoint marked the beginning of the Bible as a pièce justicative *of papal governmental pronouncements. In crucial matters, papal principles were not to rest on tradition, history, synodal statutes or other man-made organs. Among all historically evolved governments this was a unique phenomenon. Reality was to be subject to the ideology enshrined in the law, and in its basic ingredients this ideology was the sum-total of the Christian faith... For the internal substance of the papal law was said to be biblically inspired and derived. This is the same as saying that the papacy interpreted and applied the divine law of the Bible to the exigencies of the government of the Christian body itself.'*

Walter Ullman did not write this in order to support a 'Catholic' sectarian view of papal power. On the contrary, he thought that the papal monarchy in the sense of these words had ceased to exist by the end of the Middle Ages, and the verdict was Ullman's historical judgement on medieval Christendom.

Canon Law

If the claims of the Roman See were so all-embracing, to be fully effective they had to be articulated in a rational and systematic way. This was part of the meaning of the renaissance of legal studies in the twelfth century. A scholar, or perhaps more than one legal scholar, whose name has come down to us as Gratian, produced, probably in Bologna in the early 1140s, a work called the *Concord of Discordant Canons,* or the reconciliation of conflicts between Church laws. Its logical method was in many ways similar to that of Abelard's *Sic et Non* of the preceding period, which had drawn the thunders of St Bernard upon its author. However, Gratian's work was not to have the effect of disintegrating faith in Church law, but, on the contrary, of enhancing the juristic supremacy of the Roman See, of which St Bernard so much approved.

Gratian's work was to become the foundation of later medieval canon law, which amounted to a system for running the whole huge structure of the Western Church on an increasingly centralized basis, based on Roman law principles, and supervised by courts that were either located in Rome, or set up under papal mandate. Not all canonists in the Middle Ages fully accepted the maximum claims that were made for papal power, but enough support for the high view of papal supremacy existed to make it very important in Western legal culture. These tendencies had already existed before Gratian, and St Bernard wrote a work, entitled *De Consideratione,* that tried to advise his protégé, who had become pope as Pope Eugenius III, on how to preserve spiritual values when the papal institution over which he presided was effectively an overworked law court, almost continuously in session. Far from declining, and so giving the popes more room to consider spiritual matters, as Bernard had hoped, the work of the Roman bishopric as the highest Christian court overwhelmingly increased. All clerical Europe turned to Rome to ask its courts to do justice, so making the papacy into a new and different institution.

Right: Pope Innocent III, who came to office as a young man, shown in papal regalia on a fresco in the monastery of St Benedict in Subiaco (the 'Sacro Speco').

A Young Pope

Under these changing circumstances a young nobleman from the Roman countryside was elected pope in 1198 as Pope Innocent III. He was less than thirty years old when he became pope. He was already a cardinal, and the author of a treatise, *On the Misery of the Human Condition*, a subject that failed to announce that his pontificate was going to be marked by ruthless political activism. He had been accounted an 'Abraham of theology', and was also a distinguished jurist. His tenure of the Roman See (1198–1216), occurred at a critical moment in European history, and his ability and decisiveness were to prove critical in moulding the later medieval papacy.

For the forty years preceding the pontificate of Innocent III, central Italy, and the papacy with it, had been dominated by the aggressive Swabian-German dynasty of Hohenstaufen. The Italian lands of the popes had been treated as part of the Holy Roman Empire, and the popes had found it very difficult to escape Hohenstaufen political influence. But in 1197 the premature death of the Hohenstaufen Emperor Henry VI, who had been a powerful German ruler, and in Italy had ruled as far south as Sicily, gave Innocent the political opportunities he needed to free the papacy from imperial tutelage for ever. The old school of nationalist German historians judged the early death of Henry VI and its subsequent political exploitation by Innocent III to have been the most terrible disaster of medieval German history, whose consequences blocked the creation of a German national state in roughly the same period as the national states of France, England, or Spain were being formed.

Below: The imperial seal of Otto IV, the unsuccessful Saxon claimant to the Holy Roman crown.

The Struggle for Empire

Innocent III claimed to be the feudal lord and protector in the southern Italian kingdom of Sicily, of Henry VI's son, the infant Frederick II, and he claimed also to be a kind of supreme judge and arbitrator, when a disputed succession to the German kingdom and the Holy Roman Empire occurred after Henry's death. The contrasting claimants to the Empire were Philip of Swabia, the Hohenstaufen, brother of the dead emperor, and Otto IV of Saxony (c.1174–1218), son of the great ruler of the eastern German marches, Henry the Lion. There was no agreed protocol for election to the Empire, which did not fall to the successor by simple right of birth. It was widely felt that the election belonged to a 'College' of German electoral princes. The rights to the Empire of the infant papal ward, Frederick II, were also canvassed.

The uncertain situation of the Empire enabled Innocent III to seek papal political advantage. By subtle manoeuvre he represented the quarrel as one that had been referred to his court for decision. In 1200 he issued a papal 'Deliberation' that came down on the side of the Saxon Otto, and against the Hohenstaufen princes who had in the past proved unfavourable to the Holy See. Innocent did not make crude claims of supremacy over temporal rulers, but he claimed powers to intervene in their affairs in cases that involved moral or religious lapses, or when they had actually appealed to his court for decision.

The long and complex story of Innocent III's involvement in the struggle for the Empire once or twice seemed about to end in misfortune for the papacy, especially when, after Innocent's break with Otto IV, Otto's armies seemed set in 1211 to control both the kingdom of Sicily and the papal state. Innocent III riposted by supporting young Frederick II's claims to the Empire, and, after Otto IV and his English allies had been decisively defeated by France at the Battle of Bouvines in 1214, the papal gambit met with success. Innocent had played for high stakes, and won.

The Betrayal of the Eastern Church?

A not dissimilar story of risky but succesful political opportunism on the part of Innocent III was played out in the matter of the Crusade, the organization of which he was in theory responsible for. It was during the Fourth Crusade that the differences between the ideals and the reality of the Crusade came to tragic prominence. The stumbling block was the hiring of sea transport to take the armies to fight the Muslims. Under papal leadership and guidance crusading armies had been assembled in Western Europe in 1202 to fight in the East, most probably in Egypt, although Palestine was still a possibility. But the only possible carriers for the crusading armies were the fleets of the maritime republic of Venice, and money to hire their ships was not available. The only way to buy Venetian compliance was to accept their required change to the proposed route of the Crusaders, which was diverted, first to expel the Hungarians from Zara on the eastern coast of the Adriatic Sea, in pursuit of Venetian political aims, and then to sail to Constantinople. Neither had ever figured in the original programme of the Crusaders.

In Constantinople in 1204 both the Venetians and the crusading leaders had their own agenda to execute. Internal conflicts of Byzantine politics enabled the crusading force, with Venetian encouragement, to chase away the legitimate Eastern Emperor, Alexius III, and to establish its own candidate, the Emperor's nephew (also called Alexius). The Western puppet ruler, the young Alexius IV, was subsequently driven from the throne by a revolt and murdered, but the crusading armies refused to accept the ruler, the even shorter-lived Alexius V, who replaced him. In pursuance of supposedly legitimate claims, the Crusaders attacked and stormed Constantinople.

Below left: The sign of the Venetian Boat Builders' Guild. Venice controlled a seller's market supplying ships to ferry crusading armies to their destination.

Below: Frederick II on the throne of the Holy Roman Empire, which he gained with the support of Pope Innocent III.

Above: Crusading continued after Innocent III's time but was not much more successful. The knights of the Seventh Crusade (1248–54), led by Louis IX of France, took Damietta in Egypt but were captured by Turks and held to very expensive ransom.

After eight hundred years of sporadic barbarian attacks on East Rome, and as many years of bickering and quarrels between Eastern and Western Churches, the eventual decision had come as a result of a sordid bargain about ship-chartering. The sack of what was still incomparably the richest and most civilized city in the Christian world took three loot-crammed days. Not only was treasure and plunder of every conceivable sort stuffed into so-called crusading hands, but also the greatest collection of Christian relics in the world was seized with equal cupidity, for presentation or sale to the Western Church.

The absent and theoretical master of the Fourth Crusade was Pope Innocent III, who had formally forbidden an attack on Constantinople, although his earlier involvement with the Byzantine prince, Alexius, gave colour to some of the manoeuvres of the Crusaders. In his dealings with the Eastern Church he showed an inflexible and insensitive front. He gave only dusty, autocratic, legalistic answers to the spiritual problems that had accumulated between the two Churches over a period of many centuries. To the equally long history of political problems, Innocent offered the answer of armed force.

When Constantinople fell, the pope accepted the *fait accompli*, and approved the 'Latin Empire' that was set up under Baldwin of Flanders (1171–1206), albeit after a division of the spoils, made before the attack on the city, which left a sizeable slice to the Venetians. In the event, the Western adventurers managed to establish a durable Latin occupation of large parts of Greece, notably the Morea, Achaea, Epirus, Athens, and Negroponte that the Venetians had seized. But they lacked the political and military ability to hold on to anything closely resembling the former Empire of Constantinople. Constantinople became the centre of an Eastern Latin 'Empire'. But the Frankish hold on the once-great city was weak, and it is surprising that Frankish rulers held on to Constantinople as late as 1261, when the Greek Empire of Nicaea finally expelled them. Orthodox emperors once more ruled in Constantinople from 1261 until the Ottoman Turks closed the whole chapter by their capture of the city for Islam in 1453.

When he tried to sum up the new situation that had emerged after the fall of Constantinople in 1204, Innocent III wrote that the Greek Church had sailed in a ship that had caught nothing, but that the Roman Church had caught a great shoal of fish [Luke 5:5]. The Greeks had rashly dared to separate themselves from the unity of the universal Church, but now they had returned to the obedience of the Apostolic See like a daughter to a mother – or so Innocent thought. It was a strange way of referring to the sack of a great city and the attempted conquest of an Empire; it looked more like rape than like motherly love. It was an example of St Augustine's principle of 'compel them to come in', applied to a large part of the ancient Church of the East. In this way Innocent III purported to allow a feat of arms by self-interested merchants and soldiers to decide the issue of Christian unity.

Centralization and Dissent

During Innocent III's lifetime most of the big issues that were to preoccupy the Western Church for the following two or three centuries came to light, and so did many of the ways in which orthodox Catholicism was to react to them. It was a measure of the speed at which the organization of the Church had been centralized under Roman leadership, that Innocent himself became aware of the problems, and decided, in many cases, the policies by which he hoped the Church could deal with them. The degree of effective central Church organization at that time should not be exaggerated: poor communications, and the obstinate independence of medieval churches and churchmen, who were supported by a great body of legal custom and by the stout regionalism of their lay constituents, meant that papal bureaucracy and jurisdiction remained, very often, only a thin covering imposed over a chaotic and diverse reality.

When we say that one of the great problems of the Church at the turn of the twelfth century was that of dissent, we must beware of attributing to medieval society a sort of monolithic ideological unity that actually belongs to authoritarian industrial cultures, and not to pre-industrial agricultural ones. It is true that heretics were seen in the Middle Ages by ordinary Christians as demonic adversaries who ought to be savagely treated. For example, Henry II of England, who deferred to no one as an advocate of fierce central power, enacted that wandering heretics ought to be 'presented' by local juries and punished. Yet on the other hand, a lot of freedom of expression

Above: Heretics got short shrift and were lucky if mere expulsion was their lot. Here Albigensians (southern variants of the Cathars) are driven naked from Cerlesonne.

Below: Thomas Aquinas, the great Dominican theologian and philosopher. In his youth he had been known as 'the Dumb Ox' but later his intellect was to shape medieval Europe.

was available to medieval scholars and clerks, both as to their opinions and to their actions. Abelard's chequered career speaks both for the freedom that such clerks could have, and for the hazards they ran from official repression. The biggest ideological dangers, however, were deemed to be those presented by wandering strangers who proselytized for false religions.

Cathars and Dominicans

There were perhaps some historic links between medieval Catharism – the word came from the Greek word meaning 'pure' – and the Manichaeism of the late Roman Empire, but the Cathar movement of religious dissent that came to the surface in early twelfth-century France and Germany was related to religious currents in the contemporary Balkans. In it there was an underlying religious dualism that saw the universe as disputed by two opposed principles of good and evil. Like some of the earlier Gnostics, the Cathars thought that full religious enlightenment was granted to a superior class of 'perfect' believers, who were sexually chaste vegetarians in their way of life, and that a minor degree of enlightenment and a less severe regime could be allowed to the more numerous 'hearers' of the religion. For both 'perfects' and 'hearers' the supreme rite of religion was the 'consolamentum', a form of final initiation that the perfect received on being admitted to their order, and that the hearers received only on their deathbeds. The Cathars, because of their dualism, denied the sacramentalism of orthodox Catholicism, and rejected Catholic principles of Church order. They nevertheless retained a class of 'bishops', leaders who were recruited from their perfect members. They denounced the Christian holy war, and some of them rejected the idea of capital punishment.

Preaching campaigns had been conducted in the south of France, where the Cathars were especially strong, by earlier church leaders, including St Bernard, but Innocent III with typical militaristic zeal resolved on more forceful methods of persuasion. After the murder of a papal legate sent to the area, in 1209 Innocent adapted the precedent of the crusading armies sent to the East to fight for the faith, and had a Crusade preached against the Cathar heretics of Languedoc. It was a fateful decision, because it modified the whole concept of the Crusade, and became the model for many subsequent Crusades that in the later Middle Ages were to be preached against Christian dissidents, some because they were deemed heretics, others because they had offered political opposition to papal policies. The Cathar Crusade of 1209 resulted in the massacre of the population of Béziers, and the expulsion of whole populations of other areas of Languedoc from their homes, including that of the city of Carcassone.

Fighting the Cathar heresy also led to a further innovation, that of the setting up of a new order of travelling preachers, in a religious organization that had secured papal approval. Initially the preaching friars entrusted with these duties were the followers of a Spanish canon called Dominic of Caleruega (c.1170–1221), who initiated a policy of giving his friars a thorough theological training in the schools of Paris and Bologna. To these 'Dominicans' was committed the double duty of preaching the orthodox faith in areas where heresy was rife, and of acting as a religious police force to seek out and punish heresy, sometimes invoking the help of the lay power to impose the death penalty (by burning) upon the most serious offenders. Employing friars of this kind to preach without asking the permission of local bishops to do so was in itself an important act of papal power, which derogated from the authority of the bishops, and emphasized the central element in papal church government.

The policing function of the early friars led to new legal procedures being adopted that were much less favourable to the accused than earlier ones, and that were also the legal precursors for the Inquisition of heresy suspects in forms that lasted into the early modern period. Although their duties were in one way strongly repressive, and drew down on them the appellation of the 'hounds of God', the intellectual integrity of the Dominicans was established early. They acquired a reputation for the disinterested pursuit of intellectual truth; the greatest systematic theologian of the Middle Ages, St Thomas Aquinas (1225–74), was a Dominican.

The friar was a new phenomenon in the life of the Church, in the manner in which he appeared in the early thirteenth century. In another aspect friars were as old as the Church itself, and their wanderings recalled the way in which St Paul and his companions had wandered in Asia Minor and elsewhere to preach and encourage the faith. Dominic had addressed himself to what were comparatively specific problems of the Church of his time, notably the lack of preachers who were properly instructed and trained, and were free of the constraints of either the parish or the older monastic systems.

The Franciscan Way

In central Italy a very different kind of inspired figure appeared who is hard to put into any definite Church category save that of the ascetic hermit holy man, but whose huge imaginative and vital force were to have a profound effect. Francis of Assisi (1181–1226) was a layman, an early thirteenth-century contemporary of Dominic, who underwent a drastic conversion experience that made him become an immensely attractive lay preacher, the organizer of vast campfire missions. His entirely unconventional formulation of his religious experiences, and the way in which he supposed that the words of the Gospels could be followed in a spirit of literal obedience, could easily have led to his indictment and punishment as a heretic.

But the submission of Francis to Church authority, and the extraordinary tolerance and sympathy for his movement displayed by Pope Innocent III, led things in a quite different direction. Francis was a rich merchant's son, and from this aspect he represented a new 'bourgeois' variation upon the ancient theme of the penitent Christian nobleman. The immediacy of his vision, and the way in which it included all natural creation, from the sun to the birds, has made an immense impression from that day to this, especially, in modern times, because his wanderings under the wide skies of Umbria were so memorably recorded by painters working in Umbria, from the time of Giotto onwards.

Within a few years of the death of Innocent III the 'Franciscan' movement had been officially approved by the pope as a new religious order of wandering preachers, living under a vow of obedience and poverty, and under a 'Rule' that still managed to contain some of the poetic and direct moral involvement of its author and founder. The Franciscans were to prove in many

Below: St Dominic shown presiding over the burning of heretics in a painting made by Justus van Gent in the fifteenth century. The Dominicans were often given the right to detain heretics.

Above: A rendering of a dream experienced by Innocent III: Francis of Assisi is shown literally holding up the Lateran Church. The Lateran Council tightened up papal laws.

respects to be a new way in which a Church that, although it became every year more authoritarian and centralized, still managed somehow to reach and appeal to the Christian masses, and to show some concern for the Christian poor.

Lateran Law

In November 1215, Innocent III presided over the Fourth Lateran Council held at the palace of that name in Rome. It was a manifestation of the strength of medieval Latin Christendom. The main bishops of the Eastern churches did not attend, and the Council may not be called 'oecumenical', but bishops came from Eastern and Central Europe, from Bohemia, Hungary, Poland, Livonia and further east. There was diplomatic representation from all the main feudal states of the West and of the crusading East. The Council was attended by more than four hundred bishops and some eight hundred monastic abbots and provosts, and it legislated for the life of the Church on an appropriately grand scale, as well as calling for a new Crusade in the East.

Summing up the work and vision of the great pope, the new Church laws passed by the Lateran Council aimed, in the same spirit as the Reform popes of the previous two centuries, at correcting the lives of the clergy by appropriate disciplinary machinery applied by the bishops. It aimed at extirpating heresy by inquisitorial methods and at tightening up the laws that forbade the clergy to be involved in bloodshed – a rigour that went ill with inquisitorial and crusading policies which at the same time were virtually militarizing the Church.

Above all, the Lateran decrees increased the pastoral responsibilities of the lower clergy and to some extent placed them under indirect central control. For the first time in the history of the medieval Church, every adult in the entire Latin communion was to be obliged to confess his or her sins once a year, to do appropriate penance, and to receive the Eucharistic sacrament at the Easter feast. The enforcement of this canon entailed an enormous educational and disciplinary effort on the part of the clergy, who had never before been set specific pastoral aims in this manner. Tariffs of

Right: A Lateran decree meant that every adult had to confess his or her sins once a year and atone for them. This illustration of Confession is from a more secular source, John Gower's fourteenth-century poem, Confessio Amantis *(The Lover's Confession.)*

penances had often been imposed by local synods in the past, but this enactment conferred an entirely new importance upon private confession, and set a pastoral agenda that was only to be fully implemented in the Catholic Church of the so-called Counter-Reformation of early modern times.

The achievement of Innocent III cannot be summed up in some abstract formula of the attainment of papal centralization, although that was certainly one of his aims. He possessed an extraordinary consciousness of both the political and the social role of the Church, and of its historical and geographical dimension. He may be said, in some ways for the better, in others for the worse, to have defined medieval Christendom, and to have given it its mission.

1 W. Ullman, *A Short History of the Papacy in the Middle Ages* (London, 1972), pp. 17-18

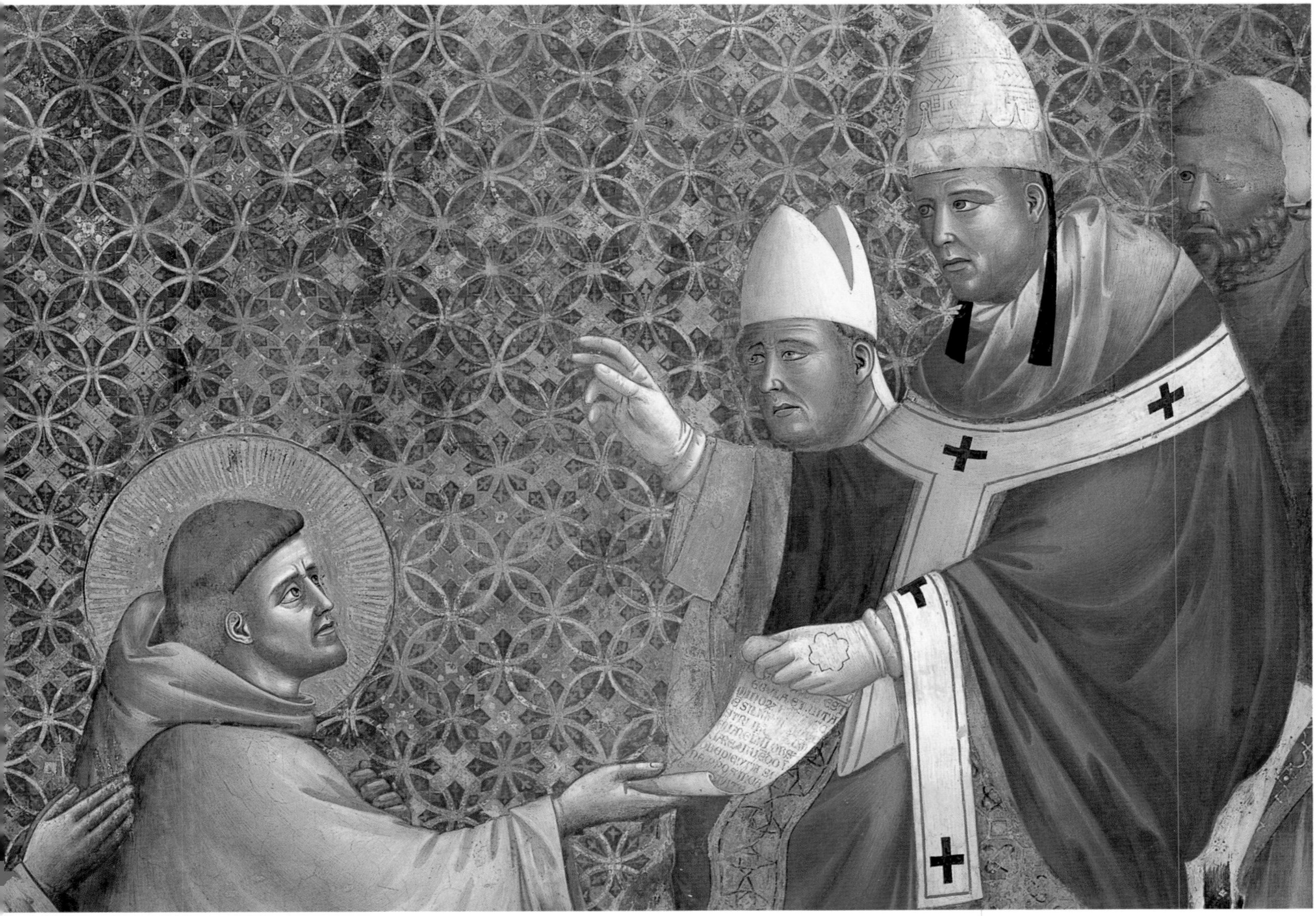

Below: Francis of Assisi's new, more humane Order was quickly recognized by Pope Innocent III and ratified his successor.

13

Inquisition, Plague and Schism

Above: Geoffrey Chaucer, author of The Canterbury Tales *and chronicler of the bawdier aspects of medieval life.*

Pope Innocent III had made the 'spiritual' power triumph over the material power; in medieval terms he had used the powers both of the spiritual and material swords that Christ had given to Peter. He had brought the moral supervision of the Church home to millions of Christian men and women. In the centuries that followed Innocent III, the Easter feast, with its Good Friday re-enactment of divine sacrifice and restitution, was made into a social fact, described in our own times as part of a 'social miracle', through which, whatever the shortcomings of individuals, salvation was accepted as a social goal.[1] Usurers and drivers of dishonest and oppressive bargains felt obliged, in huge numbers, to make restitution at their deaths for transactions whose morality they doubted. Holy men were appealed to by communities in dispute, and the feuds that tore medieval society to pieces were often settled – although usually only for a time – by such men as Francis of Assisi and his many successors.

Medieval society can easily be sentimentalized. Its personal and communal violence can still be experienced by anyone who attentively opens Chaucer – who was not innocent of using violence in his own private life. But there is still no doubt that the thickening texture of medieval

Left: Generous offerings from a layman to the clergy in return for intercession with God in the hope of salvation.

Above: The parish church became the centre of rural life.

Below: The rise of capitalism bought wages, taxes and tithes with it.

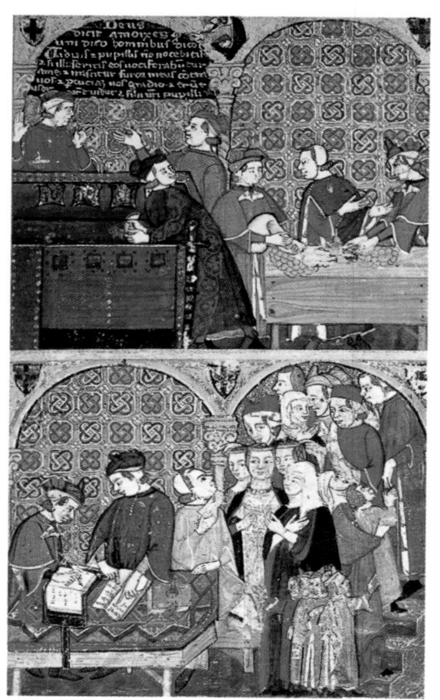

Church life, with its burgeoning 'fraternities' at local level, and its penetration of so many aspects of the village community, did a great deal to civilize Western Europe. The medieval parishes had plenty about them that was shabby in every sense, it is true. But four centuries later, the Reformation clergy were still dealing with very similar social problems as had occupied the medieval Catholic clergy, and the pastoral agenda of the churches did not change in a fundamental way until the coming of industrial society.

But a big institutional price had to be paid for the top-heavy Church of the later Middle Ages, that in spite of the undoubted moral earnestness of the Reform papacy had not really succeeded in cutting itself free of the ties that bound it to the military elites. Innocent III had, on the contrary, consummated the militarization of the Church, and especially had militarized the papacy itself. The popes became central Italian feudal rulers, with their own military needs. Big military needs meant big cash needs. The most obvious way to allow the popes to have armies was to ask the other bishoprics to pay for them. Within a few years, Pope Gregory IX (pope 1227–41) was calling on the English clergy to give him a tenth of their revenues for his wars. Such payments were fiercely resisted, and it was a further century before the European clergy could be got to pay them in something resembling an organized way. But the process of central clerical taxation had begun.

The churches throughout Europe were still collectively rich, although they were gradually being made to yield to laymen some of the immense lands they had held in the early Middle Ages. Gradually the popes became implacable and efficient tax collectors, who registered in Rome the complex transactions that took place among the European clergy, and compelled them – aided by the slowly growing European credit operations of the Italian banking firms – to pay taxes according to fixed tariffs. There was also a big clerical taxation system attached to the organization of Crusades. The popes raised very large sums indeed to finance crusading projects, and since these projects were to be effected by feudal rulers, the feudal rulers made sure that they secured early access to their crusading funds.

In Rome it did not seem to the popes that they controlled a powerful military machine; on the contrary they felt vulnerable and exposed to aggressive, powerful rulers such the Emperor Frederick II (emperor 1220–50). Frederick was Innocent III's former protégé, later the cultivated ruler of lands stretching from the North Sea to the south Sicilian coasts, and the author of a successful compromise with the Ayubid sultans in the Holy Land that guaranteed Christian access to the holy places of Jerusalem. The papal wars with Frederick II, struggles between papal allies known as 'Guelphs' and imperialist allies known as 'Ghibellines', were bitterly fought all over central and northern Italy.

The struggle with heresy continued under Innocent's successors, as did its growingly systematic suppression by Church tribunals. The Cathars were by no means the only dissenters. There were also Waldensians, Poor Men of Lyons, and other evangelical groups whose main emphasis was placed not on any form of alternative Church hierarchy, but on the action of small groups who supported wandering preachers. The aim, as it was with the Cathars and with the Catholic Church itself, was salvation, but a tragic intolerance, perhaps inevitable in a society that made social action one with religious doctrine, meant that the evangelists were seen by the Inquisitors and the bishops primarily as a problem of policing. They could not see their way to incorporating this evangelical fervour into the Church, as they had managed to do with Francis of Assisi.

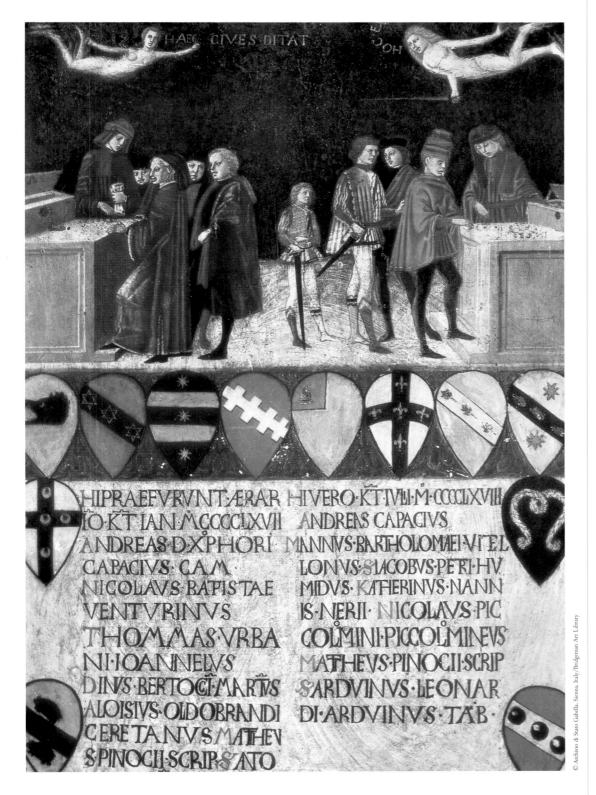

Left: Italian banking firms took charge of the war chests (filled with taxpayers' money). On the right, mercenaries are shown queuing for payment.

Above: Clement IV giving arms to the leaders of the Guelph party, supporters of the papal faction in the struggle with the forces of the Holy Roman Empire.

The Inquisition

The Inquisition was a new organ in Church government, present from the fourth decade of the thirteenth century. Outside Spain, it was not until the sixteenth century that it became a permanent organization with its own body of officials. In the late Middle Ages it was a commission given by the popes to named clerics, to investigate crimes against the faith in particular places.

In the most serious cases the Inquisitors were unable to pass a death sentence, because of the prohibition on clerics from issuing capital sentences, but this, which could not be described with any truth as a moral scruple, was dealt with by handing over the condemned person to lay authorities for punishment. The expected sentence was to be burned alive. However, it should not be supposed that the death sentence was in any way the normal condemnation for all heresy charges; it was not. The question of such punishment differed from the way in which we might expect it to be today, because hardly any medieval penal systems had any provision for imposing a term of imprisonment. Life imprisonment was quite normal, especially for clergy, but a usual lighter penalty in Inquisition courts would have been the obligation to undertake a pilgrimage.

The biggest defect of Inquisition procedures, from the point of view of natural justice, was that they removed from the defendants most of the means of defending themselves that were available either in Roman law or in the various custumary legal systems. The accused were not told the names of witnesses, nor those of people who had denounced them, nor could they call defence witnesses. Torture quickly became a normal way of examining the suspect. Confession of guilt might lead to penance and absolution, but it might equally well lead to the stake. Everything depended on the training and character of the judges, who might be people with an equitable frame of mind and some legal knowledge, but, especially in the earlier stages of the Inquisition's history, might equally well be ignorant fanatics. Bureaucratization brought to the Inquisition its normal benefits of some practical moderation and some standardization of procedure, but it remained an oppressive institution.

Cathars: the Doomed Minority

Like so many religious struggles, the conflict with the Cathars in Languedoc in the south of France was as much about regionalism as it was about religion. Behind the religious fervour against the Cathars lay the cupidity of the northern French nobles, led by Simon de Montfort (c.1208–65), who had constructed a great principality in southern France at the expense of the supposed Cathars. And behind that cupidity lay the ambition of the King of France to make his writ run in the south of the country. The true nature of the dispute had been exposed during the first series of supposedly anti-Cathar Crusades when, in 1213, Pedro II, the King of Aragon, a paladin of the war against Islam, and the recent victor of the great battle against the Muslims at Las Navas de Tolosa that had destroyed the Almohad army, decided to intervene in favour of the people of Languedoc against Simon de Montfort. He was defeated, and in fact killed, by the military ability of de Montfort, but morally the point was made, though, naturally, it was disregarded by the popes.

The tragic end of Catharism, and the end also of serious resistance to French royal power in the south, came as a result of the political defeat of the Count of Toulouse, who in 1243 finally abandoned the attempt to continue diplomatic and military resistance to northern French

Above: A fifteenth-century history book (Dicta et Facta) *shows how torture, was used to obtain evidence about the guilt of those accused of heresy.*

Left: Public shame and humiliation was the punishment of couples caught in adultery.

Left: A thirteenth-century fresco from the Palacio Aguilar showing the royal camp of King James of Aragon, who supported the Cathar minority.

intervention, and abandoned too, his long struggle to resist the action of the Inquisition in his territories. As already said, this was a critical period for the Inquisition as an institution since papal commissions of inquisition, which had in the past been issued sporadically, began to be given much more frequently. Generally, in a particular area such as the south of France, the Inquisitors preserved dossiers that could be handed on to later commissioners, so that evidence taken in one trial could be used in later ones. He reluctantly accepted a French royal bridegroom for his daughter and heiress. For the Cathar leadership this was literally a death sentence. In 1243 a royal army attacked the castle of Montségur, where most of the remaining Cathar bishops were, and at the end of a seven-month siege the place fell, on terms that meant the surrender of all the Cathars within it to the Inquisitors. Some Cathar leaders survived, and Catharism continued in Languedoc for a long time, as Emmanuel le Roy Ladourie expounded in his classic book on the mountain village of Montaillou in Foix.[2] But from the death of Raymond of Toulouse in 1249 onwards, the county of Toulouse was a royal fief, which gave full support to the Inquisitors and their formidable archive of denunciations for heresy. Catharism survived among many of the villages of Languedoc, but as a religion of an educated élite it was finished in France, although it survived for a time in Italy.

The relations of the late medieval Church with religious minorities were unhappy, because the assumption that Catholic society was close to divinely revealed truth was so absolute, and was shared at every level of society. The two religious minorities that tested Christendom's stomach for a degree of religious toleration were Jews and Muslims: Jews were present from the beginnings of medieval life; Muslims were present in small numbers after the fall of Islamic Sicily to the Normans in the late eleventh century, and in large numbers after the Christian reconquest of the Iberian peninsula began its final thrust in the early thirteenth century.

Anti-Semitism

The Jews had in the early Middle Ages held a position in Christian society that was on the whole non-segregated, and that allowed them to own and work land, so engaging in the mainstream activities of agriculture. There was plenty of prejudice against them, but it took a very long time to achieve a critical level. The catalyst that set in motion the deterioration of their social position in Europe was the Crusade. The first great massacre of European Jewry occurred at Mainz in 1096, when the archbishop of the city, having tried to protect the Jewish community against the poor 'Crusaders', himself had to flee. Closely similar and equally murderous things accompanied the Second Crusade in 1146, again in the German cities dominated by the higher clergy, although anti-Semitic persecutions were not uncommon elsewhere in Europe. The massacres were at both times connected with radical movements among the poor.

By the early twelfth century, perhaps because of increasing land scarcity, the Jews had been driven out of agriculture, and had become a more or less urban phenomenon – in fact it might be said that the Jewish urban minority was born simultaneously with the European town. In some towns Jews were allowed some self-government, and in others they were allowed to enter civic government alongside Christians; there was for a long time no universal social exclusion. Slight differences between Jewish and Christian religious tradition on how to treat the Old Testament discouragement of usury led to the Jews being more or less driven into the profession of usury, because laws of contract made it increasingly hard for them to continue as merchants.

The rapid economic expansion of Europe meant that society urgently needed a class to facilitate access to credit, and the Jews to some extent supplied that need. Bishops, who were the other great source of ready money, and princes, who saw the possibilities of skimming the profits that Jewish businessmen made from activities that to Christians were illegal, both protected the Jews, though with many reservations. For example, the English King Henry III (1207–72) over a twenty-year period raised more than a third of his cash income from levies ('tallages') on the Jews. This did not mean that the Jews were proto-Rothschilds; the vast majority of Jewish money-lenders were small pawnbrokers.

Christianity was not without its texts to justify anti-Semitic persecution. The basic one was Matthew's apparent attribution of guilt for the crucifixion of Jesus to the Jewish people: 'his blood be on us, and on our children' (Matt. 27: 25) . Latin Christianity had to wait until the end of the twentieth century for its chief bishop to repudiate that interpretation of scripture. There was also John's report (John 8: 37-47) of the debate of Jesus with the Jews in the Temple, in which the demonic element enters

Below: A late fourteenth-century manuscript showing a Jewish pawnbroker at work. Usury and money-lending were illegal for Christians and were often the only way for Jewish people to make a living.

when he says, 'Your father is the Devil... a liar and the father of lies.' Remembering such texts, terrible allegations could ensue, of which the worst was the accusation of ritual murder, first recorded at Norwich in 1144, when the Jews were charged with murdering a Christian child with the object of using the body for satanic rituals.

The Crusades continued to provoke anti-Semitic massacres into the thirteenth century. The attitude of the Church was a little ambiguous. It intervened in their favour against popular fury, and defended them against the charge of ritual murder, but at the Fourth Lateran Council early in the century, which attacked 'Jewish perfidy' in exacting usury, it insisted on their wearing a distinctive dress, and even earlier it had begun in some places to enact the formal requirement that the Jews should at set times listen to Christian sermons aimed at their conversion. There was also prohibition of sexual commerce with Jewish women, and other restriction of social intercourse between Jew and Christian. And in 1239 Pope Gregory IX called in copies of the Jewish religious writings for examination of their doctrines: this was followed three years later by the ceremonial burning of huge numbers of Jewish religious books.

Right: St Louis (Louis IX of France), pious king and lawgiver, was also fiercely anti-Semitic.

Conditions for Jews deteriorated further at the end of the thirteenth century, when the princes who had on the whole protected them began to think that there was more immediate profit and more public approbation to be obtained by expropriating them and expelling them, than by keeping them for further milking. It was possible for them to sacrifice what until that time had been to them a useful and profitable class, because the bankers of central and northern Italy had started to offer the credit and exchange functions that had previously been a Jewish monopoly. This could now be done without formal infringement of the usury prohibition of the Church, because the canon lawyers had found ways to evade it: the pioneers of modern international credit banking were Tuscan banking concerns, which transferred money across Europe on behalf of the popes. England set the trend by expelling all the Jews in 1290, an order that was only formally reversed by Oliver Cromwell, some three and a half centuries later. In France the most pious of its kings, the later-canonized Louis IX (1226–70) was also the most anti-Semitic. His successors drove the Jews from the kingdom in 1306, allowed them to return for a time, and expelled them again in 1322.

The Black Death and its Consequences

The final period of medieval anti-Semitism came with the great agricultural depression and the great plague that took place in the first half of the fourteenth century. The depression was one of under-production and scarcity, beginning with the exceptional bad weather in 1315–17. Many people lived on a subsistence economy off marginal agricultural land, and became indigent as a result. The trend continued; then from 1347 the demographic balance was thrown out by the first of a series of plagues, basically bubonic, that continued at short intervals for a couple of decades, and at rather longer intervals until well into the following century. Population loss was huge, and not restricted to urban areas. In some areas of France and Italy, war devastation added to the problems.

All over Europe, villages in the less productive locations were abandoned. Mortality was greatest among the old and the young – among the young to an extent that cut population replacement. Early population losses of up to a third and more were experienced all over Europe. Labour costs went up sharply, and remained high for about a century. The marginal agricultural land was taken out of production, but the productive farms continued to produce for a smaller market, so cereal prices stayed low, land values fell sharply, and gross national products may have gone down sharply. But, because of population decline, and because also of industrial and commercial resilience, average standards of living probably rose, or at all events rose in some areas. Or putting it slightly differently, people were richer, because they inherited from the plague victims.

The psychological social results of the Black Death (as the disease and population crisis came to be called) have to be sharply distinguished from the economic and the other social results. At birth, life expectation had never been high, but the prospect of sporadic plagues diminished life expectation for the generations that reached maturity. There was at the same time the hope of more money, and the fear of less life in which to enjoy it. *The Decamaron*, a collection of tales by the Florentine writer Boccaccio, recorded the experiences of a group of upper bourgeoisie that had sheltered, hoping to avoid the plague, in a villa in the rich Tuscan countryside. It gives an idea of the comfortable and civilized material environment of the survivors, as well as of their underlying fear.

The religious results of these experiences varied sharply between social groups. At the bottom of society there were dispossession, indigence and despair, all of which encouraged adherence to

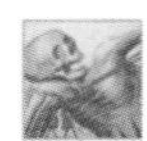

extreme religious persuasions. The Flagellant movement was not new: it had originated in the preceding century, and was a movement of mass lay penitence with an apocalyptic message carried in a letter from heaven (such letters had been a frequent vehicle for extreme prophecies of the approaching end of the world, and had figured in eighth-century dissenting movements, and in the crusading propaganda of Peter the Hermit). Its hymn-singing, wandering adherents flogged themselves with spiked scourges in solemn public rituals, convinced that their status absolved them from sin and gave them miraculous powers. Both they and the populations through which they moved thought that their mission was a reproof to a corrupt and ineffective clergy. In 1348–9 there was an especially violent and numerous Flagellant exodus from Germany, with a social-revolutionary impetus that terrified the clergy. When they approached the papal court at Avignon (see below) the pope condemned and dissolved the fraternities, and burned or imprisoned the recalcitrant.

The general direction of religious movements of the late Middle Ages is not easy to gauge. There was a big drift among lay people towards claiming some kind of active participation in church life: through fraternities (of which the Flagellants constituted only a caricature); 'tertiary' or honorary participation in religious orders, especially important among Franciscans; and other organizations represented by all sorts of honorary

Above: Flagellants at Doornik, lacerating themselves to shame a complacent clergy.

Left: A grim contemporary illustration showing the aftermath of the Black Death at Tournai. The plague wiped out whole populations and was blamed on the Jews.

and subscribing adherences, such as those, for example, to the religious crusading orders. The fraternities took part in all sorts of social work, from escorting and comforting condemned criminals to the gallows to ambulance and medical aid organizations, and the ransoming of Muslim prisoners. The great and praiseworthy army of European charity organizations was already in being, although entirely under clerical auspices. There was also a very large number of lay associations of a specifically religious sort, taking part in special devotions and revering especial shrines.

Below: Satan binds the eyes of a Jew. The desire to explain the Black Death led to conspiracy theories, the most persistent of which was the alleged Satanic bargain between Jews and the Devil.

In the closing Middle Ages there was a pious emphasis on human mortality that, in the light of the events of the Black Death, needs no emphasis. The innumerable fresco and sculptural cycles of death and judgement, sometimes in dramatic 'dances', but always emphasizing the fragility of the human body and the imminence of its divine judgement, have exercised a great fascination on modern eyes and minds, although without inspiring a complete understanding of what was involved. For example, these were not dances of death, but dances of the dead. Late medieval Christianity was in some respects a cult of the dead, but one in which the 'art of dying' was to imitate the redemptive death of Jesus. The survivors of the dead could help their lost members by causing memorial masses to be said that would assist their sojourn in purgatory, before their further passage to judgement and redemption.

In the writings of late medieval mystics, especially those of women, there is a parallel awareness, and the same emphasis on the physical details of the body, whether living or decomposing. There can be in all this an element of horror, it is true. To modern minds there can be an extravagance about it that is hard to accept. These passionate saintly women who vomited when sexual contact with their husbands was required, such as Santa Francesca Ponziani of Rome, or who rejected – not from mental instability but from other powerful internal forces – all food, all adornment, all the comforting emotional furniture of family life, may have been revolting against the hard condition of women in their society, but they were also asserting something positive.[4] Their ideals of service and suffering in the imitation of Christ were, moreover, conforming with the main religious currents of their time. It is necessary to emphasize the Christian optimism about the body that informed them. No one, towards the end of the Middle Ages, forgot that the salvation of Christian souls remains the aim of the people of God, nor that salvation, as forecast by St Paul and many others, includes the resurrection of the body.

Demonization

The implications of the Flagellant movement for the Jews were grave. The plague had convinced everyone of divine anger, but at the same time people had an urgent need to find scapegoats. The easiest way to find them was belief in a demonic conspiracy due to an unpopular minority: there had already been in France before the Great Plague a general panic that the lepers had been poisoning the wells, and with this more general crisis it became obvious to huge numbers of people that responsibility for the plague had to be laid at the door of the Jews. If the wells had been poisoned by them all over Europe, then this could only have occurred as a result of a demonic conspiracy. Scripture's ominous references to 'synagogues of Satan' (Rev. 2: 9; 3: 9) were mandate enough to demonize a whole race. As a level-headed student of extremism has written, anti-Semitism has had little to do with conflicts of interest between living people, or even with racial prejudice as such. He sees the popular medieval view of the Jews as being that of '...a league of sorcerers employed by Satan for the spiritual and physical ruination of Christendom'.[3]

All over the Holy Roman Empire, which formed a huge agglomeration of German-speaking and other countries in the centre of Europe, reaching north-west to the Rhine delta, south-west to Provence, there were massacres of Jews. There were frequent efforts by churchmen, in which the pope himself took part, to protect the Jewish communities. It was in itself a human catastrophe, but what was perhaps worse was the failure of the Church to convince Christians in general that the demonization of Jews was wrong. Too many churchmen, especially among the preaching friars, shared the popular prejudices. No authoritative voice was raised high enough to combat the general conviction that Jews were in league with demons.

The Church had had a long history, going back many centuries, of more or less courteous debate with

Above: Universities were advised to teach Hebrew but the virulent anti-Semitic atmosphere of the times made it unpopular.

Left: The statue of the Synagogue in Strasbourg Cathedral, an oasis of calm in a sea of anti-Jewish feeling.

Right and far right: Paolo Uccello's illustrations show a Christian woman handing over the sacred host to a Jewish pawnbroker as the price for redeeming her cloak. Guards break into the house of the Jew, who, together with his children, is subsequently burned at the stake.

Above: Trade between Europe and the Middle East meant that Muslims were slightly more tolerable to Christians than Jews, even though Christians had been, to some extent, persecuted under Islamic rule in Spain.

Jewish scholars. In the twelfth century, Peter Abelard had written a remarkable religious discussion that included a Jew: such works were not infrequent, and if they usually showed plenty of prejudice, they were often calm and rational. There was consciousness in the Church of the importance that knowledge of Hebrew could have, both for missionary work and for Biblical scholarship, and at the Council of Vienne in 1311–12 the universities had been advised to set up faculties to teach Hebrew and Arabic – advice that they were careful not to act upon. Right through the Middle Ages, some individual churchmen had friendly relations with learned Jews. But none of this was anything like enough to counteract a poison that worked its way into every part of the body of Christendom.

More than at any previous point in the Middle Ages, the iconic representation of the Jew became coarse and hostile. In the thirteenth-century cathedral of Strasbourg, in what seemed to be traditionally anti-Semitic territory, the statue of the Synagogue could still be tenderly executed, as that of a beautiful, if saddened, woman. But the fourteenth century representations of Jews are particularly distorted and horrible, angry prototypes that were revived in our own times. Perhaps the most frightening of all anti-Semitic pictures, because it is the work of a great Renaissance master, is the fifteenth-century predella by Paolo Ucello depicting a Christian woman who in order to redeem her cloak from a Jewish pawnbroker took him a consecrated host (the sacred element of the Christian Eucharist) to use in satanic practices. When these began, the host bled so that the blood issued under the door of the pawnbroker's house. He was apprehended and the Christian woman was hanged for her part in the affair, although her repentance secured her spiritual salvation. The Jew and his family, including his golden-haired children, are shown being burned at the stake.

Christians and Muslims

The corresponding treatment of Muslims by Christians in the lands reconquered from Islam in the Iberian peninsula, while not a model of toleration and kindness, was less drastic than that accorded

to the Jews. There are differing opinions among historians about what happened after the great collapse of Muslim arms in Spain in 1212. It seems most likely that the immediate effects of the Christian occupation of large Muslim areas were catastrophic for the Muslim population, in spite of the facts that some guarantees were given, and that many Muslim potentates made their own bargain with the invaders, sometimes at the price of conversion.

The Christian princes had to tolerate the Muslims to some extent, in order to avoid economic collapse of the lands they cultivated and exploited, and there was a certain give-and-take between the Muslim and the Christian populations. But talk of *convivencia* or coexistence seems exaggerated. As happened to Christians in Islam, public worship by the minority religion was hedged in by restrictions. The call to prayer from minarets was often forbidden in Christendom, just as Christian church bells were often forbidden in Islam. Big mosques became churches, and the funds of Muslim religious foundations were usually confiscated, distinctive clothing was required of Muslims, sexual and marriage alliances forbidden between the religions, all mirror images of what had happened to Christians in Islam.

The most severe aspect of Christian domination concerned the fate of converted Muslims, who were closely supervised, and in the fifteenth century systematically supervised by the Inquisition. Suspected backsliding was punished (as it was also on the part of converted Jews), and frequently followed by execution. For those who continued to be Muslims, the most severe step was expulsion from Christian territory. Some Muslims left voluntarily, following the Qur'anic exhortation to make the flight (*hijra*) incumbent upon Muslims, rather than to accept residence in the lands of unbelievers. But forced mass expulsion, whether or not on the model of that imposed upon Jews in some Christian lands, was another severe sanction. Portuguese rulers resorted to this before the Spanish kingdoms started to think about it in the Renaissance period.

In the fourteenth century the papacy, which had steered a steady course for most of the preceding century, began to feel the pressures exercised by the growing powers of the national state,

especially in France and England. It also began, while still powerfully developing its administration and bureaucracy, to lose a certain amount of its moral coherence. Pope Boniface VIII (pope 1294–1303), while a great jurist and administrator, displayed worrying tendencies to behave as a monomaniac dictator (in the modern sense), who placed the interests of his own family above those of the Church. In the latter part of his pontificate, when he was also sick in body, a diplomatic envoy described him as 'nothing but eyes and tongue in a putrefying body... ...a devil'.

The big political problem for the papacy was its inability, after a French prince had occupied southern Italy in 1266, to deal with the French monarchy and its offshoots. Under Boniface VIII the conflict with France became acute, and ended, when the French King Philip the Fair (1268–1314) took an extreme position and demanded the Church condemnation of Boniface and his unseating from the papal throne, in a head-on confrontation between the nascent national state and the papacy. Boniface was overwhelmed by Philip, who sent secret agents to Italy to organize a coup against the pope. In 1303, in the little papal hill town of Anagni, south of Rome, the conspirators seized the person of Pope Boniface in his palace: he died, apparently of shock, a few weeks later.

Babylonian Captivity

In spite of the violent nature of Philip the Fair's victory, it was the prelude to a French domination of the papacy that was unchallenged for three-quarters of a century. In 1309 Pope Clement V (pope 1305–14), who had been born a Gascon subject of the English kings, took up residence in the little city of Avignon, which was technically owned by the popes, and situated just outside French territory, in the 'Kingdom of Arles' that was under imperial and not under French jurisdiction. This was a fig leaf to obscure the political reality of a papacy placed under French protectorate, which endured until 1376. The nature of Philip the Fair's victory became clear after his arrest of the members of the military religious order of Templars throughout his kingdom in 1307, on charges of heresy. In spite of the tendentious nature of Philip's charges, and his dependence upon torture to obtain confessions from some Templars, Pope Clement V was over-persuaded by Philip to act against them at the Church Council held in Vienne (not far from Avignon) in 1311–12, and to dissolve the Templar Order on the grounds of its heresy.

Above: Pope Boniface VIII with the College of Cardinals. He was deposed by the French King Philip as a prelude to French control of the papacy.

The Roman bishops had for a long time previously been apt to travel far from Rome in the exercise of their duties, and they had occasionally been absent for some years. But the long exile in Avignon was something new in papal history, which could only have occurred as a result of overwhelming domination by a particular Catholic power. Curiously, the only time papal exile outside Italy was ever to be repeated happened when Pope Pius VII was carried off, again to France, by Napoleon in 1804.

The 'Babylonian Captivity' (so called from the Biblical parallel of the expulsion of the Jews from Jerusalem and their transfer to Babylon) of the popes at Avignon was especially unwelcome to Italians, although it may be observed that the first peak period of the lucrative predominance of Tuscan bankers at the Roman Court occurred during its residence at Avignon. The efficiency of these bankers in helping papal agents to collect and transmit to Avignon the papal taxes they exacted was a motive for Europe-wide discontent with the papacy on the part of both clergy and laity.

In Rome, the resentment of Romans at the enforced absence of their bishop was manifested particularly during the rule of the so-called Roman tribune, Cola di Rienzo, the flamboyant ruler of the city in 1347, who proclaimed Rome's fame and power in a manner that anticipated the rhetoric of the Renaissance Italian humanists. To symbolize his identification with Christian Rome, he ceremonially bathed in the font of the baptistry of St John Lateran, where, according to legend, Constantine had been baptized. But his rule lasted only a few months.

Italian anger at French 'Babylonian' control of the papacy was expressed by the Florentine proto-humanist poet, Petrarch (1304–74), who complained bitterly of the luxury and corruption of the papal court at Avignon. He denounced its extravagant male fashions – shoes pointed like the prow of a galley, hats with wings, curled hair with long pigtails, men with effeminate ivory combs on their foreheads – and identified the city with the harlot of the apocalypse of St John, who had written on her forehead the mysterious writing, 'Babylon the great, the mother of fornications and the abomination of the earth' (Rev. 17: 1-6).

The Great Schism

Long subjection to French political control, and the long occupation of all the key and best-rewarded offices, from the papacy downwards, by a French clerical élite, weakened the papacy as an institution. The popes at Avignon had recognized that their moral authority in Christendom was compromised by their absence in the Rhone valley, and on one occasion Pope Urban V (1362–70) had made an abortive attempt to return to Italy. At the end of 1376 Urban's successor, Pope Gregory XI (1370–78), landed in Italy, returning finally to Rome in the following year.

After his death in 1378, the first non-French pope to be chosen since 1304, a south-Italian, was elected as Urban VI (pope 1378–89). The big French faction in the College of Cardinals refused to accept defeat, and within a few months elected its own pope, a French-speaking cleric who took the name of Clement VII. Europe almost immediately split into two papal camps, dividing on political lines into pro- and anti-French positions. Within a year or so English troops left for Flanders to fight a Crusade on behalf of their own Pope Urban against his French rival.

Christendom had split along lines that were in part national, and announced the national direction of European politics for the coming centuries. The Latin Church was to remain divided among two, and from 1409 three, papal 'obediences' until 1417. The Church that uniquely prized unity and obedience to a single pastor, in a culture, what is more, that exalted wholeness in all things, was for almost forty years shamefully divided. The blow did not crush the papacy, but the institution was grievously wounded.

1 John Bossy, *Christianity in the West 1400-1700* (Oxford,1985).

2 *Montaillou: Cathars and Catholics in a French Village 1294-1324* (Scolar Press, 1978)

3 Norman Cohn, *Warrant for Genocide: the Myth of the Jewish World Conspiracy and the Protocols of the Elders of Zion* (London, 1967), p.16

4 Caroline Walker Bynum, *Holy Feast and Holy Fast: The Religious Significance of Food to Medieval Woman* (University of California Press, 1987)

14

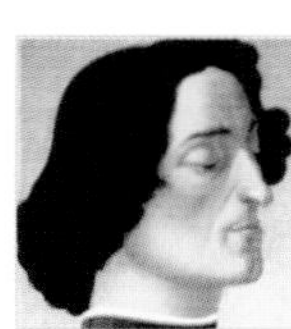

Imperishable Renaissance Monuments

The papacy was hard hit by the scandals and paradoxes of the Great Schism from 1378–1417. The Schism had been brought to a close by an expedient extremely disagreeable to the popes, that of calling a general council of bishops and other Church dignitaries. The claims of a general council to independent divine inspiration that could even authorize it to take decisions against the will of the person claiming to be God's vicar on earth, were for obvious reasons objectionable. It had been fairly evident from the turn of the fourteenth century that this was going to be the only way out of the schismatic dilemma, but the first attempt at putting it into practice, the council called at Pisa in 1409, failed to impose its solution, and resulted only in raising the number of the contesting popes from two to three.

In 1414 the Emperor Sigismund summoned a general Church council to Constance, which was imperial territory. The more powerful of the two Italian popes, John XXIII (whose reputation for integrity and good conduct was not spotless) was forced by political pressure to attend by his political weakness at the time. In 1415 John was in effect tried for misconduct and deposed. Gregory XII, who had 'been' pope for longer

Above: Mass held by Pope John XXIII at Constance during the Council of Constance held between 1414 and 1418. The illustration, by Ulrich von Riechental, comes from the Council Chronicle.

Left: The Adoration of the Magi *by Gentile da Fabriano (c.1370-1427).*

Right: Before he was deposed at the end of the Great Schism, Pope John XXIII rewarded those who supported him. In this illustration a loyal subject receives a bishopric as cardinals look on.

than John, accepted deposition. The successor of the Avignonese popes, Benedict XIII ('Avignonese' pope from 1394–1424), who had accepted the protection of the King of Aragon, refused to recognize or attend the Council of Constance, but had lost the support of the French bishops, and could only drag out a sulky exile in Spain.

In 1417 the Council of Constance elected a new pope, Martin V (pope 1417–31), a Roman, from among the cardinals of Pope John XXIII. Martin was elected with the support of the English and the Germans, and the consent of the French, and was able to re-establish the Roman papacy. He returned to Rome in 1420. Save for the brief papal exiles of the Napoleonic period, the papacy has remained in Rome ever since. For the rest of the Renaissance period the popes still occasionally wandered elsewhere according to the political and spiritual needs of the times, but far less than in the Middle Ages.

The Council of Constance (1414–18) had been a nightmare for the popes, both those who experienced it and those who came after. One of its closing acts had been to pass a decree requiring the convocation of general council every five years; the popes managed to evade the direct or regular application of this decree, but it remained a threat. 'Reform' had been the watchword at Constance: the council's own efforts in this direction were modest, but it was generally supposed that further councils, in co-operation with the popes, would bring it about. In effect Constance had been the apotheosis of the European universities, which had been directly represented in the sittings, and that had managed (with the co-operation of the English delegation) to impose their own method of corporate governance, that of voting by 'nations', upon the highest authority in the Church. The shadow of nationalism had thus already started to fall over the Church.

The popes who followed the Council of Constance were for a century and a half hag-ridden by the threat of further general Church councils that would allow the secular powers, through their control of their own senior clergy, to decide or strongly influence the destinies of both the popes and the Church. Threats of this sort came from the Council of Basle, which sat from 1431 to 1433 with the consent and to some extent with the co-operation of the pope (Pope Eugenius IV, 1431–47), and for over another ten years without either. In effect the popes were caught in a nationalistic vice: either they accepted Church councils, which claimed almost unlimited powers of Church governance, or they negotiated the affairs of the Church directly with the princely (which with major powers, excepting the Holy Roman Empire, also meant the national) governments through the diplomatic means of 'concordats' or two-party agreements. If the popes wished to govern a national clergy, they were increasingly obliged to do so by making bargains with its princely rulers.

In a Europe that was increasingly dominated by national rivalries, Pope Eugenius IV chose to emphasize the universal and oecumenical perspective of the papacy by negotiating with the Greek Emperor John Palaeologus, who was facing final political and military defeat at the hands of the Ottoman Turks. In turning to the Eastern Church, Eugenius was only following one of the oldest concerns of papal history. In 1274 Pope Gregory X had negotiated with another Palaeologus, Michael, to obtain Greek clerical representation at the Council of Lyons. At that council a form of agreement had been obtained from the Greek delegation that appeared to give their consent to the Western definition of the procession of the Holy Spirit from the Son as well as from the Father (the filioque clause), and so seemed to achieve the reunion of the churches. In Constantinople it proved impossible to persuade the Greek clergy to accept this: the majority of Eastern theologians regarded the filioque clause as a mistaken doctrinal innovation.

Above: Magnificent bronze doors at St Peter's, Rome. Created by Antonio Filarete (c.1400–69), they show scenes from the lives of Christ, the Virgin, St Peter and St Paul, and Pope Eugenius IV.

Something of the same sort happened in 1439. The Greek emperor appeared in Ferrara in north-eastern Italy, where Eugenius had initially summoned the Church council: his arrival is recorded on the great bronze doors cast by the Florentine artist, Filarete (Antonio Averlino, c. 1400–69), for St Peter's, which are still to be seen by anyone who enters the church. The Church council of reunion was prorogued to Florence, the city of Pope Eugenius's Tuscan bankers, the Medici, and the centre of Italian humanism. At this peak moment of the Florentine artistic Renaissance, when Brunelleschi's great dome for the city's cathedral was in the final stage of construction, Eugenius himself had consecrated the church building, three years earlier, in 1436.

In 1439 the council re-assembled there, assured of Florentine financial support. The pope had at his disposal a much stronger negotiating team than any pope of the Middle Ages, since the humanists surrounding the papal curia included some distinguished experts on the Eastern Church. The expectation that humanists were in general a body of people with exclusively this-worldly interests can be disappointed when we look at the Council of Florence, which anticipated some of the arguments about the reunion of Eastern and Western Churches that have resurfaced in our own times. For example, we find at Florence people such as Ambrogio Traversari, the humanist general of the Camaldoli religious order that descended from the eleventh-century hermit, Peter Damian. Traversari was a learned Hellenist, and a scholar of the Greek fathers of the Church, and also a pious ascetic.

Left: A panoramic view of Florence, the quintessential Renaissance city state, from the Carta della Catena, *1490. Brunelleschi's cathedral dome can be clearly seen in the centre of the picture.*

Below: What had been the Eastern Roman Empire disappeared for ever when Constantinople (Byzantium) fell to the Turks in 1453. This is Tintoretto's version of the event.

Traversari was responsible for drawing up the Greek and Latin texts of the final acts of the Council of Florence. The Greek delegation, which included bishops from the Russian Church, assented to another act of union that, like that of 1274, recognized papal supremacy and consented to the filioque clause. Like its predecessor, this too was rejected by the Greek clergy when the delegation returned to a Constantinople now almost defenceless against the final assaults of Ottoman Turkish power: the end was to come only fourteen years later, in 1453, when Muhammad the Conqueror finally took the city by assault, and put an end for ever to the East Roman Empire.

Renaissance Humanism and the Church

Fifteenth-century Italy was the scene of the greatest effort made in Europe to recover and understand the Greek and Latin heritage. This recovery of classical language and literature had effects far outside the new mastery of the texts. For the first time since late antiquity, educated people began to rediscover a sense of the historical origins of their own culture. To a large extent the architecture and visual arts produced by Italians of that time reflect the understanding of antiquity that had been recovered by the

scholarship that came out of what they called the 'revival of good letters', and that we call 'humanism'.

The new linguistic competence did not, however, mean an immediate revival of the philosophies of the ancient world, in a way that presented an imminent threat to Christian doctrine. Plato, for example, had been an immense influence upon the Christian thought of the Middle Ages, especially during the early and late Middle Ages. The revived Platonic interests of the fifteenth century were intense, and in many ways different, but they could not be said to be unchristian.

The long-term effects of Italian Renaissance humanism were to break the cultural monopoly that the Church had exercised over Christendom since the collapse of the Roman Empire. Breaking the monopoly was a slow process, which required the invention and use of the printing press before it could really take off. Its social achievement was even slower: teachers at Oxford and Cambridge were theoretically still bound by the obligation to clerical celibacy until the second half of the nineteenth century. Over a very long period the new classical humanism was to lead to the displacement of the clerical cultural élite by a lay cultural élite. Democracy, and the erosion of the privileges of the old secular élites by new cadres formed by democratized national education, were to develop only in times relatively close to our own.

By the late Middle Ages lay culture had in many ways been pushed out to the edges of social life. In the fifteenth century it was only genuinely active and powerful in government and the princely courts, in commerce, and in studies such as those of medicine. When it began to return, it was for a long time still in a deferential relationship to the clerks. Only after another couple of centuries was it strong enough to launch what has been called 'the trial of Christianity'.

The idea of the Renaissance is probably now one of the most widely diffused historical notions, but the way people understand it is deeply ambiguous. Greece and Rome have for the past

Right: The great humanist poet Dante, a Guelph sympathizer, reading from his own work, the Divina Commedia. *The poet has been firmly rooted in a Florentine context by the artist, Domenico di Michelino (1417–91). The Brunelleschi dome in Florence, though constructed over a century after the death of Dante, is visible in this picture as it is on that on the preceding page.*

three or four centuries, largely because of the great scholarly efforts of the Renaissance period, been seen as the cradles of the Western human spirit. From the sixteenth century to the mid-twentieth, the texts of ancient Greece were taught in European schools (and when it became relevant, American schools), although only to a limited number of pupils, and the texts of ancient Rome formed part of many secondary curriculums. The Roman Church remains today one of the main citadels where the study of Greek and Latin is defended. But it is rather dishonest to pretend, as is often done, that our modern culture is in some quite direct way based on the classical tradition. The educational method that placed these studies at the centre of the commonly received programme is moribund: both languages are now the concern of a relatively small number of specialists.

The common remark of the medieval universities – 'It's Greek, we can't read it!' – has returned to the modern universities. What has remained of the early modern version of the ancient world for people to admire today is the visual rather than the written legacy. The art of the Italian Renaissance has all the freshness of the new discovery of the ancient monuments and the ancient texts, even for us, most of whom cannot read them. It is still today the object of some of the liveliest interest that modern people can display in their cultural inheritance, as anyone can discover who tries to negotiate the queue to enter the Sistine Chapel in the Vatican in Rome. More people frequent the Italian Renaissance rooms in the big picture galleries than read Machiavelli, and hardly anyone reads Ovid (from whom so many of the Renaissance decorative programmes were taken) or Virgil, or Homer, particularly in their original tongues. A Poet Laureate of the talents of Ted Hughes could manage, at the very end of his life, to make Ovid briefly fashionable through his fine translation of some of the Metamorphoses, but even to highly educated readers much of the Ovidian material is unfamiliar.

The significance of the fifteenth-century scholars who sought out and diffused the many neglected or then unknown ancient texts, lay partly in their independence of the official clerical educational establishment in the universities. That did not mean that they had nothing to do with the Church; on the contrary, many of them were secretaries or other employees of the papal court, and all of them who could, sought out Church benefices of one sort or another, as all learned men of the time did. Nevertheless, in Italy their social context was more the world of the princely courts from which they sought patronage, than the clerical hierarchy.

It is significant that Guarino da Verona (1374–1460), the great educational theorist of the new humanist culture, educated princely and aristocratic children in a school established in his own household. In England in the preceding century the most effective reformer of the old system of secondary education had been Bishop William of Wykeham (c. 1324–1404), who had set up a new kind of residential grammar school or 'college', in order to feed the 'New College' that he had founded in Oxford. Wykeham's foundation was tied into the old university system, although intended also to supply the royal administration with trained clerks. But Wykeham's primary purpose was to supply the Church of God with educated priests: this was not the main aim of the Italian humanist pedagogues.

Christianity was itself the child of late Graeco-Roman culture, and it is probably wrong to start to contrast a 'pagan Renaissance' with a 'Christian Renaissance', as it was usual to do a century ago. On the contrary, one of the main effects of the revival of Greek and Latin studies was to revive the Christian culture of the late Roman Empire, and to bring about a great reassessment of the 'fathers of the Church', and a new understanding of the theology and Church history of the fourth and fifth

Below: A page from the Statutes of New College, founded by William of Wykeham, whose seal as bishop is shown next to the text.

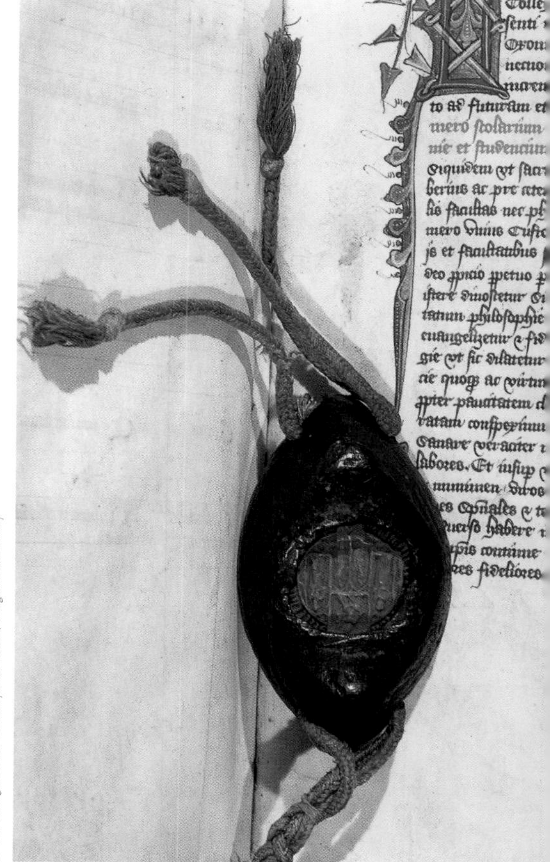

Left: Detail from Michelangelo's fresco the Creation of Adam *in the Sistine Chapel of the Vatican. God and Adam reach towards each other; they are both on the same physical scale, perhaps a metaphor for the growing emphasis that was being put on the human part of the divine plan.*

Right: The architecture of human proportions, Vitruvian Man (c.1492), by Renaissance genius Leonardo da Vinci (1452–1519). Note the mirror writing.

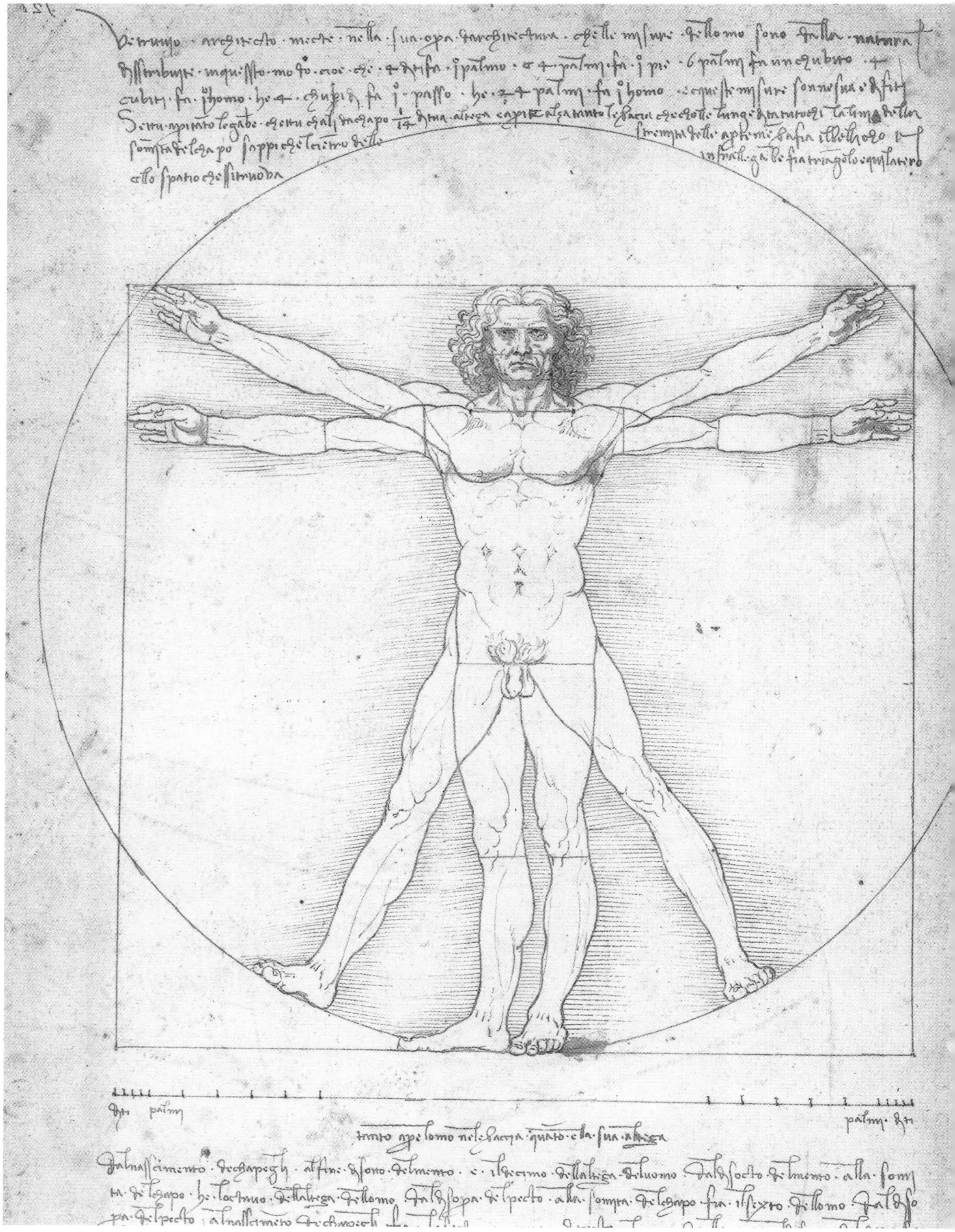

'God the Father, the supreme architect.. therefore took man as a creature of indeterminate nature and, assigning him a place in the middle of the world, addressed him thus: "You, who are confined by no limits, shall determine for yourself your own nature, in accordance with your own free will, in whose hand I have placed you. I have set you at the centre of the world, so that from there you may more easily survey whatever is in the world." ' (Giovanni Pica della Mirandola 'The Dignity of Man')

centuries. It is also a mistake to think that the Renaissance period ushered in anything resembling 'free thought' about religion. It saw a great deal of anticlericalism, and a great deal of irreligious behaviour, but these are not the same as religious disbelief. Looking not at the fifteenth century but at the sixteenth, the great French scholar, Lucien Fébvre, discussed the question in a classic book on the religion of the writer Rabelais. He concluded that there were no real free-thinkers at that period, whether inspired by humanism or by science. As he memorably remarked, it is not so easy for a man to break totally with the habits, the social customs, even the laws of a society of which he forms part, especially when these are all in full force, and when the body of knowledge available to him affords no real solid basis for religious doubt. There were people – of whom Rabelais was one – who could be called free-thinkers for their time, but that does not mean that they were like the free-thinkers of the nineteenth and twentieth centuries. Febvre's view has been challenged since his day, but his main thesis has not, to my knowledge, been disproved.

The Renaissance period inspired and developed a more lively sense of the importance and dignity of man as an individual. The dignity of man had been asserted earlier by the twelfth-century humanists, although, like earlier medieval clerics, they had also emphasized man's moral frailty. Among the Renaissance humanists, and especially among the Platonists, the assertion of human dignity was more definite, and placed in the centre of their theology. The aristocratic Platonist, Giovanni Pico della Mirandola (1463–94), an intellectual prodigy who stood close to the court of Lorenzo de' Medici in Florence, was the author of a speech on 'The Dignity of Man' that had been intended as a preliminary to the nine hundred propositions on philosophy and theology that he offered to defend, as a very young man, and which gained themselves the distinction of being condemned by the pope – although, perhaps because of Giovanni's social distinction, he was not threatened by proceedings for heresy.

The fifteenth-century Church did not, therefore, feel itself threatened by the ideological direction taken by the humanist scholars, who towards the end of the century began to turn their attention to the study of the early 'fathers' of the Church, Latin and Greek, and also towards the renewal of the study of Hebrew. There were some incipient dangers for orthodoxy there, but they took a little time to develop. Dissent and rebellion against the Church very seldom came from such quarters, although they came in from other directions.

Below: Hebrew version of the Psalms, and parallel translations into Greek, Arabic, Syriac and Latin, edited by Agostino Giustiniani (Genoa, 1516). Humanist scholars reawakened an interest in the languages used by the early Church fathers.

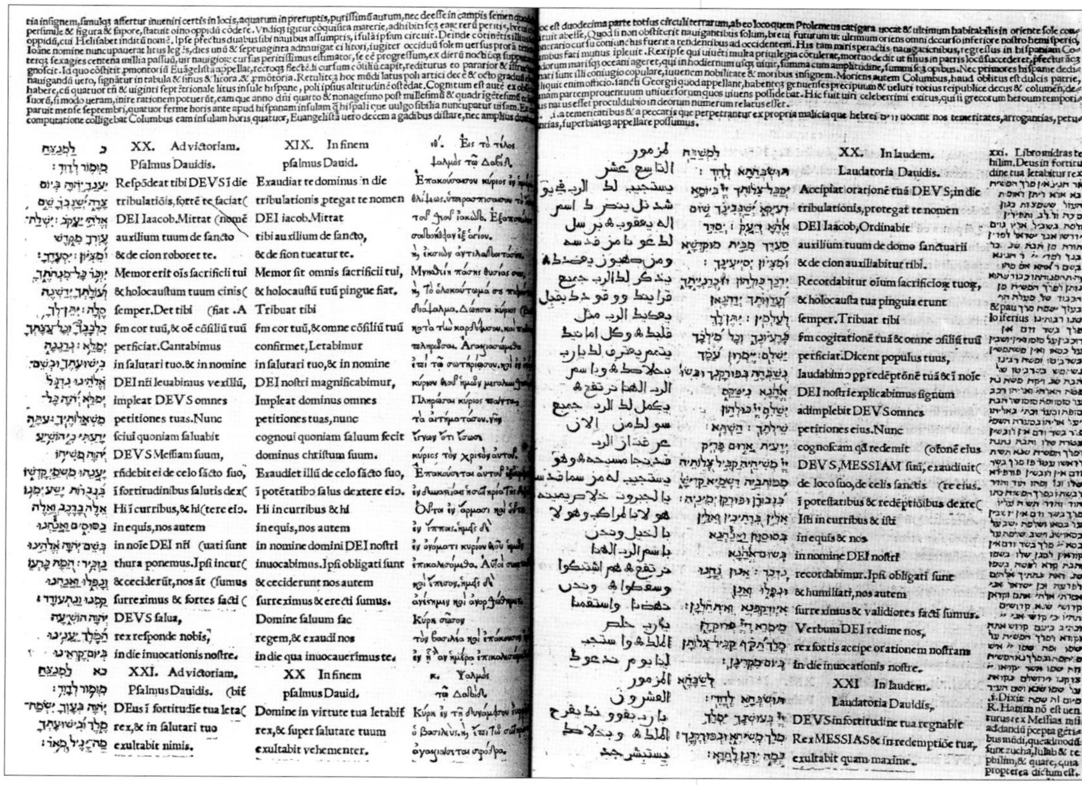

XX. Ad victoriam. Psalmus Dauidis.

XIX. In finem psalmus Dauid.

XX. In laudem. Laudatoria Dauidis.

XXI. Ad victoriam. Psalmus Dauidis.

XX In finem psalmus Dauid.

XXI In laudem. Laudatoria Dauidis.

Above: Pius II, regarded as a humanist pope.

Below: The city of Bologna viewed from the observation tower of the university, one of the first to be founded. The astrolabe and ephemeris tables indicate that astronomy was studied here.

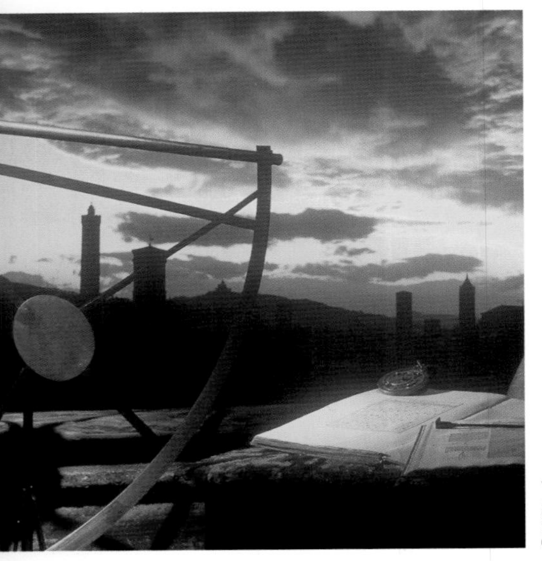

The papal court was the major employer of humanists among all the European courts, and by the end of the fifteenth century certain humanist methods and ways of expression had been officially consecrated by the usage of the papal chancery. Humanist Latin and humanist handwriting were obligatory at the papal court by this time for certain classes of papal correspondence. The only spat between popes and humanists was in a way a domestic matter: it concerned the supposedly aggressively pagan 'Academy' set up in Rome by a humanist, Pomponio Leto, in 1468. The 'conspiracy' alleged by the pope of the time to have been the work of humanist academicians seems really to have been concerned with countering papal plans to reduce the salaries of those who were employed as papal civil servants: it concerned labour relations rather than ideology.

Pope Pius II (Aeneas Silvius Piccolomini, pope 1458–64) is widely known as the humanist pope, although the emphatic definite article preceding the appellation is a little odd, since the popes had employed humanists as secretaries and propagandists from the moment that the latter could be said to have existed as a class. Pope Pius II was very far from being the last humanist pope: the successor who perhaps most resembled him in character and interests was Pope Marcellus II, pope for a time in 1555 in the early 'Counter-Reformation'. Papal Rome was the home and protector of humanists until the twentieth century: the humanism of the popes speaks from innumerable churches and public buildings of the city, and can at this day be seen in the fine recent architectural and decorative settings of the Vatican Library.

Scholars, Artists and Patronage

Early humanism depended on princely patronage more than upon anything else. The flourishing state of the Italian princely courts, and the prestige accruing to the patronage of classical learning, enabled the social world of the courtier-humanist to come into being. A few were employed in the Italian universities, which began to set up posts that employed the new style of humanist, but most had to

© AKG London

Left: The Five Masters of Florentine Art: Giotto, Uccello, Donatello, Manetti, Brunelleschi, *an oil painting on wood, c.1450, by one of the subjects, Paolo Uccello (c.1397–1475). Renaissance artists were very dependent on the Church for commissions, or on the patronage of rich families who wished to express their wealth through church decoration.*

look far outside the university world for a career: the university teachers were too wedded to the clerical careers. Only in the case of humanist-lawyers did the two worlds of humanism and university easily overlap. Humanists were valuable to their employer-patrons as propagandists who trumpeted the deeds and importance of their masters to the world in general, and also argued specific political cases for them. They could do this on behalf of the city states, but they acted also as chancellors and general intellectual factotums for the numerous lords and tyrants of the Italian peninsula.

Artists also tended to depend upon princely patronage, but in a more traditional manner than the humanists. At the end of the fifteenth century the new figure of the courtier-artist, who could sometimes even cut a fine figure in the princely court, began to assert itself. Such men were a long way from earlier Florentine artists of at least equal abilities such as Donatello, who had been given a cloak and hood to wear by Cosimo de' Medici, because his patron thought him so shabbily attired, and who then put Cosimo's gift aside because he thought wearing it was too pretentious.

Artists remained, on the whole, tied to the traditional paths of church decoration carried out for the glorification of rich or princely families. The prosperous merchant family in Italy wanted prayer to be made for the protection and salvation of its members in sacred places that were dedicated, if possible, to the privileged use of the family, and to its pride and renown. This was only a continuation of the way in which the rich and powerful had endowed and controlled sacred sites from the beginning of the Middle Ages onwards. Cosimo de' Medici exacted that the Medici coat of arms should be displayed in the Badia of Fiesole and in the church of San Lorenzo that was to be become the great family showpiece. Boasting was the order of the day. Cosimo had the cost of the marble that he paid for Michelozzo to build the tabernacle of the church of the SS Annunziata actually inscribed on the monument. And competition with other rich families was endemic: Benozzo Gozzoli's fresco of the adoration of the Magi in the Medici palace chapel was cribbed from the much earlier Gentile da Fabriano altarpiece in Santa Trinità, commissioned by the great political rivals to the Medici, the Strozzi family.

Below: A seventeenth-century view of St Peter's, Rome, and the Palace containing the Vatican Library, by Gaspar van Wittel (Vanvitelli) (1653–1736).

© Rafael Valls/Bridgeman Art Library

Right: The coat of arms of the powerful Medici family of Florence, bankers to the popes, patrons of the arts, and political movers and shakers.

Above: The secret account books of Cosimo de' Medici and his grandson Lorenzo 'the Magnificent'. The Medici dynasty was founded by the banker Giovanni (1360–1429), and lasted until the eighteenth century. It was Cosimo who set the pattern for the patronage of art and learning and whose contribution to the Italian Renaissance cannot be underestimated.

The donors often required that their portraits or other representations should be included in the chapel or church concerned, associated with the depiction of the patron saint or other religious object that was involved. Such arrangements of donor and dedicatee could be found in Renaissance Italy, and in churches all over Europe. And the donor was not necessarily a family or a family head: the very numerous religious confraternities also endowed chantries and chapels in the same ways and with the same objects. Most of the adult male population in the towns might have been expected to belong to one religious confraternity or another.

Imperishable Monuments

Humanism was not an ideology, but a body of literary and philological knowledge, which could be put to propagandist use to support whatever ideas were chosen. The oldest and most powerful ideology was still that of the Church, and humanism was naturally placed at the service of the Renaissance Church. This was far from being a strange adventure for the clerical apologists, since there had been a continuous tradition of learned praise for the Church, which stretched back into late antiquity.

The first pope to use the whole humanist propagandist machine in a conscious way in the service of the Church, and to gear it also to a big architectural and urbanist programme, was Pope Nicholas V in the mid-fifteenth century. The papal court was well served by humanists throughout the period; over the fifteenth century about eighteen per cent of papal secretaries were well-known

Left: The interior of the Chapel of the Princes, San Lorenzo, Florence showing the altar flanked by the tombs of two later Medicis, Cosimo I, 'the Great' (1519–74) and Ferdinand (1549–1609).

Below: Detail from the altarpiece in Santa Trinità. The Adoration of the Magi *(1423) by Gentile da Fabriano (c.1370–1427), at the commission of the Strozzi family, rivals to the Medicis.*

Below: A papal benediction in the square of St Peter's Church in Rome. In the background, the new dome is being built. Luther was outraged by the huge amounts that the popes spent on architectural splendour.

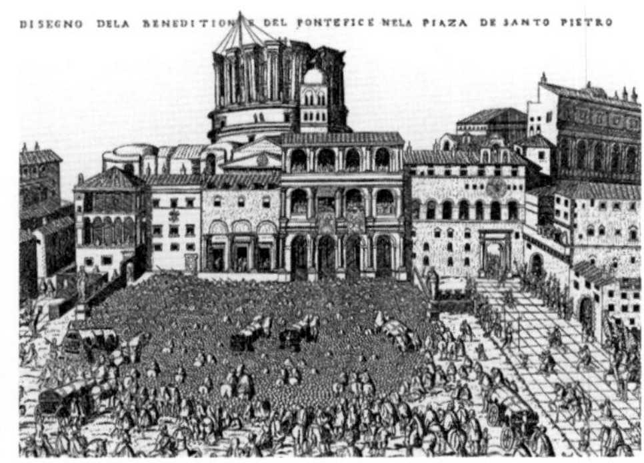

DISEGNO DELA BENEDITION DEL PONTEFICE NELA PIAZA DE SANTO PIETRO

Below: Pope Sixtus IV installing Bartolommeo Platina as Librarian of the Vatican Library. The fresco is by Melozzo da Forli (1438–94).

Greek or Latin scholars, and one secretary in four corresponded on his own account with other learned humanists. Pope Nicholas V began the long process of the re-planning of St Peter's, which lasted, with many long interruptions, until the beginning of the seventeenth century, and whose execution was to cost huge sums of money. The expenditure figured among the grievances that caused Luther's rebellion against Church authority in the early sixteenth century.

Pope Nicholas V employed the Florentine humanist Gianozzo Manetti (1396–1459), the author of a tract on the dignity and excellence of man, inferior in scope and talent to the later tract of Giovanni Pico della Mirandola, and written in a rather more conformist spirit. Manetti was Nicholas's biographer, and he recorded his papal patron's view, which he not very convincingly says was pronounced on the pope's death-bed, that:

> *'Only the learned who have studied the origin and development of the authority of the Roman Church can really understand its greatness. Thus, to create solid and stable convictions in the minds of the uncultured masses, there must be something which appeals to the eye; a popular faith, sustained only on doctrines, will never be anything but feeble and vacillating. But if the authority of the Holy See were visibly displayed in majestic buildings, imperishable memorials and witnesses seemingly planted by the hand of God himself, belief would grow and strengthen from one generation to another, and all the world would accept and revere it. Noble edifices combining taste and beauty with imposing proportions would immensely conduce to the exaltation of the chair of St Peter.'*

'Taste and beauty' meant that aesthetic standards would be imposed upon the papal propagandist programmes by the educated and cultured, in other words, that humanist taste would dictate them. The papal court was for the rest of the century equal to and probably superior to any other European court as a centre of humanist culture and excellence. The relationship between papacy and culture is unforgettably illustrated by the 1475 fresco by Melozzo da Forlì (now in the Vatican Gallery), which shows Pope Sixtus IV (1471–84) among his court scholars and his nephews, naming Bartolomeo Platina, the historian of the popes, Librarian of the Vatican Library.

The papal programmes of urban renewal for the city of Rome, which started the fifteenth century as a great farmyard full of classical ruins, and which even at its end was still a city of medieval towers, in general appearance not unlike – in part, at least – the present Tuscan town of San Gimignano, began to develop seriously under Pope Julius II (pope from 1503–13). He was the nephew of Pope Sixtus IV, as an inscription two or three metres tall still tells us from the outer wall of the great papal Belvedere. It was Pope Julius II who commissioned the Lombard architect, Bramante, to prepare the first plans for the great new church of St Peter, recorded in a papal medal of the time. The

© AKG London

Left: Interior of St Peter's, Rome. The building of this great basilica engaged the talents of almost every major Renaissance architect, including Bramante, both Sangallos, Raphael, Peruzzi, Michelangelo, della Porta, Fontana, Vignola and Bernini. The dome shown here was designed by Michelangelo and executed by della Porta, and the canopy is the creation of Bernini.

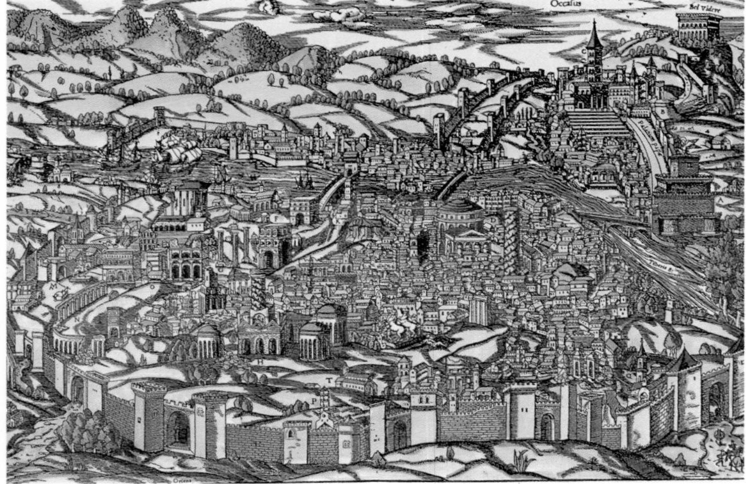

Above: A late fifteenth-century engraving of Rome at the end of the Middle Ages.

Below: The School of Athens, *a fresco made between 1510–11 by Raphael (1483–1520). Plato (modelled by the artist on Leonardo) and Aristotle can be seen in the centre of the picture. The Renaissance in Rome was led by the humanist Pope Nicolas V, many of whose staff were Latin or Greek scholars.*

construction of Bramante's proposed new church entailed the entire demolition of the old basilica of Constantine. It is not much remarked in modern times that the Rome of Raphael and Michelangelo saw one of the most ruthless campaigns for the destruction of ancient monuments in recorded history. Much of ancient Rome was literally ground to powder and burned, to provide the mortar to build Renaissance Rome.

The Unarmed Prophet: Savonarola

Girolamo Savonarola (1452–98) was a Lombard Dominican preacher brought up in Ferrara. His prominence in Florentine history, and in Church history in general, is owed to the accident that he happened to be have been a very fashionable preacher, and the prior of the Dominican convent of San Marco in Florence, favoured by the dominant Medici dynasty, at the moment of the French military intervention in Italy in 1494 that transformed Italian political life.

The invasion of Italy by the French King Charles VIII in 1494, in pursuit of a claim to the throne of the kingdom of Naples (which was to be extended by his successor to include a claim to the duchy of Milan), was a revival of French dynastic ambitions in Italy that went back to the thirteenth century. It was countered in due course by a revival of Spanish (or more narrowly, Aragonese) traditional dynastic claims in Italy, which led to long and destructive wars in the Italian peninsula between the two powers. In one way or another the wars dragged on until the middle of the sixteenth century. By the time they were over, the decentralized communal and regional independence that had marked much of Italian political life in the late medieval and earlier Renaissance period was finished, and Italy had to submit to the dominance of an external great power (Spain) and to the predominance of a much more centralized and formalized princely domination over its regional governments.

The domination of the Medici family over Florence and its subordinate zone of Tuscany had until the French wars been a delicately balanced affair, which had preserved the fiction of communal constitutional government, and represented the Medici rulers as being little more than the influential first citizens of the republic. In 1494 the approach of the French armies of Charles VIII, who had been opposed by the Florentine government in power, led to the immediate destabilization of the latter. The able and gifted Lorenzo de' Medici had died young in 1492. His son Piero, who lacked all his father's political abilities, was in short order expelled from the city, and, after a very brief French occupation, what was left of the Medici regime collapsed.

Savonarola emerged immediately as the most prominent figure of the post-Medici regime that occupied the political vacuum which occurred after the French withdrawal. It was a weak regime that depended fundamentally upon a coalition of the Florentine oligarchs most opposed to the Medicis. It spoke the language of a restoration of Florentine republicanism, and made constitutional changes intended to effect this, which to a very limited extent copied Venetian models.

Like many spokesmen for the ideologies of restored conservatism, Savonarola (who occupied no permanent political post) argued very loudly for religious revival and moral rearmament. He was fully in the tradition of the revivalist preaching of

the friars of his period, who were accustomed, almost always with the approval of their governments, to call for a new attitude of high moral seriousness to the responsibilities of communal politics. Using the pulpit as a fulcrum of the regime was no novelty. An argumentative but eloquent man, he was able to win followers over a very wide range of opinions and groupings, including some distinguished humanists: his supporters were known as Piagnoni (Pious Whiners).

The government, under Savonarola's influence, had severe laws enacted against blasphemy, sodomy – supposed to have been a widespread Florentine practice – and ostentatious frippery; the friar inspired the setting up of a morals police force at street level. His tactics included the organizing of great 'bonfires of the vanities' in which penitents (assisted by the blackmailing of the morals police) publicly burned the symbols of their proud and sinful conduct. These street dramas served to dramatize Savonarola's message and to entertain the public.

Savonarola was a formidable man. A person who could get himself treated posthumously as a major political factor by Machiavelli and attract the loyalties of Michelangelo, besides inspiring the Christian Democrat mayor of Florence in the 1950s, Giorgio la Pira, to sleep in his cell in search of holiness and inspiration, cannot have been a nonentity. He saw himself as a prophet, perhaps even as a Moses who would lead the Florentines out of the wilderness to the holy land. His prophecies were in part political: they saw the French king as a sort of Nebuchadnezzar whose power would lead to a millennial judgement (perhaps to take place in 1500) on the peoples of Italy, and to a great restoration of the spiritual Church. At a time when millennial anticipation of the end of all things was widespread, when engravings were made of a monster with the head of an ass and the body of a woman, said to have been found on the banks of the flooded River Tiber in Rome, beside the papal castle of Sant'Angelo, the pronouncements of Savonarola were readily heard.

He was no proto-Protestant: to the day of his death Savonarola saw himself as an orthodox member of a strict religious order. But in common with large numbers of people of his time, he saw the papal regime in Rome as corrupt. Pope Alexander VI (Alexander Borgia, pope 1492–1503) was the nephew of a rigorist Spanish pope, and for a long time before acceding to the papal office had been head of the papal civil service, the papal vice-chancellor. His sexual morals were certainly lax before, and very probably after, becoming pope, and he caused scandal by the political powers and the special place in his court that he accorded to his daughter, Lucrezia. His nepotism, and the ruthless and often murderous conduct of his son, Cesare, had so many precedents among earlier papal uncles and nephews that it is hard to see them as particularly shocking, and indeed the ruthlessness of Cesare is allowed to have been of probable long-term benefit to the papal state.

The puritanical eloquence of Savonarola would have no truck with the vain ecclesiastical pomp of Rome and elsewhere – for Venice and London were then held to be just as remarkable for solemn and seemly church ceremony as Rome.

After a couple of years Savonarola became unacceptable to Pope Alexander VI, not so much because of his moralistic sermons but because of his pro-French foreign policy. He also became a great deal less acceptable to the Florentines, because of the failure of the pietist government to obtain the submission of the Florentine subject-city of Pisa, which had rebelled after the first French withdrawal in 1494. The pope had plenty of weapons to use against a truculent friar; after some manoeuvring he used the most powerful, his condemnation for doctrinal unorthodoxy. The weakening political position of the Florentine republican government meant that it would no longer protect Savonarola from

Below: This portrait of a woman by Bartolommeo da Venezia (fl. 1502–46 in Ferrara) is thought to be the likeness of the notorious Lucrezia Borgia, sister to Cesare and daughter of the corrupt pope Alexander VI (Rodrigo de Borgia). Married to a series of ever more politically powerful husbands, she ended her life as the Duchess of Ferrara.

Church disciplinary measures. Excommunicated, he appealed to the judgement of a future Church council; it was a legal device invoked by many Church reformers, subsequently including Luther. In 1498, papal commissioners arrived in Florence to proceed to his trial, which ended in his being declared heretical and schismatic. He and his two closest supporters among the friars were hanged, and their bodies burned, all in the public square of the Signoria. As has often been remarked, the burning of the friars replaced the burning of the vanities.

The echoes of the Savonarola controversy continued to sound among the religious disputes of the sixteenth century. But neither they, nor the many other voices of protest and doubt in Italy, were ever to lead to a viable Italian Protestantism. The only firm line of anti-papal protest in Italy, the 'Waldensian' protest of the north Italian hills, had medieval roots, and was firmly established before Savonarola was even born. Savonarola was too deeply rooted in the political issues of provincial Italy to go very far in generalizing the theological issues of his own evangelism. He remained to his death a city preacher, who needed the approval of the surrounding urban society in order to transmit his message. In parts of Germany, a generation later, the city fathers proved willing to turn publicly to Luther: in Italy this did not happen. There was dissent against the Church in Renaissance Italy, but neither Savonarola, nor the religious rebels of the following century, managed to transform it into a revolutionary force.

Right: An unknown Italian artist has chronicled the torture and death of Savonarola, the charismatic preacher and religious reformer who was hanged and burned for heresy and sedition.

'Men feed upon these vanities and rejoice in these pomps, and say that the Church of Christ was never so flourishing, nor divine worship so well conducted as at present... ...In the primitive church the chalices were of wood, the prelates of gold; in these days the church has chalices of gold and prelates of wood. These have introduced devilish games among us; they have no belief in God, and jeer at the mysteries of our faith.. ..Arise, and come to deliver thy Church from the hands of devils, from the hands of tyrants, the hands of iniquitous prelates.' (Savonarola's Advent Sermon)

Left: Portrait of Girolamo Savonarola (1452–98), the 'puritan of Catholicism' whose philosophy opposed the humanist revival fuelled by the Medicis.

Left: *The Council of Trent, 1563.*

15

REFORM

In 1512 the warrior-pope Julius II, still at war with the French armies in Italy, had called the Fifth Lateran Council in Rome. The opening speech of the Council was pronounced by the talented head of the monastic Augustinian Order, of which friar Martin Luther was already a member. In his speech the Augustinian general, Giles of Viterbo, said that men must be changed by religion, not religion by men.

Within twenty-five years of the delivery of that speech, new 'Protestant' churches that utterly rejected the papacy and most of its key doctrines had been set up with the approval and support of the princes, in Germany and other parts of the Empire, in Scandinavia, in England. In 1536 the French reformer, Jean (John) Calvin (1509–64), then established in Basle, addressed the French King Francis I in the dedicatory preface to his *Institutes of the Christian Religion*. He asked the king to recognize that the doctrine whereby popes, cardinals, bishops, abbots and priests claimed to be the Church, was itself a deadly butchery of souls, a firebrand, a ruin, and a destruction of the Church. How had this revolutionary state of affairs come about?

Above: A seventeenth-century portrait of the French theologian Jean (John) Calvin.

The idea of an urgent, approaching general reform of the Church 'in its head and its members' had been firmly rooted in late medieval Christianity since the beginning of the fifteenth century, when Church councils had managed to end the Great

© National Gallery, London, UK/Bridgeman Art Library

Above: Raphael's portrait of Pope Julius II, instigator of the Fifth Lateran Council, at which Martin Luther spoke.

© Galleria degli Uffizi, Florence, Italy/Bridgeman Art Library

Above: Pope Leo X, the Medici pope who succeeded Julius II, bracketed by Cardinal Luigi de'Rossi and Giulio de Medici. The portrait is by the Renaissance master, Sanzio Raphael (1483–1520).

Schism of the papacy, but not to go much further. It was the councils, above all, which had created the expectation of such reform, but by the end of that century the Church leadership had signally failed to deliver it. It was an ideal to which the Borgia Pope Alexander VI had paid lip service – and even, in the months that followed the murder of his son, the Duke of Gandia, a little more than lip service. To some extent the reform idea was present in the Fifth Lateran Council, although the reform provisions of that council were pale and ineffective, like so many earlier half-measures. In 1517 the Council was closed by the Medici Pope Leo X (pope 1513–21), who succeeded Julius.

To create a general expectation within a polity, and then continually to postpone and procrastinate about it, is recognized in our own times as a way of allowing revolutionary demands to reach the point of explosion. In sixteenth-century Europe no one had formulated such an analysis, which went against the prevailing cosmological model of a hierarchy of divinely sanctioned powers. It was a theory still eloquently argued by William Shakespeare at the beginning of the following century, in the great speech about order and degree that he assigned to Ulysses in *Troilus and Cressida*:

...Degree being vizarded,
Th'unworthiest shows as fairly in the mask.
The heavens themselves, the planets and this centre,
Observe degree, priority and place,
Insisture, course, proportion, season, form,
Office and custom, all in line of order;...
... O, when degree is shak'd,
Which is the ladder of all high designs,
The enterprise is sick! How could communities,
Degrees in schools, and brotherhoods in cities,
Peaceful commerce from dividable shores,
The primogenity and due of birth,
Prerogative of age, crowns, sceptres, laurels,
But by degree, stand in authentic place ?
Take but degree away, untune that string,
And hark, what discord follows !

[Act I Sc iii]

Religious Rebellion

The repudiation, on the part of many Christian peoples, of the fundamental hierarchy of government in Christendom, in a society that professed such principles, could only have come about at the end of a long period of preparation and drift. The fifteenth century had been, it is true, rather less troubled by really radical religious movements than the thirteenth and fourteenth, but there had been a gradually increasing demand for active lay participation in religious life. Movements such as that in the Low Countries of the so-called 'modern devotion' may have proved more effective in shifting fundamental religious attitudes than the 'heretical' efforts of people who tried to mount head-on assaults on Church authority. 'Modern devotion' called for religious inspiration in all the ordinary affairs of a lay person's life, a call that applied to women equally with men. A classic manual of the movement that is still alive in Christian practice is the *Imitation of Christ*.

There were also certain ideological clefts in the religion, which enabled cataclysmic sacred events to be envisaged. Of these one of the most important was certainly the eschatological expectation of the end of all things that was written indelibly into the Book of Revelation, and present in other parts of the New and Old Testaments. Behind this lay three centuries of such

Left: The Preaching of the Antichrist, considered a sign of the imminent apocalypse, depicted in a fresco by Luca Signorelli (c.1450–1523) in the San Brixio chapel at Orvieto Cathedral.

Above: An image from John Foxe's Acts and Monuments, *1563. It shows the 'Hanging and Burning of Diverse Persons counted for Lollards, in the First Year of the reign of King Henry V'.*

expectations, which bore the mark also of the late twelfth-century Cistercian abbot and mystic Joachim of Flora (c.1135–1202), who had predicted the onset of a new era of the Spirit, to begin in 1260. The turn of the fifteenth century, as always, was a period when millennial expectation was very widely diffused. No one can look at the great fresco by the Italian artist, Luca Signorelli (c.1441–1523), in the cathedral of Orvieto, that represents the manifestation of Antichrist at the end of time, without experiencing something of the disturbance and terror of the apocalyptic vision.

There was also, by the end of the fifteenth century, the knowledge that there had already been a successful national religious rebellion. 'Hussitism' in Bohemia had actually established itself as a slightly divergent confession, which had managed to squeeze partial recognition from the official papal leadership. The great Czech religious reformer Jan (John) Hus (c.1372–1415) had been burned as a heretic by the Council of Constance in 1415, and the English 'Lollard' followers of his similar and older English contemporary, John Wyclif (c.1330–84) had been similarly persecuted and kept down. Both the English and the Czech movements owed quite a lot to theological doctrines taught in the universities. But they also had a popular base. In England this was the vernacular translation of the Bible; in Bohemia sentiment tended to find a central point in the demand for giving the cup of consecrated wine to the laity, as well as the consecrated host, when Communion was administered. The Czechs had resisted a bloodthirsty papalist 'Crusade' against them in the 1420s, in which English troops had taken part. In the end a very moderate Hussite or 'Utraquist' Church (that administered the sacraments in both kinds) had survived in Bohemia. It had wrung a very reluctant consent from the popes to lay participation in the cup, and this was its only major divergence from Catholic practice. The 'Bohemian Brethren', who professed a more radical reformist doctrine than the Hussites, had also survived.

It could have been argued on behalf of the Roman Court that a very large part of the centralized regime of papal taxation and Church appointments that aroused so much resentment in the later Middle Ages had been set up in direct response to the demands of local clerical oligarchies. Fundamentally a Church benefice, a category of Church office that included the care of parishes, but could be applied also to many other duties and dignities, was the object of private rights and not of public interests. This remained true in Protestant England, for example, until the nineteenth century. These demands had come particularly from the universities, which made such loud protests against the system in Church councils, and from the princes, who liked to give the impression that they shared nationalist resentments against Rome, while in fact they profited from Roman compliance with their wishes. The popes managed a market, but they could not have done so if the demand for the goods – in this case, Church benefices – had not existed. The endless manuscript rolls of petitions to the popes that are still recorded in the Vatican archives prove that this was so.

The critical issue, as in so many similar situations where an ancient organization defends itself against outside pressures, was the boundary between reform and rejection of the system. Like many very large and conservative bodies, the papacy was unable to deal with its own gravest problems. The real question, it already seemed to a German reformer in the Roman Court before 1400, was not whether the popes were abusing their powers, but whether they had usurped powers to which they had no right.[1] Significantly, Dietrich of Niem never pressed his question to its logical conclusion. He was an upright man, but also an important lawyer-administrator within the papal system and a connoisseur of southern Italian wines.

Sin and Salvation

Men and women need to be able to engage in some kind of transaction to try to settle the disquiet they so often experience about the way in which they manage their lives. The manner in which they experience this disquiet changes from one historical time to another, and so does the form of the transaction. In the century now ending, people in the Western world have sometimes turned to the methods proposed by Sigmund Freud: in late medieval Christendom they used the machinery of penance, very different from that in use earlier in the Middle Ages, which had been set up after the momentous requirement of annual sacramental private penance and of public sacramental reconciliation that had been established by the Fourth Lateran Council in 1215.

In the sacrament of penance there were elements of personal conversion and of submission to the divine will. But these elements were too often submerged in the formality of the occasions, which in many cases responded to the requirements of Church law rather than to the needs of individual conscience. People were conscious of these discrepancies, though not often in an analytic way. That serious discontent with the penitential regime of the Church was frequent is certain; that it was universal throughout Christendom is a great deal less certain.

In any examination of the factors that led to the 'Protestant' reform of considerable areas of Christendom in the sixteenth century, it has to be emphasized at the start that loyalty to the Catholic Church turned out, in the course of that century, to be more frequent than disloyalty. Many things of a completely secular nature were of immense weight in deciding the issue, most of all the allegiances of the princes. But the survival of majority Catholicism in Europe, which also decided much of what was to happen in the New Worlds, has to be recognized.

Indulgences, or clerically authorized remission of some of the penances required for sin, were tightly connected with the regime of penance. The most innovative transaction among them, which St Bernard himself had compared to a commercial transaction, had been the introduction of indulgence

Below: Detail from a triptych of 1547 in the church of St Marien, Wittenberg, by Lucas Cranach the Elder. It shows Martin Luther preaching.

© Galleria degli Uffizi, Florence, Italy/Bridgeman Art Library

Above: Portrait of Martin Luther by Lucas Cranach the Elder (1472–1553).

Below: Erasmus of Rotterdam, Europe's greatest humanist, after Hans Holbein the Younger.

© Hermitage, St Petersburg, Russia/Bridgeman Art Library

for sins as a reward for the pilgrimage of the Crusade, which had first appeared at the Council of Clermont in 1095. Late medieval indulgences were multiform, but they were often issued in exchange for contributions to church building funds, as was the case with the indulgences issued by Pope Leo X in 1517 to finance the rebuilding of St Peter's in Rome. To the preaching of this indulgence in Germany, the German Augustinian friar and theology professor, Martin Luther (1483–1546), published a shocked objection in the Saxon town of Wittenberg, in the same year. The objection formed part of a number of protests against clerical abuses, and a statement of his theological grounds, all cast in the academic form of 'theses', but still marked by the idiomatic power of expression that characterized all Luther's polemics.

In so far as Luther was a revolutionary, he was a remarkably unsystematic one, and the more so early in his career. What he denounced in 1517 was not the power of the visible Church to represent Christ, but the abuse by which the pope purported to remit the penalties of sin without calling for contrition on the part of the sinner. From this premise, which to modern eyes may seem still to be a conservative one, Luther moved by stages to a rather more radical position. At the heart of his theology lay the words of St Paul (Romans 1: 16–17) that the Gospel is the saving power of God for everyone who has faith: God's righteousness starts from faith and ends in faith. In this conviction lay the eventual condemnation, in Luther's eyes, of the entire priest-mediated penitential and sacramental system. In choosing Paul as the greatest of Christ's apostles, Luther was following mainstream humanist opinion of his age.

In 1520, after the failure of quite a lot of diplomatic wheeling and dealing on the part of a Roman Court that was rightly rather fearful of German public opinion, Luther was excommunicated. By this time he had secured the support of his own Saxon Electoral Duke, and of important sections of the West German nobles: as his case became a well-publicized issue, so also he secured a larger and larger following in the German cities.

The Word of God and the Printed Word

'The climate of opinion' is a treacherous and slippery phrase, but there is no doubt that that in the crucial few years between 1517 and 1525 Luther identified the *Zeitgeist* in Germany, and critically influenced it. He did so partly from a political position that turned out to be very influential among the German princes, and partly by using the new technology of the printing press. The pamphlets he wrote at this time, such as *The Babylonian Captivity of the Church*, *On the Freedom of a Christian Man*, and *To the Christian Nobility of the German Nation*, are among the most influential publications of modern Christian history. In the first of these the break with Rome was already defined as final. The pope was 'a man of sin and a son of perdition who sits in the Church like God, and by his doctrines and statutes increases the sin of the world and the destruction of souls'.

Appearing in 1521 in Augsburg before the German Emperor Charles V(emperor 1519–55) and the Imperial Diet to answer the charges against him, Luther refused to withdraw from his position, and dramatized his case before the German nation. He also calculated correctly that his political support was strong enough to discourage Charles V from repeating the acts of the Emperor Sigismund who, in 1415, had ignored the safe-conduct that he had granted and allowed the Council of Constance to burn the reformer John Hus.

Luther and like-minded reformers depended upon the word of God. But the word of God could only be known through the right understanding of the texts of the Scriptures, and such understanding demanded knowledge that could only be supplied the by humanist philology of Hellenists and Hebrew scholars. The greatest of all northern European humanists, Erasmus of Rotterdam (c.1466–1536), far the greatest man to come out of the 'new' or 'modern devotion' in the Netherlands, gave the reforming milieu his translations of the Greek fathers of the Church and of the New Testament. His commonplaces also supplied a new Christian humanist point of view. 'Dogma did not engender faith; faith came before dogma' was an observation of Erasmus.

Above: The Day of Pentecost, when believers spoke in tongues (shown by the flames coming from their mouths) from Luther's translation of the Bible into German (c. 1530). The papal dragon is powerless to interfere.

Sixteenth-century biblical criticism did not begin as a movement to bring the word of God straight to the people, although it was a necessary preliminary to such a movement. It was, on the contrary, a part of a cult of passionate humanist élitism. Modern disparaging ideas about 'popular religion' derive in part from the scorn shown by Erasmus, who wrote:

'One who aspires after Christ should be in complete disaccord with the actions and opinions of the crowd and his model of piety should be Christ and no other.'

Luther did indeed think that the reformers must bring the word of God to the people; he was to produce a translation of the Scriptures into German that was to become critical both for the development of German Protestantism and for that of the German language. Nevertheless, the élitism of the humanists was not to be irrelevant to the reformers, when the latter came to establish new churches.

The old clerical class was indeed to be abolished in the new reformed order, but the inaccessibility of the word of God to those without the learning needed to understand it was just as sure a guarantee of the continuance of a clerical order as the old Latin liturgy and dogma had been. Preaching the word of God required technical knowledge, although this was to be challenged by the sects that asserted the claims of the Spirit, and that held as Müntzer (see below) did that the common man could know the mind of Christ. To Lutherans and Calvinists this was unacceptable: university men were still to be able to find jobs in the Church.

'You bless yourself with holy water; what use is that if you fail to purify your heart from uncleanness? You venerate the saints, and love to touch their relics, but you pay no attention to their most precious example, that of a pure life. You contemplate with amazement the tunic and shroud of Christ, and you doze off when you are told what he said. You think yourselves fine folk, because you possess a relic of his cross. But that counts for nothing, if you don't store the mystery of the cross in your heart.' (Erasmus)

Reformed Churches

Luther turned out to be the precursor, and to some extent the model, for other reformers elsewhere in Europe. In Germany, naturally, his followers and allies among the learned and pious clergy were numerous, some of them to be important to him and to the development of his movement. In the Swiss Confederation, Huldrich Zwingli (1484–1531) was a similar rebel preacher, although initially not a monk in a religious order but a secular priest. In Zürich, from 1523 onwards. Zwingli launched a religious protest parallel to that of Luther, although conceived independently of Luther in most matters of dogma. Like Luther, Zwingli insisted that only faith can ensure the forgiveness of sin by God: as only the Holy Spirit can confer faith, so only the Holy Spirit can give forgiveness of sins.

Jean Calvin was the only one of the three major reformers to have been a classical and legal scholar, a humanist. He experienced religious conversion at some time around 1533–4, when he moved from being an orthodox university teacher in Paris to becoming an exiled reformer in Switzerland and Strasbourg. By 1535 Calvin was in Basle, where he wrote and in 1536 published his *Institutes of the Christian Religion*, and in 1541 he came to Geneva on the understanding that he would be one of the main leaders in establishing a new Christian polity in the city. Genevan politics denied his party absolute power there until 1555. The attempts to achieve a godly commonwealth in Geneva, 'the most perfect school of Christ that ever was on earth since the days of the apostles' (John Knox) were, almost inevitably, accompanied by something approaching totalitarian excess. It is easy to be unjust to Calvin, because of modern distaste for the closed community of the pious. But he was a man of the greatest possible literary, intellectual and spiritual gifts, and most remarkable of all for his vision of the absolute sovereignty of a merciful God.

Left: Iconoclastic Calvinists smashed Catholic religious statuary to express their objection to the Catholic hegemony over Christianity.

The iconoclasm (or in their terms, condemnation of idolatry) that accompanied the reform was in its earlier stages a rather disorderly popular movement, which perhaps represented a sentimental smashing – in a literal sense – of a side of late medieval Catholicism that had been especially cherished by ordinary people. In its later stages it simply meant that churches were built or renovated bare of the statues and pictures of saints, and free too of institutions such as the rood screen that carried a representation of the crucified Christ. The abolition of chapels dedicated to particular saints automatically carried away their representations. Lutheranism did not in the least disdain the pictorial image: one of the most powerful propagandists of the Lutheran reform (although also a troubled one) was the artist Albrecht Dürer (1471–1528).

The Reform and the Princes

The reform of the Church upon the new principles enunciated by these men depended equally upon the lateral movement of a general disposition of Christians to accept their message, and upon the vertical movement of the acceptance of such reform by the princes and the oligarchies, without whose action such reform was going to be frustrated, in the end, by the Inquisitor and the executioner. The iron law of such matters was clearly demonstrated in the Italian peninsula, where in the absence of firm support from either France or Spain, which were disputing Italy between them, the existence of widespread evangelical sympathies, even in the heart of the papal court itself, never enabled a single evangelical government. Evangelical reform depended, in fact, upon political power.

Above: The Last Supper, *a woodcut published by the artist Albrecht Dürer, who was greatly influenced by Martin Luther.*

Above: The peasants' revolt in Germany was savagely put down and received no support from Luther. Religious reform did not at that time have any social dimension.

Although everyone was more or less vaguely aware that this was so, opinions on the matter differed both among the reformers and the princes. From the beginning Luther appealed to and depended upon the German princes and nobles, and when the Peasants' War (1524–5) appeared to suggest that his movement might acquire social revolutionary undertones, he immediately came down heavily on the side of law and order – although not without some moralistic criticism of the social role of the princes. Calvin was a lawyer and in most respects a realist, and he carefully dedicated his *Institutes of the Christian Religion* to Francis I of France. But when the French monarchy failed to respond, or responded only in a reserved and half-hearted way, Calvin steered his congregations in a direction that could resist oppressive authority.

Most of the European princes came from dynasties with centuries-old traditions of diplomacy and statecraft in managing and negotiating with the Church, and their legal systems were full of provisions for the eventualities of Church-State relations. The monarchs themselves were credited with some quasi-religious powers, that became especially evident in their coronation ceremonies. These had been the medieval foundations for the seventeenth-century theory of the Divine Right of Kings. At the minimum, the reform agitation changed the conditions on which the princes came to the negotiating table to bargain with the prelates, greatly to the disadvantage of the prelates.

The 'Catholic' monarchs had their own ecclesiastical agendas, most of them unfavourable to the Roman Court in one way or another. Henry VIII of England was just such a monarch. He was the author of a tract directed against the theology of Luther, and he ironically transmitted to his Protestant successors the papally-conferred title of 'Defender of the Faith'. He only moved into anti-papal opposition when his dynastic matrimonial needs required it; medieval history is full of Catholic kings who did exactly the same thing. The Catholic Emperor Charles V was for decades regarded by the popes as a dangerous enemy: he was crowned Holy Roman Emperor in 1530 by Pope Clement VII (pope 1523–34) three years after his troops had sacked Rome and driven the pope into hiding. In the century of Machiavelli it is not surprising that the Church politics of so many rulers should have been driven by cold-blooded calculation. Although this did not stop those same rulers – the Emperor Charles V and Francis I of France are notable examples, although Henry VIII of England was not far behind – from being convinced of their own fervent and pure Catholicism.

Some princes were genuinely convinced by the new reformers, although the extent to which Lutheranism was supported by Luther's Elector Frederick could only be described as active toleration; favourable legislation only occurred after Frederick's death in 1525. In the early 1530s, after the Protestant princes had registered their 'Protest' in the Diet of 1529, the Protestant princes and towns joined in the political alliance of the League of Schmalkald, a league in which the germ of later religious war was located. In Scandinavia Gustav Vasa of Sweden (1496–1560) carried out a reformation whose aims were almost as political as those of the reformation sponsored by Henry VIII of England. Henry VIII's à la carte view of Church reform, by which he specified in a very conservative spirit the degree of Protestantism to be allowed to the reforming clergy, may be said to have embodied the politically controlled reform of the princes.

Reform in the Roman Communion

Although the pressures for a 'reform in head and members' of the Catholic Church appeared to have been frustrated by the tame and half-hearted Fifth Lateran Council, the widespread demand for a Catholic reform had not gone away. The big papal problem remained what it had been ever since the birth of the 'conciliar' movement at the end of the fourteenth century: that the popes feared above all things that an 'oecumenical council', which claimed divine inspiration like that of the first seven (or on another reckoning eight) oecumenical councils of the ancient world, might be politically used to enslave the Church. This was not necessarily a politicized view of the Church, although it was the view of men to whom political considerations were always present.

There were many Catholic bishops and holy men whose piety and good faith in the matter of reform were beyond doubt, and whose abilities as humanists and scholars of Christian history and theology were not inferior to those of the reformers. Indeed, Erasmus himself, who wrote against Luther on free will, and spent his last days between Catholic Freiburg and Protestant Basle, may be said to have belonged to the second of these categories, and to have gained from it only the lasting distaste of the Protestant reformers and the lasting distrust of Catholic orthodoxy.

Above: Francis I (1494–1547) of France, a pragmatic Catholic and a cruel persecutor of Protestants.

Right: An Allegory of the Reformation, *painted between 1568–71. Henry VIII, who moved from Catholicism to Protestantism to suit his own dynastic agenda, is seen on his death-bed handing on his work to the future Edward VI, seated on the throne. Popery is shown in a state of collapse.*

© National Portrait Gallery, London, UK/Bridgeman Art Library

© Museo de Santa Cruz, Toledo, Spain/Bridgeman Art Library

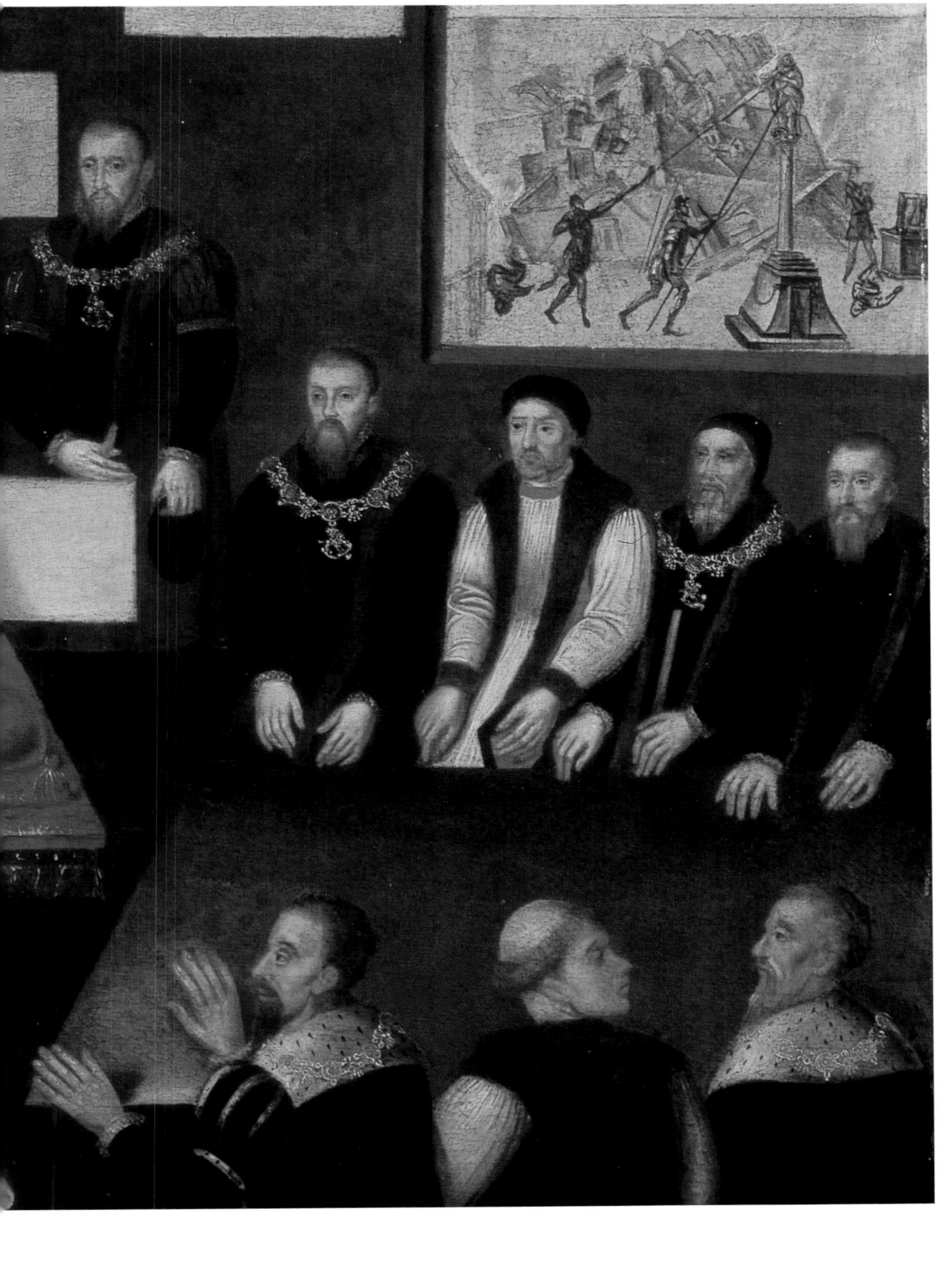

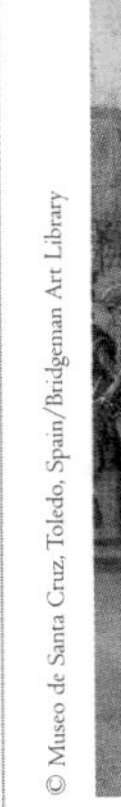

Above: Charles V of Hapsburg marching into Bologna for his coronation as Holy Roman Emperor. Charles was considered an enemy of the papacy – his troops had sacked Rome – but such was his political ascendance that he was crowned by Pope Clement VII.

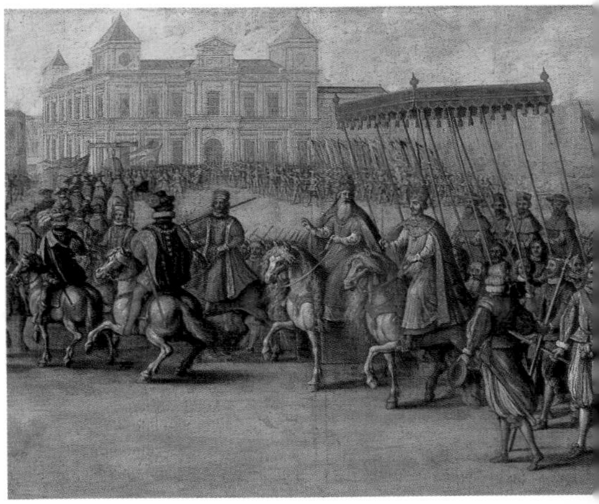

Right: A contemporary copper engraving of the interior of the cathedral at Trent (Trento) with a sitting of the Council of Trent in session.

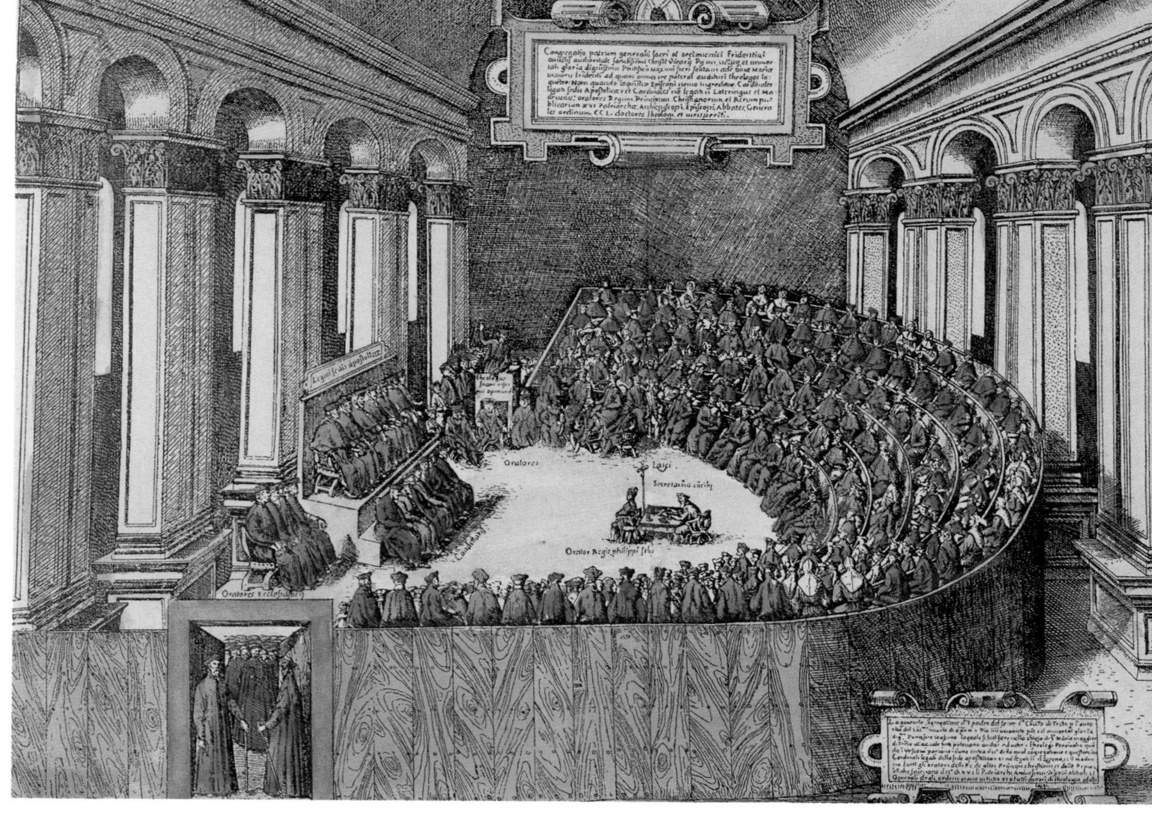

Below: Cardinal Reginald Pole (1500–58), a violent anti-Protestant, clashed with Henry VIII but was appointed Archbishop of Canterbury by the Catholic Mary I.

The choice of Trent (modern Trento), a bishopric within the Holy Roman Empire, but within geographical reach of what is now Italy, for the first sessions of a council of Catholic reformation (1545–7), already showed the concessions that the popes had been forced to make to the feared Empire. In the earlier sessions the Council of Trent was under strong German pressure to make doctrinal concessions to the Lutherans, which it resisted, so that the 'Tridentine' definitions on justification and grace (meaning, those made at Trent) allowed human merit and human free will as elements in salvation, and asserted that inner sanctification accompanies the forgiveness that Christ's salvation procures for man. The idea that justifying faith, which assures the believer of redemption, is nothing other than trust in the divine mercy that remits sins for Christ's sake was anathematized. One of the three papal cardinals to preside was the English Cardinal Pole (1500–58) who, in spite of the reputation for repression that he later acquired in his own country, was in papal terms counted as a closet evangelical. At the time of his death the Inquisition had assembled a thick and hostile dossier on his career.

Fearful of more Imperial and Lutheran pressure, Pope Paul III (pope from 1534–49) transferred the council from Trent to papal territory in Bologna: it was then prorogued, and reopened in Trent in 1551, and attended by Protestant delegates. This was the only attempt made after the Protestant Schism to achieve reunion, and it failed. In spite of the diplomatic support given to the Protestants by the emperor, who wanted a compromise to avert further civil war in Germany, theological definition had become too sharp on either side, and the attempt was abandoned, the council again prorogued.

Ignatius Loyola (1491–1556), the founder of the Company of Jesus, secured the favour of Paul III in Rome in 1538, and his new religious order received papal approval in 1540. Ignatius (born Iñigo) came from the minor nobility of the Basque country of Navarre; he had been converted while convalescing from war wounds in 1521–2. He brought to the apostolate the warrior's fervour and temperament, and the greatest ability as leader and administrator, but he had also, as the English Catholic poet Francis Thompson remarked, a great belief in that gentlemanly and soldier-like word, 'accommodate' that his followers were in the end to give a theological dimension.

The devotion that he preached was an affective piety, that was given a systematic character by the required practice of his spiritual 'exercises', in which the aspirant visualized the conflict of good and evil as a sort of sacred dramatic performance of the mind. He was the general of a new force of holy troops, whose loyalty went first absolutely to the pope, and then to the general of the spiritual order. It was an élitist concept of a small force of officers, especially educated and prepared, who were at the absolute disposal of the head of the Roman Church. The order reflected humanist ideas on élitist education, and also humanist distaste for the traditional formulae for the religious life, of regular recitation of the holy offices in choir. The constitution of the order was so deeply pondered that it did not get papal approval until two years after the death of Ignatius.

The final and decisive sessions of the council, recalled once more to Trent in 1562, are those that most confirm the title of 'Counter-Reformation' that was applied to the Catholic reform movement some three centuries after it had taken place. When the Council of Trent finally ended in January 1564, what had been achieved was to some extent a renewal of Catholic hearts and minds, but always with an eye to Protestant opposition (for example, in the repudiation of Protestant iconoclasm), and always with the intention of reinforcing the central control of Rome. So that even the decrees that were intended to renew the powers of bishops over their own dioceses were counterbalanced by others that reinforced papal authority.

The Sects

The question of authority in Protestant churches was just as central as in Catholicism, although posed in a different way. There were enormous variations in the way that Protestant congregations were governed, but broadly speaking they can be divided into those in which authority was in some way centralized – often, but not always, associated with princely power – and those in which it was not. The biggest problems for mainstream Protestantism arose from the growth of splinter movements that usually assembled around individual prophets who claimed divine inspiration, though there were also particular doctrines such as Anabaptism that spread very widely. All these were apostles of the gathered Church, the visible group of saved believers. Their saved condition was emphasized often by re-baptism (hence Anabaptism), a rite bitterly condemned by all the main reformers, but perhaps most of all by Calvin. Anabaptism proclaimed a sort of inner conversion that in a way guaranteed salvation, but that required the believer to continue to show that he or she was sanctified.

The model for sectarian extremism was the Anabaptist Thomas Müntzer (c.1490–1525), a former Catholic priest turned Lutheran, who then became convinced of the revelation vouchsafed him by the Holy Spirit. Müntzer was formidable in his belief that the elect of God were justified in

using violence to further their cause. He saw himself as a 'second Daniel, who will lead his people like Moses', and at the time of the Peasants' War he set up a tiny theocratic rule in the little town of Mühlhausen in Thuringia. Unsurprisingly the nobles suppressed his regime in blood. But Anabaptism did not die with him, and small groups survived in many places, in spite of the most fearful and barbaric treatment of its advocates almost everywhere.

Above: The massacre of St Bartholomew's Day shown in a sixteenth-century German woodcut. At the instigation of Catherine de Medici, almost 25,000 Protestant Huguenots were slaughtered in Paris between 24 August and 17 September 1572. The slaughter went on outside Paris until 3 October, and Catherine de Medici was congratulated by the pope.

The Wars of Religion

By the late sixteenth century it had become quite clear that whatever Protestantism stood for, it did not stand for toleration. The sort of élitist toleration that characterized some humanists, and the closet Protestants in Catholic lands – Nicodemists, as Calvin called them (from Nicodemus, who came to Jesus by night for fear of the Jews) – had no future at all in European power politics. The Erasmian eirenic formula of 'agree quickly and discuss little' was adopted by no one. On the Catholic side there was equal intolerance. The setting up of the Roman Inquisition and of the Roman Index of prohibited books, and institution of the Jesuits in mid-century, spoke clearly of what was to come. The one attempt to meet and reunite with the Protestants at Trent had broken down almost as soon as it began.

From the 1530s onwards German Protestantism had led to political alliances of the princes. The victory of the Emperor Charles V over the principal Protestant alliance in the war of the League of Schmalkald in 1547 brought no permanent political solution. In France, a very large and powerful faction of the nobility had passed to Protestantism. Although there was widespread desire at the top of the French monarchy to work out some kind of compromise with this very powerful group, factional violence and religious zeal in the end forbade it. France drifted towards civil war just as Germany had already done. In the 1560s what had originally been French Protestant churches started to become also paramilitary organizations. There were temporary peace arrangements for a limited toleration of Protestantism, and it was certainly the main aim of the government to avoid maximum confrontation if it could, but this policy broke down under factional pressure, and there was a paroxysm of violence in the massacre of St Bartholomew's Day in Paris (1572) and the further bloodletting that followed elsewhere.

The religious splits forced themselves into every corner of European life, and became identified with national quarrels and rebellions such as those of the Dutch Netherlands against Spain. Protestant and Catholic powers allowed their foreign policies to become to some extent dominated by religious agendas. Christendom had in many respects broken down, although it could still sometimes unite against the Turks.

1 E. F. Jacob, *Essays in the Conciliar Epoch* (Manchester, 1943).

Left: An Anti-Catholic allegory depicting Stephen Gardiner, Bishop of Winchester. Gardiner had been made bishop by Henry VIII, imprisoned by Edward VI and restored by Mary I, when he became a scourge of Protestantism. Here he is shown, with other Catholic priests, in wolf's clothing. Protestants are shown as the lambs of God, slain by the Catholics.

16

New Worlds and Old

The first Puritan settlement on the north-eastern coast of North America arose out of the persecution of the Calvinist groups of God's elect by the established Anglican Church of England. Many of the tiny group that sailed in the *Mayflower* to what they named Plymouth in Cape Cod Bay in 1620 had already been in exile for several years in Holland before they left for America. They had embarked with the intention of settling in northern Virginia, but the Atlantic winds decided otherwise. The second and much larger emigration of 1630, which settled a few miles north in Boston, came with a royal charter granted to the Company of Massachusetts Bay in New England; the scale and speed of its growth were to be much greater than those of the little church of Plymouth.

Both groups had a sense of historic destiny. William Bradford (1589–1657), the leader and governor of the Plymouth colony, wrote after 1647 that 'as one small candle may light a thousand, so the light here kindled hath shone to many, yea in some sort to our whole [English] nation.' John Winthrop (1588–1649), the leader and governor of the second (Massachusetts Bay) settlement, said to his congregation at its beginning that 'We must consider that we shall be as a city upon a hill, the eyes of all people are upon us.'

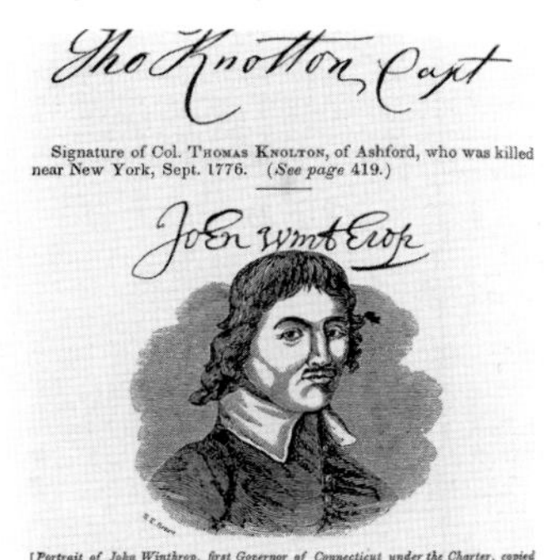

Signature of Col. THOMAS KNOLTON, of Ashford, who was killed near New York, Sept. 1776. (*See page* 419.)

[Portrait of John Winthrop, first Governor of Connecticut under the Charter, copied from an engraving in Trumbull's History of Connecticut, with a fac simile of his hand writing.]

JOHN WINTHROP, F. R. S., Governor of Connecticut, the eldest son of John Winthrop, the first Governor of Massachusetts, was born at Groton, in England, in 1605. He was educated at the University of Dublin, and afterwards traveled into France, Hol-

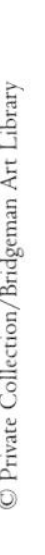

Above: John Winthrop (1588-1649) the first governor of the second Puritan settlement at Massachusetts Bay.

Zion in the Wilderness

The whole enterprise at this stage marked only the movement of a few thousand Congregationalist Calvinists to a bleak American wilderness – a wilderness that after a score of years had reduced some of the original clerical leaders to something not far off despair, and the desire, which they could not satisfy, to go home to England. But it was marked also by the imagination and energy that were to

Left: The first Puritan settlers in America make landfall from the Mayflower *on 11 December 1620.*

Above: The Peaceable Kingdom *(1833) by Quaker artist Edward Hicks. This utopian vision shows humans and animals living together under one God in the innocent state enjoyed before the Fall. In the background, true to Quaker principles, new settlers are discoursing amicably with the indigenous inhabitants.*

create in the end a widespread national belief in 'one nation under God'. Or this was how things were to seem by the nineteenth century, even if, at the time of its foundation in the eighteenth century, the American nation was already very distant from sectarian unity, and was under notoriously Enlightened – although Deist – leadership.

The Puritans were quite late among those who came to the Americas bearing a passionate Christian committment, and the sense of taking the path marked by God for Christian people to walk in. Almost a century earlier, in 1523, the twelve Franciscans who were to accompany the military force for the conquest of Central America by Hernando Cortés had been appointed by their general with the message that the world was rapidly nearing its end, and that they went to America like the son who worked at the eleventh hour in the lord's vineyard (Matt. 21: 30–31).[1]

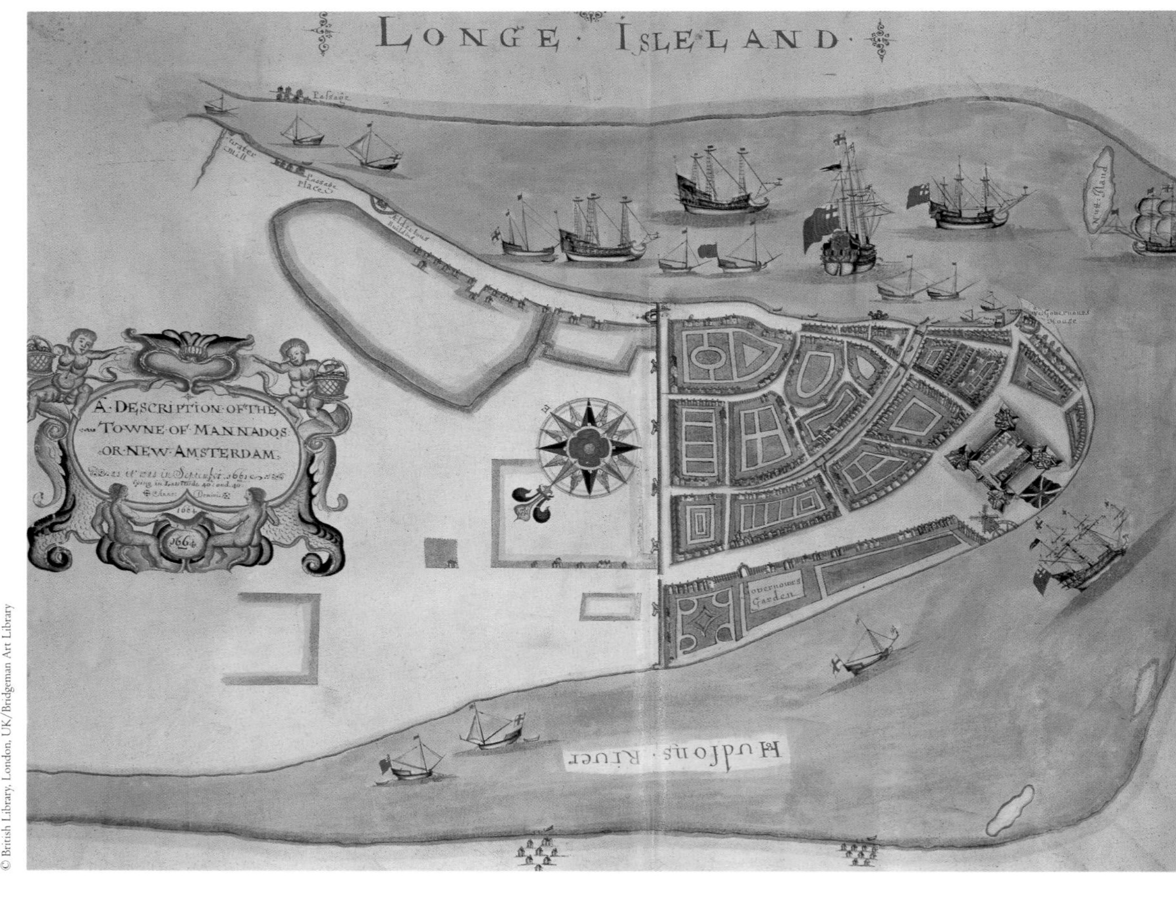

Right: An early map of New Amsterdam (later New York) showing Manhattan, Long Island and the Hudson River. Dutch Protestants were the first to settle in this area.

By the early seventeenth century, Catholic settlements and missions in the Americas had become important and populous in a way that made the tiny Puritan settlement in the north-east look for a very long time to be totally insignificant. And, indeed, its significance comes from its place in the American national myth, not from its place in the history of Christianity. The Catholic American world ran from Peru and Brazil in the south through Central America to New Mexico and Florida; in the north it was strong in French Canada (where Huguenots had also been represented). The Christian mission to the Native

Americans, which the Puritans had scarcely launched by mid-century, was in Catholic North America already significant, though slow in achieving its aims. There were also Dutch Protestant settlements on the Hudson and the Delaware, Swedish ones elsewhere. The English Anglican settlement in Virginia (originally begun in 1607–09) had provided the administrative pattern for the later Massachusetts venture.

At the heart of Puritanism lay the denial of episcopacy; the whole institution was seen as a main source of impurity in the Church. No bishops were recognized in Puritan America of the north-east. Anglicanism had been from the beginning established in Virginia, in the south, although there were no resident bishops there or elsewhere in British America during the whole colonial period. Nor was there a resident Catholic bishop for the Catholics who were present in Maryland after 1634. In Latin and French America, by contrast, bishops were ubiquitous.

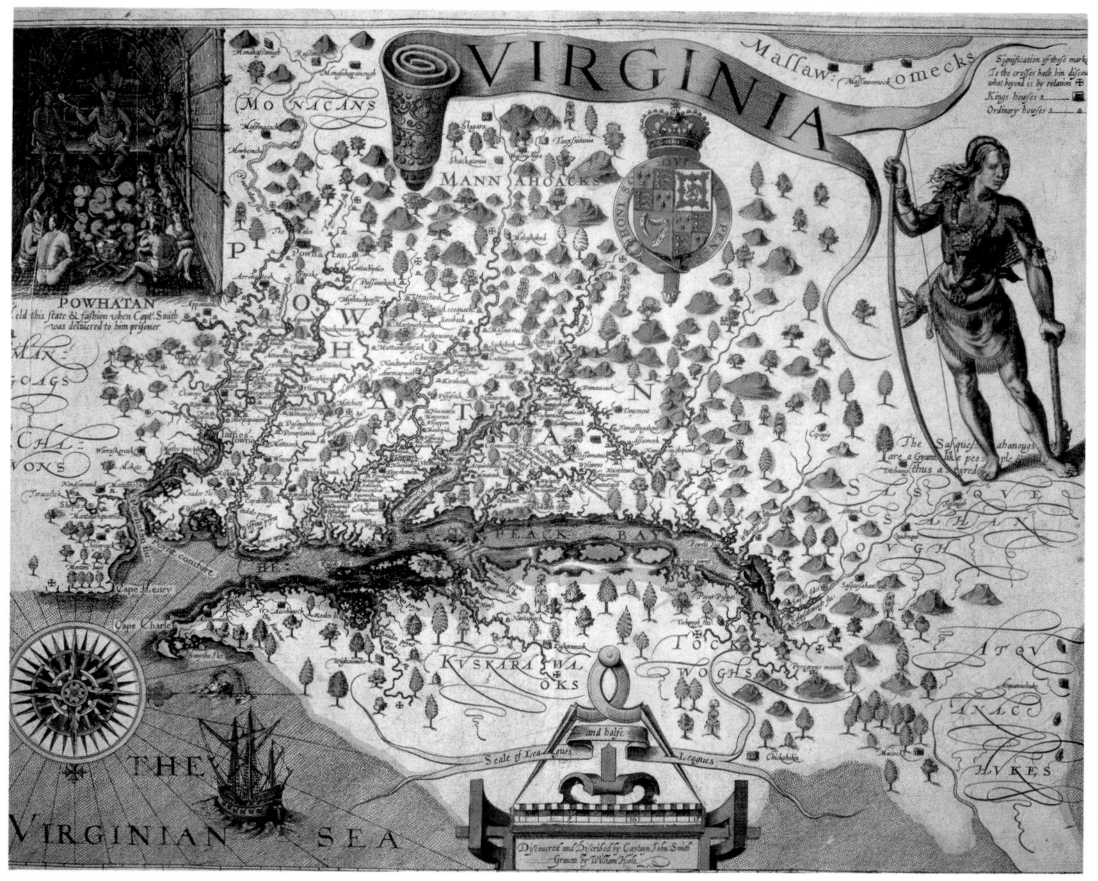

Left: A map of Virginia, the land settled by the Anglicans, showing Chief Powhatan on the left. He was the father of Pocahontas, the princess who embraced Christianity, was baptized as Rebecca, and married the Englishman John Rolfe.

The Fellowship of the Elect

American Congregationalism was in the first and most important period of its existence no more tolerant than the European churches from which it sprang. The minister Nathaniel Ward (1579–1652), who was part of the original leadership, wrote that: 'He that is willing to tolerate any Religion, or any discrepant way of Religion, besides his own, unless it be in matters merely indifferent, either doubts of his own, or is not sincere in it.'

In spite of asserting the priority of the gathered congregation of the saved, the fellowship of saints, Calvinist doctrine as understood by the early American Puritans kept a certain residual priestly element. Godly preachers meant trained preachers: in 1636, Harvard University was founded to ensure a supply of men to preach God's word. The minister's relationship with the flock he served was thought of as depending on a covenant with the congregation.

The critical issues arose early, with the appearance of vocal and articulate opposition to the ministers within their congregations. The minister's task was to preach the word of God so as be a means of grace: to do this he must be 'inwardly taught by the spiritual Schoolmaster the Holy Ghost'.[2] On the whole the ministers themselves asserted that the promise of grace could not depend upon empty works, but must be fulfilled by the promptings of the spirit. There was a successful movement to compel the members of the congregation to testify or 'relate' about their own conversions – no theoretical matter, since the colonists had no voting rights as citizens unless they were recognized as members of the church congregation.

The only long-term answer to disquiet among the congregations was to satisfy their discontents, which to some extent was done by the gloomy means of 'labouring for a sense of sin and misery' among them. They could not satisfy those who asserted the claims of spiritual inspiration. The socially well-connected Anne Hutchinson (c. 1590–1643) said that the ministers had only a legalistic way of preparing their flocks for conversion, and preached a doctrine of salvation through works. The clergy were outraged, and labelled her 'Antinomian', that taken literally meant she denied that Christians live under a moral law. The charge was untrue, but her emphasis on the inspiration of the free spirit was not unlike the things that the Quakers were to be saying in a few years. The ministers resorted, in 1637, to the very traditionalist way of calling a synod that banished her from the community; she went to Rhode Island and then to Rye, north of New York, where she was killed by hostile Native Americans.

The coming parliamentary victory in England would place the church settlement in New England in some doubt, because the new settlement in Republican England could have threatened that across the Atlantic – which had never for a moment been cited in the homeland as a possible model. The 'Cambridge Platform' that the New England congregations adopted in 1648 went along with the Parliament-dominated Westminster Confession of faith of 1646, and made significant concessions to the authority of church ministers.

New England was never a theocracy. Government under the royal charter rested with the governor and his ten officers, who had judicial powers, and possessed also a right of veto over the General Court to which all freemen belonged. The franchise rested in Massachusetts with the congregations, because membership of the General Court depended on being recognized as belonging to a congregation. When the immigrants started to include many who were not in any way saints, the absence of godliness meant exclusion from the congregation, and consequently the inability to exercise free-citizen rights. The clergy, because the material existence of the churches depended upon favourable legislation, exerted their influence in favour of the governor.

In their relations with the Native Americans, the northern colonists did not have the military power to make the forced conversions that had characterized the evangelization of Latin America. Preaching to the Indians was seen by a few of the Puritan ministers as an urgent religious duty; the majority took a different view, perhaps most of all because of the language difficulties, but also from an attitude towards the closed number of the elect that went far back into medieval Christianity. One or two learned Native American languages, and John Eliot (1604–90) made a translation of the Bible into Algonquian that he published in 1663, and distributed to learned colleges on his subsequent fund-raising trip, in England, for the Society for the Propagation of the Gospel in New England. The frontier allowed a great deal of trading, and some co-operation with Native Americans, but there were also the Indian Wars.

Troubles and Dissent in the New England Society of Saints

In England, baptism was automatically administered to the child of any Anglican Christian. In New England this had ceased to be so, because of the obligation to 'relate' conversion in order to claim membership of a congregation. By mid-century, approaching half the population were not in the full sense members of a church (although the legal obligation of church attendance continued to affect everyone), and the churches faced the classical threat to the gathered churches, of decline towards insignificance. The answer they offered was the so-called half-way covenant, that in the end was to cause a return to automatic baptism of the children of church members.

Below: Many religious settlers felt bound to preach Christianity to the inhabitants of their new home, but this was not always welcomed. Here three Jesuits are martyred by hostile Native Americans.

In the period in which the initial evangelical impulse was on the decline, the New England churches met the full impact of the sects that claimed the inspiration of the spirit as a mandate for their doctrines. The Baptists had been treated by Jean Calvin as 'Catabaptists, who deny that we have been duly baptized because we were baptized by impious and idolatrous men'. Calvin had denounced the 'follies' of adult rebaptism, because he maintained baptism to be not of man but of God, no matter who administers it, and in Geneva he had backed up this denial with persecution.

The Congregational ministers in New England initially harassed the Baptists with fines, imprisonment, disenfranchisement, the usual array of penalties. But after the Restoration in England, in 1660, and the proclamation of toleration for Protestants by the Restoration government, it proved impossible to continue with proscription of Baptists. Encouraged by English Anglicans, the colony slid quietly towards toleration.

The Quakers were treated by everyone as a different matter. They were children of the English Civil War, in that their origins lay in the peak period of the claims to proclaim doctrine by inspiration of the spirit, by divine 'openings' in the parlance of their leader, George Fox (1625–91), of a sort that were rife among the Independents. Though certainly not Ranters, who were spiritual anarchists, the Quakers had grown in the same environment, and quite a lot of the ferocious distrust and hostility they aroused came from their being, after the Restoration of the monarchy, the solitary and conspicuous survivors in England of the alarming religious sects of the early times of the Commonwealth.

Right: A French engraving of male and female Quakers at one of their controversial meetings. The Quaker on the stool is standing up to bear witness – talk about her experience of faith – part of the Quaker belief.

The toleration shown in England for Baptists and Presbyterians (the latter of whom had been of critical importance in the English Church settlement of the Commonwealth period) did not extend to Quakers, in spite of the immensely careful efforts of Quakers to give testimony without giving scandal. They went deliberately against the great shibboleth of the *ancien régime*, the outward respect for 'degree' and social order. Refusal to doff a hat or make a reverence, or to address people by their correct title, were profoundly shocking to seventeenth-century people, and the more so if the discourtesies proceeded from a woman, as in the Quaker case they often did. The Commonwealth government had never, in fact, shown itself notably favourable to Quakers. Oliver Cromwell had been willing to ride alongside the Quaker leader, George Fox, in Hyde Park, but his magistrates were quite willing to put both Fox and his followers into prison.

In New England the persecutions of Quakers were in some respects more severe than those in England. The more usual punishments were flogging, branding, or banishment, which meant Quakers fled to a more tolerant Rhode Island, or to part-Catholic Maryland. But the Quaker missionary spirit, especially among women, that took them to plead their cause with the pope and the Great Turk (the Ottoman sultan), was not going to be discouraged in the Americas. Between 1659 and 1661 four Quakers, including a woman, were executed in Boston for returning to the colony after their banishment. When George Fox came to North America in 1672–3 he went to Virginia, to North Carolina, to Maryland, but, although he attended the yearly meeting of the Friends (as the Quakers were and are called) of New England, it took place in non-hostile Rhode Island, and not in Massachusetts. In its punitive intolerance the Congregationalist establishment in New England showed that it belonged to an earlier world of rigid religious conformism, which had been weakened even in Restoration England, and which became very fragile in North America. It was to make a final, and rather tragic, intolerant gesture.

There were pressures on the colonist communities that excuse their tendency to panic, notably the danger and destruction of the Indian Wars of the 1670s. In 1692 there was a major witchcraft panic in the village of Salem just north of Boston, which led to the execution of nineteen suspects and the judicial torture to death of a twentieth. The episode has seemed especially superstitious and disgraceful to generations that have come to expect enlightenment to be conferred on people who breathe North American air; in Europe, where witch-hunts had been endemic from the fourteenth to seventeenth centuries, it would have seemed rather late in the day for such things, but not unexpected in a remote province.

The Quakers were to return in force to North America in a context that meant that they were to become big influences in the drift towards toleration and religious pluralism. This major experiment was born of old-fashioned political patronage and favouritism received from a Catholic prince. William Penn (1644–1718) was the son of an admiral to whom the Duke of York had become indebted. Penn, who had been converted to Quakerism in 1667, received the royal grant of the huge tract of land west of the River Delaware that became Pennsylvania. To this immense domain came at his invitation not only Quakers but also Baptists, principally Mennonites, from German and Dutch-speaking lands in continental Europe. The frame of government that Penn set out for the colony in 1682 gave toleration to all Christian groups that worshipped a single God, and promised that no one would be compelled to frequent or maintain a place of worship 'contrary to his mind'. This is no small matter if we think not only of the intolerance of Massachusetts, but also of the preservation of the death penalty in Maryland for those who blasphemed or denied the Trinity. The drift towards religious multiplicity in the American colonies owed a great deal to Penn.

Above: An engraving visualizing one of the 'Witches of Salem' terrorizing young girls. The hysterical witch-hunting episode ended in the hanging of nineteen people.

Below: Matthew Hopkins, the Witchfinder General, looking for clues. Hopkins was appointed in 1644 during the witch-fearing craze that swept Cromwellian England in the seventeenth century. Over 100 women were hanged as a result of his actions, but he was allegedly himself hanged as a witch in 1647.

Right: A Currier & Ives print showing the Quaker William Penn negotiating a peaceful treaty in 1661 with the Native American inhabitants of what became known as Pennsylvania.

Catholicism and American Mission

No greater contrast could exist than between the shifting world of North American Protestantism, which lived upon what was literally a moving frontier, and the hierarchic perspectives of Catholicism from south to north of the Americas. Nevertheless, the resemblances between the two apparently opposed worlds are more than might at first sight be supposed, especially as they concern the rights of indigenous Americans.

The origins of the concern of the Roman Church with the missionary field of newly-discovered overseas lands lay in the West African voyages of the Portuguese in the mid-fifteenth century. The Portuguese were authorized by the popes to rule specific named areas of lands conquered south of the Sahara, with the obligation to evangelize the populations. This did not remain a dead letter: Portuguese-imported Christianity was already a powerful influence in the African kingdom of the Congo, before Columbus sailed to America.

When the famous division of the New World between Portugal and Spain was made by Pope Alexander VI in 1493, the pope was not operating in a void, but applying some of the principles of the earlier papal concessions to help Spain and Portugal to modify an earlier treaty of 1479–80. The earlier agreement had been concerned with West Africa, but some of its clauses seemed applicable to the new Atlantic world after the discoveries of Columbus in 1492.

From the start it looked as though conversion of the new subject peoples would be easy. What their rights were to be was a different matter, though not one to which Christian missionaries were indifferent. At a very early stage – from the time of their indignation in the early fifteenth century at the horrible way in which the indigenous inhabitants of the Canary Islands were being treated – some

Left: A bronze from Benin showing a Portuguese soldier, complete with what was at the time a state-of-the-art matchlock rifle. Portugal dominated the colonization and Christianization of West Africa, of which Benin is a part.

Above: An Aztec vision of Hernando Cortés, the treacherous Spanish conquistador believed by the Aztecs to be an embodiment of their god Quetzlcoatl. His relative size in the image indicates his significance.

of the missionaries protested. Unhappily, when their protests went to the Church authorities in Europe, the reasoning of power politics intruded upon the reasoning of the Gospel.

The material interests at stake in the conquest of the Americas were huge, but religious values were not absent from Spanish or Portuguese royal policies. Because the reconquest of the Iberian peninsula provided the model for Portugese and Spanish colonialism in the New World, the popes gave the Iberian kings enormous rights over the colonial churches. The original 'Requirement' issued by the Castilian government to guide colonial policy did try to reserve some rights of peaceful possession to the indigenous inhabitants, provided that they submitted peacefully – unfortunately, it was almost impossible for the 'requirements' to be made known to them before the guns opened fire. And it was acknowledged that conversion had to be made freely and without duress – an important matter, especially because of the dire penalties imposed by the Inquisition for so-called apostasy.

The American conquests were made by a military culture that in the Iberian wars had acquired a tradition of political and religious domination, and which was not in the least ashamed of its lust for booty. They thought of themselves in the New World as entering a sort of cultural vacuum, occupied by barbarians who did not possess the coherence and aggressiveness of Islam. Hernando Cortés, the conqueror of the Aztecs, had assured the Aztec King Montezuma, shortly before he took and executed him, of the Christian principle that all men are brothers.

Among the three groups, the conquistadores, the royal officials who were supposed to supervise them, and the religious – mostly friars, for a long time – who were to undertake the missions, each pursued rather different aims. But it was the first of these who ultimately called the tune, and preferred that the Americans should live as the slaves of Christian folk, rather than as 'free beasts'. It was the victory of the principles of conquest and naked exploitation.

Right: The dead bodies of Montezuma, the Aztec king, and his courtier Itzquzuhtzin are cast into the sea by the conquering Spaniards. Cortés had assured Montezuma of the brotherhood of man, but then had him executed.

Above: After the conquest of Mexico by Cortés (1519-21), the Catholic Church made many converts.

Left: A picture catechism used as a teaching aid by Catholic missionaries to the Americas. Catholic missions were established before the arrival of the Puritans.

Below: Native South Americans are used as slave labour to build the foundations of the cathedral in Mexico City. The Catholic conquistadors claimed to believe that Americans were better off living as 'slaves of Christian folk rather than free beasts'.

Slavery was never accepted by the churchmen as being the inevitable lot of the conquered in the new lands, and to some extent the Spanish kings backed them up, although the way in which slavery was cloaked under enserfment was never taken too seriously. By the mid-sixteenth century some of the religious missionaries in Latin America had become very conscious of the terrible injustice done to the conquered peoples, part of which had been the gratuitous supposition that they had possessed no worthwhile identity and culture of their own. The missionaries began to construct, belatedly, ethnographic descriptions of some of the indigenous American cultures that recognized their independent existence.

As had happened centuries earlier in Europe, the missionary churches in the Americas had their mass conversions, but had to accept some compromises with the beliefs and cultures of the converted peoples. A notable example is the appearance of the Virgin of Guadalupe, north of Mexico City. It was reported in 1638 that a poor Indian, Juan Diego, had been told by the Virgin to take flowers to the Bishop of Mexico. He gathered the flowers in his cape, made of cactus fibre, and when he opened it to offer them, a miraculous image of the Virgin was found to have been imprinted upon the cape. The image of Guadalupe (the name was borrowed from a shrine dedicated to the Virgin in Spain) came from the Aztec shrine of Tepeyac, on the Guadalupe sierra. It was thus a product of the

Right: The Virgin of Guadaloupe, an image of the coalescence between Catholic iconography, Native American artistry and perhaps also Aztec pre-Christian tradition.

indigenous culture, even if it conformed to the European pattern of images made to honour the immaculate conception of Mary. Although reported in 1638, the miraculous appearance of the image was said to have occurred over a century earlier, which perhaps indicates that there had been a long resistance among the clergy to what was known to have been a heathen borrowing, until the reluctance was overcome by a more established Creole culture, a century later.

One or two of the Latin American clergy began to protest loudly in Europe at the magnitude of the injustices that had been done in the New World. The most widely known and influential protest was that of Bishop Bartolomé de las Casas (1484–1566), who published his account of the destruction of the 'Western Indies' in the mid-sixteenth century. De las Casas was well informed about the life and history of Central America (he was a Mexican bishop), and about South America as far south as Peru. He denounced the crimes of colonial rule in the Americas, where he arrived in 1502, in no uncertain terms, and did in fact succeed in influencing the colonial policies enunciated in Spain, although his influence on the ground in Central America was more limited. His polemic was translated and republished by the Protestants, with appropriate illustrations of the atrocities, on several occasions, although without any visible effect on the colonial policies of Protestant powers. De las Casas set a pattern for the conscientious modern defence of the rights of indigenous American peoples that has lasted into our own times, and the modern champions of conscience have included a bishop of his own diocese, Chiapas, in south Mexico. Defence of the rights of indigenous peoples has claimed at least a couple of bishop-martyrs in the present century.

Above: Illustration from Bishop Bartolomé de las Casas' Destruction of the Western Indies *showing the cruelties of colonial rule.*

In Paraguay, from the beginning of the seventeenth century until nearing the end of the eighteenth, there was a development quite different from anything else in America, that of a colony founded and run by the Christian priesthood. The Jesuit Order was so tightly disciplined, and consisted of such a dedicated band of men, that it was able to organize the population, who voluntarily accepted inclusion into what was virtually a huge religious community. Jesuit influence on the Catholic colonial powers was great enough to persuade them to accept this exceptional religious intrusion into the heart of the colonial world, that became a zone over which the Catholic princes had only the most shadowy control. Like the Massachusetts community, it was a body run by the saints, but, unlike it, the layfolk of the enterprise were Native Americans.

Below: Seventeenth-century painting of a Jesuit priest at work in India.

The Missions to the Ancient Cultures of Asia

In Asia the same pattern as in America of a colonial European domination with economic, political and religious aspects tended to impose itself, although its development took place over a very much longer period, and when the missionaries came into contact with the ancient cultures of China and Japan they were compelled to assume very different attitudes. There was also, in Asia, much missionary action that was directly controlled from the Catholic centre in Rome: the phenomenon of a colonial Church virtually granted to the colonial power was not the prevalent one. From 1622 there was a central agency for missions in Rome, called the De Propaganda Fide.

In Asia the Jesuits were, again, immensely important. The Portuguese were the key carriers by sea and the key colonizers. In India they did not come to lands entirely without Christ. There was a more than millennial history of Christianity in India when the Portuguese took their guns, troops

Above: Shah Jahangir, the third Moghul emperor known as the Conqueror of the World, holding a picture of the Madonna.

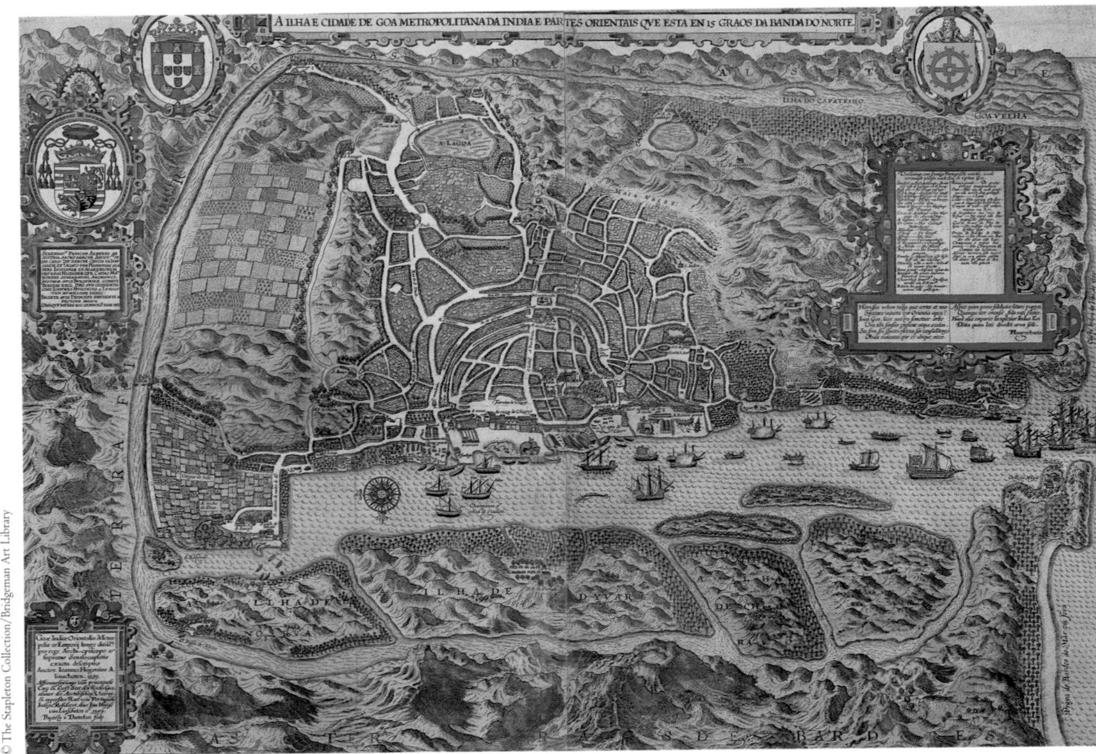

Right: A map of the city and port of Goa engraved by Johannes Doetechum. Goa was the Portuguese jumping-off point for the East, Japan in particular.

Above: A nineteenth-century engraving of the Basque-born Jesuit Francis Xavier (1506-52), known as the 'Apostle of the Indies'. In 1542, he was sent by John III of Portugal to be a missionary to the Portuguese colony of Goa, where he had great success.

and traders there – in no inconsiderable numbers – to establish 'factories' or trading posts in south India from the early sixteenth century. To a large extent the Portuguese were welcomed, but subsequently the Syriac and Eastern (believed by the Latin clergy to be Nestorian) religious culture of the native Indian Christians was unacceptable to the Portuguese, just as the bullying and interfering habits of the Portuguese priests disturbed the Indians.

It was a marriage, but a somewhat unhappy one. The 'Thomas Christians' of India had traditions that were supposed to go back to the sojourn of the apostle Thomas in India, and that certainly could have begun in the second and third centuries. Their earlier allegiance had been to the Syriac patriarch of Babylon. At the end of the sixteenth century, after the death of their last native metropolitan, the tensions between the Malabar native Christians and the Portuguese hierarchy came to a head. In 1599 an armed clash was narrowly avoided, and papal authority 'finally' reimposed – although sporadic religious resistance continued for centuries.

From Goa, the main Portuguese naval base in India, the Jesuits could embark for the Far East. St Francis Xavier (1506–52), one of the companions of Ignatius Loyola, was first in Goa in 1542, then left with two Jesuit companions and a solitary Japanese Christian convert, for Japan in 1549. The feudal samurai, engaged in internecine warfare, were not indisposed to welcoming people who might bring foreign aid and important technical military skills. Western and southern Japan saw a quite rapid growth of Christianity between 1551 and 1587, supported by a number of important nobles.

There was in the early 1580s, shortly before the beginning of the persecutions, a significant modification of cultural policy by the Jesuit leadership, that was to have more important results in

China than in Japan. The policy in India had been to fight the local indigenous Christian traditions so as to leave room for a centralized and papalist religious policy. But in the later period it was decided – although already too late – to adopt a policy that left far more religious room to the language and culture of the Japanese than the missionaries had formerly allowed.

However, the Japanese mission was unstable, principally because it depended on the goodwill of the Japanese warrior class. Perhaps because of fear of the colonial ambitions of the Spaniards (by now firmly established in the Philippines), perhaps because of the quarrels of foreign trade interests and the intervention of Dutch and English Protestants, but also because of purely internal Japanese political factors, the samurai began at the end of the penultimate decade of the century to reject and to proscribe the Christians. Twenty-six Christians were martyred at Nagasaki in 1597, and in 1614 the powerful shogun Ieyasu issued an edict which alleged that the Christians were conspiring to impose their religion and to seize power in the land. Finally, after a failed Christian peasant revolt in the island of Kyushu, a very large number of Christians were executed for rebellion or martyred for their religion (often by being crucified and left in the shallows of the inshore waters to die), and Christianity became for centuries in Japan a tiny underground sect professed only by a very few in a completely clandestine form. The persecutions are the setting for Shusaka Endo's tragic novel, *Silence*. Buddhist culture had won.

Above: A lacquer screen showing the arrival of the Portuguese Jesuits in Japan. Note how tall the Europeans are.

The fate of the Catholic mission in China was very different. The Chinese mission was launched by a gifted Italian Jesuit, Matteo Ricci (1552–1610), whose work had been enabled by the setting up of a special Jesuit training establishment for the Chinese mission in the Portuguese island factory of Macao. Ricci and another Jesuit managed to obtain admission to a city near Canton in 1583, and they remained there for some years, studying the classical language and the culture of China.

Below: A seventeenth-century engraved map of China, showing Matteo Ricci on the left.

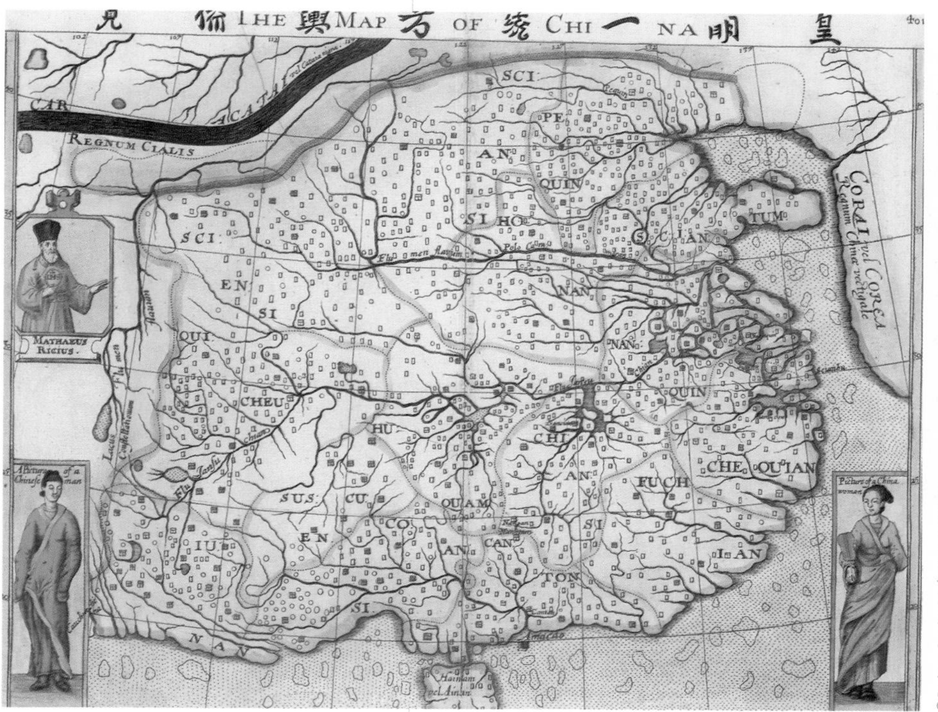

Ricci divined that the mental and social approaches of Western humanism had a great deal in common with the equally élitist culture of China, and in effect he pursued the analogy further, by realizing that the Chinese imperial court pursued a policy of the patronage of higher learning, which could get him access to the centre, if he could convince the Chinese learned élite that he had something to interest them. He managed to get admission to the imperial court in Beijing in 1601. What he had to offer particularly, was astronomical and topographic scientific knowledge: he initially drew attention to himself by identifying the exact nature and purpose of astronomical instruments that had been set up by earlier scientists in the Chinese imperial court, whose use had in later periods been forgotten. He later constructed a world map in Chinese.

Ricci remained in the court until his death. He managed to convince some of the powerful figures there that Western Christian culture was not devoid of interest, and that its morality was in many respects reconcilable with Confucianism, although the main features of the Christian religion remained unintelligible to Chinese intellectuals. At the end of the century,

Right: Portrait of the Japanese shogun Tokugawa Ieyasu, the virulently anti-Christian ruler who believed that the Christian missionaries had a more political agenda than simply spreading the Word.

a time when Christian scholars were still present at court, a Chinese scholar made these concessions, but qualified them by saying: 'It is simply a shame that they speak of a Lord of Heaven, a crude and obnoxious conception that leads them into absurdities and which our literati have a great deal of difficulty in accepting.'[3]

The key to Ricci's dealings with Chinese culture was his policy of 'accommodation', which allowed Chinese converts to Christianity to retain certain features (although only certain ones) of Confucian practice, including ancestor worship, in their lives. He also accepted some Chinese religious terminology in his ritual practice conducted in the Chinese language, notably the terms for God; later missionaries changed Ricci's practice, but still drew on traditional Chinese religious terminology. There were some parallels in early Christianity for this, though it had to be admitted that in Christianity the debate had mostly swung in an exclusive and not an inclusive direction – one thinks of St Augustine's objections to pagan-style funeral meals round the tombs of ancestors.

These 'Chinese rites' were much criticized in Catholic Europe, and eventually, in the early eighteenth century, condemned by the popes. But the real missionary problems in China were perhaps not these. A capital difficulty was that Christianity had entered China through the imperial court and remained present in that court. The way in which Chinese bureaucracy dealt with Christian matters was always as a departmental responsibility of the imperial household, which much narrowed their national importance.

Missionary activity outside the imperial court was quite widespread, but always extremely precarious, and dependent on the favour of particular local and central officials. Missionaries constantly had to move on, and to leave their flocks for years without a pastor. A Chinese clergy was ordained, although only once in this period was there a Chinese bishop. Eventually, at the end of the eighteenth century and after the abolition of the Jesuit Order by the popes, the already very sporadic toleration of Christianity ceased, and the religion survived only in a clandestine way – less clandestine than in Japan, but still only existing for small and very isolated groups, which could only be reached by missionaries who operated secretly.

The Philippines were fully colonialized and fully Christianized. There was some established Christianity in Vietnam, and Christian southern India continued to exist round its very ancient base in Malabar, and in the Portuguese colony of Goa. Elsewhere in Asia, Christianity in the period before the great colonial thrusts of the nineteenth century remained, though widely spread, very much a modest minority movement.

By 1700 the guns and sails of the Europeans had taken Christianity all over the globe, from China to Peru. But whether it was a religion of the conquerors, or also the religion of the conquered, was not at all determined. Where Europeans were not, or not yet conquerors, its status was uncertain, as it still is in China. In the Islamic lands it was still a tolerated minority religion, as it had been from the beginning. However, the Eastern Christian churches almost without exception lived as a subordinate minority, where some centuries earlier they had possessed some independent political base. Only in the Russian lands did East Rome still thrive.

Above: An orthodox Christian icon from c. 1700, of St Nicholas of Mozhaisk.

1 A. Prosperi, 'New Heaven and New Earth', in *Prophetic Rome in the High Renaissance Period* (ed. M. Reeves, Oxford, 1992).

2 David D. Hall, *The Faithful Shepherd: A History of the New England Ministry in the Seventeenth Century* (Chapel Hill, 1972).

3 Quoted by R. G. Tiedemann, in *A World History of Christianity*, ed. A. Hastings (London, 1999), p.381.

17

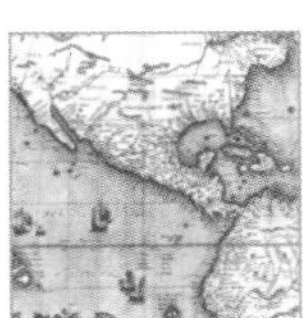

THE RIGHTS OF MAN

Christendom had, since coming into existence, accepted the spiritual leadership of the men who prayed, even if Christians followed the warriors in battle, and obeyed the warrior caste as landowners. On the whole the initiative had stayed with the men of God during the period of the Church reforms in the sixteenth and seventeenth centuries, with the difference that the Protestant pastors placed the preaching of God's word above the offer of His sacraments. But at some point in the seventeenth or eighteenth centuries, a point that until the French Revolution of 1789 is hard to identify with any precision, the social initiative began to slip out of the hands of the churches. Christendom began to travel a long, on occasion painful road, through country in which God's ministers have seemed destined to become patients rather than central actors in the social process.

For centuries the sacred realm had in some sense included all the people of God, all the denizens of Christendom. Not a small company of the elect, but all humans in Christian society had for more than a millennium been thought of as in some way resident aliens on earth, whose real citizenship was in the city of God. St Augustine's vision had not gone unchallenged, even in the Middle Ages. But in the early modern period a transmutation of the role of the churches began, which arose not only as a result of the agitation of intellectuals and publicists, but also in the sense of a shift in the mysterious subsoil that underlies all social relationships.

Above: A seventeenth-century engraving of Hugh Peter (1598–1660), a Puritan clergyman and fiery preacher, who was also actively involved in parliamentary politics. Puritan political meddling could be treated by polemicists as the work of the devil.

Left: The Patriot Oath at the Anniversary of the Federation.

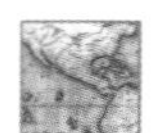

It was an extremely slow and for a long time hardly perceptible drift. Throughout Catholic Europe people continued to make Catholic deaths more or less in the way they had always done, continued to provide pious legacies, endow chapels, make penitential bequests, in ways that differed only slightly, if sometimes significantly, from the older practices. The villages, because of Tridentine reorganization and the provision of more seminaries, were subjected to more episcopal intervention, were more attentively directed, were subject to a closer penitential regime, in a sense more completely Christianized, than before. In certain country areas, it is true, there was not so much change. Even in country villages fifty or so miles from Rome, in the pope's own dominions, there were residual pagan practices and almost total religious ignorance, well into the nineteenth century.

But the fabric and decoration of the Catholic churches themselves were more closely supervised, in a manner that that was in many respects puritanical, even if certain approved images were reverenced and treasured. In the Protestant parishes there was compulsory church attendance, and pastoral supervision of the morals of the villagers. In Catholicism the great pilgrimages flourished, the Roman jubilees, the great gatherings of pilgrims in quest of special indulgences that been summoned to attend the Roman shrines at intervals of twenty-five years ever since the late Middle Ages, were well attended, and new devotions were introduced to the pious. Everywhere there was better census-taking and, on the whole, a better-disciplined Church. It did not in the least look like a gradual collapse of faith. But the social movement that enabled the brusque changes of the French Revolution to happen at ground level must in some way have been there.

The presupposition of the ancient parochial and monastic systems was the existence of lands and funds that had from much earlier times been given to the Church, that had in some sense been given to God. Such lands could still in Catholic countries amount to between a twelfth and a quarter of agricultural land, in Protestant countries much less; in the latter the pastor sometimes depended on a contract of maintenance granted by his congregation. In Catholic or in conservative Protestant countries such as England, the fact that the lands had been given to God did not stop the possessing families – or the state itself – from retaining substantial interests in them, either of a direct sort, or as a source of rights that gave employment to them or their nominees.

Beneath the ancient society other forces were at work. The state was gradually increasing its powers of intervention, so that the very ancient system – already abolished in some Protestant countries, but not in England – of treating a Church benefice as the object of private rights and not of public duties, was threatened. For example, the appearance of state educational systems was to threaten an ancient clerical monopoly in a far more fundamental way than the competition of secular private schools could have done. The birth of secular education had to wait upon the arrival of the French Revolution, but its spies were there before 1789 in some countries.

Christianity at the Court of Public Opinion

The so-called 'wars of religion' that had begun in the Reformation period, in which religion had played an increasingly minor role, ended in the 1648 Treaty of Westphalia that brought the Thirty Years War to a close in Germany. But the wars of religious opinion had yet to begin, in the sense of public controversy, not over the correct or incorrect doctrine of this Church or that, but over the principles upon which we should conduct discussion about religion, and the ways in which we should try to examine religious belief.

44 KING
My Ld Mayor & Sheriffs wait on ye Prince at Windsor

43 QVEEN
Singing O brave popery delicate Popery Oh.

48 KNAVE
Tyrconel arming ye Papists in Ireland.

51 II
L. P. Taken in disguise going to Sea

50 III
A Papist of quallity taken at Wapping

49 IIII
A Papist in disguise taken at ye Tower

45 VII
Tho. A Beckets Old Stockins 5s Ounce
A Preist selling of Relicks by Auction

41 IX
Cry ye Prince of Orange's third Declaration.

I. 30. ENGLISH.

THE REVOLUTION.

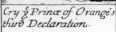

Left: Anti-Catholic playing cards commemorate the events of the Glorious Revolution of 1688. During the seventeenth century, religious debate and criticism flourished in England and Holland.

Above: A Dutch eighteenth-century engraving shows the signing of the Treaty of Utrecht, which ended the wars of Louis XIV.

Auteur d'un dangereux Sisteme
Spinosa n'a que trop repandu son erreur
Mais voyez l'Univers, et sondez vous vous même,
Vous connoîtrez un Créateur

Above: The Dutch philosopher Benedict Spinoza (1634–77). His Tractatus *published in 1670 was a devastating critique of the scriptures and a radical plea for philosophical freedom. It aroused enormous controversy and was banned in 1674.*

Such things were only possible in societies that were prepared to practise at least a selective religious toleration. Holland was intellectually the most tolerant society in Europe, and the great centre of publishing, not only of books, but also of that vehicle of early modern exchange of news and ideas, the periodical or gazette. Post-Restoration England, and even more the England that followed the Glorious Revolution of 1688, with its Anglo-Dutch leadership, was another place where religious debate was freer than elsewhere. But in the succeeding century, when the great wars of Louis XIV were over and more or less settled by the 1714 Treaty of Utrecht, the French nation that formerly had opposed a conformist Catholic front to Dutch Protestantism and secularism became the nation which, more than any other in Europe, nourished (as many believers thought) the rabid tribe of free-thinkers and libertines whose aim was to put Christianity on trial rather than to reform it.

The most radical of the early modern attempts to make a clean sweep of religious opinion, and thence a new start, was one of the earliest. Benedict (Baruch) Spinoza (1634–77) was a Dutch Jew of Iberian extraction whose change of name to Benedict had not indicated his conversion to Christianity, but perhaps pointed to his wish to show how equally things stood with him as to either religion. The *Theological-Political Treatise* that he published in Latin (*Tractatus Theologico-Politicus*) in 1670 contained a devastatingly critical examination of both Jewish and Christian scriptures, which by its exposure of their internal contradictions seemed (and still seems to the distinguished modern literary critic, George Steiner), to have left very little room for orthodox doctrine to survive in either religion. The tractate was also an attempt to establish from first principles a political philosophy of freedom, the noblest and most profound plea for freedom of opinion since the English poet Milton's *Areopagitica: A Speech for the Liberty of Unlicensed Printing* (1644). In it he wrote:

> *'...the object of government is not to change men from rational beings into beasts or puppets, but to enable them to develop their minds and bodies in security, and to employ their reason unshackled...In fact the true aim of government is liberty.'*

Spinoza was understood in his own time as an ideological wrecker, whose only aim was to destroy the foundations of religion. The powerful ethical philosophy that he expounded, especially in his posthumously published *Ethica* (1677), was disregarded, although in moral theory also he set the agenda for the eighteenth century by proposing happiness as one of the main aims of man. His determinism was based upon false premises, but he still anticipated the following century in setting out an ethics that maintained that moral questions are factual questions.

Happiness, to Spinoza, could come only from the tranquillity that goes with the understanding of truth, a truth that he understood metaphysically. Here, at least, Spinoza was more attuned to his own society, which understood (as ours does not) the Socratic testimony that a philosopher may make as much impression by his life as by his arguments.[1] A century later the American Declaration of Rights was willing to take a much less moralistic and metaphysical view of the pursuit of happiness, which it classed as an 'inalienable right', along with life and liberty. But by then the pursuit of happiness had been linked with the practice of toleration. And the question 'Am I a just man?' had been replaced by the question 'Am I a happy man' ?

The philosophies of the eighteenth-century Enlightenment are rightly said to have been based on the new knowledge of the natural world that came from the understanding of science. It has to be added that the great Enlightenment publicists were not scientists, but above all popularizers of science. The trend was set by the French writer Bernard de Fontenelle (1657–1757), who, in 1686, published a *History of Oracles*, not very polite to miracles. Fontenelle set a polemic pattern for all later rationalist publicists by the critical examination of particular cases of supposed supernatural occurrences, such as the case of the gold tooth, in which a Silesian child had, in 1599, been reported to have had a molar tooth miraculously turned to gold. It was a sort of alleged miracle which still turns up in religious life today. Fontenelle later turned to the popularization of astronomy, in an essay in which he gallantly and with great wit and clarity explained the movements of the heavenly bodies to an imagined marquise.

The aim of the new philosophy was not to abolish religion, but to tame it. The prevailing tendency, from the English Shaftesbury (Third Earl, 1671–1713) to the French Voltaire (François Marie Arouet, 1694–1778) was deist, not atheist. Voltaire spoke for so many of his generation, when he wrote that his wish was to love God, whom he sought as a father; but the God actually shown for his worship was someone he could only describe as a hateful tyrant, who offered man nothing but an insoluble enigma. The problem, of which he did not despair of an answer, was to humanize God: human nature was to be vindicated.

The English were especially fertile in ways of thought that would preserve a religion reconcilable with science, which was compatible with the principles of rational natural philosophy. In 1730 Matthew Tindal (1656–1733) published *Christianity as old as the Creation, or the Gospel – a Republication of the Law of Nature.* It was in order to preserve a rational natural theology that George Berkeley, Bishop of Cloyne (1685–1753), composed his very powerful and influential *Principles of Human Knowledge* (1710). His intention was to defend natural theology against the mechanistic tendencies that he detected in the English philosopher John Locke's *Essay Concerning Human Understanding* (1690), which Berkeley rightly interpreted as a work that would become a great support for sceptical views about religion.

Behind the endless reasonings of Voltaire lay the mathematically viewed universe of Isaac Newton (1643–1727), of whose scientific thought Voltaire was the tireless popularizer. On this basis Voltaire conceived a universe of which God was the benevolent, omnipresent sovereign, whose providence is presumed to reward good and to punish evil, and who comes to the aid of the poor and oppressed, but whose actions are entirely impenetrable to man. That Newton had in fact spent his declining years practising alchemy and speculating on biblical chronology as it could be strictly and literally understood from scripture, worried neither Voltaire nor his readers. Voltaire's universe assumed optimism, but he himself felt that optimism was impossible: that was the message of his great novel, *Candide* (1759), the doubting man's edition of the Book of Job.

Unlike Voltaire, both Denis Diderot (1713–84) and Jean d'Alembert (1717–83) were atheistic rather than than deist. In Diderot, especially, the transition between the reasonable man and the man of sentiment took place, which was to bring the new intellectuals towards the assertion of individual consciousness and of Romantic experience. With Jean-Jaques Rousseau (1712–78) this assertion was

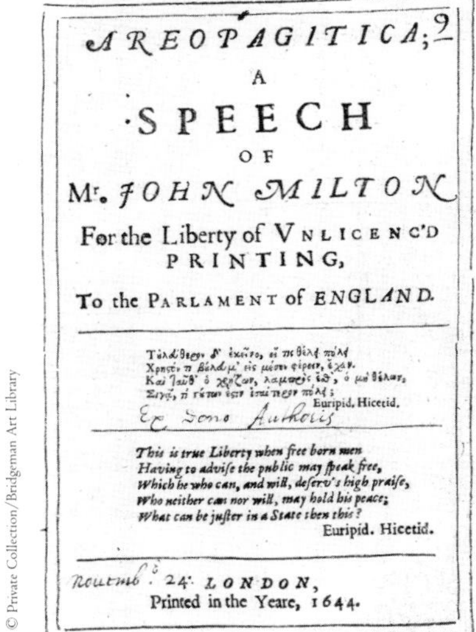

AREOPAGITICA;
A
SPEECH
OF
Mr. JOHN MILTON
For the Liberty of VNLICENC'D
PRINTING,
To the PARLAMENT of ENGLAND.

Euripid. Hicetid.

This is true Liberty when free born men
Having to advise the public may speak free,
Which he who can, and will, deserv's high praise,
Who neither can nor will, may hold his peace;
What can be juster in a State then this?
Euripid. Hicetid.

LONDON,
Printed in the Yeare, 1644.

Above: The frontispiece of John Milton's Areopagitica. *Published in 1644, it remains a rallying cry for freedom of the press.*

Below: Portrait of François Marie Arouet de Voltaire, one of the great figures of the eighteenth-century Enlightenment. He attacked religious bigotry but not God, whom he sought to humanize.

Above: A telescope belonging to Sir Isaac Newton. Newton's scientific view of the universe profoundly influenced Enlightenment thought.

Below: an engraving of an instrument-maker's workshop and tools from Diderot's Encyclopédie.

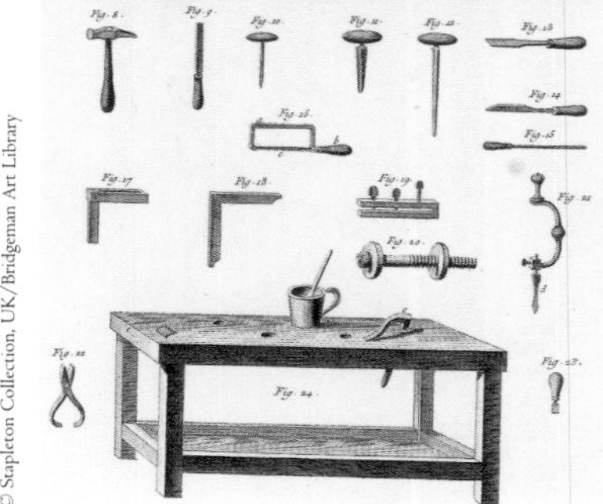

brought into the mainstream of European literary consciousness. Although Rousseau sustained that the integrity of a 'pure' religion was possible, his morality of sentiment was irreconcilable with traditional Christian doctrine:

'I have seen that, in order to act well with pleasure, I have to act freely and without fear; if I want to lose the pleasant feeling of carrying out a good work, I have only to feel it a duty.' (Sixième Promenade)

The Enlightenment, as it started to call itself within in its own lifetime, was a huge operation of public information and publication, of which the *Encyclopédie* (1751–65) of Diderot was the extraordinary and crowning achievement. In the *Encyclopédie* there lay in germ all the techniques of popular, rationalist publicity, as they were to survive in the Society for the Diffusion of Useful Knowledge (founded by the Utilitarians in 1827), in the public libraries and reading rooms of the nineteenth century, in the BBC Brains Trusts of the 1940s and 1950s, and in the CD and Internet information facilities of our own times.

Revolution in the New World

The American Revolution against British colonial government that occurred in 1776 was important to the churches both inside and outside North America. The revolution of the colonists was the first great political success of the European Enlightenment; it made the little successes of the Encyclopédistes, the currying of the favour of the 'enlightened' Frederick the Great of Prussia by Voltaire, or that of Catherine the Great by Diderot, look very petty. Those who made the American Revolution were almost to a man 'enlightened' in a general sense, and Freemasonry, the new convivial and fraternal organization that was at that time the badge of enlightened rationalism, was common among their leaders. Not for nothing was the Freemason sign of the eye and the pyramid placed on the Great Seal of the United States, and on the obverse of the one dollar bills. The English ex-Quaker Thomas Paine (1737–1809) happened to find himself in Philadelphia in 1776: his pamphlet *Common Sense*, which called clearly for independence, was one of the most important documents of the immediate prehistory of the American Revolution. To it he added a postscript that reproached the Quakers for their disavowing resistance to the English crown. Thomas Paine was among several Americans (for he became an American) who linked the American with the French Revolution, in his case by his second famous pamphlet, *The Rights of Man* (1791–2).

The American Revolution was very different from its French successor in its relationship with the Churches. In France the Revolution was to slice civil society in two, and to produce a wounding break in Europe between enlightened principles and those of the Churches, which has in some respects still, after two centuries, not fully healed. In the Amercan colonies the Churches were on the whole behind the rebellion. Catholics fought on the American side in the Revolutionary War, and a Congregational minister, George Witherspoon, and a Catholic layman, Charles Carroll, were among the signatories to the Declaration of Independence.

Internally the American Revolution only strengthened the existing Church settlement in the ex-colonies. Article 6 of the Constitution (1787) excluded any religious test as a qualification for public office in the United States, and the First Amendment (1791) forbade Congress to make any law that either concerned the establishment of religion or restricted its free exercise. Free rights to exercise

IN CONGRESS, JULY 4, 1776.

The unanimous Declaration of the thirteen united States of America,

THE DECLARATION OF INDEPENDENCE

On July 4, 1776, the Continental Congress adopted the Declaration of Independence, whereby the United Colonies of America declared themselves to be "Free and Independent States." After the Declaration had been engrossed on parchment, it was signed on August 2 by the delegates to the Congress who were present and later by others. It is now on permanent display in the National Archives. A copper-plate engraving, produced by direct impression from the document itself, was completed by William J. Stone in 1823. The above reproduction is made from one of Stone's facsimiles.

Left: The Declaration of Independence issued on 4 July 1776 by the American colonies. Signatories to this revolutionary document included a Congregational minister and Catholic layman.

Above: 'Who Wants Me?' – a cartoon by the English caricaturist Isaac Cruikshank showing the American revolutionary Tom Paine and his pamphlet The Rights of Man, *which supported the French Revolution.*

Above: Thomas Jefferson's design for the Great Seal of the United States of America. The pyramid sign of the Freemasons, symbol of enlightened rationalism, shines out between Liberty and Justice, who support a coat of arms surrounded by the initials of the thirteen colonies.

Below: Great Salt Lake, Utah, where, in the nineteenth century, the Mormons took the state option to set up a religious community.

religion were also written into the constitutions of the individual states. The New England states retained a degree of establishment of the Congregationalist churches on the English model, but in four of the thirteen colonies including Pennsylvania, there was no religious establishment of any sort. Establishment remained, however, a possible state option that was to be taken up by the Mormons in Utah in the nineteenth century.

Revolution in Europe

Churchmen were, almost as much as any other social group in the eighteenth century, penetrated by the principles of the Enlightenment. In spite of papal prohibition, the number of Freemason priests in Catholic countries was considerable. The most notable demonstration of papal weakness came about because of a chain of circumstances arising from Jesuit reluctance to go along with a Spanish-Portuguese colonial decision of 1750. This would have compelled them to submit to a huge forced movement of populations from Jesuit-run Paraguay. The decision would have inflicted – and did inflict – appalling hardship on the Paraguay Indians, compelling them to move out of the area and across the River Uruguay.

From these beginnings arose a persecution of the Jesuits in Portugal, and a virtual coalition of their many European enemies in governments all over the continent, to put pressure on Rome to their disfavour. A financial scandal in France made their situation yet worse, so far as general European opinion went. Although Pope Clement XIII refused to abandon them, his successor, Pope Clement XIV (pope 1769–74) was made of weaker stuff. In 1773 he signed the bull of suppression of the whole Jesuit Order, which the Order, bound by its own constitution to obedience to the pope, had to obey. It was a great triumph of Enlightenment political correctness that earned Pope Clement XIV a condescending pat on the back in the memoirs of the English historian, Edward Gibbon. And in a sense it was a pointer towards the direction things were later to take in France, where the most radical consequences were to follow from reformist correctness among the privileged classes.

In the critical meetings of the French Estates General in the summer of 1789, a majority of the estate of the clergy joined the Third Estate after the oath of the tennis court. The decision was influenced by the discontents of the lower clergy, but turned out to be suicidal for their order. The financial consequences were swift; in November, 1789 Church property was nationalized, and the clergy became state employees. In such circumstances the monasteries could not survive. In 1790 the Civil Constitution of the Clergy formally nationalized the Church itself. Bishoprics became the ecclesiastical shadows of the new civil departments; bishops and priests were to be elected by the congregations; papal intervention was forbidden.

There had been precedents for some of these things in earlier French Gallicanism, which the French kings had promoted from the later Middle Ages into the early modern period as a doctrine that asserted the rights of the French Church to a certain limited independence from the papacy. In theory, Church doctrine was not affected by the Civil Constitution of 1790, but in effect it created a new Church that was unacceptable to many of its own clergy. Later in the year an oath of allegiance to the state and to the civil constitution of the clergy was required, forcing many of the clergy into emigration or schism. More than half the clergy refused the oath, and in 1791 the pope condemned the civil constitution as sacrilegious. In the Terror of 1792, hundreds of the clergy were murdered or

Left: A Jesuit and his family by Marco Benefiale (1684–1764). Clement XIV suppressed the Jesuit Order in 1773.

Below: The Tennis Court Oath taken on 20 June 1789 by delegates of the Third Estate, who swore not to disband until France had a constitution.

executed, and a vast emigration, in all some 30,000, took place: the Convention continued to execute priests into 1793, and there was a second outburst of persecution at the end of the decade.

The Declaration of the Rights of Man in 1789 was integrally connected with the abolition of privilege that lay behind the huge seizures of Church property, but not the claim to complete control of the Church – that had a much more complex prehistory. In general the ideological novelty of the Revolution lay much more in its assertion of national right. This was very shortly to give rise in the Revolutionary and Napoleonic Wars to the fearsome series of modern European national wars which, until recent events in the Balkans, was thought to be over.

The settlement of the Revolutionary crisis of the French Church took place, not because of an internal movement, but as the result of external military conquests. In 1796 Napoleon's armies marched into central Italy. Military resistance collapsed, and French puppet republics were set up. Early in the following year he occupied the papal states, and plundered the remaining treasures of the great shrine to the Mother of Christ at Loreto, near the Adriatic coast. Not far from Loreto, in the little hill town of Tolentino, he imposed an onerous treaty upon Pope Pius VI (pope 1775–99), which included the concession to plunder works of art in the papal dominions. Subsequently the death of a French general in an anti-French riot in Rome led to the end of even relative independence for the pope as a secular ruler. The rest of the papal states were occupied, and a puppet Roman republic established, preparatory to the French invasion of southern Italy. Only Sicily remained Roman Catholic and non-French, defended by the Protestant fleet of Nelson.

Below: A cartoon showing Church and nobility recoiling in fear from the Third Estate. By August 1789, clergy and nobles had been forced to relinquish their privileges.

© Victoria & Albert Museum, London, UK/Bridgeman Art Library

Above: Political cartoon showing Napoleon Bonaparte as King of Rome. In 1796, during the Revolutionary Wars, Napoleon marched into Italy and in early 1797 occupied the papal states.

Right: The Declaration of the Rights of Man and Citizen, adopted by the Constituent Assembly in France in 1789. Like the American Declaration of Independence, it carries the sign of the Freemasons.

Below: The Madonna of Loretto *by the Italian artist Raphael. By a treaty signed with the pope in 1797, the conquering Napoleon could take what fine art he wished from the papal territories.*

© Giraudon/Bridgeman Art Library

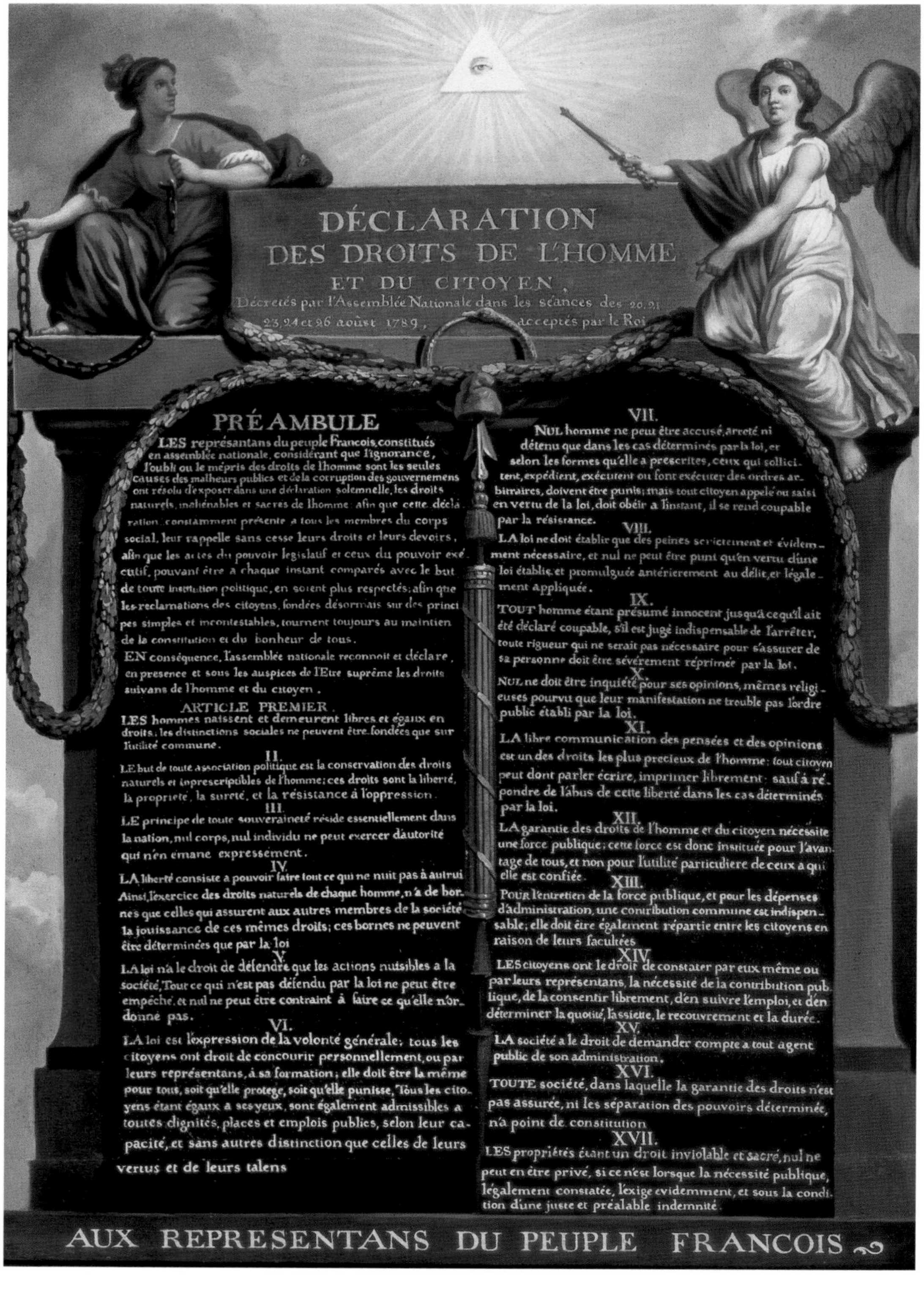

DÉCLARATION
DES DROITS DE L'HOMME
ET DU CITOYEN,
Décretés par l'Assemblée Nationale dans les séances des 20, 21 23, 24 et 26 aoust 1789, acceptés par le Roi

PRÉAMBULE

LES représantans du peuple Francois, constitués en assemblée nationale, considérant que l'ignorance, l'oubli ou le mépris des droits de l'homme sont les seules causes des malheurs publics et de la corruption des gouvernemens ont résolu d'exposer dans une déclaration solemnelle, les droits naturels, inaliénables et sacrés de l'homme: afin que cette déclaration, constamment présente a tous les membres du corps social, leur rappelle sans cesse leurs droits et leurs devoirs, afin que les actes du pouvoir legislatif et ceux du pouvoir exécutif, pouvant être a chaque instant comparés avec le but de toute institution politique, en soient plus respectés; afin que les reclamations des citoyens, fondées désormais sur des principes simples et incontestables, tournent toujours au maintien de la constitution et du bonheur de tous.

EN conséquence, l'assemblée nationale reconnoit et déclare, en presence et sous les auspices de l'Etre suprême les droits suivans de l'homme et du citoyen.

ARTICLE PREMIER.

LES hommes naissent et demeurent libres et égaux en droits; les distinctions sociales ne peuvent être fondées que sur l'utilité commune.

II.

LE but de toute association politique est la conservation des droits naturels et inprescriptibles de l'homme; ces droits sont la liberté, la propriete, la surete, et la résistance à l'oppression.

III.

LE principe de toute souveraineté réside essentiellement dans la nation, nul corps, nul individu ne peut exercer d'autorité qui n'en emane expressement.

IV.

LA liberté consiste a pouvoir faire tout ce qui ne nuit pas à autrui Ainsi, l'exercice des droits naturels de chaque homme, n'a de bornes que celles qui assurent aux autres membres de la société la jouissance de ces mêmes droits; ces bornes ne peuvent être déterminées que par la loi

V.

LA loi n'a le droit de défendre que les actions nuisibles a la société, Tout ce qui n'est pas défendu par la loi ne peut être empéché, et nul ne peut être contraint à faire ce qu'elle n'ordonné pas.

VI.

LA loi est l'expression de la volonté générale; tous les citoyens ont droit de concourir personnellement, ou par leurs représentans, à sa formation; elle doit être la même pour tous, soit qu'elle protege, soit qu'elle punisse, Tous les citoyens étant égaux a ses yeux, sont également admissibles a toutes dignités, places et emplois publics, selon leur capacité, et sans autres distinction que celles de leurs vertus et de leurs talens

VII.

NUL homme ne peut être accusé, arreté ni détenu que dans les cas déterminés par la loi, et selon les formes qu'elle a prescrites, ceux qui sollicitent, expédient, exécutent ou font exécuter des ordres arbitraires, doivent être punis; mais tout citoyen appelé ou saisi en vertu de la loi, doit obéir a l'instant, il se rend coupable par la résistance.

VIII.

LA loi ne doit établir que des peines strictement et évidemment nécessaire, et nul ne peut être puni qu'en vertu d'une loi établie et promulguée antérierement au délit, et légalement appliquée.

IX.

TOUT homme étant présumé innocent jusqu'à ce qu'il ait été déclaré coupable, s'il est jugé indispensable de l'arrêter, toute rigueur qui ne serait pas nécessaire pour s'assurer de sa personne doit être sévérement réprimée par la loi.

X.

NUL ne doit être inquiété pour ses opinions, mêmes religieuses pourvu que leur manifestation ne trouble pas l'ordre public établi par la loi.

XI.

LA libre communication des pensées et des opinions est un des droits les plus precieux de l'homme: tout citoyen peut dont parler écrire, imprimer librement: sauf à répondre de l'abus de cette liberté dans les cas déterminés par la loi.

XII.

LA garantie des droits de l'homme et du citoyen nécessite une force publique; cette force est donc instituée pour l'avantage de tous, et non pour l'utilité particuliere de ceux a qui elle est confiée.

XIII.

POUR l'entretien de la force publique, et pour les dépenses d'administration, une contribution commune est indispensable; elle doit être également répartie entre les citoyens en raison de leurs facultées

XIV.

LES citoyens ont le droit de constater par eux même ou par leurs représentans, la nécessité de la contribution publique, de la consentir librement, d'en suivre l'emploi, et d'en déterminer la quotité, l'assiette, le recouvrement et la durée.

XV.

LA société a le droit de demander compte a tout agent public de son administration.

XVI.

TOUTE société, dans laquelle la garantie des droits n'est pas assurée, ni les séparation des pouvoirs déterminée, n'a point de constitution

XVII.

LES propriétés étant un droit inviolable et sacré, nul ne peut en être privé, si ce n'est lorsque la nécessité publique, légalement constatée, l'exige evidemment, et sous la condition d'une juste et préalable indemnité.

AUX REPRESENTANS DU PEUPLE FRANCOIS

© Giraudon/Bridgeman Art Library

After a stay in Tuscany, Pope Pius VI, who was an old and dying man, was carried under guard over the Alpine passes in the spring of 1799 to Grenoble in France, to be taken as a prisoner to Valence on the Rhone, where he died that summer. In southern Italy ferocious peasant counter-revolutionary wars of rebellion were waged against the French, supported by English sea power: other similar Catholic peasant wars were fought in Belgium, Switzerland, and in the west of France itself.

Below: Napoleon at his coronation as emperor in 1804 (painted by Ingres). Pope Pius VII presided, a logical consequence of the 1801 concordat that re-established the Roman Catholic Church in France.

Pope Pius VI's successor, Pius VII (pope 1800–21) was elected in Austrian Venice. In 1801 he agreed a concordat with Napoleon that regulated the situation of the Church in France for a over a century. The new French Church was to be in some respects (but only some) the Gallican Church desired by the old French monarchy, but in others a quite different, modernized affair. Catholicism was recognized as the majority religion in France, though not as the state religion: the bishops and clergy (now salaried state employees) were to swear an oath of allegiance to the state. The pope in effect acquired new powers, not available to his predecessors, over French bishops, whom he was enabled to dismiss or confirm. The confiscation of Church property was accepted. It is significant that, after the fall and defeat of Napoleon, the restored French royalist government after 1815 was unable to find a preferable solution, and left the Napoleonic concordat intact. Napoleon and Pope Pius VII had found an agreement that was to influence all modern government thinking in Catholic countries.

Pope Pius VII's later functions at the coronation of Napoleon as French emperor in 1804 at Notre Dame in Paris were really only a postscript to the concordat. In 1806 an event of far more significance took place in Vienna: the resignation by the Austrian ruler Francis II of the title of Holy Roman Emperor. The Christendom that had come into existence after Charlemagne's coronation in 800 had come to an end, even though many of the mentalities of Christendom still persisted.

Evangelical Revival and Awakening in Protestantism

After these events in the great public world of war and revolution, the affairs of modest pastors in England and North America may seem small beer. But the evangelical revivals in Protestant lands are not to be disregarded, because they were to help decide a new social context for modern Christianity.

There is no older theme in Christianity than the awakening of the troubled soul, and the desire of the awakened soul to abide with kindred spirits who may give it some comfort. In the traditions of both Lutheranism and Calvinism there was much to this purpose that was by no means crowded out by the onset of early rationalism.

But the conversion – as it later came to be called – of the troubled soul can be a socially disturbing process. In the eighteenth century, Anglicanism was a Church that was closely tied to the defence of a particular theory of constitutional government and a particular dynasty, that of the Hanoverians. It possessed many learned and moderate bishops, who on the whole saw

 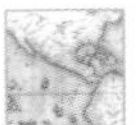

enthusiasm in religion as a threat to established and reasonable order. Hanoverian Anglicanism may from the distance of a couple of centuries seem a quiet place where clergymen ate their dinners undisturbed, but the memory of a disputed royal succession in which religion was a central issue, and even the present threat of Jacobite revolution, were very much alive. To the eighteenth-century ruling classes, for whom the clergy formed, either as preachers or as magistrates, a sort of highly privileged police force, fear of the mob was a potent thing, even when it marched to anti-papist slogans.

The onset of religious enthusiasm in the Church of England was quite a complex affair, which was bound up on one side of the Atlantic with the German connections of the Hanoverian monarchy, and on the other with the common religious world still inhabited by the Protestantism of the British homeland, and that of the North American colonists. The English religious revivalism, which could never be called religious revolution, started in a quite low-key way among young clergymen who were of modest origins, but had attended Oxford or Cambridge colleges – in fact the key figure, John Wesley (1703–91), the son of an engaging but badly organized Anglican clergyman, looked set to make a very orthodox clerical career, founded on his fellowship of Lincoln College.

Below: John Wesley, charismatic preacher and founder of Methodism, visiting his mother's grave.

The careers of John Wesley and his brother Charles, and that of their Oxford contemporary, also to become a clergyman, George Whitefield (1714–70), were for some time intertwined. John Wesley and Whitefield were both to become compelling preachers, but there was something more dramatic about Whitefield, which caused congregations practically to mob him. Wesley, on the other hand, seems to have stimulated demonstrations that would now be called charismatic. The foundation of his ministry was what his own father called 'the inward witness', an assurance of election for salvation. Of the two, Wesley was the more resistant to Calvinist formulation of doctrine, but far from doctrinally consistent.

What principally influenced Wesley in the earlier stages of his ministry was the Moravian Brethren, a sect with a long history in northern Germany, which experienced a great revival in the early eighteenth century that took them both to England and to the North American colonies. It might be said to have been part of a long on-and-off love affair between English and German intellectuals. The British intellectuals tended to be beguiled both by German devotion to intellectual 'system', which was a key word in much Enlightenment discourse, and by the powerful emotional charge that informed so much of Germanic philosophical and religious speculation.

Both John Wesley and Whitefield, at early stages of their careers, went as missionaries for a time to Georgia in the south of the American colonies. For Wesley the experience was important but not decisive; for Whitefield, whose experiences in New England were more positive, it may have been more important. But the decisive episodes in the ministries of both Whitefield and Wesley sprang out of Whitefield's open-air preaching campaigns in the mining areas outside Bristol, in 1739.

These huge outdoor gatherings – which would not have seemed strange to St Francis – inspired Wesley and his followers to preach particularly in the industrializing mining zones of the Midlands, which would seem to modern people still like open countryside, but were especially fertile for the mission field because the established parochial system did not cater for them. Both within and out of doors, the hymns that John Wesley and his brother Charles composed were to become an integral part of collective worship. The tradition and the organization for which Wesley was responsible, meant the foundation of a body that had the flexibility to respond swiftly to the enormous demands that industrialization was going to make on the Christian apostolate, especially when, as so often

happened, the new mines and factories were in areas where the existing parochial system was unable to cope with them. The members of Wesley's 'Societies' were called 'Methodists', an appellation which they owed in part to their centralized organization, based on the principle of 'connexion'. Their direct and indirect influence on English religious and social life was to be enormous, especially as it was to be transmitted in partly secularized form into the twentieth century because of Methodist influence on trade unions and the nascent Labour Party.

Below: George Whitefield, a leading figure in the English religious revivalism of the eighteenth century, preaching to a rapt audience in the countryside.

© Museum of the City of New York, USA/Bridgeman Art Library

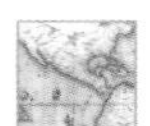

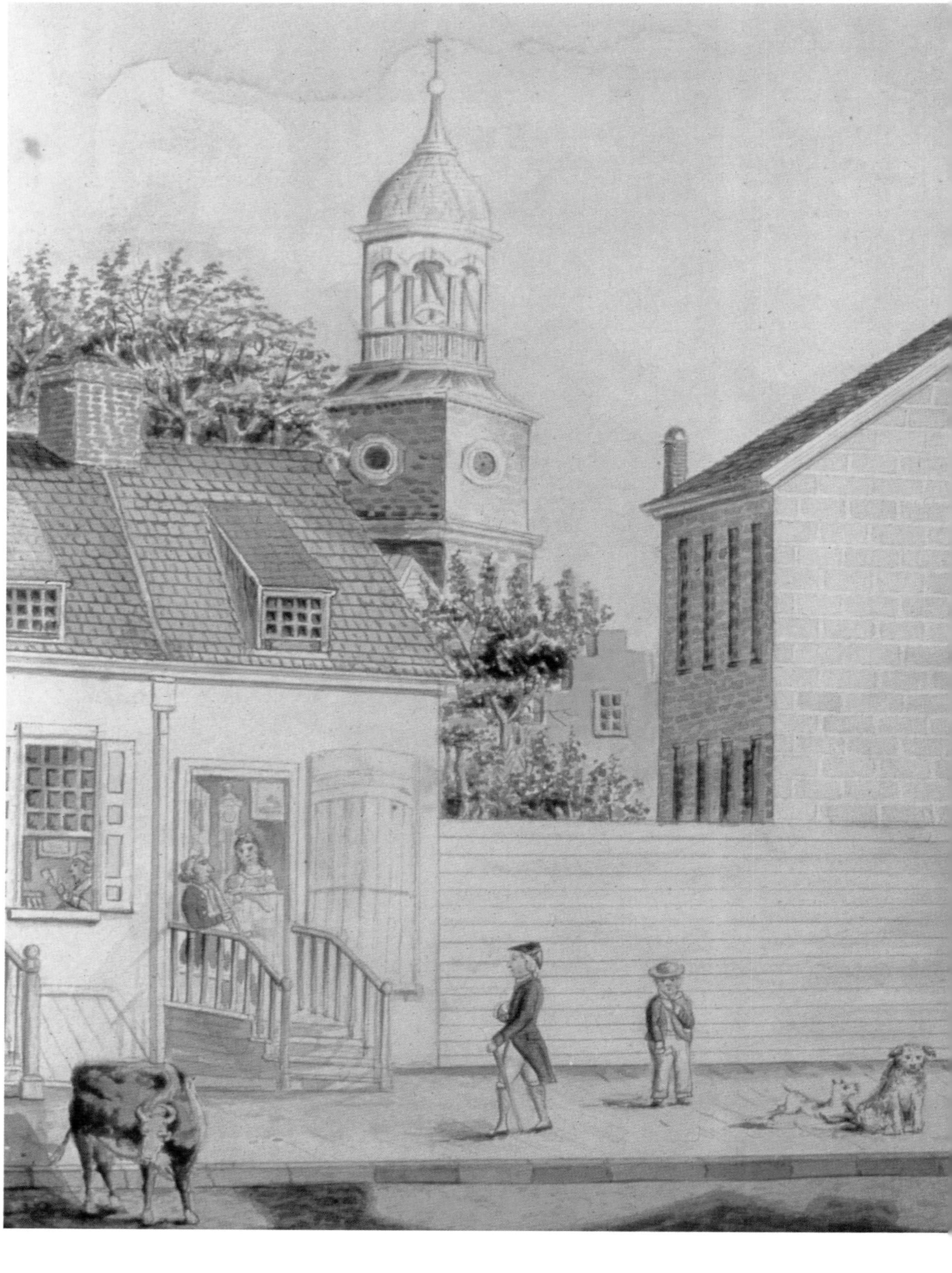

Right: The first Methodist Episcopal Church in North America. From its founding, Methodism spread rapidly, causing a clash with the Anglicans. Wesley ordained Thomas Coke (1747–1818) to superintend the 'brethren in America'.

Wesley refused to accept any limits on his preaching mission. He wrote that:

'...I look upon all the world as my parish: thus far, I mean, that in whatever part of it I am, I judge it meet, right and my bounden duty to declare unto all that are willing to hear the glad tidings of salvation.'

Wesley and his preachers were not always popular. Especially in the earlier stages, they gave cause to rioting and violence, and they were not only reviled but persecuted, and in one or two cases virtually martyred. The established order was not at all disposed to protect them, and occasionally left them under mob attack.

Wesley was to the end of his long life unwilling to admit that he had founded a dissenting sect. He declared his utter unwillingness to leave the Church of England, only a couple of years before his death. On the other hand, Methodism, as his way of doing things was called, required organization that the Anglican Church could not and would not provide. He could run the exhausting business of covering huge areas of the country with preaching 'circuits', only with the help of lay preachers whom he appointed, preachers who were to lead exacting lives of poverty and service. He also, towards the end of his life, had ordained men for the ministry in America and Scotland, some as 'superintendents'. This was not really reconcilable with continued Anglicanism.

Both in England and in North America, the eighteenth century proved to be a time in which, despite the surrounding rationalism, the Protestant churches and sects could find men and women who were profoundly convinced about religious truth, and willing to devote their lives to teaching and preaching, often in the uncongenial surroundings of the new industries. To some extent, this period of the 'Great Awakenings' made itself felt upon the black slave communities of America, but the impact was very limited.

The question of slavery and of black subjection remained. Among the sects, only the Quakers, late in the eighteenth century, denied membership to slave owners, as a result of the efforts of the Quaker tailor, John Woolman (1720–72). An American evangelical divine, Samuel Hopkins, published in 1776, at the start of the Independence war, *A Dialogue Concerning the Slavery of the Africans*, which pointed out that 'the sons of liberty' were 'oppressing and tyrannizing over many thousands of poor blacks, who have as good a claim to liberty as themselves'. But eleven years later the Constitution of the United States was to declare that 'No person held to service or labor in one State...escaping into another... shall be discharged from such service and labor, but shall be delivered up on the claim of the party to whom such service or labor may be due.' It is true that, in the draft drawn up for Congress for the Declaration of Independence, British permissiveness about the slave trade (as distinct from the institution itself) was roundly condemned, but this judgement failed to get a mention in the final version of the Declaration, and it certainly found no echo in the Constitution. Slavery had not yet become such a big issue in the Protestant conscience, as it was to be on both sides of the Atlantic in the following century.

1 The topic was discussed by Jasper Griffin in the New York Review of Books, 6 May 1999

Left: Inside the old Lutheran church, York County, USA. The sketch, which was drawn in 1800, shows the singing choir, the congregation and officers of the church.

LE CONGRÈS.

18

Romantics and Secularists

By 1815, the year of Napoleon's final defeat and of the great peace congress of Vienna that resettled the map of Europe as best it could, the continent had experienced over twenty-five years of wounding wars and revolutions that had torn the old European order to tatters both ideologically and politically. European governments felt they had to pull together to avert the entire collapse of the social order. These feelings had political effects: this was the beginning of the Great Peace in Europe, which lasted until the Crimean War in mid-century.

Russia, which had emerged during the Napoleonic Wars as the new great power, whose influence was no longer confined to the borderlands of Central Europe, was a firm part of what the foreign

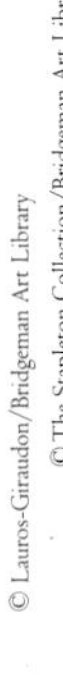

Above: The great Kremlin and cathedrals of Moscow, with their distinctive Eastern Orthodox architecture.

Left: A political cartoon showing European leaders celebrating the downfall of Napoleon and the 1815 Congress of Vienna.

© Private Collection/Bridgeman Art Library

Above: The radical English poet Samuel Taylor Coleridge (1772–1834) as a young man.

Below: An illustration of women convicts working in Brixton prison from a study of London prisons by Henry Mayhew (1812–87). Utilitarian Jeremy Bentham had a particular interest in the practical organization of prisons.

© Private Collection/Bridgeman Art Library

ministers called the 'Concert of Europe'. Russian occupying troops were in France in the years immediately following Waterloo, and Russia, representative of the Eastern Orthodox Church, had become quite a powerful influence upon the rest of Christendom. Moscow had been asserted almost from the beginnings of the Russian state as 'new Rome': in a sense the long-defeated forces of Byzantium raised their heads in Europe in the nineteenth century. In the Balkans and Greece, the Hellene and Serb nations asserted themselves against the already centuries-old domination of the Turks.

South America had during the Napoleonic period felt the full effects of the final decline of imperial Spain. By the mid-1820s the whole of South and Central America, barring the islands, had thrown off Spanish or Portuguese allegiance. The churches in Latin America were weakened by the uncertainties of political conflict: the creole, native-born European ruling classes ended by dominating in the whole area. The Church had to follow where they led, sometimes experiencing demoralizing delays. The indigenous populations were always the losers.

A Shift of Ideologies

The Revolutionary and Napoleonic periods had been a time of great political acceleration, in which huge areas of Europe had experienced not only bewilderingly swift changes of rulers, but also equally bewildering shifts of ideologies. The ancient belief systems had suddenly been directly challenged, not only in the cities but also in remote country districts where for hundreds of years the rural masses had known nothing but custom and tradition. The enlightened principles that the privileged classes had ended by more or less accepting, though often without making any real attempt to reconcile them with the religious system that continued to rule large parts of their lives, had displayed volcanic revolutionary potential. The militarization of society had suddenly been carried to a point probably unknown in Europe since the decline of the Roman Empire. National military conscription had previously been practised only in Russia; now under Napoleon it had become the rule in the most civilized country in Europe.

Faced by these challenges and threats, 'Restoration' society tried to repair the ship of the *ancien régime*, which had turned out to be in such a dangerously leaky condition. Publicists and literary folk often tended to swerve to the conservative side. There were still British literary radicals, but the poets Southey and Wordsworth represented a conformist trend. The poet Coleridge was no conformist; he was also one of the most important political philosophers of the century, the main importer into Britain of German philosophical conservatism, that had many implications for the religious outlook.

After 1815 thoughtful people tended to divide between those who consciously rejected the legacy of the eighteenth-century Enlightenment, and were either looking for or promoting a conservative alternative, and those who thought that the political and ethical values of the Enlightenment could be preserved, and that people ought to work for the progressive improvement of society in a constructive and non-revolutionary manner. Great Britain was especially encouraging to radicals of the latter sort, to people such as the philosopher Jeremy Bentham (1748–1831), who were in the last analysis Utopian Radicals, who thought that the rational reorganization of society to achieve the greatest good of the greatest number of citizens could be proceeded with indefinitely, without serious risk of social and political disturbance. Such ideas of what came later to be called 'social engineering' were under one label or another to remain influential in British society for a very long time indeed.

The British had already, in response to the challenges of the French Revolution, produced a political philosopher of great stature in Edmund Burke (1729–97). Burke's genuine traditionalism and respect for archaic custom had little equivalent in continental Europe. Curiously, the critical period of 1815–48, in which most of the ideas that lay behind twentieth-century politics were first elaborated, was one in which the most conservative thinkers were just as revolutionary and just as destructive as declared revolutionaries such as Marx. The innate intellectual conservatism of most of the Enlightenment philosophers, with their reliance on the ideas of natural virtue and natural law, has already been remarked on. Even these philosophies could get politically out of hand, as had happened in France in the last decade of the eighteenth century. But the conservative political philosophies maturing in Germany in Napoleonic times were potentially far more radical, especially in their conception of a kind of national and popular spirit, disembodied but absolutely real, that is permanent and integral to the social body. Such nationalism had terrible potential, even if for a long time it was expressed in terms that made it practically unintelligible to ordinary people.

The extreme conservatism of the French political philosopher Joseph de Maistre (1753–1821) was to some extent couched in religious language. It appeared on the surface to favour the stability of the established order. But when examined closely it was inspired by a sort of savage praise of despotism and irrationalism that included de Maistre's famous panegyric of the executioner, whom he saw as the great protector of civil and religious order. De Maistre has been said to have been in some ways a precursor of twentieth-century Fascism. In theological terms he is much stronger on punishment than on grace: forgiveness was not a word in his vocabulary.

One of the great clashes of the French Restoration period was between believers who saw the Enlightenment as a betrayal of all the values of tradition, understanding tradition in the Christian sense of the doctrine passed down through the grace conferred by the Holy Spirit, and those who (as the traditionalists saw it) to varying degrees allowed themselves to be affected by the spirit of 'liberalism'. This kind of traditionalism was essentially a religious movement led by the clergy, and very different from the innovatory and extreme politics of de Maistre.

In the Church of England the traditionalist movement became known (from its pamphlets published at an early stage) as the 'Tractarian' movement. John Henry Newman (1801–90, converted from Anglicanism to Roman Catholicism in 1845), later Cardinal of the Roman Church, in his account of his religious life as an Anglican defined liberalism in religion as 'the anti-dogmatic principle and its developments'. He described the birth of the Tractarian religious movement of 1833 as due to the sermon preached for Oxford Assizes in that year on 'National Apostasy' by a clergyman who remained firmly Anglican, namely John Keble (1792–1866), a distinguished man who is now better remembered for his hymns than for his doctrines.

The title of Keble's sermon gives some idea of the aggressive and even ferocious character of the Church conflicts of that time.[1] Liberalism, strange as this may sound to modern ears, was viewed by traditionalists as the enemy of all truth, even as the harbinger of antichrist. It is perhaps now especially difficult to see this, because contemporary people are most likely to think of the Tractarian or maybe the 'Puseyite' (from another Tractarian leader, Edward Pusey, 1800–82) movement in the context of the neo-Gothic churches that its clergymen have left behind, rather than in that of the now unfamiliar language of their books and sermons.

The Tractarians, including those among them who 'went to Rome', were characterized by strong

Left: A caricature of the British philosopher Edmund Burke (1729–97). In 1790 he published Reflections on the French Revolution, *which opposed the principles of the Revolution and was read throughout Europe.*

yearning for the Christian Middle Ages, which many of them saw as having been betrayed by the men of the 'enlightened' tendency in the churches. The vogue for medieval paraphernalia and chivalry had already, long before the Romantic-Catholic period, acquired some roots in the eighteenth-century Enlightenment, when the vogue for the neo-Gothic first appeared. It was a taste that could appear and reappear in many forms. The feeling for the lost and regretted Catholic Middle Ages was passed on from the religious right to the great prophet of art and non-dogmatic socialism, John Ruskin (1819–1900), and from Ruskin it went in a lay form to the unbelieving poet and preacher of handicraft and socialism, William Morris (1834–96) – although in the next generation a very different version of Catholic medievalism was also strong in the right-wing writers G. K. Chesterton (1874–1936) and Hilaire Belloc (1870–1953). From Morris the nostalgia was in its secular version transmitted to the twentieth century through the Arts and Crafts Movement. At the end of this century, having picked up a little romantic primitivism on the way, medievalism has found a precarious home in parts of the modern ecological movement. Perhaps we may think of some of this ideological line of descent when we next take our Pevsner guidebooks to view a Puseyite neo-Gothic church, or the Birmingham collection of Pre-Raphaelite paintings.

Above: A studio portrait of the British author and art critic John Ruskin.

Below: William Morris, British craftsman, poet and utopian socialist.

In spite of the austerities of the lives of the Tractarians and of the Catholic converts, nineteenth-century medievalism formed a link with the arts that was to flourish and endure. There was enormous interest in the study of medieval artefacts after the end of the Napoleonic Wars, and for the rest of the nineteenth century. During the Revolution the iconoclasm of republican France had been so intense that there was danger that the whole patrimony of French medieval church art would disappear. But a refuge for a large number of objects had been found by Alexandre Lenoir, who had set up the Musée des Monuments Français in Paris in 1795, which became, after a shaky start, one of the first of the national museums. After 1815 great lists and catalogues of the medieval artistic repertoire and its monuments were published in several countries: there were both religious and nationalistic aspects to this.

One of the great monuments of neo-Gothic enthusiasm in England was a national one, the reconstructed Houses of Parliament in London (1840–60), an enterprise in which the architect Sir Charles Barry was advised on Gothic decoration by A. W. N. Pugin, the son of the theologian. In England in mid-century, while Ruskin was making himself into a national figure, the Pre-Raphaelite painters launched themselves into a sort of learned primitivism, that sought to achieve a return to the condition of painting before its transformation by the supposed classicism of the High Renaissance painters. It was a heterodox movement from a religious as well as from an artistic point of view – Dante Gabriel Rossetti (1828–82), for example, was the son of an anti-clerical Italian revolutionary. Ruskin, while cautious about some of the technical aspects of Pre-Raphaelite work, nonetheless welcomed it as likely to 'lay in England the foundations of a school of art nobler than the world has seen for three hundred years'. In its religious aspects the Pre-Raphaelite paintings of William Holman Hunt (1827–1910), especially, were to make an enormous appeal to the Protestant piety of the time. The

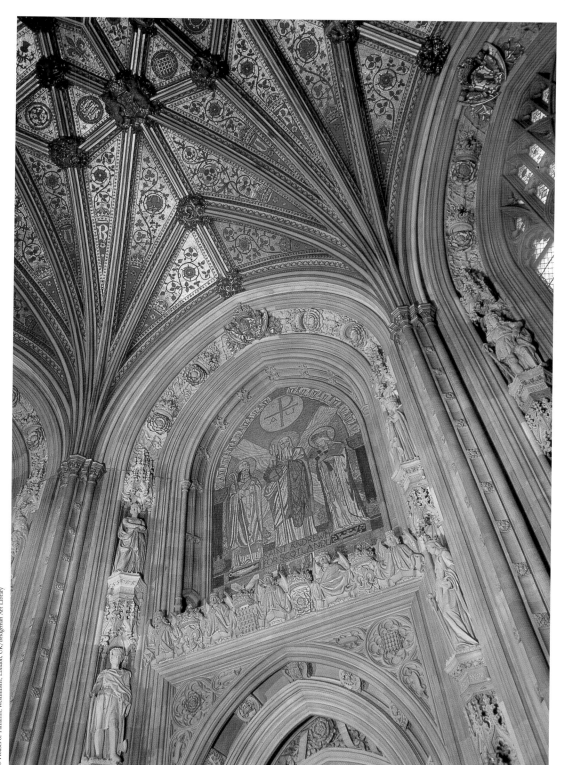

Left: The spectacular ceiling and mosaic of the Central Hall in the Houses of Parliament, London. Re-designed by the architects Pugin and Barry, the Houses of Parliament provide a prime example of the neo-Gothic architecture much loved by Victorians.

Below: The Blind Girl *by artist John Everett Millais (1829–96), one of the founder members of the Pre-Raphaelite Brotherhood.*

most emotive of them all, his *Light of the World*, was painted for the chapel of the Oxford College named after the Tractarian Keble: while working on this in 1851–53 Hunt experienced a religious conversion.

Ideological Choices

Behind all the religious controversies lay an issue that crossed the boundaries of confessions and political trends. How far were believers to defend the status quo, or the traditions of the Church as they understood them, without making any concession to the spirit and the thinking of the times? Were they a rearguard that must die at its post, as the 'ultramontane' Catholic faction of Cardinal Manning (1808–92) (who had his Protestant equivalents), sometimes tended to think? Or were they to view themselves as men of their own day, who looked at the doctrines of other men of their own time in the light of what understanding the Gospel might give them? Newman, in spite of the intransigence of his Tractarian and pre-Catholic days, belonged in a very private and discreet way to the second group rather than the first: his theory of theological development placed him among the ancestors of what came to be known as Catholic modernism. The choice is still not an obsolete one today, even if the terms in which it is put are rather different. But the contrast between traditionalists

Above: The Light of the World *by William Holman Hunt (1827–1919), shows Christ with a lantern knocking at a firmly closed door, symbol of a recalcitrant sinner.*

Right: The stirring image of Liberty Leading the People *painted by the French artist, Eugène Delacroix (1798–1863) after the French Revolution of 1830.*

and modernizers is seldom as stark as it sounds; for example, towards the end of his life Manning experienced a very modern sympathy for the situation of organized workers, a kind of understanding of the industrial world that had passed Newman by.

The test case in early nineteenth-century Catholicism was that of the French priest, Félicité de Lamennais (1782–1854), who had earlier been an admirer of Joseph de Maistre. Having started as a strong 'reactionary', de Lamennais gradually veered round to a position that wanted much more freedom for the Church from the State, even when the State was overtly Catholic. After the July Revolution of 1830, which substituted the 'liberal' Orleanist dynasty on the French throne for its Bourbon cousins, de Lamennais reached a point where he felt that the French Church needed more freedom from the papacy, as well as from the government. His political role changed: he became a liberal publicist who was in principle a democrat advocating the separation of Church and State in France and the recognition of liberty of conscience. He and one or two associates at the end of 1831 made the quixotic gesture of travelling to Rome to put their case before Pope Gregory XVI (pope 1831–46). They were perhaps received more politely than they might have been, because it was known that their requests had wide backing from the Catholics of Belgium and Poland (the Catholic nation that had just rebelled against Russia). But their case was an absolutely hopeless one, both politically and in terms of Church policy. De Lammenais was really asking the Vatican to approve French radicalism and Polish nationalism in the same breath, and it had absolutely no intention of doing either: what is amazing, and creditable to Pope Gregory XVI, is that the pope treated him with such personal courtesy.

Pope Gregory XVI's answer to the Poles came swiftly, with the condemnation of their rebellion against Russia. The pope did not condemn de Lamennais by name when the Vatican acted officially in 1832, but the doctrines Lamennais professed, and other 'modern' doctrines, were condemned generally. Freedom of conscience was described in the papal encyclical not only as a false doctrine, but as a rather insane opinion (delirium). In 1834 Pope Gregory XVI condemned de Lamennais' book, *Paroles d'un Croyant* (Words of a Believer), and from a Vatican point of view the case was closed.

Pope Pius IX (pope 1846–78) had in the first two years of his pontificate enjoyed the reputation of a liberal pope, and for a short time in 1847–48 he went through some of the motions of becoming a constitutional ruler in the papal state. In Church matters there was scarcely any relaxation of ultramontane policies until after his death. The revolutions of 1848, including that in Rome and the papal state, were defeated. But as the second half of the century unfolded, it became increasingly clear that the national and, to some extent, 'liberal' aims of the great European tribes – the Italians and the Germans, particularly – were going to be achieved. Pius IX viewed this with a defiance that was sometimes jaunty, sometimes despairing. In 1864 he issued a 'Syllabus of Errors', that in our terminology could be called the most comprehensively politically incorrect document of the century. Its most provocative denial was the refusal to admit that 'the Roman Pontiff can and should reconcile and harmonize himself with progress, with liberalism, and with recent civilization'.

In 1869, when all Italy outside Rome and its immediate surroundings had already been absorbed, sometimes peacefully but often by force, in the new Piedmontese monarchy of Italy, Pius IX called the First Vatican Council of the Church. It issued its final constitutional decree in the following year on 18 July, the day before the Franco-Prussian War broke out. Decisions of the Roman bishop were declared, when he spoke exercising the office of pastor and teacher of all

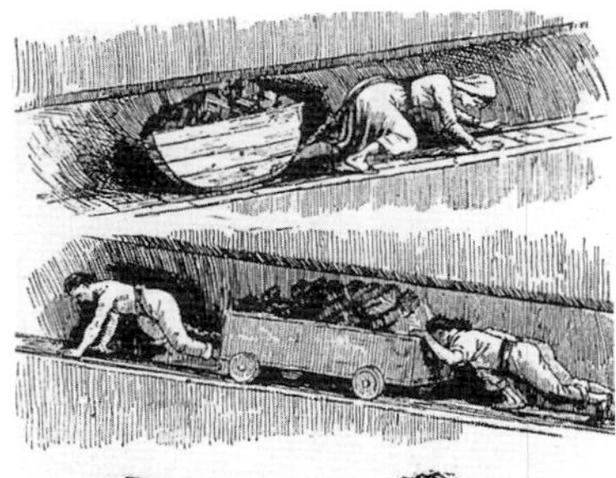

Above: Images of child mine-workers from a government report on children's employment dated 1842, the first such report to be illustrated. Atrocious conditions, and the proximity of both sexes to each other, shocked the Victorians.

Right: The industrial landscape of Bolton, Lancashire, in 1848.

Below: Over London, by Rail, *by the French painter Gustav Doré shows graphically the cramped, squalid conditions of Victorian London.*

Christians, and defined doctrine concerning faith and morals to be held by the universal Church, to be infallible [irreformable] in themselves, and not from the consent of the Church. So far as the bishops and cardinals of the council went, their agreement to the infallibility decree was far from unanimous: not less than a quarter of those attending had opposed it in the form in which it was passed. The significance of the decree goes far beyond the nineteenth century, because of its drastic implications for other Christian confessions that may seek to enter into communion with the Roman Church.

On 20 September 1870 the troops of King Victor Emmanuel entered Rome. The papal state's eleven centuries of existence ended, and the Catholic Church had to wait until 1929 before the legal position of its chief bishop in his own house was freely negotiated with the surrounding national state of Italy. The Italian 'Law of Guarantees' of 1871 that regulated the legal position at that time was a unilateral act on the part of the Italian government, which Pius IX rejected. After 1871 the pope was often described as 'the prisoner of the Vatican'.

Industrialism: Socialism: Revolution

In Britain by the early nineteenth century, the new industrial and mining areas were the most conspicuous novel feature of economic and social life. The structures of village life had not been

replaced in the new urban or quasi-urban areas, and this absence of structure extended to the Churches. The new industrial class tended to be ignorant of religion, or yet more ignorant than the old agricultural class, because its ministers were not present to teach or assist them. The same problems applied to the poor areas of the vastly expanded capital cities and great administrative centres, with the difference that very large numbers of the new population were foreigners in one sense or another, very often (like Irish Catholics and Central European Jews in London) belonging to different religions or to different religious groups from the majority culture. The minority religious leaders did their best: Catholic organization in expanding Birmingham, for example, represented a heroic effort. There was, equally, a huge Methodist and Dissenting effort to meet the needs for basic education and moral guidance of what was effectively a displaced population, which in the Methodist case had formed part of the original Wesleyan mission.

Both in Europe and in North America, the established Churches of every persuasion were slow and tepid in their response to this new challenge of the needs of the neglected poor and the disadvantaged workers. Their social attitudes tended to be strongly repressive: the pan-European conservatism of 1815 and its terror of disorder and rebellion were still alive and well. In Catholic Europe the religious orders committed to the poor, not only the Franciscans of medieval origin, but those founded by St Vincent de Paul and others in the Counter-Reformation period, did not possess the structures that were really necessary to deal with the new pastoral problems.

Far from the Vatican, Karl Marx (1818–83) and Friedrich Engels (1820–95) met and formed what was to be a lifelong friendship. In 1845, Engels published *The Condition of the English Working Class*, and the two men collaborated on *The German Ideology*. In Brussels the following year, Marx and other Socialists were pouring out pamphlets; by 1847, they were organized into the Communist League, which, in 1848, issued its declaration of faith, the *Communist Manifesto*, written by Marx. For Marx, religion was the opium of the masses, a drug that was politically administered to them by the rulers.

Marx's revolutionary doctrine was to remain, in spite of its later 'scientific' clothes and its historical paraphernalia, a secular millenarianism that looked forward to a utopian end of history. Christian concern for the poor had always existed, although in the modern period in forms that nineteenth-century Socialists very often found disgusting, and humiliating to the people they were supposed to assist. The issue between the Socialists and the Christian Socialists, when the latter began to come into existence after 1848, was not over means but over ends. The latter wanted to relieve the poor; the former wanted – in modern diction – to empower them.

By contrast, the British liberalism that was classically elaborated by John Stuart Mill (1806–73) was a restatement of many of Bentham's main utilitarian positions, qualified by an assertion of 'the free development of individuality' as one of the main essentials of a citizen's well-being. Mill was particularly strong against 'the engines of moral repression', which he regarded as not merely coming from governments, but from people who try to tyrannize by stigmatizing those whose opinions they think wrong or mistaken, in the court of public opinion. Mill quoted with approval the judgement that his age – one must ask whether the same can be said of our age – was 'destitute of faith, but terrified of scepticism'.

It was difficult for Christians to admit that there could be a political statement of the ultimate end of man: on the other hand, an attitude to the alleviation of social problems could still be taken by Christians, which recognized that part of the bad situation of the workers derived from failure to concede them full political rights. In the English case this trend appeared after 1848 – the year in

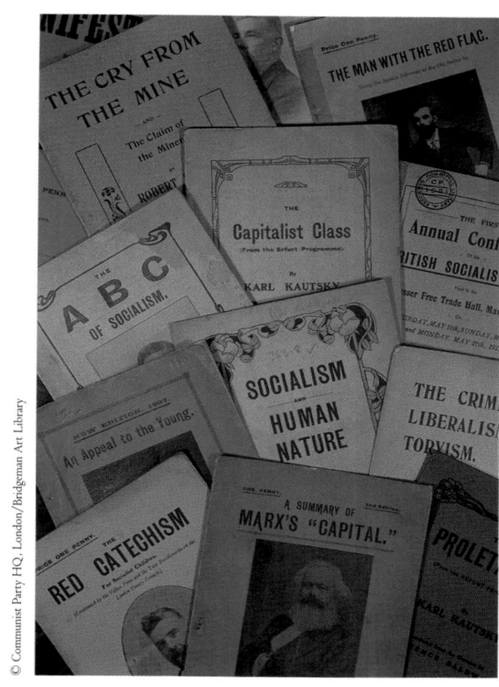

Above: Socialist and Communist pamphlets, which were published in large numbers from the mid-1800s. For Marx, religion was the 'opium of the masses'. The established Churches were slow to respond to the needs of the industrial poor and some turned to trade unionism or movements such as Chartism to improve their conditions.

Right: Dock workers on strike in 1889. Towards the end of the nineteenth century there was an upsurge of militancy, particularly among so-called 'unskilled' workers such as dockers and matchgirls.

which Britain was one of the few major European countries not to experience violent revolution – and took the form of accepting a kind of cautious recognition of some of the positions adopted before 1848 by the radical Chartist Party. The leading figure was Frederick Denison Maurice (1805–72), an Anglican theologian from a Unitarian background. Maurice, in combination with the novelist Charles Kingsley (1819–75) and others, termed their new group 'Christian Socialists'. There was very little common ideological ground between the Christian and the secular Socialists, except for a general concern about social issues, which were to become increasingly important to all the major Christian Churches in Europe. In England Cardinal Manning showed himself aware of at least some of the issues, as became apparent from his intervention in one of the London dock strikes.

Later in the century Pope Leo XIII (pope 1878–1903) turned very cautiously in the direction of social-reformist Christianity. In 1888 he allowed that a Catholic might without sin prefer a democratic form of government – the American example was compelling, although later in his pontificate Leo XIII took fright at the democratic contagion that he felt was affecting the Catholic church in North America. With Europe in mind, in 1891 he issued an encyclical, *Rerum novarum*, that, while it asserted the rights of property and condemned Socialism and Communism, recognized that justice might require the state to legislate to protect workers against unjust conditions, and that workers might associate in trade unions to protect their rights, although the same document condemned the strike weapon. Soon after, the first Catholic trade unions began to be formed.

Slavery: a Test Case

One of the greatest victories of the evangelical movement was the abolition of the slave trade. It may legitimately be asked why, after a silence of almost 1,800 years, the Christian conscience should have turned in this direction. Medieval clergy opposed the traffic in Christian slaves by other Christians, but offered no opposition to trafficking in non-Christians. Conversion to Christianity on the part of Christian-owned slaves continued to offer no prospect of manumission, and on the whole the missionaries were anxious to convince slave-owners of this, so that they might offer no opposition to slave Christianization. The Roman bishops had taken up no particular position in the matter, and, as temporal rulers in the mid-sixteenth century, they specifically legalized the ownership of slaves in their own city of Rome.

Enlightenment ideas about human rights did not necessarily lead to opposition to the institution of slavery, as the career of the slave-owning Thomas Jefferson, one of the founding fathers of independent America, shows. In Britain the anti-slavery platform found unlikely champions in the far-from-enlightened precincts of the British common law, when Lord Mansfield (1705–93) decided that slaves enjoyed the status of freedom from their presence on British soil, or even in a ship docked in a British port.

William Wilberforce (1759–1833) was one of a small group of evangelical members of Parliament. He also belonged to a group of influential evangelical laymen and laywomen (later known as the 'Clapham sect', from their place of residence). The committee for the abolition of the slave trade was set up in 1787, relying not only on evangelical sentiment (in fact Quakers were the most numerous sect among its members), but also on the general effect of two propagandist books recently published by ex-slaves under their own names. The books of the West Africans Olaudah Equiano and Ottobah Cugoano recounted their own experiences of captivity. An important part of the first push for abolition had thus come from black Protestant intellectuals, able to tell their own tales and to use the sense of the exotic and alarming to influence their readers.

The government had not been especially enthusiastic about abolition, especially as the French Revolutionary panic, and the brief revolutionary government in Haiti of the black Toussaint l'Ouverture (?1743–1803) from 1794 had made people nervous. But general public pressure had been

Above: Olaudah Equiano, a Protestant, who wrote an account of his own experiences as a slave, which played a major role in informing the abolition movement.

Left: Images such as this of a kneeling slave, entitled Am I Not A Man and a Brother, *were struck on commemorative medallions in the eighteenth century to encourage abolition of the British slave trade.*

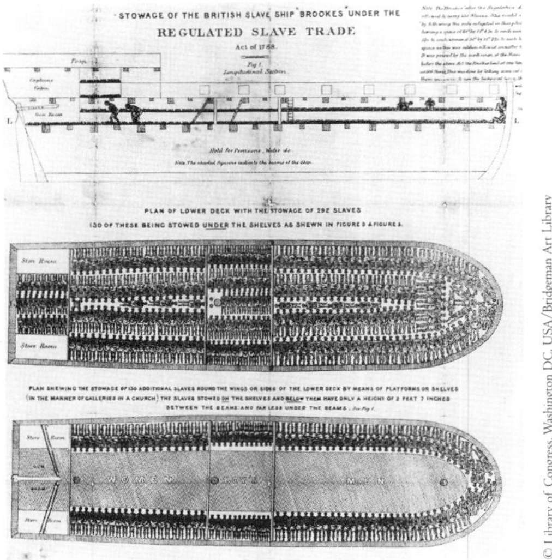

Above: An engraving showing how Africans were packed into slave ships for the transatlantic crossing. The sea trade in humans was lucrative; some 7 million were taken to the Caribbean in the eighteenth century.

strong enough to secure the passing of the Total Abolition of the Slave Trade Act in 1807, and to get it followed up by other legislation that gave the prohibition of the trade some teeth. Nothing less than British naval dominance of the seas could have enabled abolition, and in this the abolitionists were especially fortunate. There was some trouble in getting all the European powers to accept the abolition of the trade in 1815, and even more in pursuing the slavers on the high seas to enforce it. It was a cause that generally attracted at least lip service, rather like some human rights issues in our own time. It is significant that as shrewd a political operator as Napoleon, who as emperor had reintroduced slavery, decided when he had not too much to lose during the Hundred Days of 1815 that it was a good idea to swing to abolition. It was, however, idealism and not calculation that made Pope Gregory XVI condemn the the slave trade in 1839.

A Christian Century?

The nineteenth century was not a century of unbelief: to its end religious issues occasioned passionate concern, and often violent political conflict. In countries such as France, Spain, Germany and Italy, the national State attempted to exercise strict controls over the Church. These could not only affect its freedom to name its own leaders and educate the faithful, including its right to decide how to train its own seminary students, but could also involve huge uncompensated confiscations of Church property. In Britain these conflicts were not entirely absent, but were very much milder: the biggest issues of Church property and policy, for example, had been settled by the end of the sevententh century, and other less central ones were settled during the nineteenth century, not without fuss, but without the bitter struggles that happened in continental Europe. The religious disquiets of the Victorian liberal intellectuals point in one way, but there were pointers in a different direction. The big effort at church reorganization by the Anglicans and the contemporary dissenting expansion both tried to cope with the change in the industrial and social base. The enormous profusion of church-building also testifies to vitality in the Churches. These things are evidence of the power and vigour of Victorian capitalism no less than of religious zeal, but they are not merely that.

Left: A scene embroidered on to a handkerchief from a series of Illustrations of Missionary Scenes dated c. 1880. Christian missionaries were active worldwide during the nineteenth century, and the scene provides a graphic message.

In the United States the guarantees of the free exercise of religion meant that the clashes of the old world were more or less avoided, although before the emancipation of slaves at the end of the Civil War, in 1865, the blacks did not in practice have the right to organize their own churches. After the Civil War this was one of the few civil rights of self-organization that many blacks in the south of the United States enjoyed, although even this right was frequently contested, and not only in the south. In the north and the west, the great immigrations of the nineteenth and early twentieth centuries meant that the United States remained a Christian country, but became the home of very many Christian confessions, Catholic, Orthodox, and Protestant of every shade and persuasion.

Left: English officers stand at the back of an African congregation in about 1880, looking on while a white minister takes the service. Despite the expansion of Christianity, there was a reluctance on the part of Protestants to encourage or accept indigenous leadership in the churches.

Above: Afro-Americans at the Mount Olive Baptist Church in New York wait to be transported to Liberia, where in the early nineteenth century, a settlement had been created specifically for freed slaves.

Missions

Catholic missionary effort in the world had been centrally directed since 1622 from the Roman Congregation De Propaganda Fide, whose elegant headquarters, designed by Bernini, belied the deadly seriousness and huge scale of the enterprise. The Anglicans had set up the basic structures of missionary effort abroad at the end of the seventeenth century, when Thomas Bray (1656–1730) had founded the Society for the Propagation of Christian Knowledge (SPCK) in 1698, and backed it up in the following year by the Society for the Propagation of the Gospel in Foreign Parts (SPG). A further central organization, the Church Missionary Society, was added under evangelical inspiration in 1799 by the efforts of the biblical commentator, Thomas Scott (1747–1821).

The world expansion of Christianity during the nineteenth century was huge. Colonization was everywhere accompanied, sometimes preceded, by missionary effort. The impulse among the missionaries was sometimes humanitarian, sometimes strongly colonialist. There was a great reluctance among Protestants to acknowledge indigenous leadership in African churches; the only exceptions were in the colonial settlement of Sierra Leone, set up in the late eighteenth century for repatriated and freed slaves, and the later American-founded settlement of Liberia in the early nineteenth century, made for the same purpose.

Everywhere the confessional differences among the missionaries corresponded more or less to the colonial interests of the great European powers. That it was possible to serve both France and the Church in the mission field was freely – for example – asserted. On the other hand, Catholic missionary work in Africa very often antedated European colonialism by some centuries, and the popes constantly insisted with the religious missionary orders, throughout the nineteenth century and into the twentieth, that it was the duty of Catholic missionaries to respect local cultures, to avoid serving national interests, and to create an indigenous clergy. These precepts were to some extent observed by the Catholic clergy, but were a great deal less present, at all events in the high tide of nineteenth-century colonial expansion, to the minds of the Protestants.

Science, Religion, and the Higher Criticism

From Wesley to Newman, the disquiet of the troubled soul had been responsible for great changes in the faith, for trends towards rebirth and revival. But later in the nineteenth century, for the first time since such movements as the Gnosticism and Manichaeism of antiquity, the troubled Christian spirit began once more to cross thresholds that led away from the faith altogether. That was one of the factors in ethical liberalism, that in Britain had earlier been contained by the very English phenomenon of late Unitarianism, but that in the later nineteenth century was to lead numbers of very sensitive and civilized intellectuals, of whom the novelist George Eliot (1819–80) is a distinguished example, away from the churches into a world of ideas and ideals in which allegiances were very much harder to distinguish. The phenomenon was defined by Matthew Arnold (1822–88), in his poem, 'Dover Beach', written soon after his marriage to Frances Lucy Wightman in 1851, in which the metaphor of the tide retreating from the shore was memorably used of the retreat from faith:

...The Sea of Faith
Was once, too, at the full, and round earth's shore
Lay like the folds of a bright girdle furled.

But now I only hear
Its melancholy, long, withdrawing roar,
Retreating, to the breath
Of the night-wind, down the vast edges drear
And naked shingles of the world.

Ah love, let us be true
To one another ! for the world, which seems
To lie before us like a land of dreams,
So various, so beautiful, so new,
Hath really neither joy, nor love, nor light,
Nor certitude, nor peace, nor help for pain;
And we are here as on a darkling plain
Swept with confused alarms of struggle and flight,
Where ignorant armies clash by night.

Above: The Brtish novelist George Eliot (Mary Ann Evans).

The pessimism of the second of these stanzas, and its suggestion that the forces of nature are indifferent to man's plight, indicate a sadness that was to be typical of one branch of the doubting Victorians. There is no pleasure in this flight to doubt, no roll of drums in honour of the advancing forces of reason. To describe the human predicament when the tide of faith had withdrawn, the metaphors chosen are those of conflict and desolation. Arnold's was a very Christian doubt.

In continental Europe the markers had to a large extent been laid down in the Enlightenment and the French Revolution, so that the ideological emphasis in the nineteenth century was on the construction of tools with which to achieve social aims that were, at the minimum, of betterment, at the maximum, utopian. In this process the Church was assigned no role, unless an obstructive one that required its removal.

Most of the lines of thought that took shape later in the century, either in the social philosophy of positivism, or in various strands of Socialism, are to be found in the extraordinary French thinker, Henri de Saint-Simon (1760–1825). The thought of Saint-Simon was historicist, anti-egalitarian, technocratic and managerial: he could see the existence of a class war, but planned for its removal. He wished for the social control of both man and nature by a new rational order, scientific and authoritarian. He condemned the whole Church and State apparatus of the *ancien régime* as obsolete and useless. To settle the new technocratic regime he wanted the establishment of a new religion – and in the 1830s some Saint-Simonian churches were in fact set up in France.

Above: A cartoon from 1861 showing Charles Darwin with an ape-like body sitting next to an ape, both noting their common features in a mirror. It was this aspect of Darwin's theories that caused such controversy.

Saint-Simon's thought was too complicated and inconsistent to get the attention of more than a restricted circle of intellectuals, but his disciple Auguste Comte (1798–57) was important in changing the climate of opinion. Comte, like his master and like Lenin, was convinced that applied science would satisfactorily deal with all our problems, social and otherwise. His philosophy of 'positivism' applied to itself the concept of 'inevitability', a sort of apotheosis that was to be gratefully seized upon by Marxism. Because Comte had a great gift for simplification and presentation, he became for a very large number of educated Europeans and Americans a kind of prophet of the inexorable victory of the scientifically planned society. Like his master, he required the new order to be founded on a new religion, which he termed the 'religion of humanity'. It was all a bit thin, and somewhat authoritarian, and George Eliot, among many other thoughtful people, found it so.

Two main forces were publicly and widely acknowledged as the main agencies in the weakening of Christian belief. One, of which much has already been said above, was the criticism of religion that alleged its own 'scientific' basis. The other, which was really a sub-category of the first, was the 'scientific' criticism applied by biblical critics to the scriptural texts.

The latter was a department in which there had been plenty of Enlightenment precursors and some pre-Enlightment ones: the most destructive remained Spinoza. In the late nineteenth century much of the most important textual work on the Scriptures was carried out, not with the destructive aim of weakening the faith, but with the apologetic one of defending it. And it is possible that in Protestant countries, where for centuries the whole weight of Church preaching had been upon the word of God, the most disturbing knowledge was not that of the discovery of particular details in the scriptural texts that went ill with traditional emphases, but the knowledge that such enquiry was going on at all. 'Historical criticism', as it came to be known, found acceptance more easily among the churchmen who knew that its purpose was benign, than among the laymen who found it threatening.

When scholars talked about the Jesus of history, as they began to do near the end of the century, they usually meant that they were trying to deal with the history of Jesus by roughly the same scholarly methods that they would have applied to any other topic of the history of his time. The same limits on our understanding therefore apply to him, if he is looked at in this way, that would apply to anyone else. The Jesus that seemed to emerge from their work was still in many ways the loved and loving teacher, but some things about him had become disturbingly uncertain, or unfamiliar. To this extent the higher criticism was genuinely disquieting to faith.

Whether these theological doubts (if things so general can be called that) were the most potent solvent of Christian belief, or whether this priority had to be given to the great quarrels of 'science and religion' was a matter much discussed at the time. Mrs Humphrey Ward (1851–1920), the niece of Matthew Arnold, in her novel *Robert Elsmere* (1888), decided that the priority belonged to the higher scriptural criticism. But enormous publicity had attended the publication of Darwin's *On the Origin of Species* in 1859, and his subsequent very public confrontation at the meeting of the British Association for the Advancement of Science in 1860 with Bishop Wilberforce, who was a scientist.

Darwin's thesis had two quite different aspects so far as orthodox belief was concerned. On the one hand, he asserted, in a by no means revolutionary way so far as the science of his time was concerned, the validity of geological time. Biblical time, in so far as it was based on the chronology that appeared to be given in the text of Old Testament, had still preoccupied the old age of Newton: it could not possibly be fitted into the enormously long timescale that the new geology required. However, the most significant part of Darwin's thesis was not geological time, although it was necessary to it. Darwin's theories were a genuine scientific revolution, but they attracted public attention not because of the power of his abstract thought but because of the label of 'descent from apes' that was attached to them. They were only worrying to theologians if a dogmatic positivist philosophy was appended, and although plenty of contemporary positivists welcomed Darwinism, Darwin was not himself a positivist.

In the last part of the century there was a substantial body of combative rationalism that saw itself with a duty to attack and subvert the Christian faith. It was atheistic rather than agnostic, positivist in tendency. Polemicist Winwood Reade's rather breathlessly aggressive *Martyrdom of Man* (1872) contained an attempt at a rationalist philosophy of history that lacked the depth and reflective breadth that were needed for the enterprise, although there is a kind of poetic fervour to the book that impresses. He made quasi-religious claims: 'The religion that I teach is as high above Christianity as that religion was superior to the idolatry of Rome'. But his conclusion was not far from that of Matthew Arnold, twenty years earlier:

'A season of mental anguish is at hand, and through this we must pass in order that our posterity may rise. The soul must be sacrificed; the hope in immortality must die. A sweet and charming illusion must be taken from the human race, as youth and beauty vanish never to return.'

'Mental anguish' perhaps best describes the plight of the doubting Victorians. It was to take another century before doubt could become orthodox and comfortable. Religious doubt was over a long period going to lead towards a new secular morality, and social reform was the main path to lead in this direction. Gradualist Socialism was not a new religion, but it was an ethical attitude that helped to push religion out of its former dominant place in social morality. Beatrice Webb, one of the two great architects of Socialist Fabianism, and co-author of *Soviet Communism: A New Civilization?* was going to define this shift in her autobiography:

'...it was during the middle decades of the nineteenth century that in England, the impulse of self-subordination was transferred, consciously and overtly, from God to man...'.

1 There is an unusual feeling for this in the Cambridge historian Maurice Cowling's *Religion and Public Doctrine in Modern England (Cambridge, 1981-5)*

19

VIOLENCE AND DOUBT

Like so many centuries before it, the twentieth has been a time of ruthless and relentless violence. That this should have been so has been no surprise to many conservative Christians, nor, in principle, to many conservative Jews, although the planned violence that overwhelmed the Jewish communities of continental Europe in the Hitler period had no precedent in a history that already contained many terrible acts committed against them. It was also a century in which Christians almost certainly suffered no less persecution than under the Roman Empire.

Two world wars, including the unveiled threat of nuclear war with which the second ended, have inflicted grave blows both to the optimism that inspired so much Western secular rationalism in the half-century that preceded 1914, and to the general confidence in human progress in both moral and material matters, that had become integral to the whole culture of the industrialized world. Technology has continued its triumphal march; belief in moral progress perhaps still lingers among us. But injustice and terror, in spite of the great political changes in the former Soviet Union, are far from having finished with us.

Christendom has declined in the West. The idea of many nations constituting a people of God called Christendom, who know and acknowledge their Christian identity, and who have a sort of collective presence in large areas of the planet, has become

Above: War graves at Saint-Laurent-sur-Mer.

Left: Unveiling a War Memorial at Cookham *by Stanley Spencer (1891–1959).*

unfamiliar to most of the populations of the so-called First World. One way of putting this is that the principle of nationality has prevailed over the collective idea of Christianity, although there are cases such as those of Poland or Serbia where the two coincide, or have done until very recently. In most of the countries that once constituted 'Christendom' the proportion of persons who identify themselves clearly as Christians has declined sharply since the beginning of the century.

These things do not point clearly to the decline of Christianity as a world religion. To those who want to take a statistical view of morality the religion has not declined in world terms. It has declined in Europe, where it has returned to being in some countries to what it was in its early centuries – a minority religion with only weak support among the cultural and political élites. In First World democratic countries it is not persecuted, but in the course of the century Christians have in some places and at some times undergone persecution fully as severe as their predecessors experienced under the pagan Roman Empire. The minority situation is new in the very long European history of the religion, or new after the barbarian conversions of the early Middle Ages. It would be far too much to say that it has taken it back to conditions that preceded the conversion of Constantine in the fourth century, because the tenacity of institutions and mental habits means that traditional Christianity is much more widely present among us than we commonly realize. Getting a more precise idea of what this means is like trying to sketch a landscape from a moving train.

Below: French propaganda postcard reflecting the nationalist stance of the Christian Churches during World War I.

World Wars: Fascist and Communist Ideologies

In most of the main Christian countries that took part on either side in the First World War, the main local Christian churches of both Eastern and Western Christianity took a nationalist line. The connection between national Church and national struggle may have been especially strong in Britain, but many people who grew up between the wars were most conscious of the Church in its role as custodian of the memories of the war dead. During the war the Churches had not favoured Christian 'absolute' pacifism: that was confined to a few numerically small sects such as Quakers and Mennonites. Many ministers and priests fought: it was noticeable that the camaraderie that still remained among ex-combatant pastors from the trenches of 1914–18 was a factor in enabling Adolf Hitler to set up a pro-Nazi Protestant Church in 1933–4.

The Roman Catholic Church, under the leadership of Pope Benedict XV (pope 1914–22) took a humanitarian and peace-loving stance that endeared it to neither side. Pope Benedict protested against the inhuman methods of warfare used, such as poison gas, and in August 1917 launched a peace plan. The plan was entirely unacceptable to the Allies, who at that moment enjoyed military advantages they had bought at great human and material cost. It was at first cautiously welcomed by the Central Powers, but then abandoned by them when the internal collapse of Russia seemed to offer them another chance.

The peace plan offered to the combatants by Pope Pius XII (pope 1939–58) in 1939 was couched much more generally, but in fact it contained the main principles of the eventual new international post-war order (equal rights to life and national independence; a new international institution; attention to demands of racial minorities). His plan was disregarded by the combatants on either side. There was a mild and cautious attempt to draw attention to it by Cardinal Hinsley and, on the Anglican side, by Bishop Bell, but that was not the mood in Britain in 1940. It is to be regretted that the pope's other two principle – general disarmament and the recognition of the life of the spirit – did not get the attention of the victorious powers in 1945.

© Bolton Museum and Art Gallery, Lancashire, UK/Bridgeman Art Library

© AKG London

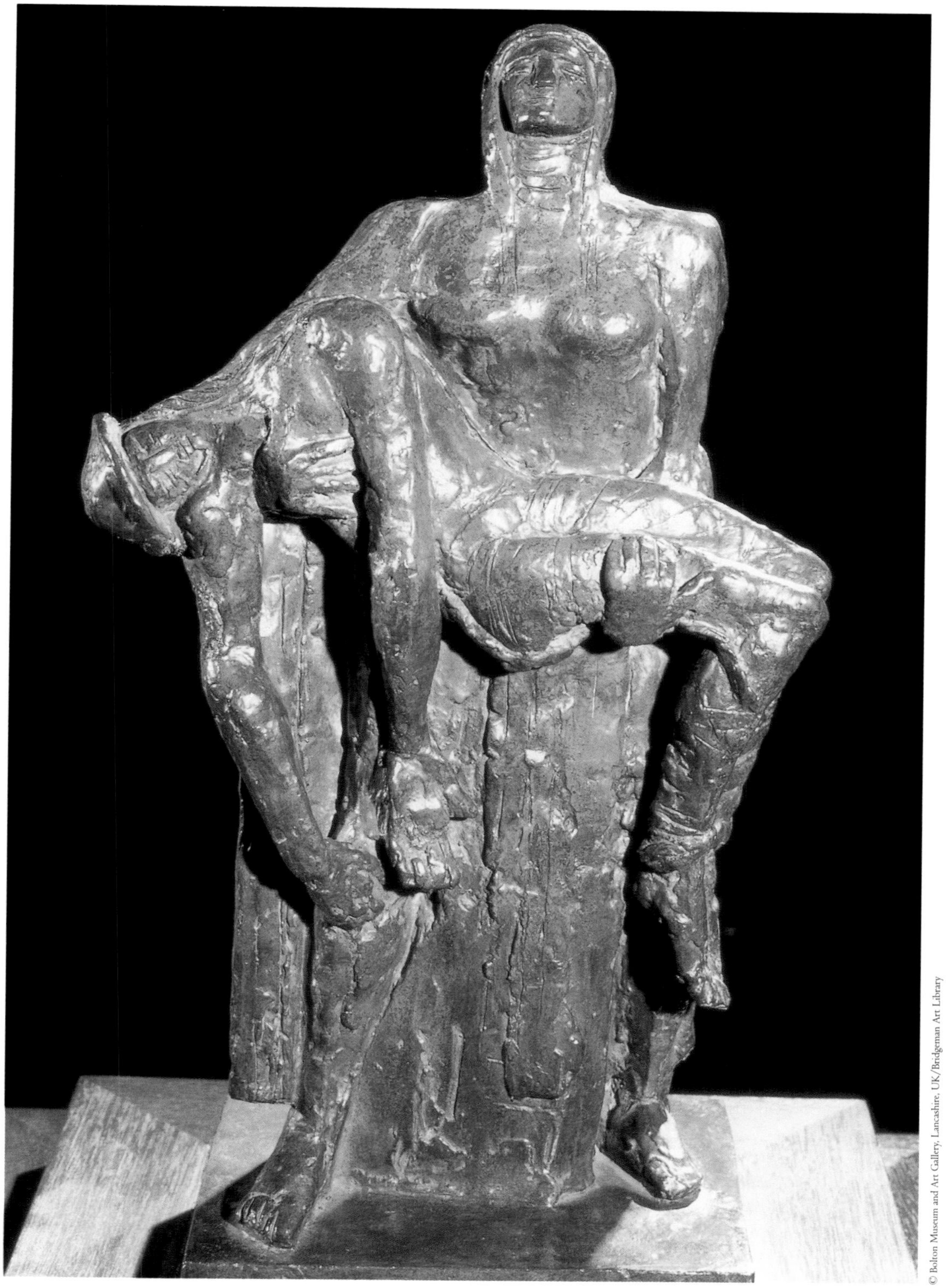

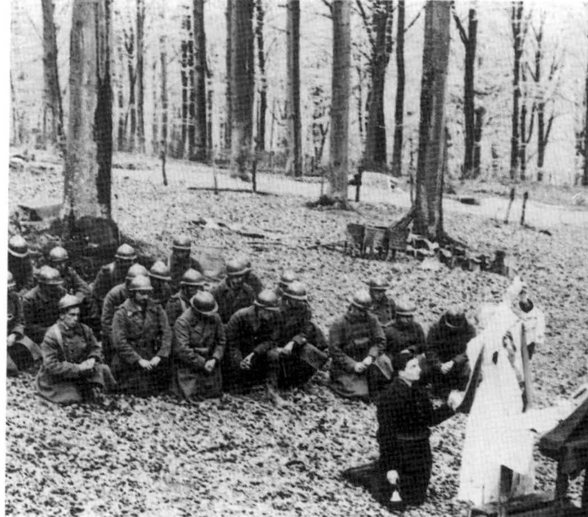

Above: A field service held for French troops just behind the battle lines during World War I. Many members of the clergy saw active service at the front.

Left: Maquette of a war memorial by Jacob Epstein (1880–1959). It was commissioned by the Trades Union Council, to commemorate the sacrifice of many of their members.

 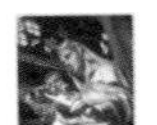

Few people had initially understood the grave problems that were to be presented to the Christian conscience by the victories of Fascist governments in the period between the wars, partly because those governments were initially so skilful in concealing the implications their doctrines had for the faith, partly because Fascist hostility to atheist Communism was accepted by many Christians as an indication that in some respects they stood on the same side as the Church. In Spain, the Fascist government enjoyed the open support of the Catholic Church; its authoritarian claims, although considerable, were much fewer than those made in Germany.

Among the more conspicuous of Hitler's dupes was Pope Pius XI (pope from 1922–39), who was tricked into thinking that because he had successfully negotiated a Church concordat with Mussolini (whom he in some respects understood) in 1929, a different sort of concordat could be satisfactorily negotiated with Hitler, whom he did not understand at all. The most skilful Church diplomat of his age was deceived in this way, and he was only sharing the same fate as many European politicians. Understanding of the moral issues presented by Nazi totalitarianism was reserved to others, notably, on the Catholic side, the German Cardinal Faulhaber, and on the Protestant side, the young German pastor, Dietrich Bonhoeffer (1906–45).

Right: Pope Pius XI, duped by Hitler, with Hermann Goering, Hitler's right-hand man, in 1933. They met to discuss the signing of a concordat between the Vatican and the Third Reich.

The German Catholic episcopate had, in fact, taken something of the measure of National Socialism by 1930, and had condemned it in absolutely definite terms. The importance of the Catholic Centre Party in German politics made it very important to the ex-Catholic Hitler somehow to outflank the German Catholic hierarchy, as he finally approached the seizure of power in 1933. He did this by letting it be known in Rome that he was willing to negotiate a Church concordat – never before offered by any national German government – on terms that conceded some of the main issues that he knew were important to the Vatican. The price was the depoliticizing of German Catholicism. Pope Pius XI took the bait, thus abandoning both the German bishops and the Centre Party to the wolves – but not before the Centre Party had consented to the fatal Enabling Law in the Reichstag that became the constitutional basis of the Nazi totalitarian regime.

© Hulton Getty/London

Left: Book burning and the Nazi salute, chilling images from the time of Hitler's ascent. It was not only art and literature by persons considered to be 'degenerate' that were destroyed; anything unbiased or not actively supporting the Nazi philosophy was also thrown on the bonfire.

In Germany in 1933 the Protestant Churches were overtaken by a whirlwind that they, too, could hardly understand. With the speed and ruthlessness that characterized everything he did, Hitler had his regime set up a new 'German Christian' Church that (by contrast with the regional German Protestant Churches) was organized on a national basis, and that repudiated such 'Jewish' Christian elements as the Old Testament and the writings of St Paul. At the same time the first great Jewish persecution was launched, to exclude Jews from public life, and the German pastorate was to be required to give its assent to these doctrines. Almost alone at first, Dietrich Bonhoeffer realized the central importance of the Jewish racial issue for the Church. Although he allowed the capacity of the state to legislate, Bonhoeffer took the traditional Lutheran position, and wrote that the Church:

> *'recognizes the absolute necessity for the use of force in this world, and also the moral injustice of certain concrete acts of the state which are necessarily bound up with the use of force.'*[1]

But he then showed, by an extraordinary leap, ability to push his thought further and to write that the Church should continually ask whether the actions of the state are such as to lead to law and order, and not to lawlessness and disorder. This must have been a reference to the requirement for legal government, a *Rechtsstaat,* that was fundamental in modern German history. Bonhoeffer was at this very early stage already looking for some kind of critique for a right of resistance to the state: it was a path that was to take him to a Nazi scaffold in 1945 and to make him one of the major figures in twentieth-century Christian history. He again showed his prescience in 1934, when rearmament was only just beginning to be an issue, at the international oecumenical Christian meeting on the Danish North Sea island of Fanø. At that meeting he made the then rather untimely-sounding appeal to:

© AKG London

Above: Pastor Dietrich Bonhoeffer, opposer of Nazi doctrine, who was executed for his defiance on 9 April 1945 at Flössenburg (Bavaria).

'issue to those who believe in Christ a radical call for peace. The hour is late. The world is choked with weapons and dreadful is the mistrust that looks out of all mens' eyes. The trumpets of war may blow tomorrow. For what are we waiting ?'

Bonhoeffer's was a lonely voice, and his close British Church contacts (of whom the most important was George Bell, Bishop of Chichester, whose conscience was a thorn in Churchill's side during the Second World War) did not inspire confidence. It seemed to many prudent conservative Christians in Germany during 1933–4 that the best thing was to recognize the nationalism that many of them shared to a certain degree with the National Socialists, and beyond that not to say too much about politics. Cardinal Faulhaber, on the other hand, asserted the Old Testament in a way that repudiated the Nazi assertion of blood and race as possible elements in Christianity, and that also strikingly held out a hand to the German Protestants (an unheard-of thing for a cardinal to do in 1933), to 'defend with them the sacred books of the Old Testament'. He said, 'We are not saved by German blood. We are saved by the blood of our crucified Lord.' What was in store for German Catholicism became clear only six months later, when on 30 June 1934 the Nazi murderers, who had a lot of work to do that day, walked into the office of the Catholic Action leader, Erich Klausener, and shot him, cynically arranging the murder so that it could be said to have been a suicide. The concordat had been signed eleven months earlier, on 20 July 1933. It took Pope Pius XI several years to realize how thoroughly Hitler had deceived him; eventually, and far too late in the day, in March, 1937 he expressed his disappointment and grief in the encyclical *Mit Brennende Sorge* (With burning concern).

In April 1934 the German evangelical Churches reorganized, in the face of what they had come to realize was a clerical part of the Nazi seizure of power, and formed, against the state-controlled and Nazi-dominated German Christian Church, the Confessing Church, which described itself as the legitimate evangelical Church of Germany. It was one of the few open gestures of resistance to the Nazi takeover in Germany, although it was very careful to declare its allegiance to the state. The

Above: Part of the aftermath of the notorious Kristallnacht *('Night of Broken Glass', 9-10 April 1938) when the Nazi militia attacked Jewish homes, shops and synagogues throughout Germany and Austria in a concerted operation. This is the devastated interior of the Okel Jaakov synagogue in Munich.*

Right: Cloth patch emblazoned with the Star of David and the German word for Jew. Hitler made it compulsory for all Jewish people over the age of six in Germany, Austria and Poland to wear the yellow star so they could be easily identified.

Below: 'Jew-baiting' in Nazi Austria. Jewish shops and services in Vienna were closed down by the Nazis after Kristallnacht *in 1938.*

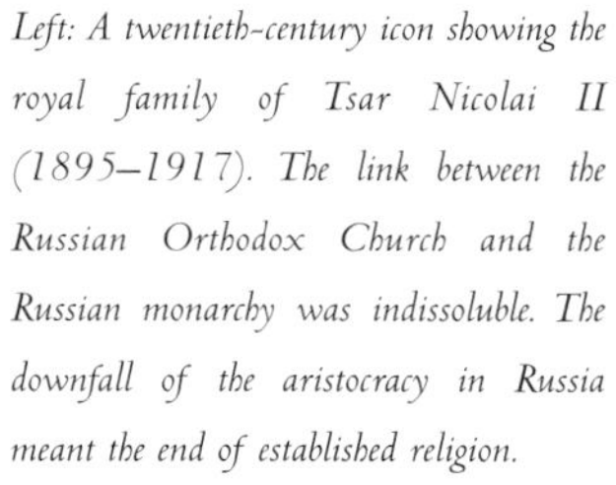

Left: A twentieth-century icon showing the royal family of Tsar Nicolai II (1895–1917). The link between the Russian Orthodox Church and the Russian monarchy was indissoluble. The downfall of the aristocracy in Russia meant the end of established religion.

Above: What People used to Fight for and What People Fight for Now, *a revolutionary poster by Dmitri Stakhievich Moor, showing how the Church and the monarchy had been replaced by the State and the people.*

Confessing Church survived precariously in the open until war broke out in 1939. The ex-submarine commander Martin Niemöller (1892–1984), the key leader of the Confessing Church movement, was sent to a concentration camp in 1937, and remained there until the end of the war, but miraculously survived the experience, which some other imprisoned Protestant pastors, besides Bonhoeffer, failed to do.

The kind of diplomatic calculation shown by Pope Pius XI in his dealings with Hitler remained in the mentality of the Roman curia under his successor. Pope Pius XII, because of his fear that frankness on his part about the threat to European Jews would make their plight even worse, chose diplomatic inactivity during the critical period of the Jewish massacres. It was a timidity that gained him a subsequent reputation, perhaps only partly deserved, for indifference.

In Soviet Russia the Church suffered one of the greatest persecutions. In the final period of imperial Russia the Orthodox lay intelligentsia, who were predominantly, but not exclusively, Slavophile, but various and creative in their thought, had made a big intellectual contribution, which after 1917 so far as it continued, continued only in exile. This was a tradition of which the writer Solzhenitsyn, who for a long time refused exile, later became a distinguished representative. In post-revolutionary Russia there were very many executions of the clergy, some public, most of them acts of terrorist power. The 1930s saw another wave of persecution and martyrdom, although by that time the clerical structures had been almost entirely destroyed. Anti-God museums and anti-religious instruction became the norm. The huge architectural patrimony of the Russian Orthodox Church came near to destruction. The monasteries as monastic communities simply disappeared. A few bishops survived, under very close state supervision. When the huge size of the old Russian empire is considered, the scale on which these things occurred is breathtaking. There was only a very partial and small relaxation of the stifling hold of state Communism, when the Russian Orthodox clergy were found to be useful by the ex-seminarist, Joseph Stalin, in mobilizing patriotic feeling in the war with Germany, after 1941.

The Cold War and its Contradictions

In the long, discouraging years of the Cold War (1947–89) the persecution of the Churches was extended to the whole area of Europe that lay under Russian leadership and domination. Everywhere east of a new long border that stretched from the Baltic to the southern Adriatic seas, the Churches in varying ways and in varying degrees suffered the most severe disabilities. There were martyrdoms, especially in Albania and Yugoslavia: Tito's post-war regime had, in any case, begun with a most fearful bloodbath. In the Soviet Union itself, and especially in the Ukraine, the old persecutions continued, sometimes with the addition of new victims such as the Protestant sect of the Jehovah's Witnesses (Watchtower Movement) and the Mormons (Latter-Day Saints).

After 1919 a phenomenon had reappeared in European, and eventually in world politics, that had last bedevilled Europe at the time of the seventeenth century Wars of Religion: the tendency to transform political conflicts into religious ones. There was a fatal temptation to turn the political struggle between the new Soviet Union and the conservative powers into a religious struggle between Christian belief and Communist atheism. It was a temptation that Communism itself had aided and abetted, principally by conceiving of itself as an international ideological and political force. Both the Republican and the Nationalist sides in the Spanish Civil War, for example, had very much to answer for in this respect – not only in a general sense but in terms of useless bloodshed. The revival of the ideas of the medieval Crusade could only be harmful, in the end, to a modern Christianity that on the whole wanted to get rid of many of the theological concepts that lay behind the Crusade. These things left long and terrible shadows across the world, which could still be seen as late as the Vietnam War.

One of the most divisive effects of the crusading spirit was a decree of the Holy Office (that is, the former Roman Inquisition) of 1949, confirmed by Pope Pius XII, which ruled that Communion could not be given in the Catholic Church to anyone who subscribed to the Communist

Above: Damage done to the Church of the Twelve Apostles in Moscow after the 1917 Revolution in Russia.

Below: The Berlin Wall, built in under a week in August 1961, blocked off the entrance to the Church of Redemption in Bernauerstrasse, consigning it to the eastern sector.

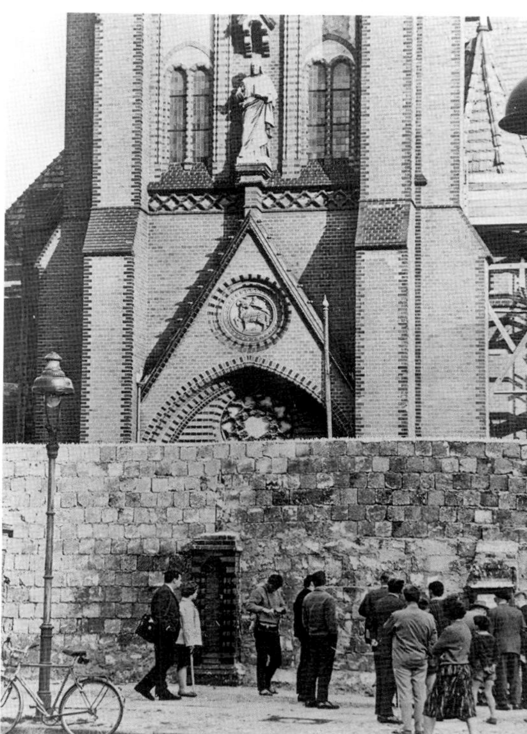

Left: Photograph made in 1970 by Marc Chaimowicz based on the Song-My massacre in Vietnam. The change in attitude to conflict since the start of the century was reflected in the public protests against the war in Vietnam.

Party or publicly advocated Communism. The decree did not say that excommunication followed for anyone who voted in democratic or undemocratic elections for the Communist Party, but it still had serious results in further politicizing the Catholic Church in Western Europe, and in further disadvantaging the position of the faithful in Eastern Europe. It also failed to take account of the position of the many believers who were troubled by the accumulation of nuclear weapons in the world: the decree tended to isolate from the Church those who took part in peace movements, which were often sponsored by the Left, and to accentuate the tendency to classify them as 'fellow-travellers' with Communism.

It occurred to practically no one in those days that before the end of the century Marxist doctrines might be moribund. Another known danger to freedom of conscience, ascendant in the 1930s, but apparently defeated in 1945, has, unlike Marxism, survived triumphantly. Right through the Cold War, the hidden issue was that of nationalism, which the Soviet Union suppressed in Eastern Europe in the name of Communism, just as the Russian government had suppressed it in the first half of the nineteenth century in the name of the conservative Holy Alliance. The Janus face of nationalism that looks at liberty from one side and at oppression from the other has been unchanging since the nineteenth century.

Nationalism can also fuse with religious particularism. The distinguished British church historian, Owen Chadwick, has recorded how the revival of a degree of Serbian government benevolence towards the Orthodox Church began in 1981 with the Albanian destruction of the historic Serbian monastery at Peć, and with the recital by the clergy of a long history of such acts against the Orthodox Church for which Albanians had been responsible in the province of Kosovo[2]. In the history of successful resistance to Soviet rule in Eastern Europe and of the disintegration of the old Warsaw Pact we have to give Polish nationalism an honoured place, just as we have to give Hungarian and Czech nationalism due honour for the parts they played in 1956 and 1968. But it is foolish to forget the debit side of the nationalist sheet, so evident in the break-up of Yugoslavia, that is light for many European nations of the post-Cold War period, especially under the influence of EEC Europeanism, but can still suddenly become heavy. Nationalism has been evident on both sides in Northern Ireland, and has left only a legacy of tears.

The Christian Oikumene

The Greek expression *oikumene* means the inhabited world, which in the days of the still universalist, but Christianized Roman Empire was taken to mean 'the universal Church'. It therefore tends to be an inclusive term, much more than Christendom, which historically has tended to be exclusive. The oecumenical councils of the Church, therefore, were those which represented the whole Church of the *oikumene*. It would be vain, however, to pretend that the *oikumene* could not also have signified the Romano-Hellenic world in opposition to external 'barbarians'. The expression did not signify 'all men', and the theological disputes of the past, whether or not Christ died for 'all men', confirm it. If we say today that Christendom is in decline, and that the oecumenical concept within Christianity is in the ascendant, we are talking about ideological and theological tendencies and not about social facts. Within the past century the oecumenical movement has come to mean, as it previously did not mean, working together for the unity of all who call themselves Christians.

The oecumenical movement has a long and complex history, mainly concerned with the Protestant Churches, but also including early contacts of some of these (mainly the Anglicans) with the Roman Catholics and with the Orthodox – the institutional relevance of the Orthodox to the Anglicans goes back at least to the eighteenth century, when Anglicans were concerned with Orthodox help in ordaining bishops to the new American Episcopalian Church. The World Council of Churches was set up in 1948. By 1998 the number of Churches involved, most but by no means all of which were Protestant, had risen to 335, coming from over a hundred countries and every continent. The Roman Catholic Church, which is itself an group of associated Churches, does not take a direct part in the World Council, but since Vatican II (1962–65, see below) various kinds of Catholic participation in the organization have developed. The ramifications of the oecumenical movement are considerable, especially in the form of regional and confessional groups of Churches.

Before 1962, the date of the convening of the Second Vatican Council (Vatican II) by Pope John XXIII (pope 1958–63), it could have been said, with some reservations, that the oecumenical movement was primarily a phenomenon of the Protestant and Orthodox communities. In order to work to set up Vatican II Pope John established a Secretariat for Promoting Christian Unity, whose duty to help to restore unity among Christians was confirmed when it became a permanent part of the restructured Roman curia in 1989. Vatican II was a critical period for the modern Roman Catholic Church, but in a sense it was also critical for the other main Church groups, which were not only directly affected by its decision to stay in touch with them and to treat them as Churches in a real sense, but were also greatly affected by its thinking and its policies. When the conservative Anglican bishop, Hensley Henson, wrote an affectionately teasing letter to Bishop Bell of Chichester in 1940 about Bell's oecumenical tendencies, he said that Bell seemed to be a spiritual acrobat riding the three horses of Quakerism, Papistry, and up to date Communism.[3] Taken in a very general and imprecise way, especially as to the last term, the observation could be applied to much of the oecumenical movement today.

Another critical opening provided by Vatican II was the decree on religious liberty. It may today seem that the affirmation of the right to freedom of religious conscience is such an obvious and fundamental matter that the Catholic Church should not have experienced the slightest hesitation or delay in making it. That this was not so was not merely due to the Counter-Reformation tradition in the Catholic Church, nor to the overhang of the mentality of the Inquisition. It seemed to many of the Fathers at Vatican II that they were not free to assert the right to affirm error: the existence of the Church depends upon the affirmation of the right tradition, and the evidence for this can be found in its history from apostolic times. At the Second Vatican Council the acceptance of such a decree was politically due to the alliance between the democratic American bishops on one hand and of the clergy from Communist-controlled Europe on the other: memories of the persecution of the Church in Germany and elsewhere by the Nazis, and the Christian failure to offer successful resistance to the Nazi racist laws were also factors.

Below: Pope Paul VI at the start of his historic visit to the Holy Land in 1964.

The right to liberty of conscience has always had to be qualified by the reservation that the affirmation of such liberty cannot be allowed to infringe the essential freedoms of others. This is a classical dilemma of liberalism, which the council met by the appeal to natural law. Bishop de Smedt of Bruges argued in 1963 in the same way that Bonhoeffer, confronted by the same problem in 1933 had argued, namely, that imposing the rule of the common good was the business of the state and should not allow people to go against the order of justice established by God.

Pope Paul VI (pope 1963–78) loyally continued the work of his predecessor, Pope John XXIII, and saw the Vatican Council through to its end. Besides the decrees just mentioned, the Council passed another concerning the Jews that referred to a spiritual patrimony that Christians hold in common with Jews. It stated that the Passion of Christ cannot be levelled against all the Jews, thus making the ancient charge of deicide against a whole religion and a whole people unsustainable by Catholic Christians. Vatican II also affirmed that the 'relationship between Jews and Christians concerns the Church as such', which made a continuing concern for that relationship the religious responsibility of all Catholics. The follow-up from these principles received public affirmation in the 1993 agreement between the Holy See and the State of Israel, which established diplomatic recognition of the State of Israel on the part of the Vatican. However, the long space of time that elapsed between Vatican II and the 1993 agreement was due to the continuing and ancient problems of relationships between the two religions, as well as the caution of Vatican diplomats.

One especially significant act of Paul VI was his visit to the Holy Land in 1964 to meet the Orthodox Patriarch of Constantinople, the Senior Orthodox bishop, in Jerusalem, where the two agreed to make the symbolic gesture of cancelling the anathemas imposed by each Church upon the other in 1054, a promise executed in 1965. There were further meetings between the two. In 1980, Pope John Paul II (pope from 1978) and the Orthodox Patriarch Dimitrios I set up the structures for an extended dialogue between the two groups of Churches, which has continued into the present decade.

In more recent times the emphasis has shifted to Christian relations with non-Christian religions other than Judaism, principally with Islam. In Europe, particularly, where large Muslim minorities exist, a big effort has been made to set up institutions of Christian religious and social co-operation with Islamic groups in most major EEC countries. In some countries, particularly the UK, these institutions have extended their activities to include other non-Christian religions, especially those of the Indian sub-continent.

Human Rights and Social Equality

The principles of human rights are enshrined in the United Nations Declaration of Human Rights of 1948, which includes the assertion of religious liberty, and the International Covenants adopted in 1966. Human rights are also protected in various regional agreements, such as those adopted within the European Convention on Human Rights in 1950.

The principles of non-discrimination between social and ethnic groups may be seen as stemming from the main human rights principles, but in practice most of these are enshrined in various bodies of national legislation. This means, of course, that such rights are not enforceable in all countries, and the manner in which they are enforceable in those countries that have the appropriate legislation varies considerably. There are enormous differences between the social philosophies that lie behind, say, the sex-discrimination laws of Great Britain and the United States, and the manner in which such legislation is discussed in Third World countries.

Very broadly, the Anglo-Saxon philosophy that lies behind such laws is one of individual rights. The way in which such things are discussed in the Third World refers much more to collective rights, and to their infringement by other collectivities such as international companies which have oppressive marketing or purchasing practices in Third World areas, or that profit from the continued exaction of interest payments from Third World countries. In other words, bad social conditions in the Third World, including, for example, the poor state of women's rights, are attributed above all to

© Hulton Getty/London

Above: A Muslim women at an Islamic rally in London. Muslim communities exist in most Western countries. Modern Christianity takes a tolerant stance and often actively seeks co-operation with religious minorities.

Below: Communion embrace at the Metropolitan Community Church of San Francisco which primarily serves gay and lesbian worshippers.

© Melanie Friend/Panos Pictures

© Panos Pictures

Left: In many Third World countries, such as Sierra Leone, shown here, multinational companies spend money advertising their products while the basic services, such as running water, are non-existent.

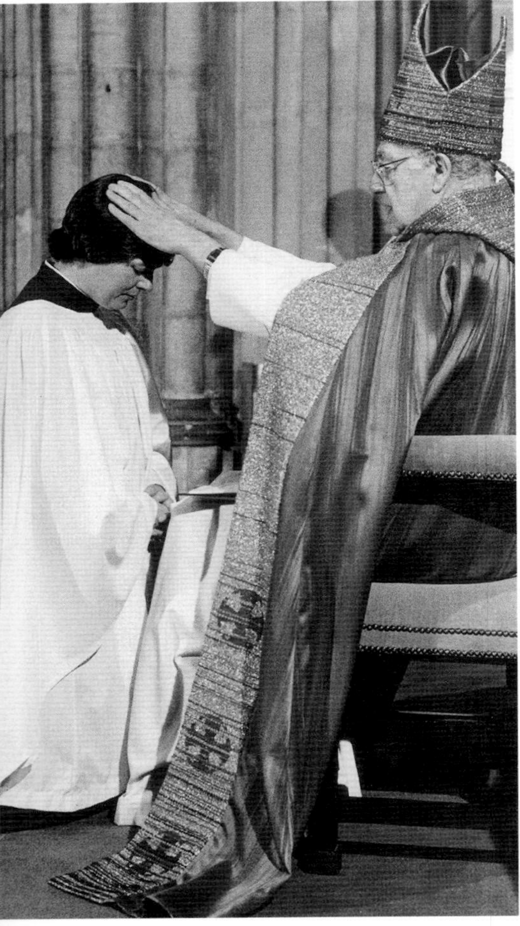

© Hulton Getty/London

Below: Robert Runcie, former Archbishop of Canterbury, ordains the first woman priest in the Anglican Church.

the 'dependent' state of the Third World economies on those of the First World, which is held morally responsible for this state of affairs. It is notorious that increasing the levels of aid to Third World countries does not have the automatic effect of righting these wrongs.

The Ordination of Women

It is not absolutely clear whether the question of the application of the principle of women's rights in the Churches, for example, in the ordination of women to priestly orders, can be discussed in the same way for the Churches of the First and Third Worlds, not only because of the enormous social and customary differences, but also because of the vast differences in the way in which the question of individual rights is approached in the north and the south. It is true that many who campaign for the rights of women to assume positions in the ministry of the Church similar to those assumed by men, would assert that their claims stem also from Church tradition that has in the past given women functions such as prophets, leaders and teachers, long before some Reformation sects such as the Anabaptists accepted a female ministry. The demand for women priests is not a part of the argument about the so-called apostolate of the laity. It is in some respects a revival of older arguments about the status and importance of the priesthood, but it is also linked to totally modern arguments about feminism, without which the debate in its present form is politically inconceivable.

That said, it is clear from the historical record that the ordination of women to the priesthood greatly preceded the feminist arguments in their modern form. The ordination of women to the priesthood (as opposed to the office of deacon) began in some Protestant Churches quite early in the twentieth century. The practice accelerated after the Second World War. Danish Lutherans elected a

© Panos Pictures

Right: A traditional religious parade in Catholic Mexico, dominated by men but dedicated to the Virgin. The dominance of female iconography in Catholicism is not translated into roles for real women in the Church.

woman priest in 1947. The US Methodists and Presbyterians ordained women on equal terms with men from 1956, Methodists in England from 1974 and Lutherans in the US from 1979. The ordination of women in the Church of Sweden in 1960 was influential on other Protestants, because of the continuity of Swedish Church orders. In Hong Kong, where an Anglican woman priest had been ordained as an emergency measure in the war, two women were ordained in 1971. US Episcopalian bishops who ordained women in 1974 found their action contested, but by 1976 this was no longer the case. A woman US Episcopalian bishop was elected in 1988. The Anglican General Synod authorized the ordination of women priests in 1994, and many such ordinations have followed.

The resistance of the Roman Catholic Church to the idea of the ordination of women to Church orders has been clear and consistent, as has been that of the Orthodox Church. After the Anglican action in 1994 Pope John Paul issued an Apostolic Letter confirming earlier rulings, and saying that the matter could not be treated as under discussion. Both Roman and Orthodox Churches maintain the tradition that reserves the main sacramental functions to male priests. It has to be remembered that 'tradition' in this context does not mean simply some sort of conservatism, but, in Catholic and Orthodox usage, the tradition that preserves Orthodox doctrine, and so the essential nature of the Church.

The question of women priests is sometimes blandly attributed to 'changing expectations about gender roles', a language that gives away a good deal about the application of social-science jargon to theology. It is not that, and the clearer-minded among feminist advocates would not say that it was. There were tendencies already apparent before the end of the Middle Ages, when late medieval Catholicism had allowed the rise of a new class of chantry priests, to introduce the principle of the labour market into the Church. At the end of a very long period of social evolution many Europeans and North Americans have come to consider the clergy as an employment that exists in order to supply a social demand: that female labour should be used is as natural as its use elsewhere. But most Protestant Churches would assert the idea of the ministry as a vocation to which men (or men and women) are called by God, and they would not allow the sacred realm to be appropriated to the needs of the individual and subjected to the laws of the market.

North and South

A century ago about half the world's Christians were located in Europe alone, without counting those of North America. The two thousand million Christians in the world today are very differently distributed. At the end of the twentieth century, the number of Christians of all denominations in Latin America, Africa and Asia is rather less than double the combined total of those in Europe and North America. Demographic change is likely to give Africa a steadily increasing importance in the pattern, although at the moment Latin America still predominates, and contains more than half the world's Roman Catholics. Nearly

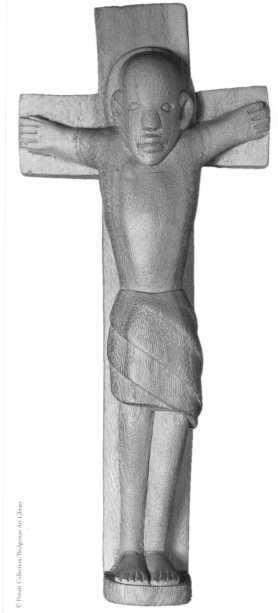

Above: Wooden crucifix from Nigeria showing Christ with noticeably African features.

Left: An exorcism being performed in Legio Maria Church, Kenya.

Right: Italian Crucifix *(1955) by Sidney Nolan (1917–92), the Australian artist.*

© Panos Pictures

Right: Some branches of Christianity have taken up the challenge of the renewed interest in pagan worship. Here members of Wolverton & Milton Keynes Christian Fellowship pray while turning to the four cardinal points of the city.

Below: Greek Orthodox priest at Monemvasia.

© Private Collection/Bridgeman Art Library

half the total African population is reckoned to be nominally Christian: the proportion of Muslims is significantly, but not drastically, smaller than that of the Christians. The world situation shows a striking predominance of non-European nationalities, but not of non-European languages. About a third of the world's Christians speak Spanish or English, in a very roughly equal proportion, and other ex-colonial languages are more or less as would be expected from the old colonial patterns.

On a world basis Roman Catholic believers are more numerous than those of any other denomination, and are thought to outnumber Protestants by something in the region of five to two. Protestants, including Anglicans, are perhaps double in numbers to Orthodox believers. All these figures are – fortunately for a none-too-numerate writer – very speculative, particularly because of the imponderable elements in the degree of religious commitment that we attribute to people classed as believers.

The consequences of this huge geographical change in Christian populations have already made themselves felt in the way that Christian Churches view themselves. The earliest major indication of this was the enormous impact made in the 1970s by the 'liberation theology' of Catholic priests in South and Central America. Their concern, first of all in their participation in the lives of very poor and disadvantaged communities, and subsequently in the political struggle to improve their conditions, sometimes led to priests giving their consent to armed rebellions. Such approval could be seen as confirming the salvation given by Christ to the poor and oppressed. Vatican theologians were extremely alarmed by this development, which threatened to turn the ancient doctrines of the armed

Left: Good Friday procession leaving from the church of Santa Domingo in Antigua, Guatemala.

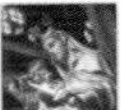

Right: Archbishop Desmond Tutu, who worked tirelessly against the apartheid regime of South Africa.

Below: Father Dan Ohmann leading a prayer meeting at a Hutu refugee camp in Tanzania. The bitter fighting and genocide in Rwanda between Hutus and Tsutsis was a challenge to Christianity in Africa.

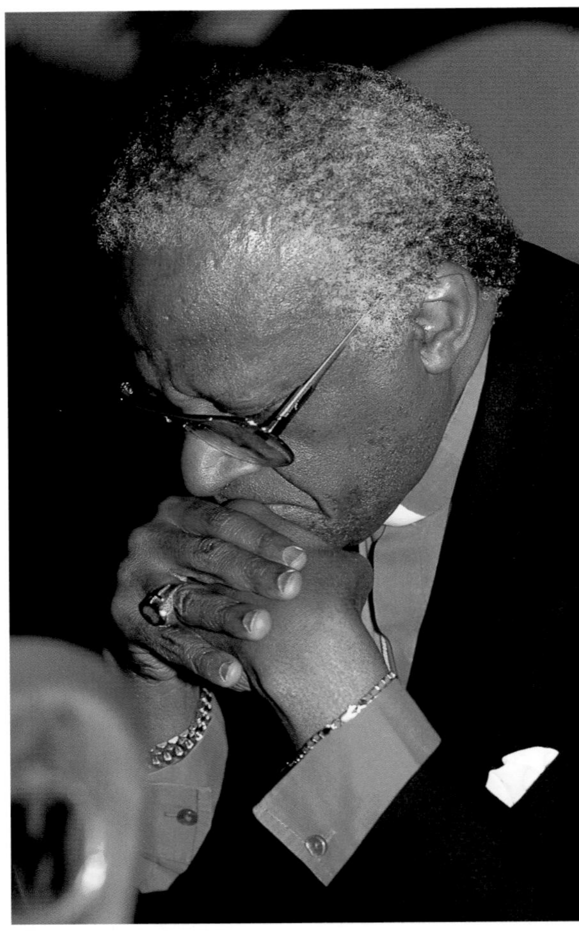

Crusade against the infidel upside-down in favour of the Marxists. However, the approach of Pope John Paul II to the problem was restrained, and in 1986 he said that some kind of liberation theology was 'not only timely but necessary'. The operation of this point of view on the ground in Latin America is likely to be through the 'Base Communities' , which are in effect parishes without parish priests. They can be viewed as a sort of compromise between the Catholic community and the trend towards evangelical Protestantism that has swept through Latin America – and also through the Hispano-American communities in the United States – since the 1970s.

In South Africa it could be argued that the Churches have come nearer, in the post-apartheid period, to claiming the social initiative and involving the whole society in a political process whose framework is overtly Christian, than any other Christian community in the present century. The Truth and Reconciliation Commission (1994–99) that has sought to reconcile South Africans of all political and religious persuasions, after the violence of the struggles of the final period of apartheid government and resistance to it, has had a very impressive degree of success. That this should have been so is due to the great qualities of understanding and leadership displayed by Archbishop Desmond Tutu of Cape Town. Political achievements of this sort are very hard to assess in the short term, and it is too early now to do more than to recognize the boldness and the great importance of the enterprise.

Africa has been in the past half-century the scene of major persecution of Christians. Uganda, especially in 1973, has seen huge persecutions, in which many priests and thousands of laymen and laywomen have died. In the past fifty years the experiences of both the African continent and Latin America have diverged so widely from the patterns expected of them in the colonial period, and their leadership has passed in such a great degree to indigenous clergies, that it has not been easy for congregations of European lay people to take these things in. It cannot be easy, even for a committed and well-informed minister, to convince a middle-class congregation in, say, Woking that it now belongs to something that can meaningfully be called 'a Church of the poor'. Yet this is an expression that has been used by many Christian leaders, including Pope John XXIII. As the demographic basis of Christianity, in a world increasingly affected by globalism, swings towards the extra-European world, the main Christian denominations are bound to reflect this in their organization and outlook.

In the north the big questions for Christians seem to relate to modernization, to oecumenism, and to pluralism: to ways in which life and doctrines are brought in some sense up to date, and to relations with members with other Christian persuasions and of other religions. But another question may lie behind these, whether the big future changes in Christianity are not more likely to come from the south than from the north. Whatever occurs, it remains true that what Christians have to offer the world is what they offered it in the beginning – hope. Was the hope justified, which the religion offered in the past to Christian societies? The question can be answered with an affirmative, as it can for some other religions, but not without remembering the long catalogue of error, failure and betrayal that accompanies the human condition. If we ask, did many individual men and women find their hopes in some way met by something that they experienced as a divine initiative, the Christian testimony is positive and overwhelming. But the injustices that the church was ready to tolerate in Christian society cannot be overlooked. We cannot forget the many millions, perhaps the historical majority of medieval Christian populations, who had little or no cause to thank Christian society for their lives, and who went to their deaths in silence.

1 Quoted in Klaus Scholder, *The Churches and the Third Reich* (tr. J. Bowden, London, SCM Press, 1987), which is fundamental for these events.

2 *The Christian Church in the Cold War* (Penguin, London, 1992).

3 Quoted by Ronald C. D. Jasper, George Bell: Bishop of Chichester (Oxford, 1967).

The great French historian, Jules Michelet (1788-1874), who saw the writing of history as a fight with death, pledged himself in The People to speak on behalf of the dead medieval generations of the poor, who 'like dumb creatures, suffered and perished in silence. Like the African who perishes of famine, they died without complaint. The European also toiled until his end was near, finished his life unknown to all...But these beings, who cannot make known to us their thoughts or their sufferings, can do so all the same by a sort of enchantment [of subsequent historical knowledge]. Learned men are needy for a drop of the sap that God poured into them [the medieval poor] brimful.'

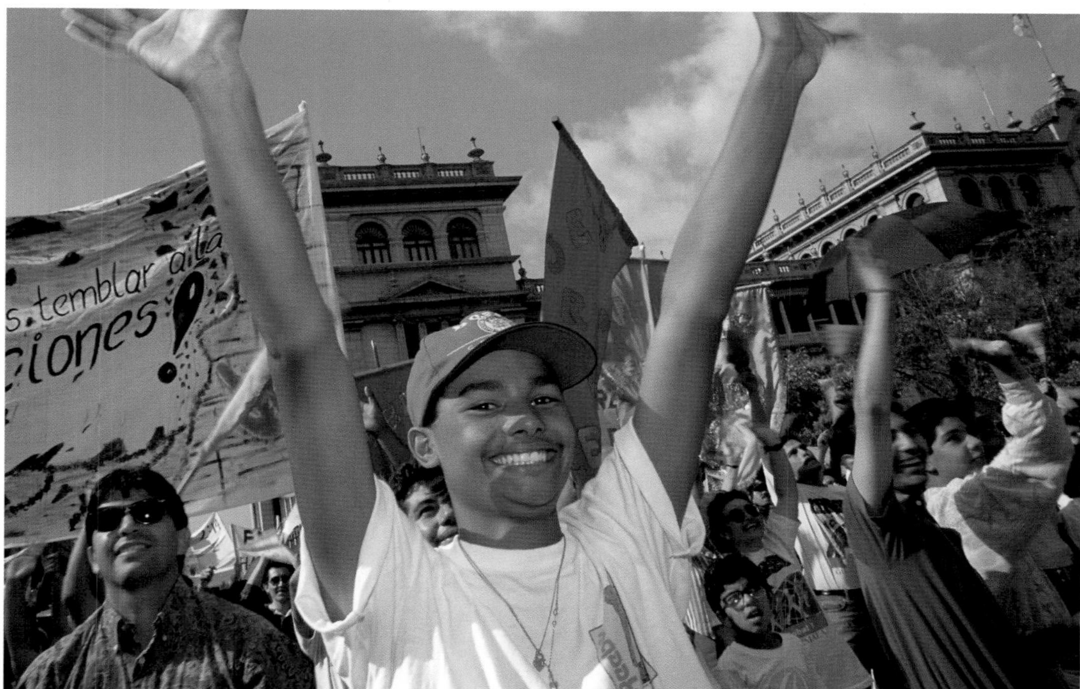

Left: The hopeful face of Christianity in Guatemala.

© Roger Harris/Science Photo Library

Left: Computer-enhanced image of sunrise over the Earth as seen from space. The perspective of humanity's place on the planet has changed since Christianity began.

Reading List

This reading list contains a few suggestions for people who would like to pursue some aspects of a huge and fascinating subject.

Chapters 1-3
E.P. Sanders, *The Historical figure of Jesus* (London, 1993)
Geza Vermes, *Jesus the Jew* (2nd edn., London, 1983)
J. Murphy-O'Connor, *Paul: A critical life* (Oxford, 1993)
W.H.C. Frend, *The Rise of Christianity* (London, 1984)
H. Chadwick, *The Early Church* (Harmondsworth, 1967)
R. Lane-Fox, *Pagans and Christians in the Mediterranean World from the Second Century AD to the Conversion of Constantine* (Harmondsworth, 1996)

Chapters 4-6
N.H. Baynes, *Constantine the Great and the Christian Church* (2nd edn., Oxford, 1972)
T.D. Barnes, *Constantine and Eusebius* (Cambridge Mass., 1981)
Eusebius, *The History of the Church from Christ to Constantine* (trs. G.A. Williamson, Harmondsworth, 1965)
P. Brown, *Augustine of Hippo: A Biography* (London, 1967)
Saint Augustine, *Confessions* (trs. R.S. Pine-Coffin, Harmondsworth, 1967)
P. Brown, *The Rise of Western Christendom: Triumph and Diversity AD 200-1000* (Oxford, 1997)
P. Brown, *The Body and Society: Men, Women and Sexual Renunciation in Early Christianity* (New York, 1988)
D. Knowles, *Christian Monasticism* (London, 1969)
Gregory of Tours, *The History of the Franks* (trs. L. Thorpe, Harmondsworth, 1974)
H. Mayr-Harting, *The Coming of Christianity to Anglo-Saxon England* (3rd edn., London, 1991)
Bede, *Ecclesiastical History of the English People* (trs. R. Collins and J. McClure, Oxford, 1994)

Chapters 7-10
A. H. Hourani, *A History of the Arab Peoples* (London, 1991)
M. Cook, *Muhammad* (Oxford, 1983)
The Koran (trs. N.J. Dawood, Harmondsworth, 1974)

Chapters 11-13

J. Riley-Smith, *What Were the Crusades?* (Macmillan, 1992)

H. E. Mayer, *The Crusades* (2nd edn., OUP, 1988)

Peter Partner, *God of Battles: Holy Wars of Christianity and Islam* (HarperCollins, 1997)

R. Fletcher, *The Conversion of Europe: From Paganism to Christianity 371–1386 AD* (HarperCollins, 1997)

Colin Morris, *The Papal Monarchy: 1050–1250* (OUP, 1991)

Michael Robson, *St Francis of Assisi, the Legend and the Life* (G. Chapman, 1997)

R. Moore, *The Origins of European Dissent* (Penguin, 1977)

Norman Cohn, (Paladin, 1970)

Chapters 14-16

Euan Cameron, *The European Reformation* (OUP, 1991)

Eamon Duffy, *The Stripping of the Altars: traditional religion in England 1400-1580* (Yale University Press, 1992)

George Holmes, *The Florentine Enlightenment 1400–50* (Weidenfeld and Nicolson, 1969)

Roberto Ridolphi, *The Life of Girolamo Savonarola* (Routledge and Kegan Paul, 1959)

Peter Partner, *Renaissance Rome 1500–1559: A Portrait of a Society* (California University Press, 1976)

Nicolas Zernov, *Eastern Christendom: a Study of the Origins and Development of the Orthodox Church* (Weidenfeld and Nicolson, 1961)

A. Hastings (ed.), *A World History of Christianity* (Cassell, 1999)

A. Hastings, *The Church in Africa 1450–1950* (OUP, 1994)

Mark A. Knoll, *A History of Christianity in the United States and Canada* (SPCK, 1992)

Martin E. Marty, *Pilgrims in Their Own Land: 500 Years of Religion in America* (Little, Brown, 1984)

Chapters 17-19

Peter Gay, *The Enlightenment, vol. 1, The Rise of Modern Paganism* (W. W. Norton, 1995)

Peter Gay, *The Enlightenment, vol. 2, The Science of Freedom* (W. W. Norton, 1996)

Stanley Ayling, *John Wesley* (Collins, 1979)

Owen Chadwick, *A History of the Popes 1830–1914* (OUP, 1998)

Owen Chadwick, *The Victorian Church* (Black, 1966)

Elizabeth Isichei, *A History of Christianity in Africa from Antiquity to the Present* (SPCK, 1995)

Stefan Collini, *Public Moralists: Political Life and Intellectual Life in Britain, 1850–1930* (OUP, 1991)

A. Hastings (ed.), *The Second Vatican Council and its Influence across 25 Years* (SPCK, 1990)

Nicholas Lossky and others (ed.), *Dictionary of the Ecumenical Movement* (WCC Publications, Geneva, 1991)

INDEX

Page references in italic indicate illustrations.